s – DARA

THE HUMANITARIAN RESPONSE INDEX 2007

Measuring Commitment to Best Practice

Silvia Hidalgo
DARA Director

Augusto López-Claros
Humanitarian Response Index Project Director

palgrave
macmillan

About DARA (Development Assistance Research Associates)

DARA is an independent not-for-profit organisation based in Madrid, Spain, committed to improving the quality of humanitarian action and development aid through evaluation and research. Through its work DARA contributes to improving the effectiveness of international aid and global efforts to reduce human suffering, vulnerability, and poverty.

Headquarters

Felipe IV, 9 - 3° Izquierda
28014 Madrid — Spain
Tel.:   +34 91 531 03 72
Fax: +34 91 522 00 39

Brussels Office

Résidence Palace
Rue de la Loi, 155, Block C
4th and 6th floor 1040
Brussels — Belgium
Tel.:   +32 2 230 33 37
Fax: +32 2 280 20 36

Washington Office

1120 19th Street NW
Washington, DC 20036 — USA
Tel.:   +1 202 721 5626
Fax: +1 202 721 5658

Email: info@daraint.org
Web: www.daraint.org

First published 2008 by
PALGRAVE MACMILLAN
Houndmills, Basingstoke, Hampshire RG21 6XS and
175 Fifth Avenue, New York, N.Y. 10010
Companies and representatives throughout the world

PALGRAVE MACMILLAN is the global academic imprint of the Palgrave Macmillan division of St. Martin's Press, LLC and of Palgrave Macmillan Ltd. Macmillan® is a registered trademark in the United States, United Kingdom and other countries. Palgrave is a registered trademark in the European Union and other countries.

ISBN-13: 978-0-230-57347-5   paperback
ISBN-10: 0-230-57347-9   paperback

This book is printed on paper suitable for recycling and made from fully managed and sustained forest sources. Logging, pulping and manufacturing processes are expected to conform to the environmental regulations of the country of origin.

A catalogue record for this book is available from the British Library.
A catalog record for this book is available from the Library of Congress.

10 9 8 7 6 5 4 3 2 1
17 16 15 14 13 12 11 10 09 08

Printed and bound in Great Britain by
Hobbs the Printers, Totton, Hampshire

Contents

(Cont'd.)

Part Four: Donor Profiles
prepared by Laura Altinger and Daniela Ruegenberg

Foreword

KOFI A. ANNAN

On 26 December 2004, the world witnessed one of the most devastating humanitarian emergencies in history, the Indian Ocean tsunami. The world's response was the largest and most generous mobilisation of humanitarian aid in history.

But this was only one of many natural and man-made catastrophes that took place during my tenure as Secretary-General of the United Nations. And to most of these—as in so many other cases—the response from the international community was, at best, wanting. It is significant that even the sudden outpouring of solidarity for the tsunami victims was not sufficient to guarantee an effective response, and many crucial lessons were learned from this experience.

I also had the privilege of presiding over an extensive course of reflection and reform across the humanitarian community, not least among donor governments themselves. One such vital initiative was the formulation of the *Principles and Good Practice of Humanitarian Donorship* (GHD), now adopted by the 23 members of the OECD Development Assistance Committee (DAC). By this means, the donor community has committed itself to safeguarding principles of humanity, neutrality, impartiality, and independence in the delivery of humanitarian assistance. The equal worth of every human life demands that humanitarian aid be equitable, that is, free from geo-strategic interests, historical ties, domestic political agendas, or the attention of the world's media.

DARA's *Humanitarian Response Index 2007* is a new and innovative attempt to evaluate the performance of the 23 OECD-DAC members against their commitment to the GHD *Principles*. The *Index* is the first of its kind to rank donor countries individually, contributing to the transparency, accountability, and quality of humanitarian aid, and thus paving the way for more effective delivery on the ground. It will be updated on an annual basis, and will serve as a scorecard of the world's progress towards good humanitarian donorship.

I have no doubt that the *Index* will serve as an indispensable tool for dialogue among all stakeholders of the humanitarian community, assisting them to improve the implementation and effectiveness of humanitarian aid. Constructive criticism and feedback on the *Index* will shape this annual publication and help it to develop further.

I share DARA's conviction that this novel benchmarking mechanism will greatly strengthen donors' voluntary commitment to the GHD *Principles*. International benchmarking has had considerable success across various fields and offers the potential, through peer pressure, to motivate actors to make their work more effective and correct deficiencies in the policy framework.

At the heart of this new publication is the promotion of fundamental humanitarian principles which will save and protect lives and livelihoods. As former Secretary-General of the United Nations and President of the *Global Humanitarian Forum*, I heartily welcome and applaud DARA's effort.

Millions of victims of natural hazards and violent conflicts will continue to depend on humanitarian relief, not only for their very survival, but for their future protection from disaster and rehabilitation on the path to escaping poverty. I firmly believe that the *Humanitarian Response Index* will serve as an important tool to help ensure that no disaster is ignored, and that every dollar spent helps those most in need.

Preface

Humanitarian action targets tens of millions of people every year. Its objectives are to save lives, alleviate suffering, and maintain human dignity during, and in the aftermath of, man-made crises and natural disasters, as well as to prevent and strengthen preparedness for the occurrence of such situations. Providing the right aid to the right people in the right way is a tremendous challenge. We in the aid community have understood for some time that much remains to be done to enable us to provide better responses to increasing numbers of affected people. In this Herculean task, we fully realise that, as human beings, we do not always learn from experience, and make repeated mistakes. And while we know that aid, with all its limitations, in these contexts has mainly remedial value, we must continue to strive for progress and quality in humanitarian action.

Given the conflicts and disasters affecting many parts of the globe, humanitarian action, in its broadest conception, is of vital importance to the millions of people who endure the effects of crises and violence year after year. Those of us remote from the turmoil are moved by the images we see of people suffering from man-made, often protracted, violence in Darfur, Somalia, the Congo, Sri Lanka, the Palestinian Territories, or Colombia, and from sudden natural disasters, such as those which befell the people of Indonesia, Pakistan, Peru, or Nicaragua. The scenes we see are real and unbearable and every attempt should be made to immediately end the plight of those affected by these tragedies.

But it is clear that there is far more than meets the eye of the ever-present camera. The year 2006 was one of many new, re-emerging, and continuing crises. The Humanitarian Response Index (HRI) presented in this publication has been constructed in the context of the continuing response to crises in eight areas: Colombia, the Democratic Republic of Congo, Haiti, Lebanon, Niger, Pakistan, Sudan, and Timor-Leste. The HRI has been designed to help improve the quality of

humanitarian action in the face of such crises, and to serve as a tool for the future, to respond more adequately to humanitarian crises which will continue to challenge us all.

In DARA we believe that donors—key actors in the humanitarian system—can improve the way humanitarian aid works. While the majority of state donors—whose role is far wider than that of funding humanitarian project—do not actually implement the aid they offer, they can have a profound influence on other parts of the aid delivery system and can be instrumental in providing the foundations for more appropriate responses. By their informed policies and practice, through increased information and analysis, cooperation, and communication, we believe that donors are already playing a pivotal role within the humanitarian system as a driving force for positive change.

The Humanitarian Response Index was conceived well over a year ago. During the first year, we faced the challenge of defining a methodology for what to measure, how to measure it, and for developing a road map for the HRI. More than a dozen different teams have carried out missions throughout the globe while a core team of experts developed comprehensive indicators. The overall project represents a unique attempt to benchmark donors and monitor progress in humanitarian action in relation to an initial baseline.

The Humanitarian Response Index presents information to help donors examine their role critically. When DARA undertook to analyse the donor studies of the Tsunami Evaluation Coalition, we found that, once donors and their overall budgets had been identified, many tried valiantly to make the best use of the funds available and to follow the *Principles* set out in the Good Humanitarian Donorship (GHD) initiative. However, despite these good intentions, and even with the GHD framework in place, they often lacked guidance and interpreted "good donorship" in completely different ways. Donors must commit and disburse funds rapidly, yet their decisions must be based on the assessment of real needs. In practice, putting the emphasis on one of the GHD *Principles* as opposed to another can result in a wide variety of approaches. By being selective, donors face less competition and feel that they are getting more "value for money." Unfortunately, in the business of humanitarian assistance, greater accountability is demanded of some than others.

The HRI has brought the GHD *Principles* closer to the field. By means of a thorough interview process, humanitarian actors in different crises and from different backgrounds have been given the opportunity to reflect on the principles of GHD and how they are actually practiced. This reflection has greatly enriched the HRI process and has stimulated our own understanding. Their responses have added a new dimension to donor accountability. Despite the difficulties faced during its first year, the enthusiasm and encouragement with which the many actors in the field have greeted this project have given us a greater clarity of purpose and made it possible for us to move forward more boldly.

The Humanitarian Response Index sets out to distil practices and rationales for the most important issues in international humanitarian aid. One of its main objectives is to monitor the progress made in official humanitarian donorship. We believe that the analysis of crisis responses offered by the HRI serves as an instrument not only to stimulate discussion and debate but to shed light on where the nations of the world stand in the task of delivering effective humanitarian assistance in the 21st century.

It is to be expected that we would want to know how our own country measures up when our governments and other donors pledge vast sums of money. The HRI provides a firm foundation of information for such reflection, for policy analysis, for reporting of data, evaluation, and monitoring.

Fully aware of the often overwhelming tasks facing humanitarian agencies and actors in all parts of the system, the authors of the HRI hope to further stimulate the political will and creativity to implement existing commitments, learn from past successes and failures, and find new responses to the work of providing and utilising humanitarian assistance in all kinds of crises.

Change demands renewed activism. The world must be repeatedly reminded of the promises made to women and children, to the uprooted, to the sick and the hungry, to ethnic and racial minorities, and to other vulnerable groups. As citizens of a shrinking world, people must be made more aware of the laws, norms and standards, resolutions and policies which have already been put in place to ensure the protection and preservation of life, of well being, and of human dignity. Equally important is the concept that aid, in and of itself, is limited if it is not viewed in the broader context of human development, local, national, and international. How assistance efforts are best integrated into local contexts, providing the right support to the right people at the right time, drawing on their knowledge and enhancing their own capacity can only be evaluated when local accountability mechanisms and the realities faced by affected populations are identified and dealt with.

It is in this spirit that we offer this first edition of the Humanitarian Response Index.

Acknowledgements

DARA wishes to express deep gratitude to the hundreds of people who actively participated in this exercise and shared their knowledge and views.

In undertaking our work across four continents, we have been assisted by a wide range of institutions and countless individuals who have generously given their time, insight, and who have been willing to share a wealth of documents. While it is not possible to name each one individually, we would like to mention several and express our appreciation for their assistance. Our first thanks go to Vidar Birkeland and the OCHA and IOM teams in Timor-Leste, to Walter Cotte from the Colombian Red Cross, and to Maurice Herson of ALNAP and Beat Schweizer of the ICRC. For their support and encouragement, we would like to express deep gratitude to the members of our Peer Review Committee, especially Johan Schaar who was gracious in sharing his knowledge and experience, both within the group and in contributing a chapter in this HRI on the birth of GHD. Heartfelt thanks are due to all the Members of the Advisory Board, especially Iqbal Riza, Jose Maria Figuéres, and Pierre Schori for their extraordinary insight and leadership. To Jan Egeland, Sarah Cliffe, Charles Petrie, and Michel Ogrizek, who contributed special chapters to this work, we offer heartfelt thanks for their experience and valuable insights.

We also wish to acknowledge the work of many NGOs, of the UN agency and the staff of the International Federation of Red Cross and Red Crescent Societies and their organisations in both North and South, who not only shared their knowledge and views about crises, donor policies, and practices, but also greatly encouraged us in our work.

Special thanks are due to the members of our survey teams who joined us in undertaking the eight crisis missions and 20 bilateral donor interviews. They worked under extreme pressure to obtain some of the data essential for the HRI and early feedback suggests that their work has already been greatly appreciated in bringing the principles of GHD closer to key stakeholders.

This project would have been entirely impossible without the knowledge, experience, and fine scholarship of Augusto López-Claros and Laura Altinger, and the work of Velina Stoianova, Carlos Oliver and Riccardo Polastro, all of whom have seen the Humanitarian Response Index through from beginning to end.

Our warmest gratitude to principal editor Nancy Ackerman of AmadeaEditing for her brilliant work and for the painstaking professionalism and skill of graphic designer Ha Nguyen.

Finally, heartfelt thanks to Igor Hodson, for the time and effort he gave to writing, research, and organisation in order to ensure that this report was produced on time.

Silvia Hidalgo, Director, DARA
November, 2007

Executive Summary

Humanitarian interventions are perceived to be falling short of existing humanitarian needs and are often not guided by recognised principles of proportionality, neutrality, impartiality, and independence. Donor policy and decision making have, at times, been compromised by conflicting domestic and foreign policy considerations, resulting in inequitable, unpredictable, and untimely funding allocations. Supply-driven aid, earmarking, short funding cycles, unrequited pledges, and late funding have all further reduced the effectiveness of humanitarian action.

The international donor community has resolved to strengthen its responses to humanitarian crises by improving effectiveness, efficiency and accountability through application of the Good Humanitarian Donorship (GHD) initiative, established in 2003, which enshrines those *Principles* that are widely accepted as representing best practice in the field, and establishing a normative benchmark for donors.

The *Principles* define the objectives of humanitarian action as "to save lives, alleviate suffering and maintain human dignity during and in the aftermath of man-made crises and natural disasters, as well as to prevent and strengthen preparedness for the occurrence of such situations." They not only spell out the ethics that should guide humanitarian action, namely humanity, impartiality, neutrality, and independence, but also reflect those principles already embedded in the body of international human rights and humanitarian law. The *Principles* also set out good practices in donor financing, management and accountability.

The aim of this publication is to present the Humanitarian Response Index (HRI) as a tool for improving humanitarian response, measuring the behaviour of donors against their commitment to the *Principles*, and promoting system-wide change for better humanitarian action.

Part One: The Humanitarian Response Index

Chapter 1, "The Humanitarian Response Index: Measuring the Commitment to Humanitarian Best Practice," by Laura Altinger, Silvia Hidalgo, and Augusto López-Claros, gives the reader an in-depth analysis of the Index, its vision and rationale, form and methodology. After outlining the GHD *Principles* in detail, the authors offer a brief overview of accountability initiatives already underway within the international humanitarian community, which are complementary to the HRI. This is followed by a detailed description of the methodological underpinnings of the Index, including its main objectives and the Survey questionnaire in which humanitarian stakeholders recorded their views about how donors active in their area of operations were faring in relation to the *Principles*. The authors then show how the content of the GHD was organized into five "pillars," each with soft and hard data indicators which formed the basis for the Index and its rankings.

A key component of the HRI is a field survey of various stakeholders involved in humanitarian activities. The aim was to record the views or opinions of implementing agencies about how donors active in the agencies' area of operations have fared in relation to the GHD *Principles*, across a representative selection of complex emergencies and natural disasters. The crises countries chosen were Colombia, the Democratic Republic of the Congo, Haiti, Lebanon, Niger, Pakistan, Sudan, and Timor-Leste.

The remainder of the chapter is devoted to the tables illustrating the rankings and summary evaluations of a representative sample of countries: Sweden, Norway, the European Commission, Ireland, New Zealand, Canada, the UK, Switzerland, the United States, Spain, France, and Italy.

The authors chose the following five categories, on the basis of the 23 GHD *Principles*, grouping them under "pillars" that deal with broadly similar aspects of humanitarian assistance:

- Responding to humanitarian needs
- Integrating relief and development
- Working with humanitarian partners
- Implementing international guiding principles
- Promoting learning and accountability

Twenty-five of the 57 indicators in the HRI constitute the hard data, capturing some dimension of the *Principles*, with the remainder drawn from the Survey and addressing, likewise, a specific GHD Principle. The methodology used resulted in the following rankings, taken from the Humanitarian Response Index 2007. Full details on the rankings are presented in Chapter 1.

Sweden is the best-ranking donor in the Humanitarian Response Index (HRI) 2007. Chapter 1 contains a description of its good performance in both hard and soft data indices, across all five pillars, and in the variables for each. This same data is presented for each of the 12 donor countries mentioned earlier.

Table 1. Humanitarian Response Index rankings 2007

Donor	HRI rankings	HRI scores
Sweden	1	5.37
Norway	2	5.13
Denmark	3	5.01
Netherlands	4	5.01
European Commission	5	4.91
Ireland	6	4.86
Canada	7	4.80
New Zealand	8	4.80
United Kingdom	9	4.76
Switzerland	10	4.68
Finland	11	4.58
Luxembourg	12	4.51
Germany	13	4.45
Australia	14	4.44
Belgium	15	4.42
United States	16	4.39
Spain	17	4.29
Japan	18	4.19
France	19	4.06
Austria	20	4.01
Portugal	21	3.95
Italy	22	3.87
Greece	23	3.17

The Humanitarian Response Index is intended to complement the voluntary endorsement donors have made to the GHD *Principles*. Its aim is to provide a platform of both qualitative and quantitative indicators to help donors assess their own humanitarian performance in relation to others, and, over time, in relation to their own past. The focus of the HRI is, therefore, on individual donor performance vis-à-vis the *Principles*.

Part Two: Perspectives on Good Humanitarian Donorship

To complement the presentation on the Humanitarian Response Index and in order to give a perspective on other dimensions of the humanitarian field, we are pleased to include a number of special chapters, written by eminent specialists, each of whom has shared insights in a particular area. These include the birth of the GHD initiative, the nature and effects of multilateral action, the link between humanitarian assistance and long-term development, and the role of the media.

In **Chapter 2**, the "Birth of Good Humanitarian Donorship," Johan Schaar tells the story of how the GHD initiative came into being. He describes how he and a number of colleagues channelled their deep concerns over the "dysfunctional," and often "irrational" situation obtaining in the field of humanitarian aid at the beginning of the millennium into a new consultative process to "move humanitarian donors towards more principled behaviour." He writes briefly about donor behaviour of the period and then presents the vision of principled action and the negotiation process that led to the GHD *Principles* and the accompanying strategy to for action. Citing the important earlier work done by many individuals and organisations, he outlines the steps taken to set up the well-known "Stockholm Conference of June 2003 and the consensus document resulting from it." He then assesses the emerging changes in donor behaviour after Stockholm, pointing out the role of "hidden assumptions" which stood in the way of improved donor practice. Finally, he expresses the factors which allow him to feel optimism about the ultimate impact of the GHD process.

Chapter 3, "Progress on the Front Lines," by Jan Egeland, shows how many of the "somber predictions" which accompanied the crises in such countries as Liberia, Sierra Leone, Eastern Congo, South Sudan, Kosovo, and Nepal, or the terrifying disasters which befell South Asia, Pakistan, and the Horn of Africa were, in large measure, "averted because multilateral action, building on local capacities, turned out to be infinitely more effective than what is even now recognized by much of the world's media and national parliaments." Stressing the collective international responsibility for humanitarian action and the vital importance of "unity of purpose," Egeland shares his conviction that "endless ongoing suffering" in a number of conflict-torn countries is "a product of either senseless bickering or passive neglect among those leading nations that could untangle these conflicts." He goes on to describe the four advocacy campaigns building in the coming years, which he feels will contribute to strengthening the core features of the Principles of GHD, many of which he concludes—based on his experience at the UN—have been ignored in recent massive humanitarian operations. Egeland ends his article with a plea, given the shrinking of the UN's relative share of the total humanitarian response, for a "broadening of partnerships" to make humanitarian efforts "less "UN-centric," offering four key recommendations for the improvement of the international humanitarian system.

Chapter 4, entitled "Opening Space for Long-Term Development in Fragile Environments," was contributed by Sarah Cliffe and Charles Petrie. As the name suggests, their paper explores the links between humanitarian aid and longer-term development. They argue that the "relief-to-development" continuum has been extensively debated in the past, but has received relatively little recent attention and is not measured in the GHD indicators. The authors explain the importance of preserving human and institutional capital in the fact of conflict, and they express the view that "global policy discussions and the experience of delivering aid in the most fragile and politically contentious environments have tended to move humanitarian and development actors in somewhat different directions as regards strategy and organisational culture." As the links between humanitarian assistance and long-term development become both more important and more complex, the authors offer some initial ideas for strengthening them in order to make the gains of the former more sustainable, focusing particularly on the post-conflict recovery period in collapsed or repressive regimes. Stressing the importance of more realistic planning between national authorities and humanitarian partners before and during the post-conflict recovery period, they urge development actors to acknowledge more fully the value of continued large-scale interim humanitarian and NGO activities, and provide better support with analysis of local conditions, advising actors in both sectors to

"strengthen the political understanding" of the post-conflict recovery period.

In **Chapter 5**, called "The Media-Driven Humanitarian Response: Public Perceptions and Humanitarian Realities as Two Faces of the Same Coin," Michel Ogrizek discusses the media not only as the conveyors of "news" about crises, but also as manipulators of public attitudes about, and the actual conduct of, humanitarian needs and responses. Ogrizek describes the humanitarian movement as a "vector of globalisation" and media networks as "the vehicle through which human suffering has become universalized and interventions borderless." He concedes the importance of images as generators of "empathy," and "indignation," but draws on a wealth of real-life examples to show how the media "capitalize on visual emotion" and "neglect the need for reason." On the positive side, he points out the critical importance of radio and new media in community development, and the role of media in exposing both delays and drawbacks in rescue operations as well as leadership responsibilities and failures, such as official denials of crisis severity or politically motivated refusals of foreign assistance. But as an experienced field practitioner, Ogrizek is critical of how the pervasive sense of critical emergency generated by "salesmen of hot news" interferes with the genuine humanitarian mission, distorts facts and priorities, purveys misinformation, arouses false anxieties, and leads journalists to corrupt footage, sometimes paying staggering sums for videos shot by "citizen journalists." He expresses concern for the way in which the frequent dependence of short-notice global network reporters on local authorities—even the military—for protection jeopardises the development of local media. Stressing the incompatibility of the "media business" with GHD Principle 11, he urges recognition of information itself as a form of humanitarian aid.

Part Three: Crisis Reports

This section of our publication presents an analysis of the eight crises analysed in this year's Humanitarian Response Index: Colombia, the Democratic Republic of Congo, Haiti, Lebanon, Niger, Pakistan, Sudan, and Timor-Leste. Each crisis report contains an initial box summarising the country and the crisis "at a glance," followed by a brief outline of the humanitarian response. The historical and factual background of each crisis is then provided, and this is followed by a detailed description and analysis of the successes and shortcomings of the international humanitarian response. A summary of 2006 emergencies is also provided.

Part Four: Donor Profiles

Part Four of this volume, prepared by Laura Altinger and Daniela Ruegenberg, offers full data on humanitarian aid for each of the 22 countries ranked in the HRI, as well as the European Commission. Taken together, they provide a comprehensive overview of countries' humanitarian aid programmes, including how much aid countries are giving, how timely it is, to which emergencies, parts of the world, and sectors it is directed, capturing essential elements of each donor's humanitarian actions.

The reader will find a list of the many acronyms used throughout these chapters, as well as a Glossary of terms referred to frequently, and an Appendix, containing the full Survey forming the basis for the qualitative measures of the Humanitarian Response Index.

1

PART ONE

The Humanitarian Reponse Index

The Humanitarian Response Index 2007

LAURA ALTINGER, SILVIA HIDALGO, and AUGUSTO LÓPEZ-CLAROS[1]

I. Introduction

Humanitarian interventions targeting persons affected by humanitarian emergencies and natural disasters around the globe are perceived to be falling far short of existing humanitarian needs and are often not guided by acknowledged principles of humanity, impartiality, neutrality, and independence. Donor policy and decision making have been criticised for being compromised by competing and sometimes inconsistent domestic and foreign policy considerations, resulting in funding allocations that are inequitable, unpredictable, and untimely in responding to crises. Earmarking and tied aid, short funding cycles, unrequited pledges, and late funding have all played a role in further reducing the effectiveness of humanitarian action.[2]

To address many of these issues, the international donor community resolved to strengthen its response to humanitarian crises by pursuing enhanced effectiveness, efficiency, and accountability in humanitarian action through the Good Humanitarian Donorship (GHD) initiative.[3] The GHD provides a forum for discussion of good practices and encouraging greater donor accountability, as well as providing a framework from which to assess official humanitarian action.[4] Most importantly, it enshrines those *Principles* that are widely accepted as representing best practice in the area of humanitarian donorship, thereby establishing a normative benchmark for humanitarian donors.

Underlying the GHD Initiative are the *Principles and Good Practice of Humanitarian Donorship* (the *Principles*) established in 2003 (Box 1), which define the objectives of humanitarian action: "to save lives, alleviate suffering and maintain human dignity during and in the aftermath of man-made crises and natural disasters, as well as to prevent and strengthen preparedness for the occurrence of such situations." Further, they spell out the principles that should guide humanitarian action, namely humanity, impartiality, neutrality, and independence, as well as

those embedded in the body of international human rights and humanitarian law. The *Principles* also set out good practices in donor financing, management, and accountability.

Recognising the need to strengthen accountability through monitoring of humanitarian donorship, the *Principles* contain a commitment to "learning and accountability initiatives for the effective and efficient implementation of humanitarian action" (Principle [P] 21) as well as to the "regular evaluations of international responses to humanitarian crises, including assessments of donor performance" (P 22).

In the spirit of these principles and to improve the effectiveness and efficiency of humanitarian action, this chapter presents the Humanitarian Response Index (HRI), a tool designed to measure how well humanitarian donors are performing relative to their commitment to the *Principles*. The HRI is intended to help identify and understand donors' strengths and weaknesses in the area of humanitarian action in order, ultimately, to improve the quality of humanitarian action and alleviate human suffering in crisis situations. This study hopes to raise awareness about the increasingly important role that good humanitarian donorship can play in setting standards in this area, both within and beyond its current core constituencies.

This chapter is organised as follows. Section II provides a brief overview of accountability initiatives already underway within the international humanitarian community and to which the HRI is complementary. Section III describes the methodological underpinnings of the HRI and provides a detailed description of the indicators used to compile the Index. Section IV presents the Index results for 2007, with the main highlights, followed by the conclusions.

Box 1. Principles and good practice of humanitarian donorship

Endorsed in Stockholm, 17 June 2003 by Germany, Australia, Belgium, Canada, the European Commission, Denmark, the United States, Finland, France, Ireland, Japan, Luxembourg, Norway, the Netherlands, the United Kingdom, Sweden and Switzerland.

Objectives and definition of humanitarian action

1. The objectives of humanitarian action are to save lives, alleviate suffering and maintain human dignity during and in the aftermath of man-made crises and natural disasters, as well as to prevent and strengthen preparedness for the occurrence of such situations.

2. Humanitarian action should be guided by the humanitarian principles of *humanity,* meaning the centrality of saving human lives and alleviating suffering wherever it is found; *impartiality,* meaning the implementation of actions solely on the basis of need, without discrimination between or within affected populations; *neutrality,* meaning that humanitarian action must not favour any side in an armed conflict or other dispute where such action is carried out; and *independence,* meaning the autonomy of humanitarian objectives from the political, economic, military or other objectives that any actor may hold with regard to areas where humanitarian action is being implemented.

3. Humanitarian action includes the protection of civilians and those no longer taking part in hostilities, and the provision of food, water and sanitation, shelter, health services and other items of assistance, undertaken for the benefit of affected people and to facilitate the return to normal lives and livelihoods.

General principles

4. Respect and promote the implementation of international humanitarian law, refugee law and human rights.

5. While reaffirming the primary responsibility of states for the victims of humanitarian emergencies within their own borders, strive to ensure flexible and timely funding, on the basis of the collective obligation of striving to meet humanitarian needs.

6. Allocate humanitarian funding in proportion to needs and on the basis of needs assessments.

7. Request implementing humanitarian organisations to ensure, to the greatest possible extent, adequate involvement of beneficiaries in the design, implementation, monitoring and evaluation of humanitarian response.

8. Strengthen the capacity of affected countries and local communities to prevent, prepare for, mitigate and respond to humanitarian crises, with the goal of ensuring that governments and local communities are better able to meet their responsibilities and co-ordinate effectively with humanitarian partners.

9. Provide humanitarian assistance in ways that are supportive of recovery and long-term development, striving to ensure support, where appropriate, to the maintenance and return of sustainable livelihoods and transitions from humanitarian relief to recovery and development activities.

10. Support and promote the central and unique role of the United Nations in providing leadership and co-ordination of international humanitarian action, the special role of the International Committee of the Red Cross, and the vital role of the United Nations, the International Red Cross and Red Crescent Movement and non-governmental organisations in implementing humanitarian action.

Good practices in donor financing, management and accountability

(a) Funding

11. Strive to ensure that funding of humanitarian action in new crises does not adversely affect the meeting of needs in ongoing crises.

12. Recognising the necessity of dynamic and flexible response to changing needs in humanitarian crises, strive to ensure predictability and flexibility in funding to United Nations agencies, funds and programmes and to other key humanitarian organisations.

13. While stressing the importance of transparent and strategic priority-setting and financial planning by implementing organisations, explore the possibility of reducing, or enhancing the flexibility of, earmarking, and of introducing longer-term funding arrangements.

14. Contribute responsibly, and on the basis of burden-sharing, to United Nations Consolidated Inter-Agency Appeals and to International Red Cross and Red Crescent Movement appeals, and actively support the formulation of Common Humanitarian Action Plans (CHAP) as the primary instrument for strategic planning, prioritisation and co-ordination in complex emergencies.

Box 1. Principles and good practice of humanitarian donorship *(cont'd.)*

(b) Promoting standards and enhancing implementation

15. Request that implementing humanitarian organisations fully adhere to good practice and are committed to promoting accountability, efficiency and effectiveness in implementing humanitarian action.

16. Promote the use of Inter-Agency Standing Committee guidelines and principles on humanitarian activities, the Guiding Principles on Internal Displacement and the 1994 Code of Conduct for the International Red Cross and Red Crescent Movement and Non-Governmental Organisations (NGOs) in Disaster Relief.

17. Maintain readiness to offer support to the implementation of humanitarian action, including the facilitation of safe humanitarian access.

18. Support mechanisms for contingency planning by humanitarian organisations, including, as appropriate, allocation of funding, to strengthen capacities for response.

19. Affirm the primary position of civilian organisations in implementing humanitarian action, particularly in areas affected by armed conflict. In situations where military capacity and assets are used to support the implementation of humanitarian action, ensure that such use is in conformity with international humanitarian law and humanitarian principles, and recognises the leading role of humanitarian organisations.

20. Support the implementation of the 1994 Guidelines on the Use of Military and Civil Defence Assets in Disaster Relief and the 2003 Guidelines on the Use of Military and Civil Defence Assets to Support United Nations Humanitarian Activities in Complex Emergencies.

(c) Learning and accountability

21. Support learning and accountability initiatives for the effective and efficient implementation of humanitarian action.

22. Encourage regular evaluations of international responses to humanitarian crises, including assessments of donor performance.

23. Ensure a high degree of accuracy, timeliness, and transparency in donor reporting on official humanitarian assistance spending, and encourage the development of standardised formats for such reporting.

II. Accountability within the international humanitarian community

The GHD Principles

At the First International Meeting on Good Humanitarian Donorship, on 17 June 2003 in Stockholm, sixteen states and the European Commission endorsed the *Principles and Good Practice of Humanitarian Donorship.*[5] Since then, seven more states have joined the GHD Initiative,[6] meaning that all 23 Member States of the Development Assistance Committee (DAC) of the Organisation for Economic Co-operation (OECD) and its Development Assistance Committee (DAC), as well as the Czech Republic, have now endorsed the *Principles*.

In practice, progress towards implementing the *Principles* has been limited, in part because of differences in priorities and approaches to implementation and in interpretation and application of humanitarian principles, but also because of limited advocacy efforts on the part of stakeholders holding donors to account for their commitments.[7] It is therefore timely to introduce a new mechanism to help strengthen donor progress towards GHD.

Existing mechanisms to strengthen accountability

At the intergovernmental level, the DAC endorsed the *Principles* in April 2005 as the standard against which the work of its 23 members should be judged and against which they can be held accountable. Humanitarian donorship is now evaluated separately within the DAC's Peer Review process[8] according to a GHD Assessment Framework.[9] The assessments are of a qualitative nature and are carried out by a Peer Review team based on a fact-finding mission to the donor capital and field locations, and aimed at monitoring implementation of GHD principles and practices. The reports maintain a common format in order to be comparable across countries and cover six key areas. In this context, peer review can play a useful role in "identifying issues of policy coherence, as well as the linkages and logic of domestic policies that have a positive or negative impact on decisions and delivery of Humanitarian Action."[10]

Individual countries have also established country-specific systems to monitor GHD implementation at the country level but these were limited in scope.[11] Canada has developed performance indicators, while the UK government has set targets in its Public Service Agreement that govern budget allocations.

Donors have also worked on collective indicators to help track *collective* progress. The indicators developed in this context focused on three elements of the *Principles*, namely, that (i) donor funding was flexible and timely; (ii) donor and agency funding for Consolidated Appeals Processes (CAPs) and Common Humanitarian Action Plans (CHAPs) was allocated on the basis of needs assessment; and (iii) donors advocated for, and supported, coordination mechanisms. Progress against these has been measured using 2004 data as a baseline and is reported in the annual *Global Humanitarian Assistance* (GHA) publications.[12] In the July 2007 GHD meeting, a new set of improved indicators of wider scope was agreed upon.

As they are directly attributable to donor action, these indicators can make an important contribution to strengthening donor accountability. However, due to their collective nature, they cannot assess individual donor performance, a central aim of the present study. Moreover, they still cover only a subset of the *Principles* and are, therefore, viewed as too narrow to provide a comprehensive assessment of the GHD framework.

At the field level, two country pilots in Burundi and the Democratic Republic of Congo (DRC) were launched to test the GHD by developing collective impact indicators derived from the *Principles*.[13] These were considerably more comprehensive in scope than the collective GHD indicators, encompassing forty-two indicators that span fourteen different *Principles*.[14] However, these indicators cannot be clearly attributed to the performance of specific humanitarian actors and are focussed heavily on the multilateral CAP/CHAP framework.[15]

Another contribution to boost the GHD's collective performance measurement system was proposed by the Overseas Development Institute (ODI).[16] Their focus was on indicators that measure donors' responsibilities in relation to Principles 4 through 10. Underlying these is the intention to establish realistic and achievable targets against which progress can be measured. However, the authors concede that baselines do not currently exist for many of the proposed indicators. Moreover, the indicators would appear to be particularly difficult and time-consuming to quantify, thereby reducing their practical value.

III. The Humanitarian Response Index

Objectives of the HRI

The overview of GHD-based donor assessments shows the importance that the donor community attributes to the GHD initiative and reinforces its status as a benchmark for best practice in humanitarian donorship. However, the lack of comprehensive impact indicators for measuring donor performance continues to be identified as an outstanding challenge.[17]

The fact remains that the endorsement of the GHD *Principles*, as any code of conduct, constitutes only a *voluntary* effort on the part of donors that is non-binding. Moreover, the environment of humanitarian action is increasingly characterised by greater donor intervention and a considerably broadened scope of humanitarian policy, reaching well beyond mere humanitarian assistance to cover development and conflict reduction objectives. These leave the humanitarian field open to donor expediency not necessarily consonant with the principles and good practices of good humanitarian donorship.

Underlying the HRI is the rationale that a benchmarking mechanism could measurably strengthen donors' voluntary commitment to the *Principles*. International benchmarking has had considerable success across various fields as a mechanism for imposing additional discipline. For example, annual benchmarking exercises carried out by organisations such as the Centre for Global Development's *Commitment to Development Index*, Transparency International in the area of the prevalence of corruption and the World Economic Forum's competitiveness indices are seen to have contributed to focussing attention on the part of policy-makers, the business community and civil society on the need for reforms to improve important elements of the institutional environment.

As an alternative to a binding (legal) obligation, benchmarking works through peer pressure to motivate actors to improve efficiency, correct deficiencies in the policy framework, and possibly even avert damage to a country's reputation, thereby achieving improved performance without resorting to more stringent disciplining mechanisms. The HRI would therefore seem particularly well suited as a complement to the voluntary endorsement donors have made to the *Principles*. It offers an important platform for assessing the quality of donors' humanitarian involvement over time in a consistent, transparent, internationally comparable, and peer-reviewed manner.

The primary value of international benchmarking through an index is less in the rankings themselves and more in the opportunities provided by the underlying data collected for meaningful comparative analysis, both as regards a country's performance in relation to that of others and over time in relation to its own past.

There are two important distinctions between international benchmarking, as used in the HRI, and some of the work on developing indicators for impact assessment in the humanitarian field, described above. First, international benchmarking does not seek to set targets for indicators, in the sense of the Millennium Development Goals, against which progress is measured. Instead, it provides a relative standard of benchmarking between countries for any given period for which the assessment is undertaken. This has the advantage of avoiding the pitfall of having to set targets for each indicator, which, especially in the case of qualitative indicators, is fraught with problems, as it is difficult to find either theoretical or empirical underpinnings for such an exercise. Second, an important aim of this study is to assess donor countries on an *individual* basis, as too strong a focus on collective targets and assessments can result in free-riding that can seriously impede progress towards implementing the GHD commitments at the country operational level.[18]

Several key considerations have been taken into account when developing the HRI. First, due to its complex nature, we came to the view that individual donor behaviour would best be described by a combination of both qualitative and quantitative indicators. Since the *Principles* encompass a number of broad objectives, it would have been too limiting to attempt to assess compliance with respect to them by focussing only on quantitative indicators, valuable as these are. Indeed, there are a number of principles that cannot be easily captured by hard data or for which readily available, internationally comparable quantified benchmarks may simply not exist or may be difficult to build in an operationally useful way. While recognising the limitations of hard data and the value that can be derived from a well-formulated survey instrument, this approach allows a more comprehensive assessment that includes donors' humanitarian procedures and practices.

It is well known that virtually all of the higher-profile international benchmarking initiatives such as Transparency International's *Corruption Perceptions Index*, the World Economic Forum's *Global Competitiveness Index*, the *World Competitiveness Yearbook* of the IMD Business School, and the World Bank's *Investment*

Climate Assessments use surveys to build a bridge between difficult-to-quantify but otherwise critically important factors (e.g., property rights, the judicial climate, various dimensions of governance, and the quality of public institutions) and a set of quantified performance indicators.

Second, donor behaviour must be seen in the context of the relationship between the donor, as the institutional principal, and the implementing agency, as the delivering agent. This relationship has been explicitly incorporated in the formulation of the *Principles* and has guided the design of the questionnaire to collect the qualitative data used for the HRI. Finally, although individual donor behaviour cannot be fully separated from collective donor behaviour, the HRI unambiguously focuses on individual donor performance, as reflected in the hard data, and as perceived by implementing agencies in their relationships with individual donors.

The Survey
The qualitative data was collected by interviewing various stakeholders involved in humanitarian activities, guided by a targeted questionnaire (Questionnaire on Good Practice in Humanitarian Donorship, henceforward referred to as the *Survey*). The aim was to record the views or opinions of implementing agencies about how donors active in the agencies' area of operations have fared in relation to the *Principles*, across a representative selection of complex emergencies and natural disasters. In designing the Survey, we endeavoured not to make it overly burdensome for respondents. The questions posed in the Survey may be broadly interpreted as capturing assessment of donor performance at the time the Survey took place.[19] (A full listing of the questions contained in the Survey is contained in the Appendix, at the end of this Report). The wording of the questions reflected closely the spirit of the *Principle* being addressed.

During each field visit, the relevant agencies that were actively working with donors and had received funding from them in that particular crisis were interviewed. The target survey group included national and international NGOs, UN agencies, funds, and programmes, as well as other international organisations active in the field. To ensure that all relevant humanitarian actors were consulted, the field visits were planned in coordination with key stakeholders[20] who could help to initiate a dialogue with agencies in each field location.

The criteria used to select the sample of representative crises involved several dimensions, including the need to have, within the sample, both natural disasters and conflicts, appropriate geographic representation, and adequate donor presence in the crises. It was also thought desirable to have some diversity in terms of the magnitude of the emergencies and a critical volume of donor funding. The crises countries chosen were the Democratic Republic of the Congo, Niger, Sudan, Timor-Leste, Pakistan, Lebanon, Colombia and Haiti and the surveys were carried out during the period May–July 2007. A pilot study was carried out in Mozambique in April 2007 to test a first draft of the Survey and to ensure a reasonable degree of clarity in its formulation.

The Survey covers a range of topics and is divided into 3 sections that broadly mirror the organisation of the *Principles*:

- Objectives of humanitarian action
- General principles
- Good practices in donor financing, management and accountability
    (a) Funding
    (b) Promoting standards and enhancing implementation
    (c) Learning and accountability

Each question has the same structure, asking participants to evaluate donor performance with respect to a particular principle on a scale from 1 to 7. At one end of the scale, 1 typically represents the least favourable possible outcome, and at the other end of the scale, 7 represents the best.

There was a concerted effort to obtain a large sample of survey responses that would provide appropriate coverage across all 23 donors being ranked. While this was not a problem for the majority of countries, there were three countries for which it proved difficult to gather at least 20 responses. Perhaps not surprisingly, small donors with relatively modest budgets in the area of humanitarian assistance operate through a correspondingly smaller number of implementing agencies than more well-established donors. On balance, it was thought better to include these countries in the ranking, particularly given that the HRI has a large number of hard data indicators which provide valuable data on the performance of all donors, and where the size of the donor was not a relevant consideration. Obviously,

future editions of the HRI will endeavour, where possible, to increase the sample size with due regard to the overall quality of the sample. Table 1 provides a breakdown of the 1,021 responses by donor and by type of respondent.

Index formulation and structure

The HRI attempts to strike a balance between the need for broad coverage of factors explaining donor performance and a reasonable degree of economy as, in principle, there is virtually no limit to the number of variables that could be used to explain donors' humanitarian aid efforts and the extent to which these mirror the GHD *Principles*. The HRI is, thus, a broad and comprehensive assessment of how individual donors are faring relative to the commitments outlined in the *Principles*. In constructing the Index, it was first necessary to identify a number of index categories capturing different aspects of the *Principles*. Each *Principle* was then mapped to a category and the most appropriate quantitative and qualitative indicators capturing donor behaviour with respect to the underlying principle were identified. It was also necessary to determine appropriate weights both for the indicators within categories, as well as for the categories within the index and, finally, to define sensible normalisation mechanisms to aggregate survey and hard data indicators.

Box 2. Example of a typical Survey question

Has the donor provided humanitarian assistance in ways that are supportive of recovery and/or long-term development?

Not at all	1 2 3 4 5 6 7	Always

1: means you agree completely with the answer on the left-hand side
2: means you largely agree with the left-hand side
3: means you somewhat agree with the left-hand side
4: means your opinion is indifferent between the two answers
5: means you somewhat agree with the right-hand side
6: means you largely agree with the right-hand side
7: means you agree completely with the answer on the right-hand side

Table 1. Humanitarian Response Index 2007: Distribution of survey responses by country

Donor	Total number of responses	Responses from headquarters	Responses from field organisations
Australia	32	8	24
Austria	21	17	4
Belgium	25	5	20
Canada	74	6	68
Denmark	22	12	10
European Commission	185	15	170
Finland	17	11	6
France	31	9	22
Germany	39	9	30
Greece	17	14	3
Ireland	31	5	26
Italy	26	7	19
Japan	33	5	28
Luxembourg	20	10	10
Netherlands	44	5	39
New Zealand	18	7	11
Norway	44	7	37
Portugal	24	21	3
Spain	39	4	35
Sweden	45	7	38
Switzerland	32	5	27
UK	87	10	77
USA	115	4	111
TOTAL	**1021**	**203**	**818**

The following five categories were chosen:

1. Responding to humanitarian needs
2. Integrating relief and development
3. Working with humanitarian partners
4. Implementing international guiding principles
5. Promoting learning and accountability

Guided by the categories set out in the *Principles*, these groups were chosen to bring together all those principles that deal with broadly similar aspects of humanitarian assistance into various "pillars." For instance, Principles 3, 4, 16, 19, and 20 highlight the importance of humanitarian action taking place in a manner that is respectful of international humanitarian law and other international protocols and guidelines. They have all been brought into pillar 4 under the heading "Implementing international guiding principles." It is evident that because the principles sometimes overlap and may, in many cases, encompass elements drawn from

a number of dimensions of humanitarian action, the above categorisation is not unique. There are, indeed, many possible ways to organise the *Principles*.[21] Box 3 presents the structure of the HRI and the distribution of all hard and soft indicators by pillar.

Table 2 shows a detailed list and definitions of the hard data indicators for each of the five pillars of the HRI.

Several remarks are in order:

The HRI contains a total of 57 indicators, 25 of which have been built up as hard data indicators capturing some dimension of the *Principles*, with the rest drawn from the Survey and addressing, likewise, a specific principle.

These indicators are broadly distributed across the *Principles*, but without a rigid formula. Some principles are more amenable to quantification, while others may be more effectively measured through the Survey. Our approach has been pragmatic. Hard data indicators have been developed where possible, when they could be formulated in a way that highlighted some essential dimension of a particular principle, but subject to the requirement that the associated data used to build it were available for all countries being ranked and were internationally comparable.

Quantitative data were collected from a variety of sources such as OCHA-FTS and website, the ECHO 14-point HAC system, the OECD-DAC, the World Bank, UNDP, IFRC, ICRC, UNHCR, UNICEF, WFP, UNRWA, and from individual donors either in donor capitals or at headquarters for operational agencies. Without any doubt, each of these data sources has its own pitfalls, either because it is incomplete (OCHA-FTS), not very current (OECD-DAC), subject to possible bias, and so on. These drawbacks arise mainly from the failure by some donors and their key partners to provide the requisite information. But another challenging problem has been the lack of an internally acceptable definition of humanitarian assistance, which means that donors each have rather different concepts of what constitutes humanitarian aid. This makes comparisons across the board very difficult. In light of these limitations, in estimating the hard data indicators we have not relied exclusively on any one data source but have consulted a variety of sources, including figures provided directly by donors. However, the FTS is currently still the most detailed and timely source of information available on humanitarian aid across the board and therefore can provide a rich source of valuable insights on specific issues pertaining to humanitarian action.

Box 3. Composition of the Humanitarian Response Index

The detailed structure of the Humanitarian Response Index is provided below. The numbers next to the survey indicators match those used in the questionnaire, shown in Box 1. In a few instances, some survey questions have been combined.[1] A full description and definitions of the hard data indicators is provided in Table 2, shown below.

1st Pillar: Responding to humanitarian needs
Survey Indicators
1.01   Alleviation of suffering
2.01   Impartiality
2.02   Neutrality
2.03 & 2.04 Independence
5.01   Reallocation of funds from other crises
5.04   Timely funding
6.01   Funding in proportion to need
11.01 Commitment to ongoing crises

Hard Data Indicators
2.01   Distribution of funding relative to historical ties and geographic proximity
2.02   Distribution of funding relative to sector, forgotten emergency and media coverage
5.01   Funding in cash
5.02   Timely funding to complex emergencies
5.03   Timely funding to onset disasters
6.01   Funding to priority sectors
6.02   Distribution of funding relative to ECHO's GNA

2nd Pillar: Integrating relief and development
Survey Indicators
7.01   Consultation with beneficiaries on design and implementation
7.02   Consultation with beneficiaries on monitoring and evaluation
1.02   Strengthening preparedness
8.01 & 8.02 Strengthening local capacity to deal with crises
8.03   Strengthening resilience to cope with crises
8.04   Encouraging better coordination with humanitarian partners
9.01   Supporting long-term development aims
9.02   Supporting rapid recovery of sustainable livelihoods

Hard Data Indicators
8.01   Funding to strengthen local capacity
8.02   Funding to international disaster risk reduction mechanisms

3rd Pillar: Working with humanitarian partners
Survey Indicators
8.05   Supporting effective coordination efforts
10.01 Promoting role of NGOs
12.01 Predictability of funding
13.01 Reducing earmarking
13.02 Flexible funding
13.03 Longer-term funding arrangements
17.01 Donor preparedness in implementation of humanitarian action
17.02 Facilitating safe humanitarian access
18.01 & 18.02 Supporting contingency planning and capacity building efforts

Hard Data Indicators
10.01 Funding UN coordination mechanisms and common services
10.02 Funding NGOs
10.03 Funding Red Cross Movement
12.01 Funding CERF
12.02 Predictability of donor funding
13.01 Unearmarked or broadly earmarked funds
14.01 Funding UN Consolidated Inter-Agency Appeals
14.02 Funding IFRC Appeals
14.03 Funding ICRC Appeals
18.01 Funding quick disbursement mechanisms
18.02 Supporting UNDAC

4th Pillar: Implementing international guiding principles
Survey Indicators
3.01   Engagement in risk mitigation
3.02   Enhancing security
4.01   Protecting human rights
19.01 Affirming primary role of civilian organisations
Hard Data Indicators
4.01   Implementing international humanitarian law
4.02   Implementing human rights law

5th Pillar: Promoting learning and accountability
Survey Indicators
15.01 Supporting accountability in humanitarian action
21.01 & 21.02 Supporting learning and accountability initiatives
22.01 Encouraging regular evaluations
Hard Data Indicators
21.01 Support to main accountability initiatives
21.02 Funding of other accountability initiatives
22.01 Number of evaluations

1 For instance, survey questions 8.01 and 8.02, addressing the issue of whether the donor has strengthened the capacity of the government and the local communities, respectively, to prevent, prepare for, mitigate, and respond to humanitarian crises have been combined, meaning responses have been averaged across both questions and a single score used for each donor.

Table 2. Humanitarian Response Index 2007: Hard data indicators

PILLAR 1: RESPONDING TO HUMANITARIAN NEEDS

H2.01 Distribution of funding to recipient countries relative to historical ties and geographic proximity with recipient country	Principle 2 calls for the implementation of humanitarian action that is humane, impartial, "solely on the basis of need" and independent from "political, economic, military or other objectives." Despite commitment to these humanitarian principles, international humanitarian financing is considered not to be equitable, with amounts allocated across various emergencies that do not reflect comparative levels of need. Donors are often motivated to intervene in a given crisis for reasons that do not necessarily match this Principles, for example, due to historical links and/or geographic proximity. Underlying this reality is the fact that there is no system-wide framework for adequately judging the relative severity of situations through global needs assessment and for prioritising response accordingly.[1] In the absence of an internationally accepted benchmark against which to measure outcomes, this indicator is based on an analysis of possible motives which donors may have in delivering humanitarian aid. Therefore, in order to proxy the adherence to concepts of impartiality and independence, a mapping of 23 donors against 113 recipient countries assesses whether the donor country enjoys strong historical links with the recipient country and whether it is within close geographic proximity. The more independent the distribution of total donor funding to recipient countries is from historical links or issues of geographic proximity, the higher the score attributed to the individual donor. There is no presumption, for example, that a donor country should not fund a former colony. Rather, the indicator assesses whether the *preponderance* of donor funding is allocated to countries with which the donor has strong historical or geographic links, adjusting for the number of such ties/links, and allocating scores across donors in a way that gives higher credit to countries who are less swayed in their funding decisions by such considerations.
H2.02 Distribution of funding to emergencies relative to degree of media coverage, sector to which funding is allocated, and whether emergency is classified as forgotten	his indicator captures the same dimensions of Principle 2 in a different way. Since donor funding should fundamentally be guided by considerations of need, this indicator rewards donors whose humanitarian interventions are not biased against forgotten emergencies, are reasonably independent from extensive media coverage, and are not unduly focused on a few media-intense sectors, such as food and health. The indicator considers 329 emergencies in 2005 and 2006 and classifies donor funding by CAP sector, by the extent of media coverage each emergency receives, and by whether the emergency in question has been classified as "forgotten," both based on the IFRC's *World Disasters Report 2006* methodology.[2] The indicator allocates higher scores to donors whose funding decisions are less swayed by media attention to particular emergencies, are not biased in favour of the high-profile food and health sectors, and pay due regard to forgotten emergencies.
H5.01 Percentage of total HA provided in cash	Principle 5 calls on donors to "strive to ensure flexible and timely funding" to meet humanitarian needs. While this concept has a number of dimensions, this indicator calculates the share of total humanitarian assistance which the donor provided in cash, as reported by the Financial Tracking Service (FTS) of the UN Office for the Coordination of Humanitarian Affairs (OCHA).[3] The emphasis here is on the "flexible" component of this principle; cash as opposed to tied or rigidly earmarked aid unambiguously adds flexibility to funding.
H5.02 Funds within an Appeal committed or disbursed to complex emergencies in first quarter after Appeal date, as percentage of total funds within an Appeal committed to those crises during year	The timely delivery of resources in the event of a humanitarian crisis is strongly supported by the *Principles*. Indicator H5.02 calculates funds within a CAP committed or disbursed to complex emergencies in the first quarter after the Appeal date as a percentage of total funds within the Appeal committed or disbursed to those crises during the period 2005–2006. It is taken as a proxy for the timely delivery of funds to such crises.

(Cont'd.)

Table 2. Humanitarian Response Index 2007: Hard data indicators *(cont'd.)*

PILLAR 1: RESPONDING TO HUMANITARIAN NEEDS *(Cont'd.)*	
H5.03 Funds committed to individual onset of disasters disbursed to complex emergencies in first quarter after Appeal date, as percentage of total funds within an Appeal committed to those crises during year	Indicator H5.03 is different from H5.02 only to the extent that the indicator applies to onset disasters (as opposed to complex emergencies) up to six months after onset and also captures funding outside a CAP.
H6.01 Funds (inside and outside Appeals) committed to priority sectors (identified for each emergency by means of the CAPs) as a percentage of total funding to those emergencies	Principle 6 calls on donors to "allocate humanitarian funding in proportion to needs and on the basis of needs assessments." Notwithstanding the lack of a widely-accepted methodology for assessing global humanitarian needs, as alluded to earlier in the related discussion of Principle 2, this indicator is based on UN needs assessment methodology—albeit imperfect—to capture the proportion of total funding, inside and outside an Appeal, to emergencies with CAPs, that is directed to those priority sectors identified by the CAPs for each emergency. It is a proxy for donor readiness to respond on the basis of needs defined by the UN, as reflected in the share of funding going to identified priority sectors.
H6.02 Distribution of donor funding relative to ECHO's 2006 Vulnerability Index/GNA	This indicator builds on ECHO's 2006 global needs and vulnerability assessment (GNA)[4] which identifies the most vulnerable countries as those most in need of humanitarian assistance. The GNA is an existing needs assessment methodology, which is also regarded as subject to pitfalls, similar to the UN needs assessment described above. The GNA indicators include human development and poverty indicators, health of children, malnutrition, mortality, access to health care, prevalence of HIV-AIDS, tuberculosis and malaria, the gender-specific human development and Gini Indices, and crisis indicators such as ongoing or recently resolved conflicts, recent natural disasters and the extent of population movements. This indicator maps donor funding to over 100 recipient countries according to the GNA's vulnerability scores and crisis index and rewards donors whose humanitarian assistance is allocated to the most needy and vulnerable countries identified.
PILLAR 2: INTEGRATING RELIEF AND DEVELOPMENT	
H8.01 Funding to strengthen capacity of countries and local communities as a percentage of total Official Development Assistance (ODA)	Integrating relief and development is considered to be essential for ensuring that outcomes initiated during a humanitarian intervention are sustainable. It is clear that the returns to investment in humanitarian assistance will be higher where long-term development issues have been addressed in a comprehensive manner during the emergency phase. However, donors often lack mechanisms for funding recovery and reconstruction work. Donors without bilateral ongoing programmes are more likely to abandon the country once the crisis is deemed to have passed. H8.01 captures a donor's commitment to local capacity building, by looking at the ratio of donor funding to projects aimed at strengthening capacity-building activities for local NGOs and local institutions engaged in humanitarian activities (as reported in OCHA/FTS) in relation to ODA.[5]
H8.02 Funding to UNDP Thematic Trust Fund for Crisis Prevention and Recovery, the IFRC's disaster management activities, to the World Bank/ISDR Global Facility for Disaster Reduction and Recovery and to ProVention as a percentage of total ODA	This indicator captures donor commitment to disaster risk reduction and crisis prevention, focusing on the biggest multilateral mechanisms available to fund disaster risk reduction and prevention projects. The indicator includes donor financing of the UNDP's Thematic Trust Fund for Crisis Prevention and Recovery (2004-2005), the World Bank's Global Facility for Disaster Reduction and Recovery (2007), IFRC's disaster management activities (2005-2006) and ProVention (2005-2006) as a percentage of total ODA.

(Cont'd.)

Table 2. Humanitarian Response Index 2007: Hard data indicators *(cont'd.)*

PILLAR 3: WORKING WITH HUMANITARIAN PARTNERS	
H10.01 Funding to UN coordination mechanisms and common services ("coordination and support services") as a percentage of requirements	Principle 10 addresses aspects of the relationship between the donor and the United Nations, the International Red Cross and Red Crescent Movement and nongovernmental organisations. Donors recognise the critical role played by these three players in the delivery of humanitarian assistance and are, therefore, called upon to maintain a balanced selection of partners between UN, NGO and the Red Cross Movement, based on their competence and capacity. Grounded in the collective indicators, indicator H10.01 recognises the leading role of the UN agencies in humanitarian action, particularly in the light of the new approaches to sector coordination, by capturing funding to the United Nations coordination mechanisms and common services as a share of total requirements, using a fair share criterion which takes into account the share of an individual donor's GDP in total DAC GDP in allocating scores across donors. Funding amounts are defined as those contributed to "coordination and support services" inside UN CAPs.
H10.02 Funding to NGOs as percentage of total HA and restrictiveness of relationship	Acknowledging the important role NGOs play in delivering humanitarian aid, donor support to, and recognition of, this key role is measured in this indicator by donor funding to NGOs in relation to total humanitarian assistance in 2005 and 2006. In addition, this indicator rewards those donors which can fund foreign NGOs, instead of being restricted to funding only NGOs of their own nationality.[6]
H10.03 Funding to Red Cross and Red Crescent Movement as percentage of total HA	This indicator measures funding to the International Committee of the Red Cross and the International Federation of Red Cross and Red Crescent Societies (IFRC) similar to that for the funding to NGOs (H10.02) above.[7] Total funding as a share of total humanitarian assistance in 2005 and 2006 is calculated and scores are allocated accordingly.
H12.01 Funding to the Central Emergency Response Fund (CERF) based on fair share	Principle 12 is derived from donor concern for the need to develop good practices in donor financing and management of financial resources. Specifically, it addresses the issue of the desirability of ensuring flexibility in funding to United Nations agencies, so as to "ensure a more predictable and timely response to humanitarian emergencies, with the objectives of promoting early action and response to reduce loss of life."[8] Indicator H12.01 takes funding to the Central Emergency Response Fund (CERF), as a percentage of total humanitarian assistance. Scores are allocated using a fair share concept based on total DAC GDP.
H12.02 Predictability of donor funding to key humanitarian partners over the last five years	Based on Principle 12, this indicator deals with the predictability of funding to key humanitarian partners. The indicator encompasses the number of times a donor has allocated funding to each of the 144 organisations involved in the delivery of humanitarian action, over the period 2002–2006. Donors which have funded their partners in each of the five years will receive higher scores than donors whose funding has been sporadic and less predictable.
H13.01 Percentage of unearmarked or broadly earmarked funds (inside and outside Appeals) out of total humanitarian assistance	Principle 13 calls upon donors to "enhance the flexibility of earmarking, and of introducing longer-term funding arrangements." This indicator gives credit to donors which provide a greater share of their humanitarian assistance in unearmarked or broadly earmarked form during the period 2004–2006.

(Cont'd.)

Table 2. Humanitarian Response Index 2007: Hard data indicators *(cont'd.)*

PILLAR 3: WORKING WITH HUMANITARIAN PARTNERS *(Cont'd.)*

H14.01 Funding to UN Consolidated Inter-Agency Appeals as fair share

Principle 14 encourages donors to respond to Appeals of the United Nations and the Red Cross and Red Crescent Movement, giving them a leading role in responding to humanitarian emergencies. The UN Consolidated Inter-Agency Appeals Process (CAPs), identifies the funding needs of the crises they apply to. This indicator calculates donor funding to the 2006 CAPs as a proportion of total needs. In estimating donor scores, we use a fair share concept which takes into account the share of an individual donor's GDP in total DAC GDP, in keeping with Principle 14's reference to the equitable burden sharing considerations in determining the size of contributions.

H14.02 Funding to IFRC Annual and Emergency Appeals as percentage of needs met for these Appeals as fair share

The Red Cross and Red Crescent Movement—consisting of the IFRC, the ICRC and Red Cross national societies—have their own annual Appeals process. This indicator captures the funds directed to IFRC Appeals, both annual and emergency, in 2005 and 2006 as a share of total needs. As with the previous indicator, a fair share criterion is used in allocating scores to individual donors.

H14.03 Funding to ICRC Annual and Emergency Appeals as percentage of total funding as fair share

This indicator calculates funding to the ICRC Annual and Emergency Appeals as a percentage of total funding in 2005 and 2006 using the fair share concept used in H14.01 and H14.02.

H18.01 Funding to quick disbursement mechanisms as fair share

Underlying this indicator is the need to allocate funding to strengthen capacities for response. This indicator aggregates donor funding to the main mechanisms—other than the CERF—for committing funding under flexible terms, using a fair share criterion. Unlike the CERF, these mechanisms allow funds to be disbursed to key humanitarian organisations more widely than to only UN agencies, funds, and programmes, and enable the Humanitarian Coordinators to act independently and robustly in support of humanitarian objectives. The funds considered for this indicator are: the IFRC's Disaster Relief Emergency Fund, the Common Humanitarian Funds piloted in Sudan and Democratic Republic of Congo in 2006, Emergency Response Funds in 2006 for the DRC, Indonesia, Somalia, the Republic of Congo and Ethiopia and country Humanitarian Response Funds in 2005 for North Korea (DPRK), the DRC, Côte d'Ivoire, and Somalia.

H18.02 Funding to and operations of UNDAC

Principle 18 encourages donors to support initiatives and mechanisms for contingency planning by humanitarian organisations. In line with General Assembly Resolution 46/182, the United Nations established a central registry of all specialised personnel and teams of technical specialists—as well as relief supplies, equipment and services from governments, among others—which can be called upon at short notice. The United Nations Disaster Assessment and Coordination (UNDAC) team is a stand-by group of disaster management professionals, nominated and funded, among others, by member governments, who can be deployed within hours to carry out rapid assessment of priority needs and to support coordination efforts. The indicator captures several dimensions of donor support to the UNDAC mechanism, including financial contributions made by donors to the costs of its operations, the availability on short notice and presence of donor country representatives in UNDAC teams, as well as their in-kind support.

(Cont'd.)

Table 2. Humanitarian Response Index 2007: Hard data indicators *(cont'd.)*

PILLAR 4: IMPLEMENTING INTERNATIONAL GUIDING PRINCIPLES

H4.01 Acceptance to be bound by principal legal instruments on International Humanitarian Law (IHL), existence of national commissions on domestic implementation of IHL and in specific case of Rome Statute, whether domestic laws are enacted or in draft stage

Principle 4 calls for donors to "respect and promote the implementation of international humanitarian law, refugee law and human rights." Indicator H4.01 captures three dimensions of implementation. First, from a total of 24 key international humanitarian law treaties,[9] it registers the total number actually ratified, accepted, approved, or acceded to by individual donor countries. Beyond this, implementation requires that states adopt a number of internal laws and regulations and spread knowledge of the relevant Conventions and Protocols as widely as possible. The indicator gives additional credit to countries that have created national committees aimed at ensuring effective application of IHL, as advocated by the ICRC.[10] Finally, in the specific case of the Rome Statute on the International Criminal Court, it gives credit to donor countries depending on whether domestic laws have been enacted or are in draft stage, based on information collected by Amnesty International.

H4.02 Acceptance to be bound by principal legal instruments on human rights, including seven core instruments and their additional protocols

This indicator gives credit to donors in proportion to the number of principal legal instruments on human rights and their additional protocols they have ratified, accepted, approved, or acceded to, including the International Convention on the Elimination of All Forms of Racial Discrimination, the International Covenant on Economic, Social and Cultural Rights, the International Covenant on Civil and Political Rights, the Optional Protocol to the International Covenant on Civil and Political Rights, the Convention on the Elimination of All Forms of Discrimination Against Women, the Optional Protocol to the Convention on the Elimination of All Forms of Discrimination Against Women, the Convention Against Torture and Other Cruel, Inhuman or Degrading Treatment or Punishment, and the Convention on the Rights of the Child.

PILLAR 5: PROMOTING LEARNING AND ACCOUNTABILITY

H21.01 Membership, attendance, and support of key accountability initiatives

Principle 21 commits donors to "support learning and accountability initiatives for the effective and efficient implementation of humanitarian action." A number of initiatives exist, including the Sphere Project and the Humanitarian Accountability Project (HAP), aimed at defining standards for field level action. Others aim to improve the overall management (Quality COMPAS), or the human resources (People in Aid) of organisations. ALNAP (Active Learning Network for Accountability and Performance in Humanitarian Action) has a unique role in promoting evaluation and learning from experience as a tool to improve overall performance of agencies and donors. The indicator seeks to measure donor support for and commitment to these initiatives by capturing various dimensions of their participation. In the case of ALNAP, membership in, and attendance to biannual meetings are considered key factors in evaluating support. The indicator assigns different weights to each initiative, reflecting their relative importance in terms of impact on humanitarian action to date, with ALNAP and Sphere accounting for 70 percent of the total weight.

H21.02 Funding of other accountability and learning initiatives and projects

This indicator measures support to learning and accountability initiatives by means of funding assigned to ALNAP and HAP, as well as to those projects that support learning and accountability and are listed in OCHA/FTS for the years 2005 and 2006.[11] The scores are calculated in relation to total humanitarian assistance funding.

(Cont'd.)

Table 2. Humanitarian Response Index 2007: Hard data indicators *(cont'd.)*

PILLAR 5: PROMOTING LEARNING AND ACCOUNTABILITY *(Cont'd.)*

H22.01 Number of self and joint evaluations of learning initiatives and projects

Principle 22 encourages donors to make "regular evaluations of international responses to humanitarian crises, including assessments of donor performance." Evaluations assess humanitarian interventions according to defined criteria such as relevance, efficiency, and impact, and are useful to assess lessons learned to enhance the effectiveness of future donor interventions. Donors can evaluate their own performance, commission evaluations of activities carried out by organisations funded by them or engage with other agencies and donors in joint exercises. This indicator counts the number of publicly available individual evaluations carried out or funded by donors in the last three years (2004–2006). It also includes a measure of joint evaluations, given their broader scope. The indicator also takes into consideration the existence of evaluation guidelines, viewed as another means of promoting the practice of evaluations.

1 See Darcy and Hofman, 2003 and Willitts-King, 2007.

2 See Tables 1.1 and 1.2 in the IFRC report. Neglected crises were defined on the basis of the following methodologies: Reuters/AlertNet; Médecins sans Frontières, 2007; ECHO; and United Nations News Service. The extent of media coverage was based on the media tracking methodology developed by Reuters/AlertNet, detailed at http://www.alertnet.org/thefacts/chart/mediamonitoringmethodology.htm

3 The value of in-kind contributions continues to be a problematic issue. In the absence of a rigorous methodology applied by all donors for calculating this, we used the values entered in the FTS. However, for three donors, some in-kind contributions were entered with a zero value, leading to a possible minor overestimate of those donors' cash contributions for this particular indicator.

4 See links for European Commission Humanitarian (Aid) Office (ECHO).

5 Search terms used were Capacity building, Local capacity, Local community, Recovery, Prevention, Preparedness, Linking relief rehabilitation development, Coordinate, Strengthen response capacity, Reconstruction, Planning mitigation, and Contingency planning, in order to identify projects funded by donors whose main focus was to build local capacity in the sense of Principle 8.

6 These data were provided directly by donors in the context of visits to donor capitals by research teams.

7 Currently, the IFRC does not systematically collect data covering the amounts of official funding to respective national Red Cross societies based in donor countries. It was therefore not possible to apportion the share of official funding within the contributions that the IFRC receives from national societies, which amount to approximately US$900 million. In addition, it also does not capture donors' contributions to national Red Cross societies that are channelled as bilateral flows from one national society to another and completely bypass the Federation. Our figures for donor funding to the Red Cross and Red Crescent Movement therefore underestimate donors' commitment.

8 General Assembly Resolution A/RES/60/124 of 15 December 2005, 63rd plenary meeting.

9 The principal legal instruments on international humanitarian law are listed in the European Union guidelines on promoting compliance with international humanitarian law (European Union, 2005).

10 See ICRC (1997) Advisory Service on International Humanitarian Law: 1) Implementing International Humanitarian Law: from law to action, and 2) national Committees for the Implementation of International Humanitarian Law.

11 Using search terms: Learning and accountability, and evaluation, to identify relevant projects funded by donors.

In this respect, we have followed the approach of Development Initiatives (DI) in its *Global Humanitarian Assistance 2006* report, which relies heavily on this source of information to calculate certain indicators for which other sources of data are not available.

It is important to emphasise that the HRI rankings reflect both relative scores on the Survey *and* the hard data indicators and that these, in turn, do not depend on a single data source, such as FTS. Indeed, the advantages of an index such as the HRI compiled on the basis of 57 indicators, means that final rankings will not unduly depend on the fact that for a given country a particular hard data indicator may suffer from reliance on a data source which, in 2007, is less than perfect in its coverage. Our aim has been to use the best data *currently* available, while endeavouring to ensure that data deficiencies, where they exist, do not unfairly penalise one country more than others. Of course, it is to be hoped that with the rising importance of humanitarian assistance, efforts currently underway to improve the timeliness and coverage of existing data sources will be further strengthened.

With one exception, within each pillar all indicators have equal weight, both as regards those drawn from the Survey and those using hard data.[22] We did take a view as to the relative importance of the individual pillars (see below), but we found no strong theoretical or empirical reason to attribute different weights to particular indicators.

The index does not weigh all 5 pillars equally, on the grounds that, *a priori*, some principles are seen by the humanitarian community to be more important than others. This applies particularly to those principles allocated to the first pillar which capture various dimensions of a needs-based response. Nevertheless, it should be stated unequivocally that the determination of weights is not a scientific process, but is based on consultation with stakeholders.[23] Table 3 below shows the distribution of weights across the five pillars as used in the calculation of the HRI.

IV. Rankings and analysis

The rankings from the Humanitarian Response Index 2007 are presented in Tables 4 through 7. In the pages that follow we analyse the performance of a number of countries, including, in some detail, that of Sweden, this year's top performer. There is no attempt to be comprehensive in our choice of countries discussed; rather, we

Table 3. Weighting of pillars in Humanitarian Response Index

Pillar	Weight (%)
Responding to humanitarian needs	30
Integrating relief and development	20
Working with humanitarian partners	20
Implementing international guiding principles	15
Promoting learning and accountability	15
Total	**100**

Table 4. Humanitarian Response Index rankings 2007

Donor	HRI rankings	HRI scores
Sweden	1	5.37
Norway	2	5.13
Denmark	3	5.01
Netherlands	4	5.01
European Commission	5	4.91
Ireland	6	4.86
Canada	7	4.80
New Zealand	8	4.80
United Kingdom	9	4.76
Switzerland	10	4.68
Finland	11	4.58
Luxembourg	12	4.51
Germany	13	4.45
Australia	14	4.44
Belgium	15	4.42
United States	16	4.39
Spain	17	4.29
Japan	18	4.19
France	19	4.06
Austria	20	4.01
Portugal	21	3.95
Italy	22	3.87
Greece	23	3.17

have chosen a group which, in our view, illustrates some particularly interesting dimension of humanitarian action. Tables 5 through 7 provide a detailed presentation of the index results and, in addition, the donor profiles at the end of this Report provide valuable additional information about individual donor performance.

Table 5. Humanitarian Response Index 2007

Donor	OVERALL INDEX		Responding to humanitarian needs		Integrating relief and development		Working with humanitarian partners		Implementing international guiding principles		Promoting learning and accountability	
	Rank	Score	Rank	Score	Rank	Score	Rank	Score	Rank	Score	Rank	Score
Sweden	1	5.37	4	5.35	7	4.47	1	5.91	1	6.12	3	5.15
Norway	2	5.13	1	5.50	3	4.72	2	5.27	3	5.79	14	4.11
Denmark	3	5.01	2	5.47	5	4.67	7	4.17	4	5.75	5	4.96
Netherlands	4	5.01	5	5.34	11	4.35	3	5.15	11	5.40	7	4.65
European Commission	5	4.91	18	4.86	2	4.77	8	4.12	8	5.44	1	5.74
Ireland	6	4.86	3	5.37	4	4.68	5	4.38	16	5.09	11	4.46
Canada	7	4.80	8	5.14	6	4.55	11	3.76	5	5.70	6	4.96
New Zealand	8	4.80	9	5.12	1	5.00	12	3.53	2	5.86	9	4.50
United Kingdom	9	4.76	11	5.07	13	4.25	4	4.44	18	5.04	4	4.99
Switzerland	10	4.68	13	4.98	8	4.43	9	4.11	14	5.34	10	4.49
Finland	11	4.58	10	5.11	19	3.93	10	3.87	13	5.39	8	4.53
Luxembourg	12	4.51	6	5.23	16	4.14	6	4.29	19	5.01	19	3.36
Germany	13	4.45	12	4.99	17	4.12	15	3.37	9	5.42	12	4.25
Australia	14	4.44	17	4.86	9	4.38	14	3.42	15	5.23	13	4.23
Belgium	15	4.42	14	4.95	12	4.27	16	3.36	7	5.60	17	3.80
United States	16	4.39	16	4.91	10	4.37	13	3.43	23	3.83	2	5.22
Spain	17	4.29	15	4.93	15	4.15	17	3.12	6	5.67	18	3.40
Japan	18	4.19	7	5.23	18	4.02	21	2.55	21	4.70	15	4.04
France	19	4.06	21	4.48	22	3.48	18	3.06	10	5.41	16	3.97
Austria	20	4.01	20	4.63	21	3.62	19	3.02	12	5.40	20	3.20
Portugal	21	3.95	19	4.71	14	4.16	22	2.48	17	5.07	22	2.98
Italy	22	3.87	22	4.46	20	3.88	20	2.84	20	4.82	21	3.08
Greece	23	3.17	23	3.43	23	3.16	23	2.17	22	4.68	23	2.44

Table 6. Humanitarian Response Index 2007: Good Practice in Humanitarian Donorship Survey

Donor	PILLAR 1: RESPONDING TO HUMANITARIAN NEEDS							
	Alleviation of suffering	Impartiality	Neutrality	Independence	Reallocation of funds from other crises	Timely funding	Funding in proportion to need	Commitment to ongoing crises
Australia	20	19	21	21	6	6	18	9
Austria	19	17	10	14	21	10	21	18
Belgium	14	3	4	12	18	18	13	7
Canada	10	9	15	10	9	12	9	8
Denmark	5	10	7	13	11	1	15	15
European Commission	13	15	17	16	22	16	5	6
Finland	12	12	14	9	8	15	21	23
France	22	22	22	22	13	20	11	1
Germany	8	13	9	7	16	14	6	19
Greece	23	23	20	19	17	23	23	21
Ireland	8	14	5	1	1	7	17	14
Italy	17	18	18	17	10	22	4	11
Japan	16	6	12	6	20	19	16	17
Luxembourg	3	5	8	4	18	8	14	3
Netherlands	7	4	16	15	4	11	8	16
New Zealand	1	1	3	2	2	2	3	5
Norway	5	8	11	8	7	4	2	4
Portugal	21	20	13	20	23	21	20	22
Spain	11	11	2	5	15	17	1	2
Sweden	2	7	6	11	5	5	10	12
Switzerland	4	2	1	3	3	3	19	10
United Kingdom	15	16	19	18	14	9	7	13
United States	18	21	23	23	12	13	12	20

Donor	PILLAR 2: INTEGRATING RELIEF AND DEVELOPMENT							
	Consultation with beneficiaries on design and implementation	Consultation with beneficiaries on monitoring and evaluation	Strengthening preparedness	Strengthening local capacity to deal with crises	Strengthening resilience to cope with crises	Encouraging better coordination with humanitarian partners	Supporting long-term development aims	Supporting rapid recovery of sustainable livelihoods
Australia	17	17	13	1	1	3	8	14
Austria	19	22	20	11	16	9	22	22
Belgium	2	6	1	18	13	20	11	3
Canada	10	3	2	4	17	6	4	15
Denmark	3	11	6	2	2	5	3	5
European Commission	13	4	5	7	8	8	10	10
Finland	11	18	22	13	19	22	20	16
France	22	20	15	21	22	17	17	21
Germany	12	7	11	14	17	16	21	18
Greece	21	23	23	23	23	23	23	23
Ireland	18	5	8	19	11	19	8	13
Italy	20	15	19	22	21	11	13	20
Japan	7	19	17	20	20	18	19	19
Luxembourg	9	16	16	17	9	21	18	4
Netherlands	5	9	7	5	14	15	14	7
New Zealand	1	21	21	2	4	1	1	1
Norway	6	10	12	12	6	4	2	6
Portugal	23	1	3	10	5	14	16	16
Spain	4	8	9	9	10	12	6	8
Sweden	14	14	10	6	12	2	15	9
Switzerland	8	12	17	8	3	10	5	11
United Kingdom	16	13	14	15	15	13	12	12
United States	15	2	4	14	7	7	7	2

Table 6. Humanitarian Response Index 2007: Good Practice in Humanitarian Donorship Survey *(cont'd.)*

Donor	PILLAR 3: WORKING WITH HUMANITARIAN PARTNERS								
	Supporting effective coordination efforts	Promoting role of NGOs	Predictability of funding	Reducing earmarking	Flexible funding	Longer-term funding arrangements	Donor preparedness in implementation of humanitarian action	Facilitating safe humanitarian access	Supporting contingency planning and capacity building efforts
Australia	17	15	15	11	12	7	8	1	12
Austria	18	16	20	21	20	21	16	20	21
Belgium	2	20	3	14	16	8	21	11	4
Canada	10	12	9	16	17	13	6	14	13
Denmark	6	1	5	4	5	1	2	13	6
European Commission	4	4	6	22	19	10	5	8	15
Finland	5	18	21	10	3	18	18	21	11
France	21	17	16	19	18	17	15	17	19
Germany	14	5	7	15	15	15	10	12	17
Greece	23	22	23	20	22	23	23	23	23
Ireland	15	13	8	8	4	2	14	18	10
Italy	19	10	18	9	5	20	20	16	18
Japan	20	21	19	23	23	19	19	22	20
Luxembourg	16	19	17	6	2	3	13	2	3
Netherlands	3	9	2	7	8	14	17	7	1
New Zealand	7	6	11	2	1	4	12	9	14
Norway	9	6	14	3	8	9	7	3	16
Portugal	22	23	22	18	21	22	22	4	22
Spain	12	3	13	13	13	6	11	19	9
Sweden	1	11	1	1	11	11	1	9	2
Switzerland	8	2	12	5	7	16	4	15	7
United Kingdom	11	14	4	12	10	5	9	5	5
United States	13	8	10	17	14	12	3	6	8

Donor	PILLAR 4: IMPLEMENTING INTERNATIONAL GUIDING PRINCIPLES			
	Engagement in risk mitigation	Enhancing security	Protecting human rights	Affirming primary role of civilian organisations
Australia	6	2	21	21
Austria	18	21	15	19
Belgium	10	12	6	14
Canada	11	8	8	5
Denmark	5	6	4	11
European Commission	8	7	11	9
Finland	14	15	16	6
France	21	20	19	17
Germany	13	17	12	4
Greece	23	22	23	20
Ireland	16	11	9	15
Italy	22	23	22	22
Japan	15	19	20	8
Luxembourg	19	14	14	1
Netherlands	4	10	10	7
New Zealand	1	1	2	3
Norway	7	3	4	13
Portugal	17	16	6	23
Spain	20	8	13	12
Sweden	2	4	3	2
Switzerland	3	5	1	10
United Kingdom	12	18	18	16
United States	9	13	17	18

Donor	PILLAR 5: PROMOTING LEARNING AND ACCOUNTABILITY		
	Supporting accountability in humanitarian action	Supporting learning and accountability initiatives	Encouraging regular evaluations
Australia	17	8	12
Austria	15	21	18
Belgium	13	2	2
Canada	5	12	8
Denmark	4	3	3
European Commission	2	9	1
Finland	9	14	6
France	18	20	19
Germany	3	17	11
Greece	23	23	23
Ireland	19	11	13
Italy	13	19	22
Japan	9	18	20
Luxembourg	20	13	7
Netherlands	6	7	10
New Zealand	11	5	5
Norway	12	16	15
Portugal	16	22	21
Spain	21	15	17
Sweden	8	1	13
Switzerland	22	6	16
United Kingdom	6	4	9
United States	1	10	4

Table 7. Humanitarian Response Index 2007: Hard data indicators

Donor	PILLAR 1: RESPONDING TO HUMANITARIAN NEEDS						
	Distribution of funding relative to historical ties and geographic proximity	Distribution of funding relative to sector, forgotten emergency and media coverage	Funding in cash	Timely funding to complex emergencies	Timely funding to onset disasters	Funding to priority sectors	Distribution of funding relative to ECHO's GNA
Australia	6	21	17	8	6	18	19
Austria	19	16	19	23	3	16	4
Belgium	22	7	9	17	10	14	3
Canada	2	18	16	16	16	4	12
Denmark	10	6	2	3	4	20	5
European Commission	n/a	8	12	9	22	12	14
Finland	9	12	6	14	17	7	7
France	20	19	20	12	5	10	17
Germany	15	11	14	20	7	13	13
Greece	18	23	23	22	23	11	20
Ireland	14	10	4	2	21	8	10
Italy	17	14	15	19	20	19	21
Japan	3	20	13	11	2	3	6
Luxembourg	8	13	11	10	8	15	16
Netherlands	12	4	7	7	13	9	9
New Zealand	7	22	8	21	18	2	15
Norway	11	5	5	4	9	17	8
Portugal	4	15	21	6	1	1	23
Spain	16	3	18	15	11	22	18
Sweden	13	1	1	1	12	23	11
Switzerland	5	2	3	18	19	21	22
United Kingdom	21	9	10	5	15	5	1
United States	1	17	22	13	14	6	2

Donor	PILLAR 2: INTEGRATING RELIEF AND DEVELOPMENT	
	Funding to strengthen local capacity	Funding to international disaster risk reduction mechanisms
Australia	11	11
Austria	22	21
Belgium	9	19
Canada	18	3
Denmark	7	4
European Commission	3	n/a
Finland	13	16
France	23	20
Germany	16	13
Greece	20	22
Ireland	1	8
Italy	19	9
Japan	17	5
Luxembourg	5	18
Netherlands	12	12
New Zealand	8	1
Norway	4	2
Portugal	14	10
Spain	21	17
Sweden	6	6
Switzerland	2	14
United Kingdom	15	7
United States	10	15

Table 7. Humanitarian Response Index 2007: Hard data indicators *(cont'd.)*

Donor	PILLAR 3: WORKING WITH HUMANITARIAN PARTNERS										
	Funding UN coordi- nation mechanisms and common services	Funding to NGOs	Funding Red Cross Movement	Funding CERF	Predictability of funding	Unearmarked or broadly ear- marked funds	Funding UN Consolidated Inter- Agency Appeals	Funding IFRC Appeals	Funding ICRC Appeals	Funding quick disbursement mechanisms	Supporting UNDAC
Australia	12	19	7	11	9	11	14	11	13	10	6
Austria	21	12	7	19	21	3	22	16	16	10	12
Belgium	13	19	1	13	15	18	9	14	9	6	16
Canada	11	15	1	9	5	5	10	7	12	7	9
Denmark	7	6	7	6	13	2	6	6	7	8	10
European Commission	n/a	1	7	n/a	1	23	11	13	11	n/a	n/a
Finland	5	19	1	8	15	9	8	4	6	10	11
France	20	7	7	17	17	13	18	22	19	10	17
Germany	19	1	7	19	11	21	19	20	17	10	8
Greece	21	19	19	18	22	19	21	19	22	10	19
Ireland	3	1	7	5	8	14	5	3	10	5	19
Italy	17	15	19	19	13	15	20	17	21	10	15
Japan	15	19	19	14	9	17	17	15	23	10	14
Luxembourg	8	7	7	1	20	10	1	10	1	10	19
Netherlands	4	7	1	4	6	1	3	5	4	1	5
New Zealand	6	12	7	19	17	16	16	8	15	10	13
Norway	1	7	7	1	7	4	4	1	5	1	3
Portugal	16	14	19	15	23	20	23	23	20	10	18
Spain	18	15	7	12	19	12	15	21	18	10	19
Sweden	1	1	1	1	4	7	1	1	1	1	1
Switzerland	10	15	1	10	11	8	12	12	1	9	2
United Kingdom	9	7	7	7	2	6	7	9	8	1	4
United States	14	1	19	16	3	22	13	18	14	10	7

Donor	PILLAR 4: IMPLEMENTING INTERNATIONAL GUIDING PRINCIPLES	
	Implementing international humanitarian law	Implementing human rights law
Australia	9	12
Austria	5	3
Belgium	9	3
Canada	5	3
Denmark	2	3
European Commission	n/a	n/a
Finland	5	12
France	2	3
Germany	5	12
Greece	16	12
Ireland	16	12
Italy	19	3
Japan	20	19
Luxembourg	21	12
Netherlands	13	12
New Zealand	13	3
Norway	2	3
Portugal	16	3
Spain	13	1
Sweden	1	1
Switzerland	9	19
United Kingdom	9	19
United States	22	22

Donor	PILLAR 5: PROMOTING LEARNING AND ACCOUNTABILITY		
	Support to main accountability initiatives	Funding of other accountability initiatives	Number of evaluations
Australia	4	15	14
Austria	20	18	18
Belgium	12	13	20
Canada	10	12	3
Denmark	9	11	5
European Commission	1	8	1
Finland	13	1	16
France	15	4	13
Germany	16	10	7
Greece	20	18	20
Ireland	2	7	10
Italy	18	18	20
Japan	17	3	12
Luxembourg	20	18	17
Netherlands	7	6	8
New Zealand	13	1	19
Norway	11	17	10
Portugal	18	18	20
Spain	20	18	15
Sweden	6	5	5
Switzerland	2	9	9
United Kingdom	4	14	4
United States	7	16	2

Figure 1. Humanitarian Response Index: Hard data indicators versus survey data

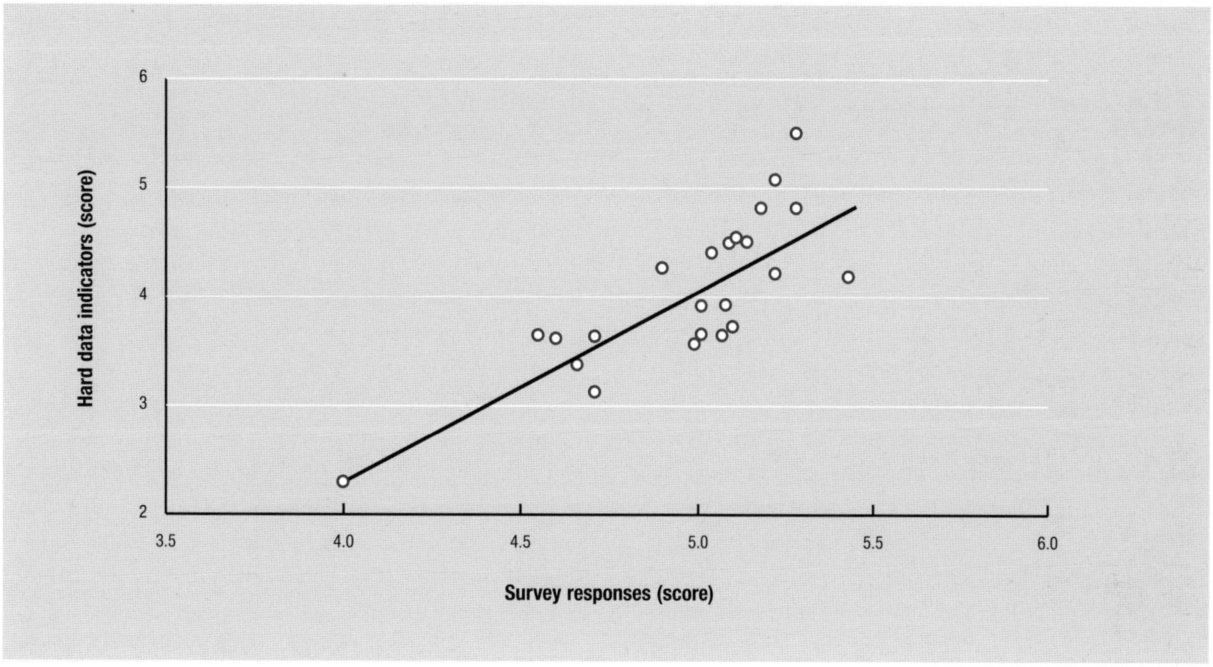

The HRI country results show a strong correlation between hard and soft data indices, suggesting that the results from both reinforce each other, thereby boosting some of the conclusions that can be drawn at the country level (Figure 1).

Country Profiles

Sweden[24]

Sweden is the best-ranking donor in the Humanitarian Response Index (HRI) 2007. Its outstanding performance is backed by both hard and soft data variables. It receives the highest score in the hard data index (5.51) and shares second place with Denmark (5.28) in the soft data index.

Sweden scores well across all five pillars, ranking first in the areas "Working with humanitarian partners" and "Implementing international guiding principles." Sweden occupies the top place in nineteen variables of the 57 variables used to construct the Index, roughly for a third of all the indicators. It receives its lowest pillar score in the area "Integrating relief and development," where it comes seventh among the 23 donors ranked.

Within the first pillar, "Responding to humanitarian needs," often referred to as the "heart" of the GHD and the pillar which attracts the highest weighting in the HRI, Sweden's strong ranking (4)[26] comes from a distribution of funding that is more focused on forgotten emergencies and on those sectors that typically receive low-profile media coverage than any other donor. This focus on forgotten emergencies appears to rest, at least in part, on its informal policy to fund all UN consolidated Appeals unless these are already well-funded, thereby reaching those crises otherwise forgotten to the world. To ensure the availability of funds for humanitarian contingencies, it caps spending on humanitarian aid within the first six months of the year at 80 percent of the available budget. It also operates a policy of transfer of funds for humanitarian action from non-humanitarian budget lines toward the end of a given year.

Equally, Sweden excels in providing the vast majority of its humanitarian assistance in the form of cash and in responding in a timely manner to complex emergencies, providing the bulk (74 percent) of its humanitarian assistance to emergencies within the first three months of their Appeal launch dates. This very favourable view of Sweden's success in responding to humanitarian needs strongly confirms findings in its OECD Peer

Review (2005), to the effect that Sweden is perceived as a timely provider of flexible funding.[25] Its ability to deliver on its commitment to the basic principles of humanitarian action is further boosted by their incorporation into its humanitarian aid policy, which reflects the GHD.

In the third pillar, "Working with humanitarian partners," which encompasses those GHD *Principles* that govern the relationship between donors and the partners they support to implement humanitarian action, Sweden unambiguously establishes itself as the foremost multilateralist in humanitarian action. According to the views of humanitarian actors in the field compiled as the soft data index, Sweden surpasses all other donors in supporting and facilitating coordination efforts and in its ability to support the implementation of humanitarian action at short notice. While Sweden does not delegate humanitarian aid to its field missions, it relies on a network of regional humanitarian coordinators to assess needs, and to monitor and follow up on its humanitarian aid portfolio. This includes close interaction with OCHA and assisting to determine needs.

In the hard data indicators, Sweden's rankings show that it has thrown its full weight behind the UN and the Red Cross Movement, proving to be among the most generous donors of the OECD-DAC group in this pillar, relative to its income. It receives top marks for funding UN coordination mechanisms and common services, the CERF, the UN, IFRC, and ICRC Appeals, and other quick disbursement mechanisms (including to pooled funds in Sudan and DRC) and for its cash and in-kind support to UNDAC.

In this context, Sweden stands out for providing predictable funding (4) to its multilateral partners, confirmed by its OECD Peer Review that reports the availability of multi-year funding arrangements that can span up to three years, subject to annual parliamentary approval. The Swedish example shows that donor accountability concerns can be met without eschewing multi-year funding arrangements, by making them subject to annual parliamentary approval. This is a formula which other donors could further explore.

Like most donors, Sweden's relationship to the NGOs it funds is governed by a trusted relationship—including pre-screening—with certain international and Swedish NGOs on whom it repeatedly relies to implement its humanitarian aid programmes. A select number of Swedish NGOs also have access to rapid-response funds for contingencies. Sweden obtains second place in the indicator on supporting contingency planning.

Its multilateralist credentials are further boosted by its top performance in the fourth pillar "Implementing international guiding principles," based on its excellent record in implementing the core instruments of international humanitarian law (1) and of human rights (joint first with Spain). Promotion and respect for IHL, refugee, and human rights law are all anchored in its humanitarian policy statement. In its GHD Implementation Plan, also Sweden cites ongoing activities in these areas, including training programmes and financial support to the ICRC, the foremost organisation with a mandate for promoting IHL.

It is also deemed by the humanitarian field to be among the top four donors for its engagement in risk mitigation, enhancing security, protecting human rights, and affirming the primary role of civilian organisations in the delivery of humanitarian aid. These are all firmly enshrined within its Policy Document. In addition, there is a strict limit on the funding that can be channeled to projects implemented by the military.

In many respects, Sweden is a model GHD donor, as it has managed to incorporate the GHD *Principles* into its own institutional operating environment. The government's humanitarian aid policy documents explicitly spells out its commitment to the Military and Civil Defence Assets (MCDA) guidelines and the primary role of civilian organisations in implementing humanitarian aid. It has also introduced a strong rights perspective into its humanitarian programme, which has been effective in promoting the rights of the child, especially in armed conflicts and during reconstruction.

The results for Sweden also point to some weaker areas, notably in pillar 2, "Integrating relief and development." Here, although it has devoted considerable attention to this area—including ensuring that implementing organisations ensure the participation of beneficiaries as per grant guidelines, spelling out a strategy[27] for the integration of humanitarian aid and development cooperation within its Policy—the opinion of the field is that it does less well in supporting long-term development aims (15), in consulting with beneficiaries on design and implementation (14), monitoring and evaluation (14), or in strengthening the resilience to cope with crises (12).

This is an area that has also been flagged in Sweden's OECD Peer Review, warning that "management of transition situations has become less flexible due to changes on what can be financed through the development cooperation budget and the budget line for humanitarian assistance and conflict management." Until 2005, SIDA could operate development cooperation programmes through its humanitarian arm but the new guidelines stipulate that transition should be covered primarily by the development cooperation budget and occasionally through the humanitarian budget.[28]

Its record in the first pillar, concerning needs-based response, also suffers from low or mediocre rankings. These suggest that its funding within the UN Appeals could be better focused towards Appeal priority sectors (23) and, to a lesser extent, the lack of timeliness of funding to onset disasters (12), with only 42 percent of its funding committed or disbursed within the first month of the onset of a disaster. The former suggests that the framework for Sweden's sector policies, the *Policy for Global Development*, may be spreading its priorities too thinly across the many sectoral priorities.

Norway

Norway (2) follows close on the heels of Sweden, achieving excellent rankings for the first four pillars. It comes in second place in the hard data index (5.08) and in fifth place (5.21) in the soft data index. Norway ranks among the top five donors in just under half of all indicators.

Norway does spectacularly well in pillar 1, coming in first place for a needs-based humanitarian response. It is perceived to be doing well at providing timely funding (4), based on needs assessments (2) and for remaining committed to ongoing crises (4). This is backed by hard data indictors, showing Norway's strengths in funding complex emergencies in a timely manner (4) and providing a large share of its funding in cash (5). It also excels in reaching forgotten crises (5), but does relatively poorly at directing its funding to priority sectors identified by the CAPs for respective emergencies (17).

Like Sweden, Norway is a multilateralist at heart, achieving overall second place in pillar 3. Relative to income, it is the most generous donor in funding UN coordination mechanisms and common services, and the second most generous in funding IFRC Appeals. It also comes a joint first for funding the CERF (representing the third most generous donor) and other quick disbursement mechanisms (fourth most generous donor), both measured relative to its income. It is also perceived by the humanitarian field to be doing well at facilitating safe humanitarian access (3).

It ranks very high (3) in pillar 4, just behind New Zealand for implementing the core instruments of international humanitarian law (2) and of human rights (3), and supported by favourable views from the field,

especially in enhancing security (3) and protecting human rights (4).

Norway does rather less well in supporting learning and accountability initiatives (pillar 5), where it achieves an overall mediocre ranking (14), due to perceived weakness in supporting learning and accountability initiatives (16) or encouraging regular evaluations (15). This is supported by the hard data showing a lack of commitment to the main humanitarian accountability initiatives (11) and of support to other accountability initiatives (17).

A major weakness in this respect is that, unlike Sweden, Norway does not have a comprehensive policy document that sets out its humanitarian policies. In this sense, it is less accountable, as it makes it difficult to assess how it sets its priorities for humanitarian action.[29]

European Commission

In fifth place overall, the European Commission's strong showing in the Index reflects a good result (7) in the hard data index.[30] However, its tenth place in the soft data index may betray some problems with its perception among humanitarian field actors.

The European Commission's stellar performance is in pillar 5, where it is perceived to be strongly supportive of accountability in humanitarian action (2) and of encouraging regular evaluations (1). This is strongly backed up by the hard data variables capturing membership of, attendance at, and funding of the main accountability initiatives and the number of evaluations, on which it does better than all other donors. This good performance may be partly explained by the fact that the European Commission's Humanitarian Office (ECHO), the main channel for the EC's humanitarian aid, is under a legal obligation to evaluate the activities it funds.[31] Evaluations are not just aimed at reviewing ECHO-funded operations, but often form the basis of wide consultation with stakeholders to improve coordination. This has paid off with a high score for consultation with beneficiaries on monitoring and evaluation (4) and for supporting effective coordination efforts (4). In this context, ECHO sees its comparative advantage over individual Member States in being able to "intervene in politically sensitive situation more flexibly,"[32] as it has a neutral past, especially in the context of colonial ties. The EC is examining how to do more to lead and coordinate Member State assistance in politically charged contexts.

The EC's wider engagement with civil society is perceived in a positive light, underscored by its excellent ranking for promoting the role of NGOs (4). ECHO has fostered strong partnerships with its 200 NGO partners that have signed its framework partnership agreement, which essentially pre-certifies NGOs that fulfill prerequisite requirements, such as sufficient financial, technical, and administrative capacity to be implementing partners. In principle, this should ensure rapid reaction times to crises, although this is not supported by its rankings for the hard data indicators on response times to complex emergencies (9) and to natural disasters (22). ECHO also applies strict criteria with regard to quality and performance of its partner NGOs and carries out an evaluation of its partner NGOs' activities every year and assesses whether they have taken up the recommendations from previous years.[33]

Despite its mandate to foster the transition from emergency aid to rehabilitation and development, the EC has had limited success in this area. It scores well on measures to reduce the vulnerability of populations at risk, for example, for funding local capacity (3) and for strengthening local capacity to deal with crises (7). It is a major supporter of IFRC work in the area of capacity-building and preparedness. However, it receives a lower rank for supporting long-term development aims (10). The ongoing decentralisation of EU aid, now largely delegated to the field, may offer scope for improvement to establish better integration of humanitarian aid with existing development instruments, especially relevant Ministries at the field level, which would build in the local dimension, an important ingredient for successful efforts in this area.

A key characteristic of the EC's humanitarian aid is its lack of flexibility. For example, in pillar 1, it is deemed to do rather poorly on the flexible allocation of funds across emergencies (22) and, similarly, in pillar 3, it receives very low ranks for reducing the earmarking of funds (22) and for the flexibility of its funding (19). This reflects the EC philosophy that funding according to needs implies earmarking funds to those needs. This is underlined by the lowest rank for any donor for the extent of earmarking (23). ECHO is an operational donor with very active field presence, with 43 field offices, including six regional support offices. This, along with its large budget allows it to carry out its own needs-assessments in the field and to "go it alone" in allocating its humanitarian budget accordingly. Its strong field presence and multilateral character enables it to play a strong role in coordination efforts.

It has, thus, been less reliant on multilateral organisations, with larger overhead costs, for implementing its

humanitarian assistance programmes and, compared to its size, channels a much smaller share through the multilateral channels than most other donors. This may be changing. Since 2002, when ECHO reported channeling an unusually high 62 percent of its funding through NGOs, there has been a shift towards a more balanced portfolio and increased funding to the UN and the Red Cross and Red Crescent Movement. The EC funding share to the UN had increased from 29 percent in 2002 to 37 percent in 2006, while the funding share to the Red Cross and Red Crescent Movement and to the International Organization for Migration (IOM) stood at 11 percent, with the remaining 52 percent going to NGOs.[34]

Although ECHO supports the new trend of pooled funding mechanisms, including the CERF and country-level funds, it has decided not to contribute to them, citing its own accountability requirements which prevent it from committing its funds to these unearmarked mechanisms, the fact that CERF funds cannot be allocated to NGOs, as well as the lack of *additional* budgetary resources, stipulated by the General Assembly.[35, 36] Its own internal financial regulations also do not allow ECHO to pay a "double overhead charge," one for the CERF or country-level fund and then again for the implementing partner that receives the funds. Because of its strong field presence, enabling it both to attend field coordination meetings and to disburse funds at least as quickly, ECHO sees no added value in contributing to pooled funding.

Relying on its own needs assessments has presumably secured the EC its good result for the indicator assessing funding based on needs assessments (5) in pillar 1, but performance in this pillar is also marred by low grades—especially vis-à-vis its overall ranking—for upholding the basic principles of humanitarian action, for example, alleviation of suffering (13), impartiality (15), neutrality (17) and independence (16). These may suggest that the there is still scope for improving the EC's decisions to grant humanitarian aid so that they are based "solely on an assessment of the beneficiary populations' needs," its stated policy.[37] Indeed, its rankings for funding to forgotten emergencies (8) and relative to its own global needs assessment methodology (14) strongly reinforce this point.

It is also hoped that the ongoing consultation round on EU humanitarian action[38] should help to refocus it towards the GHD *Principles*, giving its needs-based orientation a welcome boost and should help to strengthen EU humanitarian policy and to achieve greater efficiency and coherence in delivering its humanitarian aid.

Ireland and New Zealand

Ireland and New Zealand—by any definition small countries with correspondingly "small" humanitarian aid budgets—jointly accounted for about 1 percent of total DAC GDP in 2006. Their relative strong showings in the HRI, with ranks of 6 and 8, respectively, reflect a number of factors. First, New Zealand is an extremely strong performer in the integrating relief and development pillar and in those principles captured under pillar 4, on implementing international guiding principles, it has a rank of 1 and 2, respectively. It also earns high scores on those indicators which track commitment to learning and accountability initiatives, flexibility of funding, and funding which is committed on the basis of needs and needs assessments. Ireland has a rank of 3 in the pillar with the greatest weight in the index, responding to humanitarian needs, and also has particularly high scores in those indicators capturing the existence of flexible and timely funding arrangements, shows strong commitment to the strengthening of local capacity to deal with crises and works very well with nongovernmental organisations in the implementation of humanitarian actions. The fact that two small countries such as Ireland and New Zealand occupy relatively privileged positions in the HRI provides clear indication that the Index is able to discriminate efficiency aspects of humanitarian action from volumes of aid provided, and that it does not unfairly penalise countries which do not have large humanitarian assistance operations and the large bureaucracies that sometimes accompany them.

Canada

Canada has a very respectable ranking of 7 in the HRI, with a particularly good performance (either top 5 or 6) in the pillars integrating relief with development, implementing international guiding principles, and promoting learning and accountability. Canada's humanitarian funding is generally free of historical ties and/or geographic proximity considerations (2), and its humanitarian actions are broadly consistent with implementing international guiding principles, with ranks of 3 and 5, respectively, on support for the principal legal instruments on human rights and international humanitarian law. Canada excels in other areas as well, with top-five ranks in funding allocations to priority sectors (4), in funding which is allocated to the most needy and vulnerable

countries (12), in the predictability of its funding allocations to key humanitarian partners (5) and in delivering funds which, on the whole, are not subject to rigid earmarking constraints (5). Canada appears to take very seriously the principle which pertains to the need to undertake "regular evaluations of international responses to humanitarian crises," ranking third in terms of the number of self and joint evaluations of humanitarian assistance interventions.

Nevertheless, there are some areas of weakness where Canada's performance could improve considerably. Among them, one can point to funding allocations less driven by media coverage and/or sectoral considerations and the need to more evenly distribute resources toward forgotten emergencies from other types of emergencies (18). In the area of responding to humanitarian needs (pillar 1), Canada could improve response times as they apply to complex emergencies and onset disasters (16). Funding to strengthen the capacity of countries to respond to crises is yet another area where Canada's performance (18) could be boosted.

On the whole, Canada's performance is encouraging, with a large number of key aspects of the principles being fully reflected in its humanitarian interventions. There is broad consistency between the results of the survey and the hard data indicators and the few areas of weakness seem amenable to improvement with slight reorientations of policy.

United Kingdom

The United Kingdom, known for its important role in promoting change and reform within the system, achieves a respectable ninth place in the Index, but does better in the hard data index (8), capturing many funding indicators, than in the soft data index (13), which reflects the views of the humanitarian field. Across the whole range of indicators, it is among the top five in just under a quarter of the indicators. The UK's strengths lie in the pillars working with humanitarian partners and promoting learning and accountability, where it ranks fourth in both instances.

In pillar 3, it is perceived to be doing well at providing predictable funding (4) and at having introduced longer-term funding arrangements (5), as well as at facilitating safe humanitarian access (5) and supporting contingency planning and capacity building efforts (5). These achievements are backed to some degree by the hard data, giving the UK a high ranking for the predictability of donor funding (2). The UK also stands out for its very generous funding to the main quick disbursement mechanisms (some US$155 million or 55 percent of the total contributed by all OECD/DAC countries), coming in joint first place and representing the third most generous donor relative to income, and for its support to UNDAC (4). Despite its key role in promoting the CERF, the UK falls just short of receiving a top-five rank for the CERF indicator, mainly because, relative to its income, it comes seventh for this indicator, despite having given by far the largest absolute contribution (US$69 million in 2006).

Other strengths include "supporting learning and accountability" initiatives, strongly supported by both the soft and hard data variables. It is ranked fourth by the field for supporting learning and accountability initiatives, and also comes fourth in both hard data indicators measuring membership, attendance at and funding of the main accountability initiatives, and the number of joint and individual evaluations it undertakes.

Weaknesses are concentrated in pillars 1 and 4, supported in equal measure by hard and soft data indices. The UK achieves its lowest pillar ranking (18) for "Implementing international guiding principles," mainly because it has not implemented as many core legal instruments related to IHL and human rights as have other peer countries. However, the view from the field is also fairly critical in its assessment of the UK, leaving it with low ranks for such politically-charged indicators as enhancing security (18), protecting human rights (18), or affirming the primary role of civilian organisations (16).

Its performance in pillar 1 is mixed. Behind its eleventh place for this pillar lie some positive achievements, notably in the timeliness of its funding to complex emergencies (5), and in the concentration of its funding to identified needs, both to priority sectors identified within the CAPs (5), as well as relative to ECHO's Vulnerability Index (1). However, it does rather less well by favouring countries with which it shares historical ties or that are within its relative geographic proximity (21) when disbursing its humanitarian aid. Also, the soft data unequivocally takes a negative view of the UK's commitment to the basic principles of humanitarian action, including the alleviation of suffering (15), impartiality (16), neutrality (19), and independence (18).

Switzerland

Switzerland, on tenth place in the overall Index, enjoys a much better perception in the humanitarian field than its hard data bear out. It occupies fourth place in the soft data index and only tenth in the hard data index. It achieves a top-five ranking in just over a third of the indicators (38 percent).

Across the five pillars, Switzerland's performance is fairly equal, ranging from its best rank (8) in pillar two on "integrating relief and development" to 14th place in pillar four, which encompasses the main international guiding principles.

Switzerland undoubtedly has a number of strengths, possibly gained by its long experience in the humanitarian enterprise. For example, it is quite clear that, within the first pillar, the field takes the view that Switzerland is very much living up to its humanitarian tradition by being faithful to the basic principles of alleviation of suffering (4), impartiality (2), neutrality (1) and independence (3). Its impartiality is lent further credence by high rankings in the hard data indicators on the distribution of funding relative to historical ties or geographic proximity (5) and to forgotten emergencies (2). It is also perceived to provide timely funding (3), although this is certainly not borne out by the two hard data indicators on timely funding to complex emergencies (18) and to onset disasters (19). Moreover, the needs-based orientation of its funding is further thrown into doubt by poor rankings for funding to priority sectors identified within the CAPs and relative to ECHO's Vulnerability Index.

In the second pillar on integrating relief and development, Switzerland's perceived ability to strengthen resilience to cope with crises (3) and its funding to capacity building (2) suggest that it has had some success in reaching out to the local level. An excellent ranking for promoting NGOs (2) within pillar 3 "Working with humanitarian partners" further supports this notion. In this pillar, Switzerland also stands out for its support to UNDAC (2) and, as expected, takes first place in its funding of ICRC Appeals in its true humanitarian tradition.

United States

The United States is 16th among the 23 OECD-DAC countries in the overall ranking. It also occupies 16th place in the soft data index but only 20th place for the hard data. Its performance across the five pillars is uneven, with a strong showing (2) in pillar 5 encompassing learning and accountability, balanced against the worst performance of any country (23) in pillar 4, on implementing international guiding principles.

It stellar performance in pillar 5 is based on an excellent perception in the field that the U.S. supports accountability in humanitarian action (1) and encourages regular evaluations (4). This is strongly borne out by the hard data, with high rankings on membership, attendance of, and funding to the main accountability initiatives (7), and the number of joint and individual evaluations performed (2).

The US ranks 16th in the first pillar, capturing a needs-based response. Predictably, it attracts some of the lowest rankings for perceptions about its respect for basic humanitarian principles: alleviation of suffering (18), impartiality (21), neutrality (23), and independence (23). On the other hand, it does rather well in distributing its funding relative to identified needs, relative to both the priority sectors within CAPs (6) and to ECHO's vulnerability index (2).

In pillar 2, the US receives overall endorsement by the field for consultation with beneficiaries on monitoring and evaluation (2), strengthening preparedness for emergencies (4), and supporting rapid recovery of sustainable livelihoods (2), all suggesting a solid performance in support of civil society initiatives. This is underpinned by a good ranking for promoting the role of NGOs (8) in pillar 3.

Across the other pillars, three other points stand out. First, it receives high ranks for donor preparedness in implementing humanitarian action (3) and in facilitating safe humanitarian access (6), both possible reflections of the international clout of the U.S. Second, the U.S. performs poorly on flexibility of funding indicators, for example, for earmarking funding and for a low share of cash in total funding (both 22). Finally, it does not operate naturally as a multilateralist, appearing somewhat stingy in its funding to these mechanisms, for example, to IFRC (18) and ICRC Appeals (14), and to the UN Consolidated Inter-Agency Appeals (13).

Spain

Spain has an overall rank of 17 in the HRI. On the positive side, Spain has a good score on the indicator which gauges distribution of funding to emergencies relative to degree of media coverage, the sector to which funding is allocated, and whether the emergency is classified as forgotten (3). Spain does also well on the pillar which captures the implementation of international guiding principles, achieving a rank of 6 overall in this component of the HRI. On the whole, however, it does not score particularly well on the needs-based pillar (15), mainly due to its failure to fund priority sectors (22), vulnerable countries (18), and to free itself from its historical legacy (16).

Like Italy, however, Spain has a number of weaknesses which cut across a large number of the indicators present in virtually all the other pillars. Noteworthy are: low prioritisation of support for strengthening local capacity to prevent and mitigate crises, low levels of support to UN coordination mechanisms and non-governmental organisations, insufficient predictability in such support where it exists, low levels of support to UN Consolidated Inter-Agency Appeals and to IFRC and ICRC Annual and Emergency Appeals, low levels of funding to pooled mechanisms for contingency planning, and weak commitment to learning and accountability initiatives. In other words, it is not much of a multilateralist and does not fully embrace the culture of transparency and accountability, hallmarks of the top performers. However, Spain is not an ungenerous donor; ODA levels in relation to GDP in 2006 were somewhere in the middle range among OECD members, well below the likes of Sweden, Norway, Netherlands, and Denmark, but above many others. Its performance under the HRI suggest that, like Italy, much can be done to improve the policy and institutional framework for humanitarian action, to enhance the efficiency of those resources which are delivered in the context of various emergencies and crises.

France

France has a rank of 19 in the HRI, immediately behind Japan (18). This rank reflects uniformly low scores on the survey, with a rank of 21 overall and its best performance (19) in the pillar capturing aspects of the relationship with humanitarian partners, and a somewhat more mixed performance on the hard data indicators. Essentially, the only indicators for which France can be said to be doing well are those capturing the implementation of international guiding principles, as reflected in a rank of 3 for support for international humanitarian law and the principal legal instruments on human rights. France's humanitarian assistance is not sufficiently independent from considerations of historical ties and geographic proximity with the recipient country (20). It is, likewise, closely correlated to other factors, such as media coverage, unduly concentrated on a couple of sectors, and does not pay enough attention to the needs of forgotten emergencies. France does particularly poorly on pillar 2, capturing aspects of the integration of relief and development, where its hard data ranking (21) is strongly corroborated by its ranking in the survey (22). In relation to ODA, France allocates the lowest levels of funding (23) to strengthening the capacity of countries and local communities to deal with crises and to various multilateral mechanisms which have been established to enhance capacity for crises prevention and recovery (22).

France contributes well below its "fair share" to UN Consolidated Inter-Agency Appeals, to the IFRC and ICRC Annual and Emergency Appeals and to the CERF. In all these indicators its ranking is 17 or worse. It does no better on those variables which underscore the ability to work effectively with other humanitarian partners. Funding to UN coordination mechanisms and common services and to quick disbursement mechanisms is, likewise, well below its fair share in relation to DAC GDP. France is clearly not closely aligned with the principles enshrined in the GHD, so it is clear that a greater emphasis on better tailoring humanitarian aid policy toward the GHD can only lead to improvements in France's relative position in the HRI, particularly given the size of its aid budget and overall international presence.

Italy

Italy is a large country with a small aid budget. Official development assistance in relation to GDP in 2006 was among the lowest in the OECD, indeed only marginally higher than that of Greece and the United States, the two countries with the lowest ODA/GNI ratios in the DAC. Italy ranks 22 in the HRI, reflecting a number of weaknesses, including, but not limited to, funding practices which do not often reflect due regard for need and needs assessments, low scores on the indicators included in the pillar integrating relief and development, low levels of funding to UN coordination mechanisms, to non-governmental organisations, to the International Red Cross and Red Crescent Movement and to CERF, low levels of funding to UN Consolidated Inter-Agency Appeals and to IFRC and ICRC Annual and Emergency Appeals. Italy also scores poorly on all the indicators which capture commitment to learning and accountability initiatives. There is clearly much room for improvement in enhancing the efficiency of Italy's humanitarian actions.

V. Conclusions

This chapter sets out the underlying methodology we have developed for DARA's Humanitarian Response Index 2007, the first of its kind. The HRI combines a large number of quantitative indicators developed to assess donor country compliance with respect to the *Principles and Good Practice of Humanitarian Donorship* by means of hard data and a Survey capturing the views of a large number of agencies involved in the delivery of humanitarian assistance. Thus, it is singularly well placed to examine donor behaviour in relation to the *Principles*. The HRI is an international benchmarking exercise intended to provide a framework for the identification of a broad array of factors that play a critical role in enhancing the efficiency of humanitarian actions. It allows donors to identify their own strengths and weaknesses with respect to their actions as humanitarian donors, and permits an international cross-country comparison against best practices. Over time, as the Index is compiled on an annual basis, it will also allow each donor a vertical comparison of its own performance over time.

This study has taken the unambiguous view that for the *Principles* to be operationally meaningful, they cannot be solely interpreted as a collective undertaking. A call for "regular evaluations of international responses to humanitarian crises, including assessments of donor performance" is surely given greater meaning by initiatives, such as the HRI, that deliver a tool for assessing individual donor performance. The HRI is a powerful tool that can help donors identify and quantify their strengths and weaknesses and is complementary to other ongoing efforts to improve donor performance and accountability, with the ultimate aim of improving the quality of humanitarian assistance.

Since it is clear that the HRI country results show a strong correlation between hard and soft data indices, reinforcing each other, we may have even greater confidence in the conclusions drawn at the country level (see Figure 1).

Sweden is the best-ranking donor in the Humanitarian Response Index (HRI) 2007, excelling in a broad number of areas. Underlying its outstanding performance in responding to humanitarian needs, the heart of the GHD, is a strong policy focus on funding forgotten emergencies. Sweden provides timely and flexible funding to humanitarian crises. Its ability to deliver on its commitment to the GHD Principles is boosted by their incorporation into its comprehensive humanitarian aid policy.

Sweden is unambiguously multilateralist in its approach to humanitarian action, supporting and facilitating coordination efforts, including in the field, in order to determine needs. It is a strong financial backer of the UN and the Red Cross Movement, and has generously funded the CERF, UN, IFRC, and ICRC Appeals, as well as other quick disbursement mechanisms, thereby ensuring that its multilateral aid is timely and flexible. Sweden also offers multi-year funding arrangements. The Swedish example suggests that donors' accountability concerns can be met without eschewing multi-year funding arrangements, by making them subject to annual parliamentary approval.

Like most donors, Sweden's relationship to the NGOs it funds is governed by a trusted relationship—including pre-screening—to certain international and Swedish NGOs it repeatedly relies on to implement its humanitarian aid programmes. A select number of Swedish NGOs also have access to rapid response funds for contingencies.

The analysis has also highlighted four important concerns: a) the lack of an operating definition for humanitarian aid, b) gaps in data coverage due to conceptual inconsistencies on how to measure humanitarian aid, c) the low priority given to timely and accurate data reporting, and d) the lack of a widely accepted global needs assessment framework on which to base strategic decisions that can better tailor response to need.

References

Bijojote, S. and C. Bugnion. 2004. External Baseline Evaluation of the Burundi Good Humanitarian Donorship Pilot Final Report. 29 May. Available at: http://www.reliefweb.int/ghd/CAP_Pilots.html

Darcy, J. and C.-A. Hofmann. 2003. *According to Need? Needs assessment and decision making in the humanitarian sector."* Humanitarian Policy Group Report 15, Overseas Development Institute: London, UK

Development Initiatives. 2006. *Global Humanitarian Assistance 2006.* Chapter 6: Good Humanitarian Donorship (GHD) Indicators Report. Available at: http://www.globalhumanitarianassistance.org/pdfdownloads/GHA%202006.pdf

DFID. 2006. "Saving lives, relieving suffering, protecting dignity: DFID's Humanitarian Policy."

Emergencies/info centres: Available at: http://www.humanitarianinfo.org/

European Commission Humanitarian (Aid) Office (ECHO). "Strategy - ECHO Humanitarian activities." Available at: http://ec.europa.eu/echo/information/strategy/index_en.htm

———. 2006. "TECHNICAL NOTE: Assessment of humanitarian needs and identification of "forgotten crises." Available at: http://ec.europa.eu/echo/pdf_files/strategic_methodologies/methodology_2007_en.pdf

European Union. 2005. "European Union guidelines on promoting compliance with international humanitarian law." *Official Journal of the European Union.* 2005/C 327/04 23 December.

Graves, S. and V. Wheeler. 2006. "Good Humanitarian Donorship: Overcoming obstacles to improved collective donor performance." Humanitarian Policy Group Discussion Paper. Overseas Development Institute: London. December. Available at: http://www.odi.org.uk/hpg/papers/discussion_GHD.pdf

Harmer, A., L. Cotterrell, and A. Stoddard. 2004. "From Stockholm to Ottawa: A progress review of the Good Humanitarian Donorship initiative." Humanitarian Policy Group Research Briefing, No. 18. Overseas Development Institute: London. October. Available at: http://www.odi.org.uk/hpg/papers/HPGbrief18.pdf

Humanitarian Accountability Partnership International (HAP-I). Available at: http://www.hapinternational.org/en/pages.php?IDcat=10

International Committee of the Red Cross (ICRC). 1997. "The ICRC Advisory Service on International Humanitarian Law." Geneva. 31 August.

International Federation of the Red Cross and Red Crescent Societies. 2006. *World Disasters Report.* Geneva.

Kinkela, C., Lene Poulsen and Julie Thompson. 2004. "Baseline Survey, Good Humanitarian Donorship Pilot: Democratic Republic of Congo." Final Report, OCHA: New York. Available at: http://ochaonline.un.org/DocView.asp?DocID=3634

Macrae, J., ed. 2002. "The new humanitarianisms: A review of trends in global humanitarian action." Humanitarian Policy Group Report 11. London: Overseas Development Institute.

Médecins sans Frontières. 2007. "Top 10 Underreported Humanitarian Stories of 2006." 9 January. Available at: http://www.msf.org/msfinternational/invoke.cfm?objectid=06616F5A-5056-AA77-6CE49B621A0C195D&component=toolkit.report&method=full_html

Organisation for Economic Co-operation and Development (OECD). 2004. "Assessment Framework for Coverage of Humanitarian Action in DAC Peer Reviews." DCD/DIR(2004)11. 13 May. Paris: OECD.

———. 2005 to 2007. *DAC Peer Review* (various countries). Development Co-operation Directorate. Paris.

———. 2006a. "Humanitarian Aid in DAC Peer Reviews: A compilation of coverage 2004–5." Document DCD/DAC(2006)4. 17 January. Paris: OECD.

———. 2006b. "Humanitarian Aid in DAC Peer Reviews: A Synthesis of Findings and Experiences 2004–5." DCD/DAC(2006)3/REV1. 13 February. Paris: OECD.

Reuters-AlertNet. Available at: http://www.alertnet.org/thefacts/chart/mediamonitoringmethodology.htm

Smillie, I. and L. Minear. 2003. *The Quality of Money: Donor Behavior in Humanitarian Financing.* Study prepared for IASC, Humanitarianism and War Project. The Feinstein International Famine Center: Massachusetts: Available at: http://www.reliefweb.int/cap/CAP-SWG/Hum_Financing_Studies/DonorBehavior_FINAL.pdf

United Kingdom Department for International Development (DFID). 2006. "Saving lives, relieving suffering, protecting dignity: DFID's Humanitarian Policy." Available at: http://reliefweb.int/rw/lib.nsf/db900SID/HMYT-6QHPP2?OpenDocument

United Nations News Service. "10 Stories the World Should Hear More About." Available at: http://www.un.org/events/tenstories/

Willitts-King, B. 2004. "Good Humanitarian Donorship and the European Union: A Study of Good Practice and Recent Initiatives." Development Cooperations Ireland. 15 September.

———. 2007. "Allocating humanitarian funding according to need: towards analytical frameworks for donors." Discussion Paper.

Notes

1   The authors would like to thank the members of our Peer Review Committee: Jock Baker, Christian Bugnion, Ed Cairns, Veronique de Geoffroy, Sue Graves, Claude Hilfiker, David Roodman, Johan Schaar, Ed Schenkenberg, Ricardo Solé, Manisha Thomas, and Victoria Wheeler, for excellent contributions during the formulation and implementation phases of this project, as well as Diego Hidalgo, S. Iqbal Riza and Pierre Schori of our Advisory Board and DARA's Board of Trustees for their full support to the project. We are greatly indebted to José María Figueres for his warm encouragement and unwavering support. We also thank Lidia Hernández, Olim Latipov, and Daniela Ruegenberg for excellent research assistance, and the rest of the DARA team for their valuable feedback and comments. Finally, we would also like to thank Marcel Fortier (IFRC), Olivier van Bunnen (IFRC), Beat Schweizer (ICRC), Ann Zimmerman (DAC Contact), Dirk Reinisch (UNICEF), Elisabeth Diaz (UNDP), José Riera (UNHCR), Marcel Vaessen (UN/OCHA), Meinrad Studer (GHF), Isabelle Borgeraud (GHF), Hedwig Riegler, Johanna Mang and Robert Zeiner (Austrian Development Agency), Gerhard Weinberger (MFA Austria), Etienne Squilbin, Jan Vermeir and Antoon Delie (Belgian Development Cooperation DGDC), Victor Carvell and Stephen Salewicz (CIDA Canada), Peter Hjuler Christensen (MFA Denmark), Anne-Birgitte Albrectsen (DANIDA Denmark), Paul de Spiegeleer, Michele Lebrun, Johannes Luchner, and Julia Stewart-David (ECHO), Valerie Ramet (Europe Aid), Ulla-Maija Finskas (MFA Finland), Christian Bernard and Claire Lignières-Counathe (MFA France), Michael Ahrens and Ursula Müller (MFA Germany), A. Kosmidou, Nike-Catherine Koutrakou, and Prodormos Markoulakis (MFA Greece), Frank Kirwan (DFA Ireland), Mainardo Benardelli and Renzo Rosso (MFA Italy), Masako Sato (JICA Japan), Daniel Feypel (MFA Luxembourg), Joost Adriessen and Maikee van Koldam (MFA Netherlands), Tiffany Babington (MFAT New Zealand), Susan Eckey, Sigvald Hauge Tomin, and Geir Moe Sorensen (MFA Norway), Maria Chaves and Antonio Torres (IPAD Portugal), María Eugenia Martín-Sanz and Gonzalo Vega (AECI Spain), Susana de Funes (DGPOLDE Spain), Mikael Lindvall (MFA Sweden), Per Byman (SIDA Sweden), Marco Ferrari, Toni Frisch, Yves Mauron and Franklin Thévenaz, (DEZA Switzerland), Bill Hamminck, Ky Luu, Lynne Marie Thomas (USAID), Diane Halvorsen (DD USA), Margaret Pollack (State Department), and Joanna Macrae, Jack Jones, and Moazzam Malik (DfID UK) for their inputs into the data collection, information gathering, and consultation process. The usual disclaimer applies.

2   See Smillie and Minear, 2003.

3   See http://www.goodhumanitariandonorship.org

4   The term humanitarian *action* is wider than humanitarian *assistance* in that it includes protection as a central element.

5   Australia, Belgium, Canada, Denmark, Finland, France, Germany, Ireland, Japan, Luxembourg, the Netherlands, Norway, Sweden, Switzerland, the United Kingdom, and the United States.

6   Austria, the Czech Republic, Greece, Italy, New Zealand, Portugal and Spain.

7   See Graves and Wheeler, 2006; Harmer et al., 2004; Willitts-King, 2004.

8   See www.oecd.org/dac/peerreviews

9   In addition to the *Principles*, OECD (2004) suggests that other relevant principles and guidelines that can guide the Peer Review process include the *UN General Assembly Resolution 46/182*, designed to strengthen the United Nations' response to both complex emergencies and natural disasters, and to improve the overall effectiveness of humanitarian operations in the field; the Sphere standards; the *Red Cross and NGO Code of Conduct;* and the 2001 DAC guidelines *Helping Prevent Violent Conflict.*

10 OECD, 2004, p.11.

11 These were Canada, Denmark, Ireland, the Netherlands, Sweden, and the UK.

12 See Development Initiatives, 2006.

13 See http://www.reliefweb.int/ghd/GHDDRC-indicatorsrevised18-12-2003.doc for a listing of the indicators. The reader is also referred to Bijojote and Bugnion (2004) for a comprehensive evaluation of the Burundi Good Humanitarian Donorship Pilot.

14 The categories are: donor funding was flexible and timely (P 5); donor and agency funding was allocated on the basis of needs assessment (P 6); local capacities were strengthened (P 8); donors supported the UN leadership and coordination role (P 10a); ear-marking was reduced (P 13a); funding was made available on a long-term basis (P 13b); recovery and long-term development was linked to humanitarian programmes (P 9); funding requirements for assistance effort was shared equitably among donors (P 14a); established good practices were adhered to by humanitarian implementing partners (P 15); safe humanitarian access was promoted (P 17); contingency planning was supported by donors (P 18); military assets were used appropriately (P 19b); performance was evaluated (P 22); contributions were reported in a timely and accurate fashion (P 23a).

15 See Kinkela et al., 2004.

16 See Graves and Wheeler, 2006.

17 See OECD, 2006b; Graves and Wheeler, 2006; DFID, 2006, p.16.

18 A collective indicator may show improvement over time for the members of the group. But this could, for instance, reflect outstanding performance by a handful of countries and mediocre performance by the majority. A monitoring mechanism which is prone to free-riding behaviour would not appear to be consistent which the spirit of Principle 22 which calls for "regular evaluations of international responses to humanitarian crises, including assessments of donor performance."

19 This is in line with, for instance, the World Economic Forum's Executive Opinion Survey, which captures the contemporary views of senior enterprise managers regarding obstacles to the creation of a better business environment, and the several surveys which go into the formulation of Transparency International's *Corruption Perceptions Index.*

20 For example, OCHA, the Resident or Humanitarian Coordinator, the International Committee of the Red Cross (ICRC) and representations of the Inter-Agency Standing Committee (IASC).

21 Note that OECD (2004), p. 10, uses the following (overlapping) categorisation: (1) Humanitarian Policies (P1–10); Funding (P5, 6, 11–14); Promotion of Standards and enhanced implementation (P14–P0); Learning and Accountability (P7, 21–23).

22 The exception concerns the three hard data indicators used in pillar 5, where the indicator on the number of evaluations is given twice the weight of the indicators on promoting learning and accountability initiatives.

23 Other organisations have dealt with this methodological issue in different ways. For instance, in the World Economic Forum's *Global Competitiveness Index 2006–2007*, a total of 90 factors have been grouped in nine distinct pillars, capturing different dimensions of the business environment. Each pillar, however, has been weighed equally within each of three separate subgroups (stages of development) and, within each pillar, each factor has, in turn, also received equal weighting. In deciding this approach, the primary consideration was whether there was *a priori* information, either empirical or based on theory, which suggested that some indicators were more important than others. In the case of the WEF's competitiveness index, those involved in its design came to the view that although intuition and empirical experience suggested that some indicators might indeed be more important than others within each pillar, there were no sound theoretical considerations that would credibly justify

allocating different weights to different factors. However, the HRI is linked to the *Principles* and there seems to be broad consensus among humanitarian experts that some are more important than others, thus justifying a more flexible weighting structure.

24   References on Sweden: DARA questionnaire 2007; Swedish Government Communication 2004/05:52 (The Government's Humanitarian Aid Policy); OECD (2005) DAC Peer Review: Sweden; GHD Domestic Implementation Plan for Sweden (2005).

25   OECD, 2005 (Sweden), p. 36.

26   Numbers in parentheses in the country descriptions refer to rankings on the HRI.

27   Swedish Development Cooperation Agency (SIDA, 2005), "Reducing the risk of disasters: SIDA's effort to reduce poor people's vulnerability to hazards."

28   OECD, 2005, Sweden, p. 37.

29   See OECD (2005), Norway.

30   In contrast to other countries, there are a few hard data indicators which do not apply in the case of the European Commission, and in these cases, the HRI estimation for the EC excluded these. For instance, the indicators on the funding of UN coordination mechanisms and common services or of the CERF were judged not to apply to the EC due to its own size, field presence, and rapid response capacity, which means that it needs to rely much less on UN mechanisms than other smaller donors.

31   Specifically, the legal basis is Article 18 of the Humanitarian Regulation that stipulates that the Commission is required to "regularly assess humanitarian aid operations financed by the Community in order to establish whether they have achieved their objectives and to produce guidelines for improving the effectiveness of subsequent operations."

32   OECD, 2007, European Community DAC Peer Review, p. 97.

33   ECHO (2006), 2006 Operational Strategy, available at: http://ec.europa.eu/echo/information/strategy/strat_rep_en.htm

34   Directorate-General ECHO, Financial Report 2006, p. 13.

35   General Assembly Resolution 46/182 (A/RES/46/182), 78th plenary meeting, 19 December 1991, para. 24, specifies that contributions to the fund should be on an "additional basis."

36   OECD (2007), DAC Peer Review of the European Community.

37   Ibid., Council Regulation (EC) No. 1257/96 concerning humanitarian aid states that humanitarian aid decisions "must be taken impartially and solely according to the victims' needs and interests" and "must not be guided by, or subject to, political considerations."

38   Communication from the Commission to the European Parliament and the Council: Towards a European Consensus on Humanitarian Aid, COM (2007) 317 final, 13.6.2007: Brussels.

2

PART TWO

Perspectives on Good Humanitarian Donorship

The Birth of the Good Humanitarian Donorship Initiative

JOHAN SCHAAR, Special Representative for the Tsunami Operation, International Federation of Red Cross and Red Crescent Societies, former Head of Division, Humanitarian Assistance and Conflict Management, Swedish International Development Cooperation Agency

Introduction

Our everyday actions towards fellow human beings are guided by principles, most of which form part of cultural norms which we inherit and pass on. Some of these become domestic law, and even international law, thereby guiding the actions of states. This is the case when it comes to the protection of civilian populations under armed conflict.

The obligation to help a person in acute need is a norm in almost all cultures, but has only become law in a few countries. At the international level, humanitarian assistance in connection with man-made or natural hazards—funded by governments and carried out by humanitarian organisations—is only partly regulated through soft law, such as resolutions in the UN General Assembly or in the International Conference of the Red Cross and Red Crescent.

The volume of international humanitarian assistance increased dramatically during the decade after the Cold War. Thus, its nature as an unregulated and uncoordinated aid sector—in terms of donor behaviour—became increasingly clear. This had serious consequences for people in need of protection and assistance, living in desperate conditions.

In my role as head of the humanitarian division in one of the government donor agencies, I became part of an effort to do something about what my colleagues and I felt was an unacceptable situation. The initiative was called Good Humanitarian Donorship (GHD). What follows is the story of the birth of this initiative. It is a subjective story, written by one who has been in an implementing as well as a donor role for more than twenty years in the international humanitarian system. In this article, I begin by describing donor behaviour at the beginning of the millennium and then present the vision of principled action and the negotiation process that led to the GHD Principles and to the strategy to for action. Following this, I assess the emerging changes in donor behaviour after Stockholm, in part linked to the humanitarian reform process which began in 2005. Finally, I point to the factors that give cause for optimism about the ultimate impact of the GHD process, including the existence of independent initiatives aimed at promoting the GHD Principles, such as the DARA Humanitarian Response Index.

What was wrong?

At the turn of the millennium, my colleagues and I found donor behaviour to be dysfunctional, irrational, and sometimes arrogant. Whether people who were living in desperate conditions because of conflict or natural calamities would be assisted at a level guaranteeing some dignity seemed to depend on no real assessment of what threatened their safety and survival. Some crises received more resources than seemed to be required, while others, particularly those lingering year after year, received a pittance. And although a balance of sustenance, services, and protection must be provided to ensure a dignified life, this was far from the rule. Food was most often there, although not always of the most appropriate kind, while support for reproductive health or livelihoods was not readily forthcoming. In some crises, donors and international agencies were tripping over themselves to find operational space, while in others they were few and far between, if they existed at all.

We found this situation both embarrassing and outrageous. How could we accept to represent a sector which functioned with such anarchy? How could we accept that people living in conditions of desperate adversity were used by donor governments to make grand gestures of generosity, while others in even greater need were ignored? If humanitarian action was impartial and neutral, only motivated by need, how could we accept the political considerations of some donor countries when making their funding decisions? Was there a way of moving humanitarian donors towards more principled behaviour? Could well established practices among development donors be adapted to the admittedly more unpredictable humanitarian arena? Were there not already universally accepted customary norms that could provide guidance and structure for our sector?

These deficiencies were criticised, but not in such a way as to reach the public domain. With some exceptions, there seemed to be few politicians or journalists in donor countries with a good grasp of the issues. This lack of public debate insulated donor governments from any serious scrutiny. If anything, what was perceived as life-saving assistance was little questioned while development aid was sometimes struggling to demonstrate the tangible results that would satisfy critics. Only events such as the war in Kosovo in 1999 triggered discussions, when an almost surreal influx of international organisations and NGOs took place in the wake of unprecedented media attention. That discussion, however, was less about donor behaviour and more about competition and lack of coordination between implementing organisations.

Significant initiatives had been taken among implementing organisations in the 1990s to improve their performance and accountability. The Red Cross Red Crescent Code of Conduct, the Humanitarian Accountability Project (later renamed Humanitarian Accountability Partnership International) and the SPHERE project on a Humanitarian Charter and Minimum Standards in Disaster Response grew out of operational experiences, although they did not address donor performance directly. However, many donors introduced conditions stipulating that organisations applying for funding must adhere to specific performance and accountability initiatives.

Several independent and influential voices critiqued the humanitarian "enterprise," even if they did not reach the public discourse. The series of publications from the Humanitarianism and War Project, led by Larry Minear and Thomas Weiss of Brown University, analysed humanitarian action in a large number of armed conflicts starting in 1990. The Humanitarian Policy Group (HPG) at the Overseas Development Institute (ODI) in London conducted research on humanitarian policy and practice, led by Margie Buchanan-Smith and Joanna Macrae. Following the multi-actor evaluation of the humanitarian response to the genocide in Rwanda in 1994, the Active Learning Network for Accountability and Performance in Humanitarian Action (ALNAP), formed in 1997 and led by John Borton for many years,

provided regular analyses of reviews and evaluations of humanitarian operations. Its meta-evaluations and annual reports were particularly valuable in analysing trends in the humanitarian sector. And Development Initiatives, a small British NGO under the leadership of Judith Randel, led the Global Humanitarian Assistance project, analysing flows and trends in humanitarian financing, official aid as well as resources contributed to NGOs by the public.

Research by HPG on the bilateralisation of aid was particularly important in analysing the flaws and negative impact of donor behaviour, and had strong influence on the GHD process.

Most of the donor debate occurred in closed rooms between mid-level officials in the humanitarian departments of donor agencies and foreign ministries. Opportunities for open discussion were offered at such occasions as the bi-annual informal meetings of the Humanitarian Aid Committee (hosted by each EU presidency and attended by member state representatives), the annual meetings of the Donor Support Group of the Office for the Coordination of Humanitarian Affairs (OCHA), and the meetings each spring in Montreux, where the donor group met OCHA and other humanitarian agencies to review experiences and discuss improvements to the Consolidated Appeals Process (CAP). As far as their own role in the humanitarian sector was concerned, some in the small travelling circus that met regularly in these forums easily found common ground when discussing weaknesses. Thus, in 2002, eight donor representatives[1] agreed to launch the Humanitarian Financing Work Programme and commissioned three studies to further analyse problems and find solutions.

A vision of principles

Building on the comprehensive and critical analysis that thus became available,[2] and the experience among donor "practitioners," a vision of what was needed began to take shape, initially among government colleagues in the Netherlands, Canada, and Sweden. In many ways, the vision was the mirror image of the practice we were observing, as summarised by the UN Deputy Emergency Relief Coordinator Carolyn McAskie: "Most donor behaviour is rational from a donor point of view. However, the sum total of all donor behaviours doesn't produce a rational whole."[3] Thus, the notion of a code of conduct, or principles that would characterise a good donor entered our discussions.

If memory serves me, the first mention of the idea of a good humanitarian donorship initiative occurred during an informal meeting of EU's Humanitarian Aid Committee in Copenhagen during the Danish EU presidency in October 2002. If we expected UN agencies, the Red Cross Red Crescent Movement, and NGOs to work according to good or even best practice, why not demand the same of ourselves? Development donors had a history of reform and had come a long way towards greater coherence and harmonisation. Why should humanitarian donors lag so dismally behind and with such serious consequences? Dutch colleagues suggested a conference on good donor practice. After taking the issue back to Stockholm for consultation, Sweden then offered to host a conference on good humanitarian donorship, to be held in Stockholm in June, 2003.

Our idea was to organise an inclusive conference, bringing senior donor government representatives to the table together with humanitarian organisations and independent researchers. Representatives from HPG were invited as technical advisors to the conference organisers. We wanted the critique to be present and heard in the room, although we realised that this might be viewed as somewhat unorthodox by government representatives, given our intention to discuss and most likely negotiate an outcome document in the way normal to diplomats. To do this in the presence of a number of independent participants was certain to make for an interesting event for both sides.

What did we want to achieve? What was our vision? Put simply: aid should be given according to need, when and where it was required, in sufficient amounts and with appropriate quality, and it should include measures to prevent and prepare for emergencies, while also helping people rebuild their lives and livelihoods after a crisis.

As we were drafting documents for the conference, an op-ed on the topic before us appeared in the International Herald Tribune, written by Dr. Mukesh Kapila.[4] A visionary, who had recently left his position as head of the British government's agency for humanitarian assistance, Kapila forcefully outlined the weaknesses of the humanitarian system and called on "the richer world to commit to meeting basic humanitarian needs in their entirety. Not here or there, not now and then, but everywhere and everytime." In recognition of Kapila's role in promoting and advocating humanitarian reform, he was invited as one of the key-note speakers to the Stockholm conference.

Negotiating the principles

The vision required clarity of objective and principles to guide action, in addition to what constituted good donor practice. A draft document, "Suggested Elements for Conclusions," was circulated to participants ahead of the meeting to stimulate both discussion and final agreement in Stockholm. A few issues were of particular importance, but were also challenged in the negotiations of the text, both before the meeting and later in Stockholm. As might have been expected, the resulting document was less ambitious than the original draft—the usual price to be paid for a consensus document. The task before us was to bring the feasible, politically and practically, as close as possible to the desirable.

As the important foundation for what was to come, we first needed to articulate *what humanitarian action is*, its purpose and the actions it entails, starting with the protection of civilians. To evoke its legal foundations and strong roots, we purposely used some well established and accepted language—e.g., that acting impartially means to respond *solely on the basis of need*—the wording used by the International Federation of the Red Cross and Red Crescent Societies (GHD, Principles 1, 2, 3, and 4).

Francis Deng, the Secretary-General's Special Representative for the Internally Displaced, appealed eloquently during the conference to give the same recognition for the politically and operationally highly significant Guiding Principles on Internal Displacement as was already given to international humanitarian law. This was not achieved, even though the Guiding Principles are all derived from existing international and domestic law. However, the Guiding Principles found their place under the less prominent heading "Promoting standards and enhancing implementation" (GHD, Principle 16).

The draft also addressed the problems of disaster preparedness and transition from crisis to recovery, often exacerbated by the strict division between donor humanitarian and other budget lines. It was important for donors to recognise that funds invested in disaster reduction and preparedness would reduce the costs of responding to disasters, and that donor responsibility goes beyond immediate relief and protection, and includes helping to restore lives and livelihoods after an emergency (GHD, Principles 1, 3, 8, and 9).

If donors and agencies are to meet needs, they must know what they are. Humanitarian response must be based on proper needs assessments, carried out as a joint and continuous process and involving the different humanitarian actors. This leads to shared problem analysis and a much improved potential for coordination (GHD, Principle 6).

And in order to allow agencies to tailor their programmes to meet evolving needs, and plan with sufficient time frames, funds for humanitarian action must be predictable, sufficient in volume, and given with as few conditions as possible. In the draft document, we used Kapila's strong recommendation that donors commit to *meeting basic humanitarian needs in their entirety*. This commitment went too far for some of the governments at the Stockholm conference, and was watered down to "the collective obligation of striving to meet humanitarian needs." Our ambition to reduce earmarking to a minimum also sounded considerably weaker when donors were encouraged to "explore the possibility of reducing, or enhancing the flexibility of, earmarking" (GHD, Principles 5, 12, and 13).

From our point of view, reduced earmarking and making long-term funding from donors more predictable implied *greater respect for the mandates and roles of implementing agencies*. Ill-adapted, ill-timed and inappropriate humanitarian response, especially when accompanied by donor micromanagement and conditionality, would be corrected if agencies were provided with the necessary resources and the time, space, and authority to use them in response to actual and evolving needs. As a result, decisions would be taken as close to the ground as possible. The different but complementary roles of the three key humanitarian actors were made explicit by naming the UN, the International Federation of the Red Cross and Red Crescent Societies and nongovernmental organisations (GHD, Principle 10).

Some years see peaks in the number of severe disasters, while other years are less challenging. Predetermined and finite humanitarian budgets obviously do not take such fluctuations into consideration, so there have to be built-in contingencies. In order not to make humanitarian funding a zero-sum game, the practice of ensuring that new crises would not "adversely affect the meeting of needs in ongoing crises" was introduced (GHD, Principle 11).

The Stockholm conference took place in June, 2003, three months after the invasion of Iraq. At that time, the role of the military in humanitarian operations was intensely debated, and then US Secretary of State Colin Powell was describing NGOs in Iraq as "force extenders" or "multipliers." However, the humanitarian community viewed the mixed role of the Provincial Reconstruction Teams of international military forces in Afghanistan as highly controversial, blurring the lines between humanitarian and military action. Conventional military doctrine mentioned civil-military cooperation —"winning hearts and minds"—as an integral part of force protection. Although some of the governments present in Stockholm had troops in Iraq and Afghanistan, it was necessary to make a clear statement about the civilian nature of humanitarian action in the GHD Principles.

In this, we were greatly helped by the fact that states had recently negotiated the Guidelines on the Use of Military and Civil Defence Assets to Support United Nations Humanitarian Activities in Complex Emergencies, building on the so-called Oslo Guidelines for natural disasters, and outlining roles more clearly. The meeting agreed that civilian organisations would have priority and take the lead in humanitarian response, and that any use of military resources would be in conformity with international humanitarian law (GHD, Principle 19).

Improved coordination was obviously embedded in the spirit of the document, but it also specifically mentioned the importance of supporting the formulation of Common Humanitarian Action Plans (CHAP) as the primary instrument for planning, prioritisation and coordination in complex emergencies. Although some significant organisations, such as the International Committee of the Red Cross (ICRC) and Médecins Sans Frontières (MSF), would never seek funding through the UN Consolidated Appeals, donors still expected them to coordinate with other agencies for the purpose of comprehensive and effective humanitarian action (GHD, Principle 14).

Finally, the document acknowledged the importance of continued reflection, analysis, and learning in order to improve the ongoing performance and accountability of the humanitarian actors, including donors, and their obligation to support such activities (GHD, Principles 21, 22, and 23).

From principles to practice: a post-conference strategy

More than agreement on principles was needed to effect real change in donor practice and to ensure that the GHD process would not end with yet another document. Participating governments agreed on an implementation plan, specifying five measures:

1. Identifying at least one crisis country in which the GHD Principles were to be piloted;

2. Inviting the OECD's Development Assistance Committee (DAC) to include donor performance in the humanitarian sector in peer reviews;

3. Harmonising reporting demands on implementing organisations, in the spirit of the Rome Declaration;[5]

4. Beginning the process of finding a common definition of humanitarian assistance for reporting and statistical purposes;

5. Promoting the broad application among all donors of the GHD Principles, with different donor countries offering to take the lead on the various action points.

There was a sense of urgency among the humanitarian agencies present and a hope that there would be fast action. Carolyn McAskie, UN Deputy Emergency Coordinator, asked the donors present to immediately select pilot countries in time for the 2004 Consolidated Appeals Process. Burundi and the Democratic Republic of Congo (DRC) were proposed.

Of the different measures planned, the invitation to DAC to join the process was particularly important. The effectiveness of peer pressure and exchange of good practice had been well demonstrated through the DAC peer reviews of development donor performance. If the Principles were to become normative they would have to be built into a performance assessment framework.

In early contacts, DAC was reluctant to add another task to its already full work plan. On the Swedish side, we therefore offered to second a full time staff person to OECD-DAC in Paris to start working on an assessment framework for coverage of humanitarian action in DAC peer reviews, based directly on the GHD Principles. The drafting of an assessment framework could then start a few months after Stockholm.

A new and active DAC role was meant to strengthen donor accountability, using well established checks and balances developed by the donor community itself. But we also felt that it was important for independent and external voices to continue to follow critically the

process initiated in Stockholm. The Humanitarian Policy Group (HPG) at the Overseas Development Institute (ODI) in London was therefore encouraged not to drop its analysis of the issues that had triggered the initiative, but to continuously follow the process over the coming years, particularly as pilots and new practices were being rolled out. HPG accepted this proposal, and has published a number of studies on GHD over the past several years.

There were a number of implicit assumptions which, although not articulated in the GHD Principles or implementation plan, nevertheless had to be addressed if improved donor practice was to translate into action and meet real needs "everywhere and every time." Since donors were actors in a humanitarian system, these assumptions required reciprocal measures from other actors. If donors reduced earmarking, increased flexible multilateral funding, and offered more support to the Consolidated Appeals, underlying humanitarian strategies, and action plans, this would potentially lead to—and was intended to lead to—a stronger coordinating role for the UN in crisis countries. This, in turn, required that the UN be able to field humanitarian coordinators who would not only have the requisite high-level competence, but who would have institutional support and enjoy the confidence of both the UN country teams and the wider group of humanitarian organisations in the country in question.[6]

Moreover, critics of the humanitarian system had pointed to another fundamental flaw that was not within the purview of donors to influence directly. Donors were criticised for not basing their funding decisions on accurate information. However, there was, in fact, little evidence-based data about needs, and since there was no baseline, there was little relevant information about the outcomes and impact of humanitarian programmes.[7] Any action plan and appeal for resources rested on shaky ground. There were also questions as to whether organisations appealing for funds tended to describe needs in terms of the resources and services they were able to provide. In other words, there were potential conflicts of interest that could lead to doubts about the objectivity of needs assessments. Mukesh Kapila had proposed that needs be assessed by independent organisations which were not implicated in implementation.

To address this problem, humanitarian organisations had to jointly agree on methodologies and procedures that would provide an accurate image of the threats and risks faced by a particular population in crisis. The picture had to be not only comprehensive and multidimensional, but provided at regular intervals and agreed upon and trusted by the majority of implementing organisations. This was not an easy task, but if it could be achieved, there would be significant additional indirect benefits. If humanitarian organisations engaged in a joint analysis and shared these findings and conclusions, then relationships of trust could begin to grow among them during the strategic phase which would, in turn, facilitate coordination and cooperation as operations got under way. Despite the obvious methodological challenges, it was understood that the effort was worthwhile and that it would have a positive impact on the functioning of the system as a whole.

Two organisations, UNICEF and the World Health Organization (WHO), took the lead and decided to focus on the two pilot countries (Burundi and the Democratic Republic of Congo) proposed by the donor group in order to test a broad needs assessment framework for use by all organisations active in these two countries.

After Stockholm

In early February, 2005, after my active involvement in the process leading up to the Stockholm conference and the ensuing efforts at starting to change donor practice, I left the Swedish International Development Agency to lead the tsunami operation of the IFRC in Geneva—certainly a crisis situation in which good donorship principles were thoroughly tested! Therefore, I am not in a position to judge the results and impact of GHD from an insider perspective after Stockholm. But it is, indeed, interesting to witness changes in some of the specific areas which were identified as being in need of improvement in 2003. As with any external observer, I will have to take a long distance snapshot. And from this vantage point, I do see a great deal of improvement, both in evident donor policy change and in a number of recent studies and evaluations of new practices and funding models.

Some recent results are especially encouraging, along with new issues and unforeseen problems which have also emerged. First, it is very satisfying to note that humanitarian action is now firmly placed within the mainstream of DAC analysis and identification of good donor practice. This was viewed by some critics as a rather bureaucratic and humdrum objective, but it means that humanitarian assistance is now judged against a set of codified norms and principles, like other forms of aid, as endorsed at the OECD-DAC ministerial

level in 2006. Since the Stockholm conference, peer reviews of humanitarian assistance from thirteen OECD members[8] have been carried out, all publicly available on the DAC website. As the reader can plainly see, reviews are clear in identifying areas where individual donors are in need of improvement. Although shortcomings are still evident, such as the common absence of explicit humanitarian policies, the fact that they are being addressed in open discourse where good practice is shared means that there are opportunities for speedy correction.

A number of initiatives have been taken to make funding more flexible and allow for a more needs-based response in the spirit of GHD. Then UN Emergency Relief Coordinator Jan Egeland, with strong political backing from the British and other governments involved in GHD, took the initiative to substantially increase the volume of the UN's Central Emergency Response Fund (CERF) and to change the criteria for its use. With a target at US$500 million, the CERF is now aimed at immediate response to emergencies—before donors make their funding decisions—and at humanitarian emergency actions that tend to be neglected and receive insufficient funding. In the first allocation for 2007, little-publicised emergencies in fifteen countries received funding from the new CERF.

The British government is also responding to the GHD call for donors to prevent and strengthen preparedness for the occurrence of man-made crises and natural disasters, by investing 10 percent of its spending on emergency disaster response, setting an example for other donor governments.

In order to provide flexible and non-earmarked funding and allocate financial resources in the field, pilot efforts are being conducted in Sudan and the Democratic Republic of Congo, where a group of donors that were part of launching the GHD initiative have pooled resources into a Common Fund. Allocation decisions are vested in the UN Humanitarian Coordinator, supported by an advisory group consisting of major agencies and donors. A recent evaluation[9] found that the Common Fund has improved the planning, prioritisation, and coordination of humanitarian response. While strengthening the position of the Humanitarian Coordinator, it has created strong incentives for coordination.

However, the review found that some important organisations with specific roles and mandates, but which do not take part in the UN strategic planning process—such as the ICRC and MSF—risk receiving less support from donors, although they coordinate at the field level with other organisations. Application procedures for NGOs were cumbersome and donors did not make their funding decisions early enough to improve the predictability of available funds.

Although this first attempt at pooled funding may have become too UN-centred, there was still strong support among organisations for the ethos and objectives of the Common Fund, whose flaws were found to be significant, but reparable. As pilots, the results from Sudan and the DRC are encouraging.

Another recent review has analysed the impact of OCHA Emergency Response Funds (ERF)[10] in five crisis countries. ERFs have been in use for several years, aimed at providing rapid and flexible funding to organisations at the country level, mainly NGOs, to address unforeseen humanitarian needs. They prove particularly valuable for filling a range of gaps in humanitarian response, increasing humanitarian access, and enabling NGOs to scale up their activities, not least in the transition from emergency to early recovery. The role of the OCHA in coordinating response has been strengthened through its ability to both identify needs and solicit NGOs to submit funding applications. It appears that this role is close to the independent and impartial non-implementing actor that Kapila proposed for the carrying out of needs assessments.

Work has also continued, based on the early pilots in Burundi and the DRC, to develop multi-sector Needs Assessment Frameworks (NAF) which provide a consolidated understanding of needs. Most of the Consolidated Appeals in 2007 will be based on NAFs, and the OCHA has accepted to review its own role in managing future needs assessments.

In addition to these encouraging results, the public and the aid community can track progress made by donor countries through a set of indicators presented on the GHD website.[11] It is also clear that the GHD initiative has provided a significant platform for donor dialogue on policy and practice. All of this is well and good, but another recent review[12] of donor performance—as measured against the GHD Principles—still found that more work is needed to improve indicators and the performance framework. Much can be learned from the experience of turning the Rome and Paris harmonisation agendas into practice, not least in terms of guidance to donor agency staff with practical instructions on how to monitor and report on measures to improve performance in line with the GHD Principles.

There is also the perennial problem of insufficient recognition and support to those local organisations

which inevitably respond first when crises occur, but which do not fit comfortably within the international structures for assessing humanitarian needs and coordinating action. Sometimes this occurs simply because of language barriers, as was amply demonstrated after the Indian Ocean tsunami. The role of local actors in early response, bridging the gap to recovery and sustaining long term efforts is critical. Donors and implementing actors still have serious work to do in this area.

Conclusion

The deep frustration felt by various individuals concerning donor practice was one of the triggers leading to the GHD initiative. What staff felt accountable for and able to influence as part of a system spurred them to action. Realising that binding agreements between donor governments in this area would not be feasible, they set a process in motion whereby a set of principles was codified through the articulation of good practice and its institutionalisation as a performance framework. This represents a kind of "seeping upwards" normative process. Was it successful, or was the meeting in Stockholm in June 2003 just one more conference "for powerless bureaucrats"[13] with "almost no agreement on anything that extended beyond a platitude and a vague undertaking to strive to do better"?[14]

One thing is certain: we tend to declare success or failure much too early when assessing social processes. What makes me somewhat optimistic in the case of GHD are some additional factors. Some were part of our strategy, while others evolved as part of the larger, unpredictable social and political processes in which humanitarian action occurs. First, the GHD initiative was able to feed its ideas into a process of more comprehensive humanitarian reform. Energised through political leadership, the reform has had strong momentum and continues. Contributing to a broader and more forceful stream has been beneficial for the translation of the basic premises of GHD into action.

Second, as this account intends to illustrate, the GHD process has been accompanied by a constructive commentary from independent policy research bodies and individuals, including the yearly publication of DARA's innovative Humanitarian Response Index, which will undoubtedly build on these efforts. Open and public discourse is fundamental for making governments accountable, not least in an area which has been largely protected from scrutiny and where public perception has been so far from reality.

But even as we acknowledge that donor practice is improving, much remains to be done. There are still insufficient resources to meet the needs for the protection of all the men, women, and children who face the terrible adversity brought about by natural hazards and man-made crises. If we are to meet the challenges now on the horizon, we must get the humanitarian system right.

Bibliography

Darcy, James and Charles-Antoine Hofmann. 2003. *According to Need? Needs Assessment and Decision-Making in the Humanitarian Sector*. HPG Report 15. September.

Development Initiatives. 2003. *Global Humanitarian Assistance Flows 2003*. January.

Good Humanitarian Donorship, available at: www.goodhumanitarian-donorship.org

Graves, Sue and Victoria Wheeler. 2006. *Good Humanitarian Donorship: Overcoming Obstacles to Improved Collective Donor Performance*. Humanitarian Policy Group Discussion Paper. December.

Kapila, Mukesh. 2003. "Everywhere: Time for a humanitarian compact." International Herald Tribune. 8 January.

Mowjee, Tasneem and Judith Randel. 2007. *Review of OCHA Emergency Response Funds*. United Nations Office for the Coordination of Humanitarian Affairs. January.

The Rome Declaration on Aid Harmonization. 2003. Rome, Italy. February. Available at: http://www.aidharmonization.org/ah-overview/second-ary-pages/why-RomeDeclaration

Smillie, Ian and Larry Minear. 2003. *The Quality of Money: Donor Behaviour in Humanitarian Financing*. Tufts University.

———. 2004. *The Charity of Nations. Humanitarian Action in a Calculating World*. Bloomfield, CT: Kumarian Press.

Stoddard, Abby, Dirk Salomons, Katherine Haver, and Adele Harmer. 2006. *Common Funds for Humanitarian Action in Sudan and the Democratic Republic of Congo: Monitoring and Evaluation Study*. Centre on International Cooperation, New York University, in collaboration with the Humanitarian Policy Group at the Overseas Development Institute, London.

Notes

1 Australia, Canada, the European Community, the Netherlands, Sweden, Switzerland, the United Kingdom, and the United States.

2 Darcy and Hofmann, 2003; Development Initiatives, 2003; Smillie and Minear, 2003, a report later developed into a book, *The Charity of Nations*, which included a critical and ironic review of the Stockholm conference and its outcomes.

3 Smillie and Minear, 2003, p. 5.

4 Kapila, 2003.

5 The Rome Declaration on Aid Harmonization was announced in February, 2003, setting forth the agreement between donor and recipient countries, development agencies, and international financial institutions, streamlining donor procedures and practices, and giving assurance that donor assistance would be aligned with the recipient's policy priorities.

6 Ed. note: this reform process is outlined by Jan Egeland, former UN Under-Secretary General for Humanitarian Affairs, in Chapter 5.

7 Darcy and Hofmann, 2003.

8 Australia, Belgium, Germany, Norway, Sweden, Switzerland, the United Kingdom, Portugal, Greece, the United States, the Czech Republic, Denmark, and the European Commission.

9 Stoddard et al., 2006.

10 Mowjee and Randel, 2007.

11 Available at: http://www.goodhumanitariandonorship.org

12 Graves and Wheeler, 2006.

13 Smillie and Minear, 2004, p. 241.

14 Ibid, p. 227.

Progress on the Front Lines

JAN EGELAND, President of the Norwegian Institute of International Affairs (NUPI) and former United Nations Under-Secretary-General for Humanitarian Affairs

Introduction

During my years as a member of Secretary-General Kofi Annan's senior management team, I saw first hand how effective multilateral action, in collaboration with important local and regional efforts, helped to build progress and peace in such war-torn societies as Liberia and Sierra Leone, Eastern Congo and Burundi, Angola and South Sudan, Northern Uganda, Kosovo, Timor-Leste, and Nepal.

The United Nations also coordinated massive, life-saving international relief following the Indian Ocean tsunami, the South Asian earthquake, the droughts in the Horn of Africa, the threatening hunger in Southern Africa, the July 2006 war in Lebanon, and the Darfur crisis. In several of these overwhelming emergencies, it was expected that hundreds of thousands of lives would be lost. But in all of these wars and disasters these sombre predictions were averted because multilateral action, building on local capacities, turned out to be infinitely more effective than what is even now recognised by much of world's media and national parliaments. This commitment to multilateralism and improved delivery of humanitarian assistance to save lives and alleviate suffering are at the heart of the Principles and Good Practice of Humanitarian Donorship (GHD), a commitment the Humanitarian Response Index aims to support.

Collective international responsibility for humanitarian action

Humanity fails collectively when multilateral action by member states of the United Nations lacks unity of purpose. We fail, tragically and repeatedly, when the United Nations and regional organisations do not have political will and are not provided with the minimum of economic and security resources needed from their member states. The endless ongoing suffering in Darfur, in Iraq, among Palestinians, and among the growing numbers of climate-change victims in southern nations is a product of either senseless bickering or passive neglect among those leading nations that could untangle these conflicts.

Back in 2003 and early 2004, I naïvely believed that the growing but forgotten Darfur crisis would be resolved if we managed to bring it to the attention of world leaders. This was, after all not a tsunami, an earthquake, or a natural disaster. The violence and ethnic cleansing was man-made from start to finish. But even after the issue of Darfur was brought to the Security Council in April 2004, and after we did achieve the media attention we asked for, world leaders still did not exert the political pressure or offer the physical protection that were critical to stopping the atrocities. Instead, donor nations responded generously to enable us to bring emergency relief to the peoples of Darfur. As a result, the achievements of close to 14,000 Sudanese and international aid workers in Darfur in undertaking the world's largest humanitarian operation were nothing less than heroic.

Until the summer of 2007, and against all odds, my colleagues in Darfur were able to deliver life-saving relief every month since late 2004 to most of those in dire need. A comprehensive survey undertaken by UN and NGO experts in August 2006 showed that overall malnutrition had been reduced by half since we first obtained access to carry out our large international operation in mid-2004. When relief workers were finally able to get into the country in June of 2004, mortality rates fell to a fifth of what they had been when we did our first survey. Seventy-three percent of all Darfurians had access to safe drinking water. In 2006 alone, 550,000 tons of food had been delivered.

To my intense dismay, by the time of my fourth and final visit to Darfur in late 2006, I was told by the UN, nongovernmental, and Red Cross colleagues who gathered to see me in El Geneina in Western Darfur that all of these humanitarian achievements were "under massive attack." Their elected spokesman summed up the tragic situation: "Militia attacks and banditry have rendered more than 95 percent of all roads in West Darfur no-go areas for humanitarian operations. As a result, an increasing number of camps are cut off from adequate and reliable assistance; in some instances, all basic humanitarian services have had to be shut down."

Clearly, without a negotiated and political solution to the bitter conflict in Darfur, humanitarian efforts are rendered impossible or actually regress. I recall a long night from 2 to 3 July 2003 spent in negotiations with the Foreign Minister of Sudan to cement the first agreement on access for humanitarian organisations to Darfur. President Bashir and Secretary-General Kofi Annan then announced the so-called moratorium on aid restrictions at the end of our first visit, which saw the beginning of what was to be one of the largest humanitarian operations ever undertaken. But since then, new walls of administrative obstacles have slowly but surely been erected both in Khartoum and in Darfur, walls which have all but strangled our operations.

A similar paralysis of collective multilateral action is costing lives in a very different area. If our generation had managed to unite around curbing greenhouse gas emissions—as member states generally agreed in Rio de Janeiro as early as 1992—we might not have seen the relentless increase in natural disasters produced by extreme weather and climate change—as seen in Haiti and Niger. Seven times more livelihoods are devastated in our age by natural hazards as by war and strife. Humanitarian field workers cannot believe their eyes or their ears when some politicians and industrialists still insist on arguing that explosive global economic growth has not changed the climate. For many years we have seen how the lives of increasing numbers of people are destroyed by ever more extreme drought, hurricanes, and floods. In terms of loss of human life, the effects are almost always much greater in poor, developing countries. But even in Europe the great heat wave of 2003 took 71,000 lives. Decades ago, leading scientists on United Nations climate panels had already agreed that policy and behavioural change was urgently needed. If North Americans, Europeans, Chinese, and others had all started the process of change there and then, we would have had earlier positive results, and at a lower cost.

Just as Iraq is the symbol of unilateral impotence in the new millennium, the positive change that has taken place in the worst war zone of our generation, the Democratic Republic of Congo (DRC), is symbolic of a multilateral success story. During six terrible years of war, from 1998 to 2004, nearly 4 million Congolese

died from malnutrition, preventable disease, and violence, according to the International Rescue Service. That loss of human life equals the entire population of Norway, or five Rwandan genocides, or nearly twenty times the human toll in the wars in Bosnia of the 1990s. Nowhere else have so many died from war during the last generation.[1]

When I visited the DRC in 2003, a dozen or more armies were still fighting in Eastern Congo. Armed groups and militias roamed the land, made up of hundreds of thousands of ruthless, undisciplined men from neighbouring states, from the main ethnic groups, and from massive organised crime fuelled by illegal exploitation of Congo's vast natural resources. Among them were some 30,000 child soldiers. In the crossfire of the many parallel armed conflicts was the defenceless civilian population.

But when I visited again in the autumn of 2006, much positive change was taking place. More than half of the 3.5 million displaced people had returned home. A series of militias had been disarmed. In conflict-prone areas of Katanga, Ituri and the Kivus, we met many other fighters who were waiting impatiently for small sums of money and support from the World Bank and the UN for demobilisation and reintegration, men who for more than a decade had preyed on others and lived by the gun, but who now told us they wanted to earn their livelihoods as workers in a peaceful society. For the first time, my humanitarian colleagues had access to nearly all major communities in that huge, conflicted, disaster-prone country. By 2006 and 2007, the death toll of more than one thousand per day during 1998–2004 was finally coming down.

What caused the turnaround in Congo? By 2004, after years of indecision, neglect, and penny-pinching in United Nations operations, a united Security Council finally made a concerted effort to provide a more robust peacekeeping force, and the European Union term pushed for generous funding for the enormous UN-led electoral process, and for our efforts to provide coordinated relief in all parts of the country. On the front lines of this increasingly effective operation were the good efforts of dozens of Congolese and international nongovernmental organisations, all UN humanitarian agencies, and a peacekeeping force consisting primarily of soldiers from the Asian and African nations, which have—with little publicity—helped pacify and secure larger regions of these enormous, lawless territories.

The challenges for humanitarian action

The world is currently witnessing the largest and best network of like-minded intergovernmental, governmental, and nongovernmental organisations acting as a channel for future investments in peace and development. By using highly specialised experts, operating on a large scale, utilising local networks and manpower, continuously building in quality controls and improved coordination mechanisms, humanitarian agencies can feed, vaccinate, and provide primary school education for children for a mere US$2 dollars a day, even in the remotest crisis areas. Dollar for dollar, the investment is more cost-effective than anything I have experienced in the private and public sector in any society in the North or the West. Moreover, these nongovernmental and UN organisations are speaking out more systematically on behalf of neglected peoples and communities. Throughout my three and a half years as UN Emergency Relief Coordinator, I had a pulpit from which I could advocate more effectively for what I saw as the unvarnished truth than I had dreamed was possible when I took up the job in 2003. Every working week for more than three years, I could speak in the leading international media about unmet relief needs in exploding disasters, forgotten emergencies, and the abuse of civilians.

The several hundred humanitarian and human rights organisations can and will be mobilised to hold leaders around the world accountable both for their failings and for the good things they refrain from doing locally, regionally and internationally. I see four major advocacy campaigns building in the coming years, all of which are linked to and will contribute to strengthening the core features of the Principles of GHD: first, the political leadership in an increasing number of industrialised and affluent nations will have to fulfil the agreed upon United Nations goal stipulating that at least 0.7 percent of gross national income (GNI) should go to foreign assistance. It now stands at a pitiful 0.3 percent among the twenty-two major donors organised in the OECD. The goal of providing 0.7 percent to combat poverty, disease, and hunger has been reaffirmed several times by world leaders in New York, in Monterrey, and, more important, as a legal commitment by the European Union member states. It can hardly be considered an overly ambitious goal. When economies on all continents are witnessing exploding consumption of luxury goods, it is shamefully inadequate that most of these same economies have endorsed no realistic domestic plans to achieve the 0.7 percent goal.

Countries such as Sweden, the Netherlands, and Norway have for decades overshot this goal—despite unmet domestic needs—and enjoy widespread public support for giving 1 percent or more to the poorest and the neediest.

Upon the wise initiative of their British hosts, the G-8 nations, the self-proclaimed group of the world's leading economies, agreed in 2005 to pledge an additional US$50 billion in foreign assistance by 2010, of which half was to go to Africa. In 2006, these same leaders and countries gave *less*, not more, to the two billion people on the planet who subsist on less than US$2 dollars a day. Except for the UK, all the others failed to honour their commitments. The OECD reported an overall *decrease* of 5 percent in foreign assistance from 2005 to 2006, and the wealthiest G-8 countries were no exception. The total amount of foreign assistance registered was a mere US$104 billion—less than the annual US cost of waging the war in Iraq. Many of these "world leaders" now make pitifully small investments to combat poverty, some of them less than 0.2 percent of GNI. Furthermore, it is no surprise to anyone that it is the poorest who suffer most during humanitarian disasters. As recognised by the GHD Principles, prevention is better than cure and investment in disaster risk-reduction strategies and long-term economic and human development are fundamental to humanitarian action.

But it is not only the G-8 nations that must be targeted by aggressive advocacy campaigns. The many newly rich nations in South East Asia, in the Gulf region, and elsewhere should be held accountable for playing their part in the effort to end mass misery. Today we are still far from achieving the goal of predictable minimum levels of support. Each year from 2003 to 2006, I launched global humanitarian Appeals with Secretary-General Kofi Annan on behalf of 25 to 30 million of the most vulnerable war and disaster victims in the world. We did not ask for more than US$3 to 4 billion each of these years, the equivalent of less than two café lattés per person in the industrialised world, or less than two days' worth of global military spending. We always received less than two-thirds of what we asked for, even in response to these calls for life-saving assistance. With the exception of the tsunami and Lebanon war Appeals, no Emergency Appeal was fully funded. Each year, many places such as Haiti, Somalia, or the Congo, where children died in the thousands for lack of funding, do not receive more than 50 or 60 percent of what our field workers said they needed to save the lives at risk.

The second major campaign that is gaining momentum will be to hold world leaders accountable for their obligation to protect defenceless civilians who are threatened by armed men and violent thugs in lawless places around the world. World leaders from the United States, China, Russia, Europe, the Islamic world, Africa, and from all other continents—some 190 heads of state and governments in all—solemnly swore at the United Nations summit in September 2005 to uphold their "responsibility to protect" vulnerable communities, when their national authorities cannot or will not provide such protection. I was there when it happened. For many months, diplomats from all UN member states had sat in the windowless basement meeting rooms to ponder on the "Millennium + 5" Summit Declaration. For the first time, there was a decisive majority of states who went beyond the medieval principle of "not interfering in the internal affairs of sovereign states," and the following text was agreed upon by consensus when the kings, presidents and prime ministers met in the General Assembly Hall of the UN:

> "…we are prepared to take collective action, in a timely and decisive manner, through the Security Council, in accordance with the Charter, including Chapter VII…, should peaceful means be inadequate and national authorities are manifestly failing to protect their populations from genocide, war crimes, ethnic cleansing and crimes against humanity."[2]

This "responsibility to protect" is more revolutionary than many world powers and developing world leaders seem now willing to admit, because they can no longer be passive bystanders to the carnage in Darfur, Chad, Western Ivory Coast, Eastern Congo, Gaza, Lebanon, or Burma. The campaign we must undertake aims to see this responsibility translated into predictable and adequate action to provide protection for all beleaguered and threatened communities, regardless of time, place, or circumstance.

What does this mean? Simply that more countries must allocate more manpower to peacekeeping and peace-enforcing operations undertaken by the United Nations or by such regional organisations as the African Union. These joint forces have to be operationally capable of protecting women and children against armed militias and of disarming those groups when they are not part of legitimate law enforcement units. It also means that more governments, such as those of China, India, Nigeria, South Africa, Egypt, Saudi Arabia, Brazil, and Mexico, will enforce protection by an international security presence in cases where their national elites fail to end the abuse. It means that these and other UN member states will uphold the use of economic sanctions and individual judicial accountability when political and military leaders attack civilian populations. If the new and emerging powers were to do more to defend women and children worldwide, then certain Western powers would have to do less to push such moral causes. More than anything, it means an end to standing by complacently when there is killing, rape, and mutilation of civilians or non-combatants in any crisis area, when they are your neighbours, when they occur in a country with cultural or political links to your own, or when you are simply rich or powerful. You, your government, and your nation have a responsibility to act immediately, forcefully, and coherently with other UN members to end the abuse.

Third, there will have to be a far stronger international campaign to control the proliferation of modern weapons of mass destruction, including small arms and light weapons, in particular military-style automatic guns. Even though there has been a marked decline in full-scale wars and outright genocides since the fall of the Berlin Wall, the number of violent attacks against civilians has increased since the end of the cold war in 1989. In ongoing contemporary conflicts, the contending parties have demonstrated a wilful disregard for the basic tenets of the humanitarian law governing armed conflict. I have seen, first hand, how mass murderers, mafias and terrorists in Colombia, Darfur, Northern Uganda, Eastern Congo, Iraq, and elsewhere in the Middle East never seem to lack the tools to maim, kill, and terrorise civilians. There is an alarming increase in government-sponsored and private illegal armies, ethnic militias, and non-state guerrilla forces. And they are supplied as never before with lethal automatic military weapons, often including the sophisticated overflow from the cold war, from both East and West. In recent years, the arms suppliers from the South are entirely without scruple and rival the traditional warlord-friendly supplier in Eastern Europe. Only when there is a concerted effort to curb production, control and publish all weapons sales, and vigorously prosecute the networks of illegal arms brokers will it be possible to reverse the floodtide of current weapons of mass destruction.

Reform of the UN humanitarian system

An important precondition for effective future multilateral action is true reform of the United Nations system from today's old fashioned model to a much improved operational approach and structure. The UN can no longer continue to reflect the world as it appeared to the victors after World War II.

In all areas where UN reform and restructuring are urgently needed, Secretary-General Kofi Annan provided detailed and well argued proposals to the 2005 General Assembly for approval by the member states. In most of these areas, Northern or Southern member states came together as spoilers and blocked real progress. In many key areas historic opportunities for change were lost. The United Nations is today more often than not an effective tool for the international community not because of, but in spite of its structure and its procedures. Fortunately, the humanitarian area is an exception.

In 2005, given the ample proof of the slow UN and non-UN response to the overwhelming humanitarian needs in Darfur, I initiated an ambitious humanitarian reform process. Our old systems for funding, preparedness, and coordination did not work as they should have. We were simply too slow to come to the rescue of the one million souls displaced in Western Sudan, even after we succeeded, in June 2004, in lifting many of the Sudanese government's immoral restrictions on our access to Darfur. Even with the so called "CNN-effect" working to our advantage and with numerous development ministers attending our fundraising meetings, it took months before we actually received the necessary funds to jump start the large and expensive operation. Even though we had agreement from all the executive directors of the main operational organisations on the critical importance of deploying large numbers of relief workers inside Darfur, for many months we had far too few experienced logistics and protection experts, water engineers, and camp managers on the ground. And even though we agreed on which life-saving services had the highest priority, we were not able to get the organisations to focus cooperatively on first things first.

Realising that it is usually easier to be forgiven than to obtain permission, I decided to start the reform process with humanitarian colleagues immediately and seek formal diplomatic approval later. A Humanitarian Response Review was first undertaken by experienced experts who interviewed operational organisations and field workers. The question was simple: how could we best ensure the provision of a minimum of life-saving relief and recovery assistance to all those with emergency needs, irrespective of time, place, and cultural background? Through the Inter-Agency Standing Committee—which I chaired as Emergency Relief Coordinator—we came to an agreement that reform should seek to improve the effectiveness of humanitarian response by ensuring predictability, accountability, and partnership. In short, in line with the basic GHD Principles, we aimed to reach more beneficiaries with more comprehensive needs-based relief and protection, and in a more effective and timely manner.

Three key pillars characterised the humanitarian reform programme launched at the end of 2005: first, we agreed through the Inter Agency Committee—consisting of three large NGO federations, the Red Cross and Red Crescent Societies as well as the UN agencies—to establish a series of operational partnerships. We called this the "cluster" approach. These clusters were to improve coordination and accountability in providing humanitarian services in the key aspects of emergency relief, including such gap areas as water and sanitation, emergency health, and protection of the civilian population. We asked specific operational agencies to take the lead in each of these clusters and to ensure that materials and expertise were planned, mobilised, and applied to good effect. Before the reform went into effect, our response capacity varied widely from one area and population to the other. More often than not, we succeeded in providing food, largely because the World Food Programme is a highly effective, well resourced organisation, dedicated to this purpose. But tons of corn or lentils are of no use to a mother if her child is dying for lack of clean water. So it was of crucial importance that UNICEF, in partnership with NGOs such as OXFAM, took the lead in providing water supplies and latrines in a more predictable manner.

Slowly but surely, the cluster approach is becoming more effective at assisting more people in more places.[3] Some good donors have given funds to the cluster leaders—the UN organisations, the NGOs and the Red Cross and Red Crescent Societies—to build preparedness in the key subject areas and in all geographic regions. At the July 2007 meeting of the UN Economic and Social Council, my successor as Emergency Relief Coordinator, John Holmes, concluded that host governments have welcomed the cluster approach in the ten new and ongoing emergencies where it has so far been applied as the new method for bringing about a more coherent response. At the global level, clusters have been able to rebuild emergency stocks of relief supplies and develop stand-by rosters of technical experts. At a country level, clusters have improved dialogue with government line ministries, by designating clear focal points for all key areas of activity, by defining roles and responsibilities more quickly in emergencies and by focusing on national and local capacity in 'gap' areas.

Secondly, as called for in the GHD Principles, we needed more predictable overall funding for this improved response capacity, not only for new emergencies such as Darfur in 2004, but equally in the neglected emergencies where there was no "CNN-effect." We had an old UN Central Emergency Revolving Fund, launched in 1992 after the Kurdish refugee crisis, but even a decade later, it consisted of a modest US$50 million and could only provide loans to relief organisations, which, in turn, were afraid to become indebted themselves. For this reason, I suggested to the Secretary-General that he include in his ambitious reform agenda to the Millennium + 5 Summit the proposal for a new Central Emergency Response Fund (CERF), with US$500 million in voluntary contributions from UN member states. We secured important allies for this through the British Minister for Development, Hillary Benn. In addition, Sweden, Norway, and Luxemburg all expressed willingness to invest in and campaign for a fund that could guarantee that, in Benn's words, we would have "water in our hose when a fire was detected."

When the proposal to dramatically upgrade the Emergency Fund was brought to the General Assembly in late 2005, it was already an uncontroversial *fait accompli* and the first element of the reform package to be agreed upon. All regional groups had been consulted, donors had promised sufficient money to move forward, and humanitarian organisations had been included in the planning process. Only four months later, the CERF was launched with an impressive initial US$260 million from 48 governments and private sector groups, representing all continents and as many traditional as non-traditional donors. In the first four months of activity, we allocated more than US$100 million for 130 relief projects in nineteen war- and disaster-stricken countries. From the beginning, the fund provided two-thirds to jump start operations in sudden-onset emergencies and one-third for neglected and severely underfunded continuous crisis areas. Since 2006, from Timor-Leste and Somalia to the Congo and Côte d'Ivoire, the CERF has helped make humanitarian relief more predictable where it is most needed. Further fundraising progress was made in 2007, and by July, commitments for that year already stood at US$346 million, with a threshold of US$133 million in multiyear pledges.

Of course, there will be neither successful operational clusters nor efficient use of early and additional funding if there is no guarantee of effective leadership on the ground. The third element of the humanitarian reform, therefore, became a systematic effort to recruit and train a standby pool of highly qualified "Field Marshalls" for emergency relief operations. For many years, there has been a system of Humanitarian Coordinators to facilitate the work of relief groups and to stimulate cooperation among humanitarian agencies. The work done by these key representatives has often been enormously impressive, and carried out under extremely difficult circumstances. But these individuals have varied widely in terms of their leadership qualities and creativity. Too often, a UN Resident Coordinator would continue business as usual when given additional responsibilities for humanitarian intervention. The roster of experienced candidates from inside and outside the UN system of experienced leaders is now ready for immediate deployment and can replace those coordinators who are not up to the challenge.

Humanitarian action: A joint effort

Finally, we began a process of broadening partnerships in an effort to be less "UN-centric" and less "Northern" in a world that is rapidly changing. The United Nations system is engaged in larger and more numerous relief and recovery operations than ever before. However, its relative share of the total humanitarian response is shrinking. The UN is needed for standard setting, coordination, and facilitation, and for seeing that political, security, and humanitarian efforts come together coherently. Most of the actual delivery of assistance on the ground is undertaken by the dramatically growing number of non-UN public and private actors in humanitarian response, including NGOs from the North and increasingly, and impressively, from the South. A total of some 400 international relief groups converged on Ache in Indonesia and Sri Lanka in the first month of the tsunami relief effort. This was clearly too many—perhaps even 200 to 300 too many—for the local communities to bear, given that many of their own organisations and authorities were pushed aside and not consulted in the course of recovery and reconstruction planning and operations.

The conclusions reached in the voluminous set of evaluation reports from independent experts, and published under the name of the Tsunami Evaluation Coalition[4] make for interesting reading. They confirmed that "generous relief provided affected populations with the security they needed to begin planning what to do next. Large amounts of funding allowed rapid initial recovery activities…Within a few months there was palpable evidence of recovery. In all countries, children were back in school quickly and health facilities and services were partly restored and, in some cases, much improved….The international response was most effective when enabling, facilitating and supporting (local and national) actors, and when accountable to them. Overall, international relief personnel were less successful in their recovery and risk reduction activities than they were in the relief phase."[5]

The tsunami aftermath witnessed the most rapidly and generously funded disaster response in history, yet many of the GHD Principles, already in existence, were largely ignored. The global total of US$13.5 billion represented an astonishing US$7,100 for every affected person, in stark contrast to the meagre US$3 per person spent on those affected by floods in Bangladesh in 2004. Sadly, however, the evaluators found that, in four key areas, the colossal tsunami effort represented a "missed opportunity," and offered the following key recommendations:

1. The international humanitarian community requires a fundamental reorientation from supplying aid to supporting and facilitating communities' own relief and recovery priorities;

2. All actors should strive to increase their disaster response capacities and to improve the linkages and coherence between themselves and other actors in the international disaster response system, including those from the affected countries;

3. The international relief system should establish an accreditation and certification system to distinguish agencies that work to a professional standard in a particular sector;

4. All actors need to make the current funding system impartial, more efficient, flexible, transparent, and better aligned with the GHD Principles.

In summary, we must think more strategically and more locally in the way we undertake our long term efforts to make societies resilient to hazards and strife. As stated in the GHD Principles, we must work more closely with local governments and civil society to strengthen *their* capacity for handling crisis and exercising good governance. We must find better ways to forge coordination and partnerships internationally, nationally, and locally. In this way we will be better able to tap local resources and local expertise. Time and again, we see that more lives are saved in earthquakes, floods, and tsunamis by local groups than by any expensive airborne fire brigade. Similarly, it is usually local and regional actors who are most committed to peace-building efforts and reconciliation. In July 2006, in Geneva, recognising the need to discuss a new approach to forging effective partnerships beyond borders and artificial organisational barriers, we called a first meeting of executive leaders of leading humanitarian organisations from the North and the South and from UN and non-UN agencies with the aim of forming a "Global Humanitarian Platform." A second successful meeting of this broad platform took place in July 2007.

The growth in high quality civil society movements, especially within third world societies, is probably the single most important trend in global efforts to combat poverty and conflict. They are vastly more important than the governments and intergovernmental organisations which the UN tends to recognise. All over Asia, Africa, Latin America, and the Middle East, I could see how religious organisations, and groups of women, peasants, students, and trade unions stand up for humanitarian principles, for local development, and for peace and reconciliation. Their existence offers the greatest hope for those who shoulder the weighty responsibility for ending overwhelming human misery and preventing conflict and disasters.

References

Telford, John and John Cosgrave, with Rachel Houghton. 2006. "South Asia: Joint evaluation of the international response to the Indian Ocean tsunami - Synthesis Report." Tsunami Evaluation Coalition. 14 July. Available at: http://www.reliefweb.int/rw/rwb.nsf/db900sid/EKOI-6S39GX?OpenDocument

United Nations General Assembly. 2005. "2005 World Summit Outcome." New York: United Nations. Available at: http://www.responsibilityto-protect.org/

Notes

1   Editor's note: As illustrated in Chapter 9, the victims of the crisis in the Democratic Republic of Congo received scant donor funding and attention in comparison with many other crises across the globe, contrary to the principles of impartiality and needs-based funding central to GHD.

2   United Nations World Summit Outcome, 2005, Paragraph 139, available at: http://www.responsibilitytoprotect.org/

3   Editor's note: see the crisis reports used as case studies by DARA for the Humanitarian Response Index, which include: Colombia, Democratic Republic of Congo, Haiti, Lebanon, Níger, Pakistan, Sudan, and Timor-Leste.

4   Editor's note: DARA was a member of this coalition.

5   Telford et al., 2006.

Opening Space for Long-Term Development in Fragile Environments

The critical role of humanitarian aid

SARAH CLIFFE and CHARLES PETRIE[1]

The Good Humanitarian Donorship (GHD) Principles commit donors to "provide humanitarian assistance in ways that are supportive of recovery and long-term development." The linkage with longer-term development, while extensively debated in the past in connection to the "relief to development" continuum, has received relatively little recent attention and is not measured in the GHD indicators. This paper argues that these links are becoming both more important and more complex, and outlines some initial ideas strengthening these links.

Background

The range of situations in which large-scale humanitarian aid is being provided has increased dramatically in the last decade. In 1995, twelve countries received humanitarian aid of over US$20 million.[2] By 2005, this had increased to thirty-eight countries. Countries where humanitarian aid volumes have increased substantially include Afghanistan, Burundi, Chad, Côte d'Ivoire, the Democratic Republic of the Congo (DRC), Guinea, Kenya, Sierra Leone, Myanmar, Nepal, and Somalia. These are complex environments, ranging from new post-conflict governments with reasonably broad popular support to those with fragile ongoing peace processes, as well as countries where social vulnerability has been caused by deteriorating political governance conditions and increased conflict or repression. For some long-standing recipients of humanitarian aid, all these conditions have prevailed at different times over the last two decades, or continue to prevail in different parts of the country.

The same period, in particular the post 9/11 years, has also seen increasingly *simultaneous* provision of humanitarian and development aid, along with significant increases in international assistance for peacekeeping.[3] The existence, side-by-side, of humanitarian activities, development assistance, and peacekeeping operations—all on a large scale—poses new challenges for both humanitarian and development actors.

Thinking among humanitarian and development actors on the provision of aid in crisis and post-crisis situations has also evolved. Several trends are worth underlining. First, development actors have become "more engaged with how to engage" in the most fragile and conflict-affected environments, a challenge which was previously left principally to the humanitarian actors. This debate focuses on the centrality of state-building and peace-building goals as a prerequisite for making sustainable progress in poverty reduction in weakly-governed, fragile environments, such as DRC, Timor-Leste, Sudan, and Haiti.[4]

Second, increased attention to security goals and the rise in peacekeeping operations has led to a new emphasis on security/development and security/humanitarian linkages, including the concept of integrated missions, and the creation of the UN Peacebuilding Commission.

Third, while the conceptual frameworks of the Millennium Development Goals, human security and social protection offer the potential for increased consensus on objectives between humanitarian and development actors, the initial, rather apolitical, discourse on the "relief to development continuum" has become more complex. A comprehensive 2004 survey of the academic literature and policy debates underlines the impact of the Iraq and Afghanistan experiences in increasing caution within the humanitarian community with regard to linkages with other forms of assistance, together with renewed attempts to "brand" humanitarianism's distinctive principles of impartiality, independence and neutrality."[5]

Both the complementarity and the contradictions between these policy debates are summarised in the two sets of internationally endorsed principles covering, respectively, Good Humanitarian Donorship and Good International Engagement in Fragile States and

Situations.[6] Both sets of principles stress the need for flexible, yet predictable, responses and for links between humanitarian assistance and longer-term development. However, they also differ in emphasis, in particular as regards the "independence of humanitarian objectives from political, economic and military objectives" (GHD Principles), versus the need to "recognize the link between political, security, and development objectives."

Given this context, how can humanitarian aid fulfill the GHD aspiration to "support recovery and long-term development"? Should humanitarian actors even attempt to insulate humanitarian activities from local political governance conditions and from the goals of longer-term political, peacekeeping, or development assistance? What should development actors do to strengthen positive linkages with humanitarian activities? This paper attempts to address these questions in two specific contexts: first, where there is government-led recovery and second, where the international community is unwilling or unable to engage with national authorities.[7] These contexts are not mutually exclusive and may coexist in one country in different sectors or different geographical areas.

Humanitarian-development linkages in situations of government-led recovery

In Liberia, Haiti, DRC, Burundi, Afghanistan, and Timor, as well as in post-conflict, post-tsunami Aceh, donors are attempting to support a government-led programme of reconstruction and recovery, involving both continued humanitarian assistance and a concerted effort to build capacity and accountability in state institutions. Similarly, in South Sudan and Kosovo, while the eventual status of these territories is not yet determined, it is clear that local leadership and functioning local institutions are critical to the success of recovery efforts. In all these situations, international actors have recognised that:

- While national institutions and some individual leaders may not be free from accusations of previous involvement in corruption or human rights abuses, the national leadership commands broad popular support and is, in varying degrees, willing to undertake pro-peace, pro-governance, and pro-poor reforms, making government-led recovery a viable hope for exit from crisis;

- Delivery of rapid results, visible to the population, is a priority for consolidating peace-building or political transition efforts, yet state institutions do not have sufficient capacity to deliver rapid results across the country;

- In the medium term, without state institutions which are both capable and accountable at a basic level, no exit from the crisis is possible.

Many of these recovery programmes display a gap between immediate humanitarian provision and developmental activities, where the latter move too slowly to avoid a vacuum in service provision and economic recovery on the ground. This gap is often seen either as a funding problem—leading to policy prescriptions for new funding instruments for transition financing—or the result of slow and bureaucratic procedures in development agencies. Such criticisms have merit, in particular with regard to donor procedures. Development institutions must reform their approach to the processing of funding decisions, deployment of experienced staff on the ground, and contracting and payment systems. Many have already started to do so.

Procedural and funding difficulties, however, do not adequately explain delays in early recovery. In many of the situations above,[8] large-scale funds were available under quick-disbursing procedures throughout the two-year period following the crisis. Problems in accelerating the pace of recovery activities—even where ample funding and flexible international procedures are available—have reinforced the renewed focus on institutional issues. The transition from humanitarian to development activities is not only a funding transition, but also a shift from execution primarily by international agencies to execution primarily by national institutions—"doing it themselves, rather than our doing it for them." Thus a significant gap between humanitarian and development activities can occur if national institutions do not have the necessary capacity to take programme decisions, let contracts, oversee activities, and make payments. The pace of efforts to build capacity and accountability within national institutions, therefore, plays a key role in determining how quickly developmental activities can take over from humanitarian interventions. In this sense the gap is an institutional as much as—in some cases more than—a funding or procedural problem.

What does this context mean for the planning and delivery of humanitarian activities and the linkages to development aid? If we accept that a reasonable level of capacity and accountability in state institutions is a critical basis for peace and longer-term development, and that weak institutions are central to the relief-to-development gap, it means that humanitarian actors must give greater consideration to the links between humanitarian activities and efforts to build capacity and accountability in national institutions. For development actors (and national authorities), it means questioning the assumption that humanitarian assistance under a government-led recovery programme should be short and sweet, and acknowledging that in some situations a more gradual transition to state-provided services may allow a better balance between the delivery of rapid benefits to the population, and the time needed to build capable and accountable state institutions. For both humanitarian and multilateral development actors, it means engaging with the inherently *political* nature of state-building and peace-building efforts, without compromising the basic principles which govern our assistance.

The technical level: Clear planning for transition

Bridging the institutional gap requires a much more systematic transition from international agency or NGO-led assistance to state-led service delivery and social protection. In a government-led recovery situation, this implies joint planning on post-conflict humanitarian activities—as opposed to ad hoc consultation—with a country's national leadership.

The need for joint transition planning applies particularly to sectors of humanitarian assistance which concern a *temporary incapacity* of the state to deliver services (in response to an ongoing need of the population) rather than a *temporary need*. For example, humanitarian programmes may span both life-saving services which are only provided in a crisis—such as untargeted food aid, temporary shelter, or emergency health services in refugee or IDP camps—as well as services which the state or other national institutions normally provide in a functioning administration, such as primary education and healthcare, water and sanitation, and maintenance of transport links. These latter sectors are both much more central to long-term issues of state-building, and (often) more politically sensitive for governments who seek to build their own credibility in delivering to the population. For these latter activities, a clear transition plan can help ensure that state institutions take over coordination and provision of services as they build national capacity.

Box 1 illustrates the close collaboration between national counterparts, UN agencies and the World Bank to provide for this type of transition in the health sector in Timor and a similar programme in Afghanistan.

Box 1: Transition from non-government to state provision of services

In both Timor and Afghanistan, recovery in the health sector has drawn on the capacity of humanitarian NGOs for immediate service provision as part of (rather than separate from) a programme to gradually transfer management and delivery skills and responsibilities to national institutions. This allowed for a positive balance between quick visible services to the population and longer-term institution-building. The Timor process was phased as follows:

- Phase 1: NGOs provided emergency health services; the framework for a national health system was created by a coordinated assessment and planning process by Timorese health professionals, UNTAET, WHO, and the World Bank;

- Phase 2: Government-signed memoranda of understanding with international NGOs to deliver priority health services; a national policy and training programme was conducted and a basic pharmaceuticals distribution system created;

- Phase 3: Government assumed financing of NGO services and conducted management training for national staff;

- Phase 4: NGOs transferred responsibility for district health-management systems to government, which continued to contract international doctors, while Timorese doctors were in training overseas.

The programme generated significant development results: child mortality declined dramatically, immunisation rates increased from 26 to 73 percent of all children, and from 26 to 41 percent for skilled attendance at birth; institutions created also proved resilient; during the political crisis of 2005, the health ministry continued to deliver services.

While the programme is at an earlier stage in Afghanistan, similar results have been achieved: a fourfold increase in the number of people receiving care at rural health centres, and an increase from 5 to 63 percent of women receiving prenatal care. The program operates even in the most insecure areas.

A similar approach could be taken to refugee and IDP return and the provision of local infrastructure, social protection, and livelihood support to assist reintegration. Each sector will need different institutional arrangements[9] for such transitional programmes. For example, using the capacity of international NGOs may make sense in health, while community structures may be better suited to function as transitional delivery mechanisms for local infrastructure rehabilitation, education, or livelihood-support in the period prior to the building of local level government capacity.

Timing of the handover from non-government to state provision of services also varies for different functions and areas of a country, with the state capable of assuming and being accountable for some functions earlier than others. Insecure areas or those in which local state institutions are particularly weak may require a longer handover period. For example, as described in Box 1, Timorese institutions were ready to take on the administration of public finances and social services by the time of independence, but not those of justice and security, where a short transition period had disastrous effects for governance and, ultimately, human security.

Such systematic planning early in the recovery period remains rare in practice. More frequently, there is a gap between high government expectations around the authority and capacity of the state to channel external funds for service delivery, and continued donor funding of independent humanitarian activities through UN agencies or NGOs. This creates a disconnect between the Consolidated Appeal Process (CAP) and nationally-led recovery planning. A commonly agreed results framework, as adopted in Liberia in 2005, would help bridge this divide. Such an approach will often require development actors to engage in more realistic planning with national authorities and humanitarian partners, bearing in mind the time it will take to rebuild and transform basic state functions, and the need for continued large-scale humanitarian activities in the interim.

There are significant potential benefits both for crisis-affected countries and international donors in making these changes. Governments—which are often suspicious of humanitarian Appeals—tend to be reassured by a dialogue on their increasing role in coordination and service provision, and by the identification of specific benchmarks for the transition from non-government to state service provision. Dialogue early in the recovery phase can also help clarify expectations. For example, in South Sudan, if there had been a more in-depth dialogue with leadership of the Sudan People's Liberation Movement about the time required to build state institutions capable of channeling large-scale aid for service delivery, it is likely that there would have been more realistic planning of development assistance, with an explicit longer-term role for humanitarian activities.

Clear transition planning also has the potential to improve the predictability of humanitarian funding. Consolidated Appeals are typically underfunded, especially in those sectors which respond to temporary state incapacity rather than temporary need (Box 2).

The presentation to donors of a clear transition plan, where humanitarian funding needs decrease gradually over time as state capacity increases, is likely to result in more secure funding for those humanitarian activities needed while state institutions are being established. This would also facilitate joint support for external financing needs from both humanitarian and development institutions, bringing greater pressure to bear from the IFIs, UNDP, and other multilateral development agencies in support of humanitarian financing needs.

Box 2: Lack of credible transition frameworks affects humanitarian financing

Global figures on humanitarian financing demonstrate the constraints faced in financing sectors where national counterparts and donors expect to see a strong framework for the transition to state service provision. The Humanitarian Appeal 2007 reports that 89 percent of the support requested for food was received in 2006, but only 16 percent of that requested for education, 26 percent for health, and 30 percent for water and sanitation. These latter are the sectors where humanitarian agencies are responding to a *temporary incapacity of the state* rather than to a *temporary need of the population*. There is, therefore, a much greater imperative to plan a transition back to regular state service provision in these sectors. It is likely that one of the principal reasons that these sectors are so chronically underfunded is that donors perceive a high overlap with government-led reconstruction plans, and are hence unwilling to provide long-term humanitarian funds in the absence of a clear plan and funding requirement for the transition from humanitarian to national institutional provision.

Source: OCHA, Humanitarian Appeal 2007.

The political level:
Accepting and mitigating political risk

Creating a positive role for national institutions[10] which associates them with humanitarian and early service delivery is key to the credibility of a post-conflict settlement. Schools and clinics which are rebuilt with the logo of the European Commission Humanitarian Aid Office or USAID provide concrete benefits to the local population, but they do little to build the credibility of national institutions in the eyes of the population in a manner which will sustain longer-term peace and recovery.[11] In situations where there is genuine government will to reform and rebuild, there are therefore enormous political benefits, in a positive sense, to adjusting the traditional humanitarian approach to incorporate increased engagement with the state. But there are also risks involved for international actors in associating too closely with weak state institutions which are vulnerable to corruption and political manipulation.

Closer engagement with national institutions does not necessarily imply co-option or naivety. It is reasonable for international actors to ask that a government-led framework for recovery demonstrate a growing commitment to political inclusion and equity, human rights, pro-poor policies, and action to diminish corruption. This is an area where development actors could usefully learn from humanitarian approaches. If the structural and cultural tendency of humanitarian actors is to be state-avoiding, the structural and cultural tendency of development actors is to be state-supporting, often to the detriment of early awareness of increasing abuses by state institutions. While efforts to boost the credibility of post-conflict state institutions may require an adjustment on the part of humanitarian actors, they also require that development actors guard against human rights abuses or the punitive use of aid, encourage a clear division of state functions from partisan political activities and transparency in government claims of progress. Development actors have often been slow to recognise emerging problems in these areas.[12]

Dealing more directly with the political risks and opportunities involved in government-led post-conflict recovery, therefore, requires increased efforts to understand the politics of post-conflict peace-building and state-building, as well as how to mitigate the risks. Both the character of staff and organisational culture can affect one's understanding of the political dynamics involved. For humanitarian actors, the principled independence of humanitarian aid from political objectives is, for good reasons, crucial. Although most development actors have improved their understanding of political governance as a development issue, they may frequently view short-term political concerns as corrupt or opportunistic, weakening their focus on poverty reduction.

The concept of peacebuilding provides a framework to differentiate between the positive and negative political impact of aid decisions which may be more acceptable to both humanitarian and development practitioners, due to the focus on local political impact, rather than international political interest.[13] For example, attempts to stop humanitarian or development aid from reaching villages or population groups which have supported rebel groups or opposition political parties would be deemed unacceptable on peacebuilding grounds. But, while political in nature, attempts by national politicians to *prioritise* aid to insecure opposition-held areas or population segments which might be susceptible to recruitment by armed groups (such as urban youth), may be seen as a more positive and healthy manifestation of a commitment to peacebuilding and to normal, peace time political dynamics. That said, these are always grey areas. Closer engagement requires strong analysis, staff with the experience needed to make the required judgments and better links with institutions leading peacebuilding and mediation efforts.

Military-humanitarian engagement

Before we look at the links between humanitarian activities and medium-term development in collapsed and deteriorating environments, let us briefly consider the recent debate regarding military-humanitarian linkages for long-term development and recovery. While humanitarian principles have long included independence from military objectives (reiterated in the GHD Principles), the position of the humanitarian community on interacting with military forces has evolved significantly since the end of the Cold War, with increased, although still cautious, coordination. This evolution has paralleled or mirrored the increasingly violent and complex nature of many of the contexts in which humanitarian assistance has been and is being provided. In more recent years, the development of Provincial Reconstruction Teams in Afghanistan, and later Iraq, has renewed heated discussion about the appropriate role of the military in humanitarian activities. This is an important issue for long-term governance in conflict-affected countries. Box 3 outlines some of the development considerations involved.

Box 3: Role of the military in humanitarian activities: Long-term development impact

The use of Provincial Reconstruction Teams (PRTs) has renewed debate about involvement of international armed forces in humanitarian and development activities. This has focused on two types of risk:

- from the humanitarian side, that military involvement in distributing aid will obscure an already fragile understanding of the independent nature of humanitarian assistance, and that the utilisation by the military of humanitarian projects for intelligence-gathering purposes will compromise the security of other humanitarian aid efforts;

- from the military side, that deploying key military assets into humanitarian functions will undermine concentration of effort on military objectives.

There is yet another risk to consider from a long-term development perspective, that of the inappropriate example set by the military in fragile post-conflict societies. In most societies with high governance ratings, the military does play a role in responding to crises, as in the aftermath of natural disasters or terrorist attacks, through critical functions such as search-and-rescue and the restoration of key infrastructure and transport links. These functions should therefore not be contentious in weaker societies, provided international or national forces are perceived to be neutral actors, and have not become partisan players in a local conflict.

When the armed forces go beyond this and become responsible for local administrative, humanitarian and service delivery functions, there is a considerable risk for longer-term development. For example, if international forces are involved in the oversight of local civil servants and the investigation of criminal activity, it becomes extremely difficult to explain to local political and military leaders why a clear separation of roles between the military, police, and civilian authorities is a critical part of good governance. This is particularly important in fragile post-conflict societies, because the role of the military is often at the heart of the conflict, with security sector reform one of the key priorities for sustainable peace-building.

Thus, the valid contribution of external peacekeeping forces is linked to their ability to assist in establishing a more secure local environment in both the short and long term. Explicitly modeling the limitations on the role of the military in a democratic society is an important effect to achieve to support this goal. Of course, this requires that national government, humanitarian and development agencies respond with sufficient speed and scale to support civilian governance and social protection functions.

Humanitarian aid in "unacceptable" governance environments

Government-led recovery forms one important context for the provision of humanitarian aid. But humanitarian activities also play a critical role in environments where the international community is unwilling or unable to engage with state authorities. These include:

- collapsed administrations, where the steady erosion of central state authority has allowed local economic strongmen to compete freely and violently for control over resource rich areas;

- strong states, in which closed political systems impose high levels of suffering and hardship on the populations they administer.

In the first case, the international community cannot engage with national institutions because responsible state institutions either do not exist or do not control all their territory. In the second case, the international community is unwilling to support a government-led process of social protection. In such situations the aid community finds itself under the humanitarian obligation of delivering the basic services and life-saving support that would otherwise be the responsibility of the national authorities to provide.

Other writers have commented that the debate on linking relief and development has tended to ignore these "prolonged crisis" situations, presuming a clear transition along the lines of the government-led recovery program described above.[14] Yet, many of the most difficult humanitarian interventions of the last 15 years have been characterised by just such non-linear progress and multidimensional layers of conflict and governance problems. Indeed, the two situations may exist simultaneously within one country, as is arguably the case with regard to different state functions and different geographical areas in Afghanistan and DRC at present.

In these contexts in particular, the humanitarian principles of impartiality and independence have been key to positioning international aid efforts outside of the politics that define the "unacceptable" governance environment. Upholding the GHD Principles has been central to the humanitarian community's strategy to oppose attempts by local warlords or repressive state authorities to instrumentalise, politicise, and constrain activities. Similarly, advocacy over the independence and impartiality of humanitarian aid has been used successfully to counter externally-driven advocacy positions which question or seek to halt humanitarian assistance on political grounds.

In hindsight, however, the question can be posed as to whether the humanitarian community's strict adherence to the non-political or independent nature of its obligations has not, in some cases, hindered its ability to appreciate socio-political changes as they occur, blinding itself to the emergence of both risks and opportunities.[15] The risks of an excessively "apolitical" approach were demonstrated in the DRC by the re-establishment of control by genocidal forces from the Rwandan conflict over the population in the Goma camps in 1994, and the setback faced in the humanitarian community's attempts to address the violence in the early stages of the Ituri conflict (see Box 4).

In both cases, the primary issue was the change in local leadership dynamics, with responsible traditional and community structures losing authority in relation to violent and unscrupulous local leadership.[16]

The ease with which the genocidal forces were able to re-establish control over the population in the Goma camps in 1994, under the eyes of a large assistance presence, hindered the humanitarian community's ability to provide much needed humanitarian assistance to large numbers of innocent refugees in the camps, complicated the post-genocide humanitarian and recovery efforts inside Rwanda, and compromised peace and reconciliation in the Great Lakes region. In Ituri, where some of the lessons from Goma had been taken into account, the humanitarian community's attempts to address the violence in the early stages of the conflict faced setbacks, as the sole humanitarian focus of engagement with the local leadership proved to be insufficient.

The problems of the international response in Goma and Ituri have long been recognised by humanitarian practitioners. While the debate that such situations have generated frequently focuses on the question of security, one could argue that, in the preliminary stages, the real issue is that of political engagement at the local level. In the context of Ituri, a more intense and sustained political effort to work with local community leaders in their conflict-resolution efforts was needed. In order to counter the emerging authority of extremist criminal elements, specific actions should have been identified to signal the international community's confidence in traditional leaders, such as involving them in the planning and monitoring of the response, and making it clear from the outset that the international community

Box 4: Humanitarian intervention in Goma and Ituri

From the outset of the massive humanitarian intervention in Goma in 1994, the international community moved quickly, reluctant to acknowledge the nature of the political leadership which had provoked the massive movement of refugees into Zaire. The speed and intensity of the international response in this situation contrasted sharply with the much-discussed international *inaction* during the genocide in Rwanda. It was only in November 1994, when fifteen international NGOs threatened to withdraw from a number of the camps in Goma and Bukavu that the issue of politicisation of the camps was seriously raised. The subsequent discussions occurred months after the perpetrators of genocide had regained control of the camps, a process started in September 1994 with the murder of community leaders who were working with aid agencies. By the time the international community had recognised the need to act, it was too late. There was no alternative leadership structure left in the camps.

Until six Red Cross workers were killed in Ituri in April 2001, the humanitarian community worked closely with local community leaders to contain the violence which periodically flared. What was not fully appreciated at the time was the extent to which the attempt to support traditional authority directly countered the interests of local economic warlords. Thus, the more successful the humanitarian community's efforts to support conflict management at the community level, the more these extremists resorted to sophisticated forms of manipulation to reignite intercommunity tensions. Every spike in violence corresponded to a further weakening of traditional authority. Though aware of increasing tensions, the aid community did not immediately detect a significant increase in the degree of violence and were not attuned to the extent to which this was increasingly undermining the overall humanitarian effort.

unequivocally condemned the acts that had been committed in Rwanda during the preceding 100 days.

Humanitarian aid organisations raised the valid concern that implementing such measures introduces an unacceptable level of political involvement on the part of individual agencies. It must be recognised that, on the one hand, an emphasis on safeguarding the neutrality and independence of humanitarian aid delivery, and, on the other, the notion that political engagement is critical to avert much of the suffering in some of the most violent contexts, are, in fact, not contradictory. Understanding local political dynamics does not mean that humanitarian agencies have to lead political efforts. It does, however, imply the ability to adjust delivery mechanisms to emerging political opportunities and risks. Such an approach would be consistent with both the humanitarian donorship principle of supporting long-term development, and the fragile-states principle of "taking the context as the starting point."

A stronger focus on the interaction of humanitarian activities with local political dynamics may also indicate in some cases the need to advocate for stronger and more formalised international support at the political level. Although the international community has recently attempted to integrate political, security, and humanitarian responses, the focus of much of this effort has been on the security, rather than political aspects. Political initiatives have been weakly resourced, and, where they exist, have concentrated more on resolving national conflicts than on facilitating sub-national or local conflict resolution and political development. A better mix of international instruments is needed to make local humanitarian, political, and security strategies coherent, and thus ensure stronger political support to sustain the gains made through humanitarian activities.

The extent to which humanitarian assistance is asked to operate beyond its intended scope is one that is even more relevant in "unacceptable" governance environments. In a situation where sanctions have been imposed, disallowing development aid, a conventional interpretation of humanitarian aid[17] accepts the provision of basic food and medical aid to vulnerable populations, but does not authorise support for education, sustainable livelihoods, or other long-term, essential services.

In cases where governments are unwilling or unable to deliver essential services to their population— sometimes for prolonged periods of time—the humanitarian community is faced with the difficult question of whether humanitarian aid should fill the void in order to prevent an even greater crisis. The counter-argument is that such substitute services inadvertently support delinquent or negligent governments by allowing them to redeploy fungible domestic resources for their own political or personal gain, rather than investing them in public services. While the latter is a valid concern, the medium to long-term implications of *not* supporting interventions that strengthen the ability of communities and individuals to sustain themselves—and eventually to participate in a transition process—is an equally important consideration. Attention to longer-term development linkages in such circumstances, in particular the local institution-building elements of humanitarian aid,

necessitates recognising the special political and operational risks at play, and taking active steps to mitigate these.

If properly applied, the Good Humanitarian Donorship Principles provide a solid framework for these "unacceptable" governance environments, where the aid provided should:

- be fully transparent and accountable;
- reinforce the primary responsibility of states for assisting victims of humanitarian emergencies within their own borders;
- strengthen the capacity of local communities.

From the outset, every opportunity should be seized to make clear to authorities that engagement is based on the understanding that it is the state's responsibility to provide services to its people according to international standards, and carries the expectation that global goals, such as the MDGs and international human rights Conventions, are adhered to. In closed environments, attempts have been made to provide assistance with performance-based, phased implementation criteria, which include the acceptance of monitoring and accountability mechanisms.

Transparency in a humanitarian crisis can also contribute to opening debate within closed systems. To view pariah regimes as homogeneous structures is, in many cases, an oversimplification. Mid-level civil servants, civil society and opposition groupings, and community leadership, aware of the deficiencies and injustices of the system to which they belong, may be open to finding entry points to improve governance. Humanitarian issues may also offer possibilities for dialogue between opposing parties.[18] Thus, part of the value of a principled and robust humanitarian response for longer-term development is to provoke internal debate. In part, this can be done through the dissemination of fact-based needs assessments, and continuous attempts to dialogue with the authorities, opposition, and civil society groups at all levels.[19]

Thus, key to the effective provision of assistance in contexts of deteriorating governance is the maintenance of a strong and visible international presence which can provide independent information about the situation on the ground. While donor "branding" of assistance should be discouraged in situations of government-led recovery, the case can be made that in cases of "unacceptable" governance such international visibility is both justified and desirable. In the best case scenario, the identification of humanitarian activities as independent and international allows the process of aid delivery to model more accountable and inclusive governance, which would not be possible if humanitarian activities were to be strongly associated with the state.

The deliberate retention of an international flag for aid in these circumstances does not negate the value of participatory approaches at the local level. Engaging community recipients in the identification of aid priorities and in the delivery of services furthers an understanding of the premise under which the assistance is provided—avoiding misinformation about the role of government or political affiliation in humanitarian provision. More important, it offers an opportunity for positive longer-term governance impact. The strength of local communities emerges as much from the organisational opportunities provided by a participatory approach to aid delivery as it does from the protective deterrence provided by the physical presence of international organisations. Box 5 looks at this issue in greater detail.

Nor, in situations of deteriorating governance, should the international branding of humanitarian efforts—focused on community-driven rather than state-driven delivery mechanisms—imply the complete exclusion of state social service provision entities. Governance structures in many of these contexts do not consist merely of the political leadership/elites considered "unacceptable." Civil service administrations often do provide social services, albeit limited. And in the event of a political transition, many of the civil servants involved in service delivery will remain in place.[20] Institutional capital must be preserved, not only to address suffering today, but to strengthen the ability of communities and individuals to participate in the transition process.

In cases of collapsed administrations and states under sanctions, development actors tend to have little direct presence or financing role, and linkages are therefore less immediate than in the context of government-led recovery programmes. As with adjustments to humanitarian responses, discussed earlier, there are some critical areas where development actors can adjust their practice as well. These include devising ways for development institutions to play a supportive role behind humanitarian efforts—for example, by contributing expert analysis of local social and economic conditions, supporting community structures, or offering innovative institutional and financing arrangements. Similarly,

development actors could draw more on the expertise and knowledge of local conditions developed by humanitarian practitioners when a potential transition opportunity emerges.

Box 5: Community empowerment in difficult governance environments

In many prolonged crises, given limited donor support and restrictive environments, there are often constraints on the scale of the field presence of humanitarian actors. Engaging community structures becomes one of the most effective means of ensuring and extending the impact of a humanitarian response. Though support for community networks can take various forms, it invariably involves focusing mobilisation efforts on specific needs, in part to protect the non-political label of the response. For example, communities may be mobilised to address primary education through parent-teacher interaction. Similar local self-reliance structures may be set up to address food distribution and livelihood needs.

The use of community structures as a conduit for humanitarian aid has strong potential for longer-term development benefits, through increased empowerment and local transformation, especially leadership development; demonstration of a participatory model of local decision-making; strengthened community debates about poverty, exclusion, and local conflict resolution; and demonstration of transparent and accountable public expenditure approaches.

Essential to the support of local communities is the establishment of a localised presence of humanitarian organisations—even if staffed by nationals of the country—as technical facilitators rather than direct providers. To be truly effective, the localised humanitarian presence must seek to gain acceptance of the local authorities. Initially, it can serve as a deterrent to abusive local authorities, who may hesitate to commit exactions in front of witnesses whose influence they have yet to gauge. Thus, one of the functions of a localised presence is to facilitate the interaction between the authorities and local communities, and, more specifically, to assist local communities in articulating their needs and concerns. An effective local presence also provides a recourse mechanism for communities, who then have an additional channel through which to present their grievances. The more principled—hence independent—the response, the more effective it becomes, and the greater the ability of local communities to resist pressures.

Conclusion

In recent years, debates on the linkage between humanitarian assistance and long-term development have stagnated. There have been positive examples of cooperation between humanitarian and development actors on the ground, and these offer lessons which can be applied in emerging and post-crisis situations. At the same time, global policy discussions and the experience of delivering aid in the most fragile and politically contentious environments have tended to move humanitarian and development actors in somewhat different directions as regards strategy and organisational culture, with development actors increasingly stressing support for statebuilding, and humanitarian policy-makers focusing on efforts to enhance the real and perceived independence of humanitarian aid.

We have argued that the emphasis in the GHD Principles on safeguarding the neutrality, impartiality, and independence of humanitarian aid delivery is compatible with political engagement, and that the strengthening of national institutions is critical to the alleviation of suffering and fostering a sustainable exit from crisis. Humanitarian, like development activities, always have political impact, via decisions on when, where, and to whom to provide assistance, and with whom to consult in decision-making. Efforts to understand and address the political impact of humanitarian intervention does not in any way compromise its neutrality or independence. It does, however, allow a greater adjustment to local realities and hence greater potential to support sustainable recovery and long-term development.

The recommendation to strengthen the political understanding of post-conflict recovery applies equally to humanitarian and development actors. While humanitarian actors tend to be structurally and culturally stateavoiding, development actors tend to be structurally and culturally state-supporting. Both need to adjust these approaches to take into consideration the local political context. Specifically, there is an opportunity for both communities to differentiate their approaches and their partnerships in response to situations of government-led recovery, in contrast to those characterised by collapsed administrations or repressive regimes. An increased focus on peacebuilding would assist in shifting organisational culture so as to fully incorporate analysis of, and appropriate engagement with, local political dynamics in humanitarian and development responses.

In government-led recovery contexts, greater willingness to associate humanitarian activities with emerging post-conflict state institutions and to plan the transition from nongovernmental to state provision of services has the potential to make the gains from humanitarian interventions more sustainable, while also ensuring more predictable humanitarian funding. On the development side, a parallel willingness to discard the standard assumption that conflict periods represent a short break in "normal" state provision of services is needed. This would mean efforts to engage in more realistic planning with national authorities and humanitarian partners concerning the time it takes to rebuild and transform basic state functions. It also means that development actors must acknowledge the value of continued large-scale humanitarian or other nongovernmental activities in the interim. In situations of collapsed administrations and repressive regimes, development actors could play a stronger supportive role by providing analysis of local conditions and developing innovative institutional and funding arrangements.

Responding to the complexity of these situations stretches the capacities of humanitarian and development actors to their limit. An effective response also requires combined and complementary efforts from political and security actors. Considerable progress has been made in recent years in strengthening security-humanitarian and security-development linkages. The political element is also crucial, yet tends to be under-resourced and under-valued, in particular at the subnational and local level.

Finally, renewed efforts to improve the effectiveness of humanitarian-development cooperation would be supported by a push from the donors and authorising structures of the key multilateral institutions to adapt planning and results-monitoring frameworks This is particularly important in government-led recovery contexts, where large-scale humanitarian assistance is provided simultaneously with development aid. A requirement to develop and report on common results frameworks which link programmes under Consolidated Appeals with longer-term frameworks such as government-led recovery plans and poverty reduction strategies would assist in shifting organisational culture of both the humanitarian and development communities towards closer and more effective cooperation.

References

Cliffe, Sarah and Manning, Nick. *Building Institutions after Conflict. International Peace Academy*. Forthcoming.

Ghani, Ashraf, Clare Lockhart, and Michael Carnahan. 2005. *Closing the Sovereignty Gap: An Approach to State-Building*. London: Overseas Development Institute.

Hammer, Adele and Joanna Macrae, eds. 2004. "Beyond the Continuum: The Changing Role of Aid Policy in Protracted Crises." Humanitarian Policy Group. Available at: http://www.odi.org.uk/hpg/papers/HPGreport18.pdf

Lange, Maria and Mick Quinn. 2003. *Conflict, Humanitarian Assistance and Peace-building: Meeting the Challenges*. International Alert.

OECD-DAC. 1997. *Guidelines on Conflict, Peace and Development Co-operation*. Paris. Available at: http://www1.umn.edu/humanrts/instree/OECDdev.htm

Office for the Coordination of Humanitarian Affairs. 2007. *Humanitarian Appeal 2007*. Available at: http://ochaonline.un.org/humanitarianappeal/webpage.asp?Page=1501

Principles and Good Practice of Humanitarian Donorship. 2003. Stockholm. 17 June.

Principles of Good International Engagement in Fragile States. 2007. Paris: OECD-DAC. April.

Notes

1 Sarah Cliffe is Head of the Fragile and Conflict-Affected Countries Group at the World Bank. Charles Petrie is United Nations Humanitarian Coordinator and Resident Coordinator for Myanmar. This article reflects the personal views of the authors, and not those of the World Bank or the United Nations.

2 In constant 2005 dollars.

3 The correlation between emergency aid and development aid in the years 1995–1997 was negligible (.02); by 2003–2005 it had increased to .23.

4 OECD-DAC literature from the Conflict, Peace and Development Co-operation and Fragile States Groups summarise much of this evolving thinking among development actors.

5 Hammer and Macrae, eds., 2004.

6 See Principles of and Good Practice of Humanitarian Donorship, 2003; Principles of Good International Engagement in Fragile States, 2007.

7 The paper focuses on the delivery of aid in political and conflict-related crises rather than natural disasters, although some of the conclusions may also be relevant to post-disaster recovery.

8 The Aceh situation was particularly notable for the flood of international funds made available after the tsunami. But it is also difficult to argue that lack of funding availability was the binding constraint in Afghanistan, Haiti, Kosovo, South Sudan, or Timor.

9 See Ghani et al., 2005, for a discussion of core state functions; see Cliffe and Manning (forthcoming) for a discussion of varied transitional approaches to different sectors.

10 The terms "National authorities/institutions" are used synonymously with "the state," although during an ongoing peace process, the appropriate counterpart structure may be transitional structures involving parties to the peace process, in addition to government.

11 In general, donors rather than UN agencies and NGOs are at fault here, in insisting on donor visibility in order to boost the credibility of their own institutions, to the detriment of efforts to build the credibility of post-conflict states. It is, of course, critical to maintain support for humanitarian aid amongst the governments, parliaments, and interest groups of donor countries. A better compromise, however, would be to "double (or triple) brand" the humanitarian activities taking place within a government-led program, giving credit to the donor, the implementing agencies, *and* the counterpart government agency.

12 A clear set of agreed benchmarks between national and international actors—as in the case of the Results Focused Transition Framework in Liberia—can expose problems early and galvanise international response.

13 See for example OECD-DAC, 1997 and 2001 and Quinn and Lange, 2003.

14 Hammer and Macrae, eds. 2004.

15 This is equally true of the development community.

16 In Ituri, insecurity had reached a state of equilibrium, as alternative authorities used intimidation and violence to retain their control over populations and resources. Hence, the act of scaling up humanitarian aid in itself tended to destabilise this equilibrium, with the attendant risk of escalating the conflict.

17 Conventional interpretations of humanitarian assistance would consider life-saving interventions to be part of humanitarian assistance, in addition to meeting temporary needs in other sectors.

18 The potential of humanitarian activities for initiating dialogue is the basis of the important work performed by the Centre for Humanitarian Dialogue.

19 Engagement and dialogue with closed regimes frequently raises the concern that *any* form of interaction only strengthens them, and may undermine the population's confidence in the international community's willingness/ability to address their suffering. However, in contexts of "unacceptable" governance, the confidence that populations have in international assistance organizations and the wider international community is based far more on the ability of the most vulnerable to voice their needs and grievances—and the perception that assistance/services can be trusted—than on whether or not there is discussion with authorities. In fact, it can be argued that in complex political environments, local populations view as reassuring the fact that organisations defending their interests are able to access those with local or national power, and see abandonment as a far greater international sin than dialogue with the officials of a repressive regime.

20 The attempt to purge the Iraq administration of all Baathist party members demonstrates the inadvisability of a strategy which excludes efforts to preserve the human and institutional capital of previous administrations.

Opening Space for Long-Term Development in Fragile Environments

The Media-Driven Humanitarian Response
Public perceptions and humanitarian realities as two faces of the same coin

MICHEL OGRIZEK, M.D., Senior Adviser to DARA

Media business is news coverage and distribution in real time. Humanitarian catastrophes are extreme events, characterised by all the attributes of striking news, and capable of mobilising public opinion worldwide within hours.

The problem is that a media-driven humanitarian response focuses only on fresh crises, making it incompatible with Principle 11 of the Good Humanitarian Donorship Practice Code, which says: "Strive to ensure that funding of humanitarian action in new crises does not adversely affect the meeting of needs in ongoing crises."

This paper reviews how media processes influence humanitarian intervention and the various options for managing that response. In particular, we will look at the future of the relationship between media and humanitarian action, in the context of "new media" and "citizen journalism." In the words of one contributor to the World Disasters Report, "one must recognize information itself as a form of disaster response."[1]

Modern communications and the growth of humanitarian aid[2]

The 20th century information revolution paved the way for contemporary humanitarian aid by exposing to the whole world the misfortunes of people living in areas never seen and sharing their suffering in real time with an affluent, protected public. Thus, the humanitarian movement has become a vector of globalisation. Today's interconnected media networks are the vehicle through which human suffering has become universalised and interventions borderless. In short, the media spurs governments and public opinion into humanitarian action to such an extent that Boutros Boutros Ghali once called CNN the 16th member of the United Nations Security Council.[3]

The 1960s and 1970s saw the increasing solidarity of what Rony Brauman, former President of Médecins

Sans Frontières (MSF), called "an international morality in action," characterised by the routeing of emergency care and "media fuss."[4] There is even a "before" and "after," marked by the 1967 civil war in Biafra (Nigeria), which killed over 1.5 million people. Following this, the humanitarian aid strategy "moved from explanation to emotion, compassion to pity, quest for justice to complaint, information to communication, meaning to feeling."[5] As a result, the complexity of political and historical realities has been reduced to sentiment. The active mobilisation of Western public opinion opened the floodgate for funds. This marriage of media and aid supported the development of nongovernmental humanitarian organisations such as Oxfam and Médecins Sans Frontières. Today, humanitarian organisations and the media, in concert, continue to sell tragic events to the public and donor governments. In the words of Bernard Kouchner, founder of Nobel prize-winning MSF, an event in our modern societies "is valued exclusively by the audience rating which it is likely to garner."

Media and NGOs as "co-producers"[6] of humanitarian events

It is not by chance that some catastrophes create more news than others. Stéphanie Dupont argues that they simply match TV rating criteria; "Media turn humanitarian causes into audience figures."[7] Rony Brauman has demonstrated that broad press coverage results if events meet four basic conditions:

1. **Continuous flow of images:** Representations of the drama are allowed to accumulate in the collective unconsciousness and reach a polarising critical mass; these images then become part of daily life due to their proximity; they then marginalise other events in the private sphere; according to Brauman, TV news becomes an "open tap with images."

2. **No competition:** Only one disaster at a time is the rule of the game when communicating about a catastrophe; this reinforces the impact of the story and avoids trivialisation that would push viewers' emotional tolerance level beyond their limit. As we say, "too many calamities cheapen misfortune."

3. **Innocence of the victims:** This explains the media's preference for natural disasters, as opposed to armed conflicts, in which victims—other than children—are often presumed guilty; this is why images of young people dominate television reports.

4. **Presence of a mediator:** These are usually represented by doctors, international or nongovernmental organisations, and peacekeepers, who accompany the suffering with a remedy at hand; the mediator effects "the exchange of money for moral worth."[8] In recent years, the use of celebrities as mediators—labelled "ambassadors"—has developed a glamour version of humanitarian aid. These celebrities are supposed to create greater awareness—that is, more media interest—and therefore attract more donor money.

Positive complementarities risk exploitation and excess

No one disputes the fact that it is vital and philosophically reassuring that human beings are moved by images of catastrophes, since it demonstrates our humanity and generates a dynamic of empathy and solidarity. It is easy to agree with Bernard Kouchner when he says that "without images, there is no indignation. The enemy of dictatorships and underdevelopment remains photography, and the outburst of anger which it activates."

However, people are seldom informed about *why* the calamities which make them cry occur. What is worse, they do not know why the crises repeat themselves year after year. Unfortunately, the universal presence of digital images leads to excess on the part of both media and humanitarian actors: "the weight of words is ridiculously light compared to the shock of shots."[9]

Since the 1980s, humanitarian communication strategy has not refrained from capitalising on visual emotion and, as a consequence, has neglected the need for reason. The emotional strategy eliminates analysis, questioning, and political engagement. In time, this has led humanitarian aid organisations to focus on what I

call "hopeless cases," to cohabit with the military, and to lend themselves to being used as good will insurance by politicians. Thus, in October 1984, international public emotion was at a peak in the face of distressing images from more than 400 television channels of the Ethiopian famine. Tragically, this charitable smoke screen facilitated the massive displacement of the population towards the south of the country by the totalitarian government in power. These deportations left more than 200,000 dead, while, at the same time, Western youth, with the best of intentions, called for international solidarity with local authorities by singing "We Are the World"!

Today, modern technologies make it possible for journalists to transmit images from isolated and devastated sites in real time. But once on the ground, they often remain dependent on NGOs or soldiers to facilitate their logistics. This "embeddedness" compromises their independence of movement and coverage, and their capacity for analysis of the crisis. This is all the more the case since the majority of them are foreign correspondents, deposited suddenly in the country for a few days, often having landed only a few hours prior to the shoot.[10] The pervasive sense of critical emergency generated by these "salesmen of hot news" interferes with humanitarian aid and its genuine mission, namely to provide the most urgent medical assistance, anticipate the needs for rebuilding and implement prevention programmes.

Today, however, experts know that an immediate presence at the heart of the drama often gives only the illusion of effectiveness. Nonetheless, it remains a cornerstone of humanitarian aid marketing techniques. NGOs seen as the first on the battle field by their donors demonstrate they are more operational than their competitors. Answering questions in front of TV cameras, NGO spokespersons are becoming true "special media correspondents" in the eyes of spectators. Thus, on today's medical assistance missions, the "stethoscope and the microphone are two essential pieces of emergency equipment."[11]

The commercial pressure to show stereotypes of misfortune to viewers worldwide is so demanding that journalists even seek elsewhere what they cannot find on the spot. Thus, many photos of Rwanda victims were, in fact, shot in Zaire.[12] Some reporters even manipulated images to give them a more dramatic character by means of such techniques as cleaning, changing colours, correcting the level of saturation, modifying the landscape, amplifying smoke and fire, and even re-setting the entire scene—for example, by adding children's toys—all of which contributed to the creation of new legends.

Corpses are central to media stories. The ethical problem stems not so much from the statistics—which, after all, aims to give an indication of the horror and scale of a catastrophe—but, rather, the "reality show" of dead bodies. To report death "live" can even make journalists liable for the crime of not assisting people in danger. Everyone still remembers the little Colombian girl caught in moving sand and dying on air in November 1985. "The cameraman was desperate. He did not know what to do. The first-aid workers hopelessly awaited a wrecking crane to release the child whose legs were blocked under a concrete beam. But the crane never arrived. Between two shots, the TV team tried to release the child but in vain."[13]

Not all deaths carry the same weight. "There are those which elicit more compassion than others."[14] For example, in its coverage of the Indian Ocean tsunami, the *Daily Mail*, carried front page headlines on the tiny percentage of British casualties.[15] Thus, for many local readers and viewers in Europe, it was not the 300,000 local people killed by the tsunami that had the shock value, but the plight of their own nationals who had the misfortune to be caught in the disaster.

The representation by the media of an imaginary risk that corpses represent for the living creates public anxiety that generates irrational security requirements, cultural, religious, economic, political and social tensions, even civil disorder and panic. Indeed, one of the rumours most difficult to manage after a catastrophe is the assumed health hazard of corpses. This myth leads to hurried collective burials or cremations, which seriously disturb the normal mourning process, and later pose painful and delicate problems for the identification of victims by their families.

On the contrary, it has been known for a long time that corpses do not represent a tangible medical risk.[16] Sometimes, despite assurances from international organisations experienced in managing natural disasters, the physical anguish at the sight of the corpses, which inspire revulsion, fear, and a sense of guilt among survivors, and which provide an unending reminder of the misfortune that struck the community, has an impact on local official declarations in the media. The real risk is the precarious living conditions of survivors. Unfortunately, the media all too often prefer to present macabre scenes of mass graves rather than the continued suffering of the survivors.[17] In fact, when journalists describe survivors, they tend to dismiss them as "virtual living" because they are "socially dead." They are portrayed as "deaths forgotten by destiny," that is, those who should have died in the catastrophe, but who are still alive.[18] In fact, most of the survivors do not understand why God saved their lives, and often feel guilty that they are still among the living.

The media and a new global culture of risk

By selecting which catastrophic events are worthy of being seen and remembered, the media is one of the cornerstones of our collective memory and therefore contributes to building a new global culture of risk.[19] By showing all kind of anonymous "heroes" in action, in circumstances of emergency or physical danger, the media divides humanity into "God's people"—worthy of being cared for—and the "Devil's people"—condemned to become collateral damage, as in a video game.[20]

In the chaos of disasters, both local people and decision-makers become victims capable of functioning only in the immediate present. Their minds are not able to design future scenarios in the vacuum left by the disaster. "Many of those who survived the tsunami were left without a recognizable world… they became 'strangers,' their estrangement coming not from leaving home, but from having their homes leave them."[21] Such extreme situations can generate irrational behaviour, which adds to the difficulties in managing the crisis effectively. This is why the intervention of external actors who are capable of identifying risks, applying immediate concrete solutions and communicating hope for the future is so essential. "This is the role of international organisations and NGOs. Journalists cannot play such a part, as their professional objective is not crisis management, but the narration of the stories of people's misfortune."[22]

Nevertheless, the media has become more proactive and engaged, particularly in documenting and exposing leadership responsibilities as well as failures in the face of catastrophic events. Journalists not only identify delays and drawbacks in rescue operations, but are quick to criticise official declarations which deny the severity of a crisis, or the refusal of foreign assistance for political reasons. The reluctance of the Indian and Thai governments to call for international humanitarian aid after the tsunami was described by the national media as evidence of their incompetence and incapacity to cope with such an event. Today, global public opinion will not accept half-hearted efforts in humanitarian assistance to the victims of disasters, whoever they are and wherever they may be—as President George W. Bush learned, to his chagrin, after the disastrous crisis management after Hurricane Katrina.

Nevertheless, the question remains whether the media can act as a watchdog for the accountability and effective governance of states and NGOs regarding risk management, transparency in the funding of operations, the reconstruction of livelihoods, the evaluation of local populations' real needs, ethnic discrimination, and other humanitarian issues. In 2005, roundtable meetings bringing together government officials, civil society representatives, tsunami victims, and journalists were held in Hyderabad and Kerala by the Asian Media Information and Communication Centre of India, with the support of UNESCO and the Friedrich Ebert Foundation. The outcome was a call for "more investigating reporting probing the needs and conditions of ordinary people and communities… whose stories remain untold, in addition to the fishermen who already had made headlines."[23] Victims who are not making news may be forgotten.

Memory lapse, the cornerstone of media stories

Do the media have a memory? When reporting certain cases the media will not fail to point out the long list of similar past events. However, in other situations, history will be buried in the tomb of silence. The tsunami of 26 December 2004 was regarded by the media as "extraordinary," "unique," and "of a quasi unequalled significance." "While it is true that the death of 300,000 victims represents a terrible tragedy, it is no less true that, in strictly scientific terms, this tsunami was an event of average proportions. The wave hardly exceeded ten meters in height, not as high as other waves seen in the past and in other parts of the planet."[24] The history of tsunamis began in Lisbon, in November 1755, events which caused deaths in the hundreds of thousands. No one had done anything to prevent these phenomena from happening again and again. Two months after the tragic days of Christmas 2004, none of the international media was speaking about Sumatra and *its* tsunami. The media will recall the disaster only on annual anniversaries, but probably not for more than five years.

Proper funding means institutional independence, but also marketing techniques

Humanitarian aid organisations cannot be completely independent from states if they are not able to raise funds separately. With this in mind, it is therefore necessary for them to be able to both mobilise public opinion and provoke a donor response. Marketing studies demonstrate that "it is not so much the magnitude of the catastrophe and the number of deaths, but the breadth of the press coverage which makes donors react."[25]

By emotionally engaging people with the victims of a disaster and refusing to portray the catastrophe as an inevitable accident of fate, humanitarian action becomes an act of empathy and economic engagement. Public emotion is directed and shaped by the global media. Humanitarian aid becomes a player on the stage and is part of the spectacle which aims to attract the generosity of small, rather than institutional, donors. Regretfully, this transforms citizens into consumers of tragedies, even voyeurs.[26] In fact, there exists a "televised dramaturgy of humanitarian aid, with its emblematic characters, its scenic conventions, its linguistic rules… the victim/first aid worker "couple" are made to dance ad nauseum to the music of our feelings."[27] Since the 1980's, one can even see the development of a new form of aesthetics in the photographic representations of misfortune, often exhibited and awarded international prizes.

Competition in the field of humanitarian aid is intense and driven by the need to protect and/or enlarge an organisation's market share and its presence in the media. This is why actors increasingly position their services by using what is known in the trade as a USP (Unique Selling Proposition) such as hunger, disability, or child adoption. Some develop broadly universal discourses; others denounce political responsibilities and failures; still others defend the duty of governments to intervene. The result of this humanitarian market segmentation has been the creation of a congestion of myriad organisations and messages working on the ground after any spectacular disaster.

The development of local media and the sustainability of humanitarian aid

UNESCO's Belgrade Declaration, adopted in 2004, emphasises both "the responsibility of the international community in making reliable information available during times of crisis, as well as the necessity of strengthening local media and ensuring its independence throughout transition processes."[28]

In the field, there is, indeed, an interaction between peacekeeping forces, humanitarian organisations, and the local media, but in many situations it is hard to differentiate information from public relations, or worse, from strict censorship. In countries where the humanitarian situation is severe, freedom of speech is often virtually non-existent, and, at times, even the physical safety of journalists is uncertain. The local media, particularly in conflict zones, is condemned to work not only under the direct control of local authorities but, increasingly, under threat from insurgent groups. In these circumstances, international peacekeeping forces often choose to communicate primarily with global media representatives, because relationship-building with the local media remains delicate and sometimes counterproductive, particularly when considering the poor working standards. As a result, local access to information, one of the fundamental pillars of democracy and sustainable peace, is seriously hampered.

As it is sometimes hard for local populations to believe that a humanitarian organisation is truly neutral, it is crucial to provide accurate information to the local media "in order to raise awareness about what assistance they [NGOs] can provide, secondly, to win trust and enhance security for the staff and the chance of success in their work, and thirdly, to raise awareness about international law."[29]

In remote areas, broadcast or non-print media is the medium of choice for reaching people who live with the threat of natural hazards. "Radio in particular is a very accessible medium for poor people, especially women in their homes. Apart from radio's usefulness in supplying information after the sudden onset of disasters, skilfully produced radio dramas can be used to help reduce ongoing disaster risks… In Cuba, for example, a high public awareness of disasters has ensured that death tolls from hurricanes are far lower than in neighbouring countries. Cubans understand the warnings issued by their meteorologists and relayed by the media. They know what to do and where to go. Vulnerable communities keep in close contact with government at all levels—unlike in Haiti which… suffers many more disaster deaths. Cuba's success shows that scientific knowledge alone isn't enough; information only becomes useful when it is shared with people at risk."[30]

These issues raise a number of questions for donors on how best to approach the challenge of local media development. Access to free media on the ground, i.e.,

strengthening local media capacity, should in fact be one of the criteria used to evaluate the success of a humanitarian intervention. For example, Novicki states that, "in Liberia, Charles Taylor persecuted the media and at the time of his departure the media was in a poor state, with only a few functioning print and broadcast outlets. One year on from the start of the UN mission, there were 10 radio stations in Monrovia, 30 newspapers, and two TV stations."[31]

Traditional and new media convergence

Access to information is decisive in life-threatening situations. In this context, new information technology is seen as a vital component of natural hazard Early Warning Systems (EWS), although many have yet to be implemented in the zones most at risk.

In the space of a few years, the Internet has not only become a privileged media channel to access and share life-saving information, but it has also created a virtual global space where isolated people and those under state control and censorship can have a voice. It has also become an extremely powerful tool through which to collect "new money" from people who are "younger than traditional donors."[32] Today, one third of donations received come through the Internet.

The mobile phone is also becoming an essential instrument in the event an emergency, particularly through the use of Short Message Service (SMS). In 2004, "Operation *SMS for Asia* in France made it possible to collect more than 3 million SMS in one week according to telecommunication operators."[33] SMS were also used by the French authorities to contact isolated tourists in Asia during the tsunami, thus informing them in real time of the developing situation and to locate the missing. Another example, from the IFRC's *World Disasters Report*: "After Gujarat's 2001 earthquake, the local women's union Self-Employed Women's Association (SEWA) distributed 200 handsets to its staff, enabling them to communicate without returning to headquarters. SEWA also used satellite TV to conduct video conferences with its field staff and to broadcast public interviews with government officials."[34]

The birth and multiplication of mobile phone paparazzi and video-bloggers is a perfect example of how new communication technology has created an epistemological explosion in the media coverage of catastrophes.[35] Citizen journalism has become a flourishing business.

"Some of the most striking film of the tsunami was taken not by professionals, but by amateurs. They used relatively cheap, relatively simple digital video cameras to shoot the footage. They then put their video images up on the Internet… The clips are short, grainy and jumpy, and the sound is marginal . . . It took only hours for videos like this to make it from Thailand, Sri Lanka, and Indonesia to the Internet… Some did get their videos to the websites of mainstream news outlets such as *The Washington Post* and Britain's *Guardian* newspaper. Some of the amateur footage appeared on broadcast outlets such as *CNN* and the *BBC*."[36]

Such "citizen journalism" represents a gold mine for the media. The *BBC* has set up teams of full-time journalists to collect amateur video and photographic material. The agency "Scoopt" is the first of its kind to act as intermediary between amateur photographers and the professional media. Television outlets now send journalists with cash on the ground to buy amateur material, often for an exhorbitant price, and then make it available to television viewers around the world."[37]

This proliferating amateur footage intensifies the emotional dimension of already tragic events. The primitive techniques used by frontline witnesses add to the feeling of chaos and highlight the fragility of our lives. Violent and hideous realities are seen in the rough, no longer filtered through professional eyes.

Media business is incompatible with Principle 11 of Good Humanitarian Donorship (GHD)

The key questions for donors are: how much, why, and to whom. There are no easy answers to these questions, which have become more complex because perception has increasingly become reality, often driven by media "logic." The business of media is news coverage and distribution in real time. Humanitarian catastrophes are extreme events, capturing all attributes of striking news, and capable of mobilising public opinion worldwide within hours. Television coverage and NGO marketing efforts thus operate hand in hand to target the general public. Broadcasting triggers the attention of 33 percent and direct mailing another 37 percent of potential donors.[38]

The problem is that a media-driven humanitarian response focuses on new crisis only, which makes it incompatible with the Principle 11 of the GHD, namely, "Strive to ensure that funding of humanitarian action in new crises does not adversely affect the meeting of

needs in ongoing crises." In fact, the December 2004 tsunami washed out other crises, such as the famine in Somalia or the spread of AIDS in Africa. It took three years to rebuild public awareness about the humanitarian tragedy in Darfur!

Lessons from the controversy created by the overabundance of resources available in response to the 2004 tsunami should be taken into consideration when marketing humanitarian aid in future disasters. Eight days after the tragic event, Pierre Salignon, managing director of MSF—which had collected €40 million from donors around the world—decided to close their appeal for funds, arguing that their capacity to use this money in the affected regions was overburdened. He said they were acting transparently and honestly with respect to the donors. Nevertheless, this decision triggered much criticism. Through the response to the tsunami, many donors discovered the heterogeneity of the NGO world, as well as the wide variety of the missions and mandates of these agencies and their sometimes limited capacity to act on the ground. Financial evaluations following the relief effort, investigating how funds were used, illustrated that the concerns raised by MSF should have been taken more seriously. Operational capability and accountability, not media publicity, should be the main criteria by which donors fund NGOs.

Prime Minister Tony Blair accurately observed that there are emergencies equivalent to a tsunami each week across Africa, and that it is possible to prevent these because many are man-made. How refreshing it was to hear this honest appraisal. Indeed, governments should adopt a more rational and sustainable approach when allotting humanitarian aid. Unfortunately, they are too often under the spell of the media. Equally problematic is the fact that government promises of humanitarian aid are frequently driven by national public opinion or foreign policy interests. At the time of the tsunami, the secondary benefits for the United States of helping the Muslim world were obvious, as were those for Japan in counterbalancing the power of China in Asia. Even Blair was accused of using this opportunity to improve his public image at home vis-à-vis his political rival Gordon Brown.

Media-driven humanitarian aid strengthens international civil society

It is difficult not to agree with Zsuzsa Ferenczy when she says that, "NGOs no longer limit their activities to humanitarian aid development on the ground. Their engagement implies also powerful testimonials which are able to create awareness and mobilise public opinion through communication strategies. Thanks to this new expertise and power, some NGOs are often seen as more capable of managing misfortunes than governments; they are not only active on the ground, but are an important source of information for the media and the state."[39] As a result of this new awareness, NGOs are increasingly influencing international debates and negotiations.

This situation raises even more fundamental questions about the functioning of our present model of democracy. Elected leaders appear more and more to be unable to address and solve crises in a complex and fragile world. Who then decides what issues are worthy of our attention and which ones warrant mobilising citizens? The answer is straightforward: on the one hand, there are nongovernmental organisations—representing only themselves and speaking on behalf of a limited number of stakeholders—who advocate their viewpoints or beliefs and defend their interests; on the other hand, there is a global media hub— controlled increasingly by a few powerful individuals.[40]

What is the future of the media/humanitarian action relationship?

The media industry is under heavy economic pressure for market shares and advertising revenue. This pressure will, no doubt, reinforce the present global trend to hook audiences with cut-and-paste news clips, popular local "soap" stories, and the occasional global event that floods viewers with violent emotion. As a consequence, it is highly unlikely that media treatment of humanitarian catastrophes is going to change in the near future.

The Internet, blogs, and citizen journalism are often idealised as the hoped-for transparent and free global communications network. However, it must be pointed out that it is still difficult to be sure of the credibility, much less the relevance of much information currently on the Internet, even in a social and political environment scanned by watchdogs. Needless to say, it is virtually impossible to detect misinformation or rumour in conflict situations, especially when dealing with countries under dictatorial control or disconnected from the rest of the world. Grassroots digital information is often purely emotional and self-centred and therefore lacking

the necessary strategic relevance regarding community needs and action priorities.

In humanitarian situations, international organisations, no doubt, have a role to play in ensuring that global and local media work in cooperation with humanitarian actors and in harmony with the Good Humanitarian Donorship Practice Code. Having said this, international bodies do not have sufficient budgets or enough trained communication experts on the ground to implement this worthy goal. Nor, it must be said, does this important function even figure as part of their core mandate.

Conclusion

Following are two recommendations for improving the information interaction among all stakeholders in humanitarian crises:

- Journalists and NGOs must acknowledge that *information alone is a form of humanitarian response.* Therefore, as part of their ethical code of conduct, they must accept to be fully transparent in coordinating their coverage of disasters.

- Donors should always be aware that they are manipulated emotionally by both media and NGOs. When making decisions, they must remember that public perceptions and humanitarian realities are two faces of the same coin—the very coin that first-aid workers ask for and collect on behalf of victims. Donors should then take time to consider carefully and dispassionately before giving money and ask whether their chosen NGO fully represents the victims' interests, or those of the organisation. In order to answer this delicate but crucial question, it must be realised that information supplied by the media is often not very useful. Rather, reading reports from agencies which specialise in evaluating humanitarian aid—much the same way that institutional investors study the recommendations of financial analysts—is probably the best approach.

References

Aigle Royal (pseud.). 2005. "Polémique humanitaire." 5 January 2005. Available at: http://www.oulala.net/Portail/article.php3?id_article=1602

Arboit, Gerald. 2003. «Rôles et fonctions des images de cadavres dans les medias—l'actualité permanente du 'massacre des saints innocents.'» Centre d'Etudes et de Recherches Interdisciplinaires sur les Médias en Europe. *AFRI* IV.

Backmann, René and Rony Brauman. 2001. « Les médias et l'humanitaire.» Paris. Centre de Formation et de Perfectionnement des Journalistes (CFPJ).

Barre, Michel. 2001. «La Communication de crise: un apprentissage réciproque.» Les Cahiers du Conseil 4. 1 October.

Boyd, Clark. 2005. "Tsunami disaster spurs video blogs." BBC.com 4 January.

Brauman, Rony and René Backmann. 1996. «Les médias et l'humanitaire: Ethique de l'information ou charité spectacle.» Paris. CFPJ Editions (Coll. Médias et société).

Clark, Nigel. 2005. "Disaster and generosity." *Geographical Journal* 171(4):384–386.

CSA. 2005. Survey. 27 September.

Dupont, Stéphanie. 2002. «Les enjeux d'Internet dans la communication des associations humanitaires.» Diplôme d'études supérieures spécialisées (DESS).

Ferenczy, Zsuzsa Anna. 2005. «Les ONG humanitaires, leur financement et les médias.» Memorandum. Centre International de Formation Européenne. Institut Européen des Hautes Etudes Internationales. June.

Good, Robin. 2005. Full Tsunami Video Footage, Pictures, Clips and TV News Stories. Available at: http://www.masternewmedia.org/2005/01/02/full_tsunami_video_footage_pictures.htm

Guillet, Alexandre. 2002. «Asie: le boom des dons par Internet.» *La Chaîne Info (LCI)*. 9 January.

International Federation of Red Cross and Red Crescent Societies (IFRC). 2005. *World Disasters Report 2005*. Geneva.

Jacquemin, Marie. 2006. «Media et humanitaire: émotion ou information?» Presented at Festival International du Grand Reportage d'Actualité (FIGRA).

Mesnard, Philippe. 2002. «La victime écran: la représentation humanitaire en question.» Paris. Available at: http://www.hcci.gouv.fr/lecture/note/victime-humanitaire.html

Morgan, Oliver. 2004. "Infectious disease risks from dead bodies following natural disasters." Rev Panam Salud Publica 15(5):307–12.

Nouvo. Website available at: http://www.nouvo.ch/108–3

Novicki, Margaret. 2004. "Friends or Foes?" Presentation at Peacekeeping Forces, Humanitarian Aid and Media Development, International Media Support Conference. Copenhagen. 26–27 November.

Ogrizek, Michel. 2005. «Communi-risquer, Séminaire sur la Gestion des Risques.» Faculty of Economic and Social Sciences. University of Geneva. April.

Ogrizek, Michel and Jean-Michel Guillery. 1990. «La communication de crise.» Collection *Que Sais-je?* Presses Universitaires de France.

de Senarclens, Pierre. 1999. *L'humanitaire en catastrophe*. La bibliothèque du citoyen. Paris.

Talles, Olivier. 2005. «Plus de trois millions de SMS envoyés en France pour autant d'euros.» *La Croix*. 11 January.

UNESCO. 2004. *Belgrade Declaration*. 3 May.

———. 2006. Website: NEWS – Communication and Information Sector's Daily Service. 20 June.

Vaux, Tony. 2005. "Data or dialogue? The role of information in disasters." In *World Disasters Report* 2005. IFRC. Geneva.

Veyret, Yvette. 2004. «Réflexions géographiques sur le tsunami du 26 décembre 2004.» University of Paris X. Nanterre.

Westphal, Florian. 2004. "The human deadline—when aid organisations need urgent information dissemination." Presentation at Peacekeeping Forces, Humanitarian Aid and Media Development, International Media Support Conference. Copenhagen. 26–27 November.

Wood, Graham. 2005. "Tsunami media convergence: Not a fair guiding principle for aid." Christian Science Monitor. 24 January.

Notes

1. Vaux, 2005.

2. Ferenczy, 2005.

3. Boutros Boutros Ghali, Former Secretary-General of the United Nations, in a speech at ResPublica Conference, 6 June 2005.

4. Brauman and Backmann, 1996.

5. Backmann and Brauman, 2001.

6. According to Philippe Juhem, Maître de Conférence en Sciences Politiques, Strasbourg.

7. Dupont, 2002.

8. Mesnard, 2002.

9. Backmann and Brauman, 2001.

10. Some broadcasters on FR3 (French regional television) organised training sessions for their journalists on how to cover technological accidents and natural disasters.

11. Brauman and Backmann, 1996.

12. Mesnard , 2002.

13. Jacquemin, 2006.

14. Arboit, 2003.

15. Wood, 2005.

16. Morgan, 2004.

17. Ogrizek, 2005.

18. Ogrizek, 1990.

19. Notes from the introduction to the Third International Symposium on the History of Natural Risks: Media and Memory of Natural Risks, Grenoble, 10–11 April.

20. According to the International Federation of Red Cross and Red Crescent Societies (IFRC, 2005), "in Afghanistan, for example, a long-running BBC soap opera in local languages has been shown to change listeners' attitudes and behaviour towards such risks as landmines and infectious diseases."

21. Clark, 2005.

22. Barre, 2001.

23. UNESCO, 2006.

24. Veyret, 2004.

25. Aigle Royal (pseud.), 2005.

26. de Senarclens, 1999.

27   Brauman and Backmann, 1996.

28   UNESCO, 2004.

29   Westphal (International Committee of the Red Cross), 2004.

30   Ibid.

31   Novicki, former Chief of Public Information and Spokesperson for the United Mission in Liberia, 2004.

32   Guillet, 2005; Dupont, 2002.

33   Talles, 2005.

34   Vaux, 2005.

35   See Website at: http://www.masternewmedia.org/2005/01/02/full_tsunami_video_footage_pictures.htm

36   Boyd, 2005.

37   See Website at: http://www.nouvo.ch/108-3

38   CSA Survey, 2005.

39   Ferenczy, 2005.

40   For example, 80 percent of the French media is owned by two private groups, both of which are global leaders in the armaments business; this illustrates the well known fact that humanitarian crises and wars are two sides of one coin.

3

PART THREE

Crisis Reports

Introduction

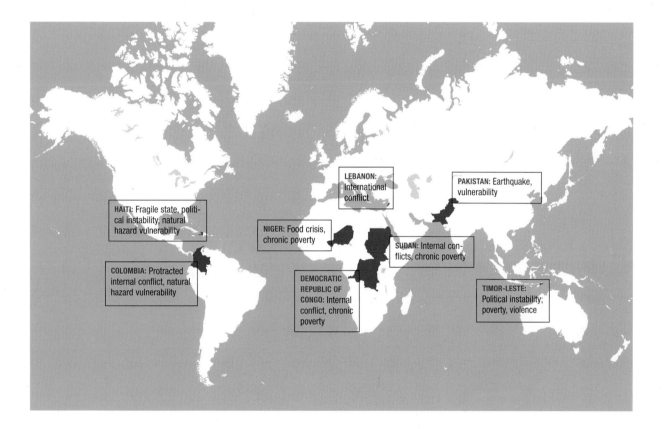

HAITI: Fragile state, political instability, natural hazard vulnerability

LEBANON: International conflict

PAKISTAN: Earthquake, vulnerability

NIGER: Food crisis, chronic poverty

SUDAN: Internal conflicts, chronic poverty

COLOMBIA: Protracted internal conflict, natural hazard vulnerability

DEMOCRATIC REPUBLIC OF CONGO: Internal conflict, chronic poverty

TIMOR-LESTE: Political instability; poverty, violence

The Humanitarian Response Index is based, in part, on a survey of implementing agencies working in eight humanitarian crises across the globe. The Survey collected over 1,000 responses assessing OECD DAC donor performance in these countries in relation to the Good Humanitarian Donorship (GHD) *Principles*. The eight crises represent a variety of disasters and complex emergencies resulting from natural hazards and violence and conflict, in different phases of the humanitarian response, and with contrasting levels of funding. The following reports, based on field missions conducted by DARA teams in 2007, review the key features and debates surrounding the causes and nature of the crises, the international donor response, and the implementation of humanitarian action on the ground. They therefore illustrate the complexity of humanitarian operations and the challenges faced in putting the GHD *Principles* into practice.

Colombia

AT A GLANCE

Country data *(2005 figures, unless otherwise noted)*

- 2006 Human Development Index: 0.790, ranked 70 of 177 countries
- Population (2006): 45.6 million
- GNI per capita Atlas method (2006, current US$): 2,740
- Life expectancy: 72.8
- Under five infant mortality rate: 21.4 per 1,000
- Population undernourished (2001–2003): 14 percent
- Population with sustainable access to improved water source (2004): 93 percent
- Primary education completion rate: 96.9 percent
- Gender-related development index (2006): 0.78, ranked 55 of 177 countries
- Official development assistance (ODA): 511.1 million
- 2006 Corruption Perception Index: 3.9, ranked 59 of 163 countries

Sources: World Bank, 2006; UNDP, 2006; Transparency International, 2006.

The crisis

- From 1990 to 2000, the conflict claimed 27,000 civilian and 2,887 military casualties;
- Over 4,000 people are kidnapped annually;
- Colombia has the highest number of anti-personnel mine-related deaths and injuries: 1,110 casualties in 2005;
- After Sudan, Colombia has the highest number of internally displaced persons (IDPs) in the world (3.8 million in the last 20 years), 1.2 million since 2002, and more than 215,000 in 2006 alone;
- In 2006, an average of 602 persons were displaced every day in Colombia;
- Afro-Colombians and indigenous people—the country's poorest, representing 30 percent of the population—account for 40 percent of IDPs;
- In 2006, 200 persons died and some 685,000 were affected by landslides, floods, avalanches, and storms.

Sources: Council for Human Rights and Displacement (CODHES), 2007; Land Mine Monitor; Colombian Red Cross, 2006.

The humanitarian response

- There is no UN Consolidated Appeal for Colombia;
- OECD-DAC donors committed over US$36 million in humanitarian assistance in 2006; the largest donors were: the EC/ECHO (US$12,356,614 or 33.8 percent), Norway (US$5,286,663 or 14.5 percent), Netherlands (US$3,468,054 or 9.5 percent), Switzerland (US$3,445,904 or 9.4 percent) and Germany (US$3,444,157 or 9.4 percent);
- Colombia has increased its financial response to the crisis; in 2006, the Colombian Congress approved a budget of US$365 million to assist IDPs;
- Plan Colombia has strong military components, both social and developmental; in 2006, the United States provided US$138.52 million for development, and US$641.15 million (82.2 percent) in military and police aid.

Sources: UNHCR, 2007; Centre for International Policy (CIP), 2007; OCHA, Financial Tracking Service.

Colombia
A Crisis Concealed

SILVIA HIDALGO, Director, DARA

Introduction[1]

The inclusion of Colombia in the 2007 Humanitarian Response Index (HRI) may surprise some, especially Colombians. Indeed, Colombia takes pride in its well established democracy, strong economic growth, and high levels of human development. However, these achievements mask a humanitarian crisis brought on by continued armed conflict. Because the government is unwilling to recognise the crisis—for both political reasons and out of anxiety to avoid the application of international humanitarian law—there is ineffective state presence in many parts of the country. As a consequence, whole segments of the population face a protracted humanitarian crisis in which thousands die and tens of thousands are displaced every year. The effects of the conflict are exacerbated by poverty and inequality.

What began as an uprising over inequality and poverty has become an endless war among guerrillas, paramilitaries, and state forces. The lucrative drug trade is deeply emmeshed in the violence, which invades rural villages and isolated indigenous communities, creates urban slums, and leaves many Colombians living with pervasive fear. The international response is conditioned by the government's reluctant approach to the conflict and humanitarian situation, as well as donors' political interests, in particular, the drug trade. The discrepancy between official figures and those of implementing agencies makes it difficult to justify an adequate response. Aid personnel working in Colombia consistently claim that the crisis is underfunded, when compared to the needs and to past responses to other crises.

Causes and dynamics of the crisis: An impasse fuelled by profit

After more than 40 years of internal armed conflict and several failed attempts at negotiating peace, Colombia remains engulfed in violence. The main actors are the state security forces, two rival leftist guerrilla organisations—the Ejercito de Liberación Nacional (ELN)[2] and Fuerzas Armadas Revolucionarias de Colombia (FARC)[3] —and the Autodefensas Unidas de Colombia (AUC),[4] formed in 1997 by several right-wing paramilitary groups. The civilian population is caught in the middle and in the course of the violence all sides have been accused of gross human rights violations.

FARC, the largest armed group, with up to 18,000 members, is one of the richest and most powerful guerrilla armies in the world and operates across half of Colombia. The ELN, operating mainly in the northeast, has some 4,000 members. Although both the FARC and ELN emerged as independent forces in the 1960s, their roots can be traced to violent political struggles in the 1950s, revolving around social inequalities, poverty, land control, injustice, corruption, and impunity, as well as the development of the state and internal colonisation of the country.[5]

By the 1980s, illegal drug trade expansion changed the nature and contours of the conflict. Paramilitary groups such as the group Muerte a Secuestradores (MAS),[6] linked to wealthy landowners, drug cartels, and segments of the Colombian military, emerged to combat the guerrillas and non-violent leftwing movements. Paramilitary forces have assassinated members of the ELN and FARC, as well as leftwing politicians, activists, trade unionists, and numerous civilians. Violence became so widespread that state institutions were virtually paralysed, as members of the paramilitary organisations continued to engage in kidnapping, drug trafficking, and attacking civilians. Control of the drug trade, kidnapping, and extortion became part of the rationale and means for illegal armed groups to fund the conflict, with military and economic objectives overriding political and social ones. The FARC and paramilitaries are reportedly responsible for 80 percent of the world's cocaine trade.[7] Throughout 2006, paramilitary leaders were on the US wanted list for drug trafficking.

Despite numerous negotiation processes throughout the 1980s and 1990s and the disbanding of smaller armed groups, the conflict continues to rage. In 2006, President Álvaro Uribe Vélez was re-elected on a pledge to strengthen state authority, improve security, and combat armed groups. His government struggled militarily against FARC, but for the time being, efforts to find a negotiated settlement with the ELN have failed. While the government convinced many paramilitaries to disarm, demobilisation has neither ended the influence of the AUC nor dismantled its criminal and drug-trafficking operations, but merely left a void readily filled by others. In fact, at the time of the DARA mission in May 2007, revelations were made linking outlawed right-wing paramilitary groups with top government officials, including the Vice President and the former Foreign Minister. Despite a significant counter-narcotics strategy, Colombia's role in the drug trade has actually increased.

The government has adopted a military, law-and-order approach to the conflict, portraying it as a struggle against narco-guerrillas and terrorists, part of the global anti-narcotics campaign and the "war against terror." At the same time, it has played down the humanitarian crisis, and sought to control the language used by international agencies, sending instructions to foreign ambassadors and representatives of international agencies in June 2005 discouraging the use of such terms as "armed conflict," "non-state actors," "civil protection," "peace communities," "peace territories," or "humanitarian space."[8]

Humanitarian impact of the crisis: Civilian targets and forced displacement

Violence against civilians and forced displacement are not an unintended consequence of the conflict; rather, they are a strategic objective, aimed at forcing them from their homes and lands. In fact, the conflict has been described by all humanitarian organisations, academics, and the Internal Displacement Monitoring Centre (IDMC) as a war against civilians, nearly 27,000 of whom were victims of the conflict from 1990 to 2000. In contrast, there were 12,887 "military" fatalities during that period.[9] Forced displacement allows agricultural land to be seized from peasants and small farmers, among the poorest and most vulnerable of Colombia's people. As part of Plan Colombia, aerial chemical spraying by the government of areas of coca cultivation has forced thousands to flee their homes, particularly in the guerrilla-controlled regions.

Almost 4 million of the country's 40 million people were displaced by violence between 1985 and 2007, with an estimated 500,000 now refugees in neighbouring countries. More than 215,000 were displaced in 2006 alone. Since 2002, 1.2 million people have been displaced, among them a disproportionate number of Afro-Colombians and indigenous people, among the country's poorest.[10] Many NGOs argue that the real figure is much higher, as the numbers do not account for the growing number of besieged communities, under-registration due to fear, people displaced by anti-narcotics fumigations, and intra-urban displacement. The majority of these live in precarious conditions without access to water or sanitation, or effective protection, and at risk of being displaced several times. Because of their IDP status, they are often suspected of collaboration with the armed groups and risk being targeted. Many lack formal title to their land, have no identity papers, documentation, or benefits.

Afro-Colombian or indigenous IDPs are subject to greater discrimination. Although the indigenous peoples represent only one percent of the population,[11] all indigenous groups in Colombia—more than 80—have experienced displacement, in part, because of their location in isolated and marginalised areas where the armed groups operate and where drug crops are grown. Tribes such as the Wounaan and the Nukaks, forced from their ancestral lands by armed incursions in 2006, now face extinction.[12]

In addition to displacement, civilians in Colombia are victims of violence, kidnapping, robbery, confinement, and persecution. Over 4,000 people are abducted annually, the majority by the ELN.[13] In addition to outright massacre, violent attacks, and intimidation, most committed by the armed paramilitary groups, Colombia has become one of the hemisphere's major suppliers of women and girls for international sex trafficking, with IDPs among the most vulnerable. Colombia ranks highest for anti-personnel and mine-related deaths and injuries, which claimed 1,110 casualties in 2005.[14]

Confinement is defined as "the arbitrary obstruction by armed actors of civilians' free movement and access to goods essential to survival," and has grown in frequency and intensity.[15] The combination of land mines, confinement, and blockades of goods and persons, targeting primarily civilians, exacerbated poverty and social instability, and prevented access to basic necessities, such as food and medicine.

Despite its rank of 70 out of 177 countries in the UNDP Human Development Index in 2006, Colombia

is considered a middle-income country. However, vast swathes of the country are affected by the conflict and beyond the control and provision of state social services. Economic inequality in Colombia is among Latin America's highest: the country's top quintile possesses 60 percent of the national income, and 3 percent of landowners own 70 percent of arable land.[16]

Colombians, especially the displaced living in poverty belts around major urban cities, are also exposed to many natural hazards. At the time of the HRI mission, heavy rains caused landslides in the outskirts of Medellin, seriously affecting displaced people.

The international donor response: Compensating for an insufficient national response

The international response to the crisis in Colombia is distinct from that of other interventions largely because of three of its main features:

First, the fact that Colombia is not considered a failed state, but, rather, a middle-income country, has implications for international donors. The Colombian government has resources, strong institutions, and services in Acción Social, the government department primarily responsible for those who have been displaced, and important social programmes, such as Familias en Acción.[17] Both of these state agencies address humanitarian needs. The strategy of the international community has been to encourage the state to take greater responsibility for the provision of assistance to IDPs. In the case of UNDP, Colombian funding outweighs international funding 11 to 1.[18] International organisations and NGOs are constantly explaining to IDPs and residents their rights under Colombian legislation.[19] The Colombian Congress approved a budget of US$365 million for assistance to IDPs in 2006.[20] And even if the Colombian government is legally obliged to ensure that IDPs have access to services such as health care, this is far from being the case in reality.[21] Thus, a major issue continued to be the lack of protection and assistance for those not officially registered as IDPs. In January 2005, OCHA recommended that the registration standards be redefined to include, for example, those who flee within the same municipality, or as a result of the aerial spraying of coca plantations with toxic herbicides.[22]

Second, a genuine UN Consolidated Appeals Process (CAP) for Colombia does not exist. The UN devised a Humanitarian Plan of Action for 2003, requesting US$62 million. The main objective was "to promote respect for, access to, and enjoyment of the human rights and basic humanitarian principles by the population affected by the humanitarian crisis caused by the armed conflict."[23] However, the Plan was rejected by the Colombian authorities, who resisted prioritising human rights issues and refused to acknowledge the presence of an internal armed conflict, despite the urging of UN agencies that the government meet its responsibilities under international human rights and humanitarian law.[24]

As a result, UN political and humanitarian representatives and NGOs are prohibited from dealing with the armed actors even on humanitarian issues. What is more significant, OCHA is unable to issue a Consolidated Appeal through which donors can fund humanitarian activities. The absence of a CAP and the concealment or lack of visibility of the crisis has made raising funds and attracting donor attention extremely difficult. A regional donor commented that "the dead in Colombia are less visible and funding for this country only comes at the end of the fiscal year and depends on whether no hurricanes or earthquakes take place elsewhere on the continent."[25] Therefore, it is not surprising that most implementing agencies view their funding and programmes in Colombia as inadequate.

Third, the international community is divided in its response. For many donors, this is conditioned by their relationship to the government, that is, to political concerns. Plan Colombia with its strong military component and some social and development schemes in the regions most affected by coca farming, epitomises this division. For example, the United States provided US$138.52 million in 2006 for social and development schemes, but US$641.15 million (82.23 percent) in military and police aid to the Plan.[26] The consequences of the Plan's implementation are complex and affect not only large drug producers, but also small peasants involved in the cultivation of illegal crops and indigenous communities. Colombia is the source of nearly 90 percent of the cocaine entering the United States.[27] As a result, US policy towards Colombia is influenced by its anti-narcotics strategy and commercial and strategic regional interests, including Colombia's oil reserves, its opposition to Venezuela, and its concern for regional stability. The Uribe government is considered a US ally in both the war against drugs and against terrorism, with the FARC, ELN, and AUC listed as terrorist organisations, by the United States and the EU.

According to OCHA's Financial Tracking Service, OECD-DAC donors committed over US$36 million in humanitarian assistance to Colombia in 2006. The largest donors were: the EC/ECHO with US$12,356,614 (33.8 percent), Norway US$5,286,663 (14.5 percent), Netherlands US$3,468,054 (9.5 percent), Switzerland US$3,445,904 (9.4 percent) and Germany US$3,444,157 (9.4 percent). In fact, through ECHO, the European Commission has provided over €100 million in humanitarian assistance since 1994, with additional EC support channelled through the uprooted budget line. Certain donors, including some of those above, have engaged in conflict-resolution efforts and human rights programmes, in addition to providing humanitarian assistance. Implementing agencies commented that Spain was only interested in funding projects in the West, especially in tourist areas.[28] France is also known for providing humanitarian support alongside its efforts to liberate Ingrid Betancourt, a French national and Colombian politician, held hostage by the FARC since early 2002.

Implementation of the humanitarian response: Need for protection and longer-term strategies

Displacement is a daily reality in Colombia, illustrating a chronic emergency. Protection, therefore, remains a key feature of the required response. Implementing agencies point out that many donors not only do not fully understand protection, but, aside from supporting the Red Cross operations in Colombia, do not foresee flexible support mechanisms for successful protection efforts, despite the fact that these are fundamental issues covered in GHD Principles 3, 4, 7, and 16. Security issues and humanitarian access remain a constraint and affect the delivery of protection and assistance across large parts of the country. Violent incidents were reported in border areas throughout 2006, such as the imposition of ransom demands, death threats to humanitarian workers, and assassinations. Given that medical personnel are often attacked by armed groups, the International Committee Red Cross (ICRC) accompanies Colombian medical teams in many areas. Agencies were in fact critical of donors, complaining that they were inconsistent by focussing on cost-per-beneficiary ratios and neglecting to provide sufficient funds for logistics and security measures needed to reach those in greatest need.[29] The latter is contrary to GHD Principle 17 and the facilitation of safe humanitarian access. A key feature of the international response through the ICRC involves supporting protection-related activities and facilitating humanitarian organisations' efforts and access. With the exception of the ICRC, organisations (including UN agencies) prohibited by the government from dealing with the armed actors even on humanitarian issues, created an additional obstacle. In contrast, the Colombian army provided humanitarian assistance in many instances, and some implementing agencies worked alongside them, channelling assistance through them, theoretically contrary to GHD Principle 19.[30]

In relation to the humanitarian principles of neutrality and impartiality in addressing needs, it should be noted that a number of large international NGOs refused donor funding for activities in support of demobilised paramilitaries, as they felt this would represent a contradiction of their activities supporting the victims of paramilitary violence.[31] Some organisations felt that donors were discriminating against returnees, and that many returnees were worse off than the displaced and received *no* assistance. This was confirmed by a major donor,[32] and suggests that the response was category-based as opposed to needs-based, since the latter would take into account additional vulnerability criteria, such as ethnicity and exposure to the conflict. GHD Principle 6 promotes just such a needs-based approach and is absolutely fundamental to humanitarian action. Nevertheless, the vast scale of the crisis and the fact that organisations in Colombia are kept in check and lack access to many areas and groups, have impeded a more targeted and long-term approach. Because agencies have less room to manoeuvre because of the government's attitude and are also limited by the security situation, they have great difficulty in carrying out vulnerability surveys, and cannot ensure adequate coverage and reach.

Since aid in Colombia is not driven by the need to respond to emergencies, timeliness is a less important factor than full fledged support and consistent, predictable funding in key areas, such as protection. Implementation involves responding to both mass and individual displacement. Since the government's response to the IDP situation was imperfect but well funded, the international humanitarian response did not match the scale of the crisis. Although the UNHCR received sufficient funding for its regional programme, it faced a budget shortfall for Colombia in 2006. Thus, some core protection activities, such as the reinforcement of national registration capacities and the profiling of unregistered IDPs were not implemented.[33] However, the government response did not always cover these gaps. While local organisations and IDP representatives saw the May 2006 presidential elections as an opportunity to address humanitarian issues, the UNHCR argued that

electoral campaigning actually postponed significant decisions.[34] In fact, despite OCHA's recommendation in January 2005, the criteria for IDP status were not redefined in 2006. The government's humanitarian response focused only on the immediate needs of IDPs for the first three months of displacement—mainly food, shelter, and access to healthcare, leaving significant problems in the medium to long term. Livelihood strategies for the displaced in urban settings are complex as the vast majority are farmers. Moreover, there was also insufficient funding for UNHCR community support, local integration programmes in rural areas, and microcredit projects for urban refugees.

Nevertheless, some progress was made with the issuing of more than 400,000 identity cards and the protection of some 1.2 million hectares of land belonging to IDPs and persons at risk of displacement.[35] Independent organisations, such as the ICRC—the only organisation that has a presence in the entire country—provided assistance to 45,000 IDPs in 2006. National NGOs and civil society organisations, including the Catholic Church, also played a crucial role in protecting and assisting IDPs. The Church has a local presence throughout the country, is actively involved in the IDP problem— documenting IDPs displaced at the parish level—and promotes "pastoral dialogue for peace" initiatives. National NGO efforts were also wide-ranging, from the provision of aid to advocacy for IDP rights. Moreover, Colombia has an extensive civil society peace movement. For this reason, given the limited presence and response of the state to the IDP crisis, international agencies have often sought to strengthen Colombian civil society. Thus, the capacity, level of involvement, and ownership by Colombians themselves constitutes a positive and distinct feature of the humanitarian response. Partly because of their level of preparedness, the duration of the conflict, and the fact that many Colombians have been displaced several times, it is common for Colombian nationals to head international NGOs and occupy key positions in implementing agencies.

As regards coordination, in September 2006 the UN Inter-Agency Standing Committee (IASC) activated the cluster approach, introducing three thematic groups under the overall leadership of the UN Humanitarian Coordinator. Despite some skepticism on the part of humanitarian actors concerning coordination and meeting overkill in Bogotá, OCHA was well funded and played an important role in linking international and national government agencies and providing updated information on the humanitarian situation. In contrast, coordination among donors regarding funding of humanitarian activities was inadequate, prompting Sweden to ask OCHA to facilitate monthly or bi-monthly coordination meetings among donors to monitor humanitarian issues on a permanent basis.[36] However, the UN in Colombia has a difficult relationship with the government. After criticising the government's security policy, UN Secretary-General's Special Envoy, James Lemoyne, was not reappointed in 2005.[37]

Conclusion

Paradoxically, Colombia's ongoing humanitarian crisis still remains largely invisible. Its inclusion in the *Index* is important, not only because of the scale of the crisis, but because of its complexity and political overtones. Lack of visibility and denial—in the context of a relatively strong, functioning state, economy and society—severely limits the level of international funding. Many donors have a delicate relationship with the government due to political and strategic interests, in particular, the "war on terror" and the fight against drugs. Thus, funding is not proportional to need. The prosperity of many in the capital, Bogotá, where the international community is based, stands in stark contrast to the situation of the displaced—the majority Afro-Colombian and indigenous people—in urban slums and rural areas. Despite the disputed figures, it is clear from reports[38] that large segments of the population, often the most vulnerable and marginalised, are trapped in the middle of the conflict and risk forced displacement, confinement, and continued human rights abuse. Humanitarian access is another key problem.

Although government policy regarding the humanitarian crisis is advanced and well-funded, it is lacking in coverage, short-term in approach, and category-, rather than needs-based, aimed at blending the displaced population into the same social programmes as poverty-stricken Colombians. Ironically, the very existence of the government's limited response to the crisis poses an obstacle to international funding, which does not meet the dire need and is undermined by the lack of a CAP. Donors have consistently advocated for increased governmental involvement and responsibility.

In light of the complex, highly politicised situation, many implementing agencies argue that political support and backing from donors to address the crisis is just as important, if not more significant, than funding. This is especially true with regard to protection and human rights-related activities and on issues of humanitarian access. There is considerable room for the donor community to further support and promote many of the key Principles of Good Humanitarian Donorship.

References

Amnesty International. 2007. *Colombia: Killings, Arbitrary Detentions, and Death Threats - the Reality of Trade Unionism in Colombia.* 3 July. AMR 23/001/2007.

Castro, Nelson Fredy Padilla. 2001. "Toxic rain kills more than the coca." UNESCO Courier. May Available at: http://www.unesco.org/courier/2001_05/uk/planet.htm

Centre for International Policy. 2007. "US Aid to Colombia since 1997: Summary Tables." Available at: http://ciponline.org/colombia/aidtable.htm

Colombian Red Cross. 2006. "Balance preliminar de los desastres 2006." [Preliminary Report of Disasters in 2006]. 28 December. Reliefweb. Available at: http://www.reliefweb.int/rw/RWB.NSF/db900SID/SNAO-6X3LP6?OpenDocument

Council for Human Rights and Displacement (CODHES). "Más o menos desplazados." Available at: http://www.codhes.org/Info/Boletines/BOLETIN69DEFINITIVO.pdf

El Espectador. 2005. "Se va LeMoyne y cierran la oficina." 25 April. Available at: http://www.reliefweb.int/rw/rwb.nsf/db900SID/EVIU-6BSC9B?OpenDocument

González, Fernán, E. 2004. *The Colombian conflict in historical perspective.* London: Conciliation Resources.

Human Rights Watch. 2007. "Maiming the People: Guerrilla Use of Antipersonnel Landmines and other Indiscriminate Weapons in Colombia." 25 July. Available at: Maiming the People Guerrilla Use of Antipersonnel Landmines and other Indiscriminate Weapons in Colombia. Available at: http://hrw.org/reports/2007/colombia0707/

Internal Displacement Monitoring Centre (IDMC). 2006. "Colombia: Government "Peace Process" Cements Injustice for IDPs." 30 June. Available at: http://www.internal-displacement.org/8025708F004CE90B/(httpCountrySummaries)/BC16D950C7D18F37C12571870042838B?OpenDocument&count=10000

International Committee of the Red Cross (ICRC). 2006a. *ICRC Annual Report 2006?Colombia.* 24 May. Available at: http://www.icrc.org/Web/eng/siteeng0.nsf/html/colombia

———. 2006b. Colombia: no reprieve for victims of enduring conflict. ICRC Activity Report. Available at: http://www.icrc.org/web/eng/siteeng0.nsf/html/colombia-update-311206

International Crisis Group. 2007. "Introduction: Colombia." Available at: http://www.crisisgroup.org/home/index.cfm?id=1269&l=1

Land Mine Monitor. 2006. "Mine Ban policy."Available at: http://www.icbl.org/lm/2006/colombia.html

Minear, Larry. 2006. "Humanitarian Agenda 2015 Colombia country study." July. Tufts University. Available at: http://fic.tufts.edu/downloads/HA2015ColombiaCountryStudies.pdf

Office for the Coordination of Humanitarian Affairs (OCHA). 2005. Retreat Notes. Available at: http://www.humanitarianinfo.org/IMToolBox/07_Info_Centres/Colombia_Humanitarian%20Situation%20Room/Acta_Final_Encerrona_OCHA_Diciembre_2005.doc

Republic of Colombia. 2005. "Lineamientos para el enfoque de los proyectos de cooperación internacional [High Commission for Peace]." 13 June. Available at: http://www.altocomisionadoparala-paz.gov.co/noticias/2005/junio/documentos/lineamientos.pdf

United Nations High Commissioner for Refugees (UNHCR). 2007. *UNHCR Global Report 2006—Colombia*. June. Available at: http://www.unhcr.org/home/PUBL/4666d2360.pdf

United Nations Human Rights Council. 2007. *UN Human Rights Council: Report of the United Nations High Commissioner for Human Rights on the Situation of Human Rights in Colombia*. PLACE OF PUBLICATION. 5 March.

United Nations System Thematic Group on Internal Displacement. 2007. "Humanitarian Action Plan 2002–2003 Colombia." Available at: http://www.reliefweb.int/library/documents/2002/unct-col2-29nov.pdf

United States Department of State. 2007. *Trafficking in Persons Report—Colombia*. Washington. 12 June.

World Bank. 2006. "Colombia Country Brief." Available at: http://web.worldbank.org/WBSITE/EXTERNAL/COUNTRIES/LACEXT/COLOMBIAEXTN/0,,contentMDK:20214628~pagePK:141137~piPK:141127~theSitePK:324946,00.html

Notes

1. The opinions expressed here are those of the author and do not necessarily reflect those of DARA.

2. [Army of National Liberation]

3. [Revolutionary Armed Forces of Colombia]

4. [United Self-Defence Forces of Colombia]

5. González, 2004.

6. [Death to Kidnappers]

7. International Crisis Group, 2007.

8. Republic of Colombia, 2005.

9. González, 2004.

10. UNHCR, 2006.

11. Organización Nacional Indígena de Colombia [National Indigenous Organization of Colombia].

12. UNHCR, 2006.

13. International Crisis Group, 2007.

14. Land Mine Monitor, 2007.

15. CODHES.

16. The World Bank (2006) estimated that if Colombia had achieved peace 20 years ago, the income of an average Colombian today would be 50 percent higher and a further 2.5 million children would be living above the poverty line today (US$2 per day).

17. Familias en Acción is a cash-transfer programme directed towards Colombia's poorest families.

18. DARA field interview, May 2007.

19. A National Displacement Plan, drafted in January 2004 found the government's response to the IDP situation unconstitutional.

20. UNHCR, 2007.

21. ICRC, 2006a; Human Rights Watch, 2007.

22. Castro, 2001.

23. United Nations System Thematic Group on Internal Displacement, 2007.

24. Minear, 2006.

25. DARA field interview, May 2007.

26. Centre for International Policy, 2007.

27. International Crisis Group, 2007.

28. DARA field interview, May 2007.

29. Ibid.

30. Ibid.

31. Ibid.

32. Ibid.

33. UNHCR, 2007.

34. DARA field interview, May 2007.

35. UNHCR, 2007.

36. OCHA, 2005.

37. El Espectador, 2005.

38. ICRC, 2006b.

The Democratic Republic of the Congo

AT A GLANCE

Country data *(2005 figures, unless otherwise noted)*

- 2006 Human Development Index: 0.391, ranked 167 of 177 countries
- Population (2006): 59.3 million
- GNI per capita Atlas method (2006, current US$): 130
- Life expectancy: 44
- Under five infant mortality rate: 205 per 1,000
- Population undernourished (2001–2003): 72 percent
- Population with sustainable access to improved water source (2004): 46 percent
- Primary education completion rate: NA
- Gender-related development index (2006): 0.373, ranked 131 of 177 countries
- Official development assistance (ODA): US$1.8 billion
- 2006 Corruption Perception Index: 2.0, ranked 156 of 163 countries

Sources: World Bank; UNDP, 2006; Transparency International, 2006.

The crisis

- From 1996–2003, almost 4 million people died from the conflict—called Africa's world war—the equivalent of six Rwandan genocides;
- In 2006, 1,200 people died *daily* as a consequence of the war;
- In addition to a new wave of displacement in 2006, between 1.4 and 1.6 million persons were still displaced and 1.3 million returnees required urgent support;
- High levels of sexual violence and rape, described by then UN Under Secretary-General for Humanitarian Affairs as "a cancer… out of control;" sexual violence used as a weapon of war; therefore, incidence of HIV/AIDS believed to be high;
- 30,000 boys and girls were used by armed groups as combatants, camp porters, or sex slaves;
- Despite first democratic elections in 40 years held in 2006, violence and human rights abuses continued in some areas throughout 2006 and 2007.

Sources: Brennan, 2006; OCHA, 2006; UNICEF, 2006; Oxfam, 2006; Watchlist on Children and Armed Conflict, 2006.

The humanitarian response

- The DRC has been considered a "neglected" crisis; in 2000, the UN Appeal received 31.8 percent of requested funds; the 2005 Appeal received 64.8 percent;
- The 2006 UN Humanitarian Action Plan (HAP) requested US$696 million to assist 30 million people, and received US$287 million, or 42 percent of funding requested, although this represented 2.5 times more than funding received in 2005;
- Of the 21 OECD-DAC members providing humanitarian aid in 2006, the UK, the EC/ECHO and the United States provided 49 percent of funds;
- The Congo crisis served as the impetus for several initiatives for reform of humanitarian action: the Needs Assessment Framework Matrix (NAFM), the Pooled Fund, the Central Emergency Response Fund (CERF), the cluster approach, and the GHD initiative; DRC was selected by OECD-DAC as a pilot country for application of the GHD *Principles*;
- Humanitarian actors have estimated their funding requirements for 2007 at US$687 million.

Source: OCHA, Financial Tracking Service.

The Democratic Republic of the Congo
Sick Giant of Africa

GILLES GASSER, Independent Consultant on Development and Humanitarian Aid

42-17043152I DPI © Lynsey Addario/Corbis

Introduction[1]

The Democratic Republic of Congo (DRC) is the site of one of the world's worst ongoing humanitarian crises. The country suffered what has been called "Africa's world war" from 1996 to 2003 from which almost 4 million people died, compared to the 228,000 dead and missing from the 2004 tsunami.[2] Following a peace agreement in 2003, and with the help of the world's largest and most expensive peacekeeping operation, the country held its first democratic elections in 40 years in 2006.

However, 2006 did not mark an end to instability and violence in a country no longer at war but still not at peace. Protection issues continued on a large scale. Throughout 2006, killings, human rights violations, widespread rape, and forced displacement of civilians continued, in particular in the east. Many communities were still being deprived of basic services and humanitarian assistance.

Despite the scale of the disaster, the crisis has traditionally been considered "neglected" and the UN Appeal in 2006, as in previous years, was underfunded. However, 2006 saw a sharp increase in the volume of funding and the introduction of a number of humanitarian reform initiatives, in part due to the fact that the DRC was selected as a pilot country for the application of the Good Humanitarian Donorship *Principles*.

Causes of the crisis:
Regional warfare fuelled by natural wealth

The causes of the conflict and humanitarian crisis which erupted in 1996 were a volatile mix of long- and short-term factors, including the country's brutal colonial past, violent struggles over state power and control of natural resources—often delineated along ethnic lines—regional state rivalry, and spillover from conflicts in neighbouring countries.

The country's population and natural resources were exploited under Belgian colonial rule until independence in 1960, when the Congo became embroiled in the Cold War and a violent conflict over its future. Colonel Joseph Desiré Mobutu (later known as Mobutu Sese Seko) came to power in a military coup in 1965 and installed a repressive regime which was to last 32 years. Political rule through violent repression, corruption, patronage, and the manipulation of ethnic divisions, along with the exploitation of natural resources by national and foreign interests, and the devastation of the broader economy were hallmarks of the regime. This troubled history was perpetuated in and shaped the current conflict.

In 1997, Mobutu was ousted in a rebellion led by Laurent Kabila and backed by Rwanda and Uganda. However, when, in August 1998, Kabila purged Tutsis from his government, Rwandan troops backed Congolese Tutsi rebels and entered eastern DRC. The conflict escalated, with Zimbabwean, Angolan, and Namibian troops supporting Kabila. Numerous local militias emerged, following ethnic lines and supporting the various state actors. At least seven states and seven rebel groups were involved in the fighting. Internal conflicts, such as that in Rwanda, were played out in eastern DRC and control of territory for the exploitation of natural mineral wealth became a key objective for all sides. Following the signing of the Lusaka ceasefire and the deployment of the UN peacekeeping force (MONUC) in 1999 and 2000, respectively, along with Kabila's assassination in 2001 and succession by his son Joseph Kabila, a peace agreement was finally signed in 2002. This included the withdrawal of foreign troops and the introduction of a transitional government which paved the way for elections in 2006.

Nevertheless, this failed to stop the violence in eastern Congo, specifically in Ituri, North Kivu, South Kivu, and Katanga provinces. Rebel groups continued to combat the government and rival groups for control of mineral wealth, with a potent admixture of ethnic competition and insecurity. The election, in which Joseph Kabila was voted President, was marred by violence, with supporters of Presidential candidate Jean-Pierre Bemba refusing to accept the vote. Political instability and violence continued into 2007, with former militias—including Bemba's supporters and Tutsi rebels in the east—refusing to integrate into the national army.

While there has been considerable progress in improving security, the situation remains unstable, with very weak state institutions and services and human rights abuses routinely committed by both army and police, as well as armed groups. The causes of the conflict, including corruption, the exploitation of natural resources, ethnic divisions, and authoritarian government, continue to haunt the country.

Humanitarian impact of the crisis:
The deadliest conflict since World War II

The crisis in the Democratic Republic of Congo has been called the deadliest humanitarian catastrophe since the Second World War.[3] The greatest number of victims of the conflict, many of them children, dying of malnutrition and disease, were civilians caught in the middle of the violence. Human rights abuses such as murder, torture, rape, abduction, and the use of child soldiers were rampant and committed by all sides. Civilian belongings were looted, and they were displaced from areas of mineral resources, and out of retribution. The conflict also devastated the economy, destroyed livelihoods, created mass food insecurity, and denied local communities the basic healthcare, food security, and education. With access virtually impossible in many areas, humanitarian actors were obliged to adapt their strategies in favour of advocacy activities in support of humanitarian access, respect for humanitarian principles, and the protection of civilians.

As difficult as it is to contemplate, almost 4 million people have lost their lives since 1998, as a direct or indirect result of the conflict, the vast majority due to malnutrition and preventable disease.[4] This is equivalent to *six* Rwandan genocides.[5] Equally difficult to comprehend is the fact that, as late as 2006, more than 1,200 people continued to die every day as a direct or indirect consequence of the war.[6] In 2006, between 1.4 and 1.6 million persons were still displaced and unable to return due to continuing violence.[7] In fact, 2006 saw a new wave of displacement, caused by renewed violence in the east. IDPs were exposed to multiple threats, such as cholera and malnutrition, and were denied basic social services. In addition, over 400,000 refugees were still living in neighbouring countries, and 1.3 million returnees required urgent support.[8]

The impact of the war on the civilian population must itself be understood within the existing context of chronic poverty and the virtual collapse of state institutions and services, inherited from the Mobutu regime. Income per capita peaked at US$1.31 per day in 1973, and by 1998 had dropped to just US$0.30 cents.[9] By 2006, it was estimated that 80 percent of the population lived on less than a dollar a day.[10] In 2006, Oxfam estimated that 75 percent of the population faced a precarious food situation, with the DRC government calculating that severe malnutrition affected over 16 percent of the population. A 2005 report by Médecins Sans Frontières estimated that the mother and child mortality rate stood at 1,289 per 100,000 live births, representing the death of 585,000 children a year. One in every five children died before the age of five.[11] In 2006, food security was still one of the worst in the world. The public health system had collapsed in large parts of the country and the privatised health system was beyond the means of a large majority of the population.

Macroeconomic indicators improved following the 2003 peace agreement, but the fact that the country slipped to 167th out of 177 countries in the 2006 UNDP Human Development Index—having previously ranked 152nd in 1998—would suggest that these agreements had little direct impact on the lives of most Congolese.[12]

Despite the increase in numbers and more robust mandate of UN peacekeeping forces in 2006, and the progress made in repatriating foreign armed forces and disarming and reintegrating militias, interethnic and rebel clashes continued and human rights abuses were ubiquitous. Civilians were targeted not only by armed groups which had not demobilised, but also by members of the new national army and police force. Clearly, the introduction of procedural democracy has yet to address impunity, corruption, and governance issues.

An extremely worrying trend was the high level of sexual violence and rape, described by former UN Under-Secretary-General Jan Egeland as "a cancer… out of control."[13] An average of 40 women were raped daily in and around Uvira in South Kivu between October 2002 and February 2003, as documented by a specialised local NGO. During the conflict, sexual violence was used as a weapon of war and the HIV/AIDS rate is thought to be extremely high. A report by

Watchlist on Children and Armed Conflict also documents high levels of abuse and human rights violations against children in 2006. Some 30,000 boys and girls are estimated to be attached to armed groups as combatants, camp porters, or sex slaves.[14]

These problems will not be solved rapidly and it will take many years to design, finance, and implement sustainable responses, requiring long-term financial and political donor commitment. In the meantime, the civilian population is deprived of their basic rights and many remain dependent on humanitarian aid for their barest survive.

International donor response: From forgotten crisis to GHD flagship

The humanitarian crisis, despite being described as one of the world's worst, is also regularly referred to as "neglected." For several years, the international community paid but scant attention to the DRC. Funding remained low compared to higher profile emergencies, such as the 2004 tsunami and Iraq. Conflict in the Great Lakes region had been going on for so long that the media had lost interest. Reflecting this neglect, the 2000 UN Appeal received only US$11 million (31.8 percent), although the 2005 Appeal had received US$142 million (64.8 percent).[15]

The 2006 UN Humanitarian Action Plan (HAP) requested US$696 million to assist 30 million people. As of 11 September 2007, the donor community had responded by providing US$287 million, representing a low funding level of only 42 percent. Nevertheless, the absolute amount of funds received was two and a half times the entire amount of funding received in 2005. The 2006 HAP represented a radical shift in the humanitarian community's approach to the crisis: for years, large parts of the country remained inaccessible and humanitarian assistance had only scratched the surface. The successful transition process, reinforcement of the MONUC mandate, and improved security allowed humanitarian actors to reach unassisted communities and realise a more comprehensive needs assessment covering all areas of the country. The successful election process, in which donors invested considerable resources and political effort—including EU troops—attracted increased international attention and funding. Arguably, therefore, some donor behaviour was not driven by needs assessments, but by changes in the broader context. Increased funding and attention was also in response to the GHD *Principles*, specifically because the DRC was chosen by donors as a pilot country (along with Burundi) in which to put the GHD *Principles* into practice.

As an instrument consistent with the GHD *Principles*, the Pooled Fund was created as a pilot initiative in 2005, aimed at strengthening the role of the Humanitarian Coordinator, improving coordination, and increasing the extent to which funding was allocated to priority humanitarian needs. Six countries contributed 27 percent of the financing of the HAP through the Pooled Fund, to which three (the UK, the Netherlands, and Sweden) contributed 90 percent of the total budget. Their contributions to the overall financing of the HAP were made almost exclusively through the Pooled Fund (95 percent for Sweden, 89 percent for the Netherlands and 88 percent for the UK).

From among the 21 OECD-DAC members who supported humanitarian aid in-country,[16] three contributors alone (the UK, the EC/ECHO and the USA), financed 49 percent of humanitarian aid in 2006. It should be emphasised that these donors were closely involved in the GHD pilot initiative which promotes needs-based funding and mid- to long-term donor support. Nevertheless, organisations such as Oxfam considered that the United States could have contributed more to the 2006 Appeal and criticised France, Germany, and Japan for their small commitments.[17]

Humanitarian actors have estimated their funding requirements for 2007 at US$687 million. The major differences in comparison to the previous year are that 20 percent more of the funds are directed towards the immediate saving of lives and 70 percent are destined for eastern areas. Budgets are based on regional action plans developed by technical experts in the field to target priority humanitarian zones and the most vulnerable populations.

Despite the engagement of the international community through MONUC and the support for the 2006 elections, many actors believe that the international community could do more to promote peace and human security in the DRC. In fact, MONUC has one of the lowest number of peacekeepers per capita of all UN missions and more could be done in the area of protection. This is one of the reasons why the situation remains fragile and why donors must be make long-term commitments. Yet, in July 2007, the International Crisis Group warned that "without clear signs of improvement before year end, donor support will drift

to other post-conflict theatres, and Congo could lose the peace-building gains made over the past five years."[18]

Implementation of the humanitarian response: GHD reforms

The international humanitarian community has implemented a number of reforms, including the Needs Assessment Framework Matrix (NAFM), the Pooled Fund, the Central Emergency Response Fund (CERF), the GHD initiative, and the cluster approach.

The 2006 Humanitarian Action Plan was the first to bring together the broadest possible cross-section of humanitarian actors (UN, NGOs, and civil society). The 2007 HAP is also the result of a collaborative effort, bringing together Congolese government officials and donors. OCHA also formulated and introduced the Needs Assessment Framework Matrix (NAFM), a standardised multi-sectoral needs assessment questionnaire that could be used by UN agencies and NGOs in countrywide needs assessments. However, the NAFM was only partially operational in 2006, because its format was rejected for being too complex and technical, and no agreement was reached on the measuring units and benchmarks. Implementing agencies felt that it was too constricting, and although donors were supportive of the initiative, no funds were made available.

The Pooled Fund was created as a pilot initiative in 2005, in the context of UN humanitarian reform and the implementation of the GHD *Principles*. Among other goals, the PF aims to support the role of the Humanitarian Coordinator by making available a tool to augment the efficiency of the humanitarian response and thereby better respond to priority needs. The PF became operational from April 2006 and has become the largest single source of funding for humanitarian activities. A PF team was created within OCHA to facilitate the overall management of the funding allocation process. It also provides guidance on identification and project prioritisation in the various regions and ensures the completion of the allocation process. In its role as the administrative agent, UNDP has also put a special team in charge of the financial aspects of the fund and of monitoring the projects implemented by NGOs, as well as by the International Organization for Migration (IOM) in its capacity as a UN participating agency.

At the end of October 2006, approximately US$83 million had been given to a total of 136 projects through the PF mechanism. UN agencies received 63 percent, NGOs 25 percent, with the remaining 12 percent allocated to the Rapid Reaction Mechanism (RRM), thus largely benefiting the three NGOs that are RRM focal points in the field.

Although the Pooled Fund is largely supported and accepted by the humanitarian community, problems have been identified at different levels. In the allocation process, there is a potential conflict of interests, as some UN agencies have benefited greatly from the PF mechanism, both financially and in terms of visibility. In contrast, there have been difficulties of access and participation for some NGOs, with accusations that funds are not always allocated to the most capable actors. Finally, as a result of administrative complications and delays resulting from UNDP internal regulations and guidelines, there were complaints from NGOs about UNDP leadership. Some implementing agencies suggested that a development agency like the UNDP did not function with sufficient flexibility and speed to make it the appropriate body for administering humanitarian programmes.[19]

In addition to the PF, another key mechanism implemented as part of the UN humanitarian reform agenda, and consistent with GHD objectives, was CERF, the Central Emergency Response Fund. The financial contribution to the 2006 HAP reached US$38 million, as part of the funding directed at "underfunded crises." In contrast to the PF, CERF funding is earmarked exclusively for UN agencies, including the IOM. Nevertheless, NGOs benefited from it indirectly, as implementing partners or the RRM in the field. However, the CERF itself has been criticised for its hierarchical decision-making structure, the lack of access to funds by local NGOs and government, and delays in disbursement.[20] As a result, many NGOs call for direct access to CERF funds.

The UN cluster approach to improve coordination and the effective delivery of aid was introduced in January 2006, with the establishment of ten clusters: Protection, Water and Sanitation, Health, Non Food Items and Shelter, Logistics, Nutrition, Food Security, Return and Reintegration, Education, and Emergency Telecommunications. In addition, OCHA was in charge of geographical coordination. However, OCHA focussed on the zones of conflict or post-conflict where there was greatest humanitarian need—particularly in the provinces of North Kivu, South Kivu, Katanga, and Ituri—and then began to focus attention on issues of long-term development.

Most implementing agencies were aware of the GHD *Principles* and pilot project, but the degree of their detailed knowledge and interest varied. Those who were sceptical of the initiative viewed the GHD *Principles* as a vague intellectual concept unrelated to daily priorities. However, NGOs do not have equal capacity and means to understand, absorb, and participate in the GHD initiative, and there is a risk that smaller NGOs, in particular local ones, will be marginalised. So there is a need to improve the information flow on GHD and encourage the participation of smaller, local NGOs.

Nevertheless, these new mechanisms and instruments were largely accepted by humanitarian actors, who recognised their positive impact in the field. Since the implementation of the GHD pilot project, the perception among implementing agencies was that coherency, effectiveness, flexibility, and accountability had improved.[21] However, some difficult questions remain, such as the availability of funds in proportion to identified needs or the comprehensiveness of assessments in a constantly changing situation.

Conclusion

The scale of the tragedy of the crisis in the DRC cannot be underestimated. However, it is also a clear example of some of the key contradictions and challenges that exist in the humanitarian system vis-à-vis the GHD *Principles*. The 1,200 deaths every day in the DRC represent the death toll of the 2004 tsunami every six months. Yet, while the tsunami has received over US$6.2 billion to date, the DRC received only US$445 million in 2006, fourteen times less. Granted this is a crude comparison, but it raises serious questions regarding the application of GHD *Principles* 2, 6, and 11, and in particular the fundamental principles of humanity and impartiality, complicated though they are in practice by issues of humanitarian access and reduced implementation capacity.

Nevertheless, there was dramatic progress in 2006, with improvement in the security situation in most regions and a significant increase in the volume of humanitarian aid. The selection of the DRC as a pilot country for the application of the GHD *Principles* contributed to this improved scenario. Moreover, the introduction of new instruments based on the GHD *Principles* deserves praise, although in practice, some have yielded mixed results. This illustrates the complexity of operationalising the GHD *Principles* in a difficult and fluid environment and in light of overwhelming humanitarian needs. Efforts must be matched by donor funds and a stronger partnership should be created with implementing agencies regarding the GHD pilot scheme.

Finally, despite these improvements and the much lauded elections, continuing violence in the east throughout 2006 and into 2007, as well as staggering and persistent levels of humanitarian needs, indicate that a long-term solution to the crisis is still far off.

References

Brennan, Richard and Anna Husarska. 2006. "Inside Congo, An Unspeakable Toll." *Washington Post.* 16 July. Available at: http://www.theirc.org/news/latest/inside-congo-an-unspeakable.html

Faubert, Carrol. 2006. "Case study Democratic Republic of the Congo." Evaluation of UNDP assistance in conflict affected countries. New York: UNDP

International Crisis Group. 2007. "Conflict in Congo: Consolidating the Peace." Africa Report N°128. 5 July. Available at: http://www.crisis-group.org/home/index.cfm?id=4933&l=1

International Rescue Committee. 2003. "Conflict in Congo deadliest since World War II." 8 April. Available at: http://www.theirc.org/news/con-flict_in_congo_deadliest_since_world_war_ii_says_the_irc.html

Médecins Sans Frontières. 2005. "Access to healthcare, mortality and vio-lence in Democratic Republic of the Congo. Results of five epidemi-ological surveys: Kilwa, Inongo, Basankusu, Lubutu, Bunkeya March to May 2005." Brussels. October.

Office for the Coordination of Humanitarian Affairs (OCHA). 2006. Briefing to the Security Council by Under Secretary-General for Humanitarian Affairs and Emergency Relief Coordinator Jan Egeland. 15 September.

Oxfam. 2006. "Meeting real needs: a major challenge for donors to the Democratic Republic of the Congo." http://www.oxfam.org/en/policy/briefingnotes/bn_DRC_donor_conference_060213

———. 2007. "The UN Central Emergency Response Fund one Year on." March. http://www.oxfam.org/en/policy/briefingpapers/bp100_CERF_oneyear_0703

Transparency International. 2006. *Corruption Perception Index.* Berlin.

Tsunami Evaluation Coalition. 2006. *Synthesis Report.* London

UNICEF. 2006. "Democratic Republic of Congo: Martin Bell Reports on Children Caught in War. CHILD ALERT. Available at: http://www.unicef.org/childalert/drc/martinbell.php

United Nations Development Programme. 2006. *Human Development Report 2006. Beyond scarcity: Power, poverty and the global water crisis.* New York.

Watchlist on Children and Armed Conflict. 2006. "Struggling to Survive: Children and Armed Conflict in the Democratic Republic of Congo." Available at: http://www.watchlist.org/reports/pdf/dr_congo.report.20060426.pdf

World Bank. http://devdata.worldbank.org/external/CPProfile.asp?PTYPE=CP&CCODE=ZAR

Notes

1   The opinions expressed here are those of the author and do not necessarily reflect those of DARA.

2   Brennan, 2006; Tsunami Evaluation Coalition, 2006.

3   International Rescue Committee, 2003.

4   Ibid.

5   OCHA, 2006.

6   UNICEF, 2006.

7   Oxfam, 2006.

8   Ibid.

9   Cited in Faubert, 2006.

10 Faubert, 2006.

11 Médecins Sans Frontières, 2005.

12 UNDP, 2006

13 OCHA, 2006.

14 Watchlist on Children and Armed Conflict, 2006.

15 OCHA, Financial Tracking Service, August 2007.

16 Australia, Belgium, Canada, Denmark, European Commission, Finland, France, Germany, Greece, Ireland, Italy, Japan, Luxembourg, the Netherlands, New Zealand, Norway, Spain, Sweden, Switzerland, United Kingdom, and United States

17 Oxfam, 2006.

18 International Crisis Group, 2007.

19 DARA field interviews, May 2007.

20 Oxfam, 2007.

21 DARA field interviews, May 2007.

Haiti

AT A GLANCE

Country data *(2005 figures, unless otherwise noted)*

- 2006 Human Development Index: 0.482, ranked 154 of 177 countries
- Population (2006): 8.6 million
- GNI per capita Atlas method (2006, current US$): 480
- Life expectancy: 53
- Under-five infant mortality rate: 120 per 1,000
- Population undernourished (2001–03): 47 percent
- Population with sustainable access to improved water source: 54 percent
- Primary education completion rate: NA
- Gender-related development index (2006): NA
- Official development assistance (ODA): US$515 million
- 2006 Corruption Perception Index: 1.8, ranked 163 out of 163 countries

Sources: World Bank; United Nations Development Programme, 2006; Transparency International, 2006

The crisis

- 37 percent of the population, or 3 million people, were affected by the crisis;
- Violence and deteriorating security resulted in civilian deaths, looting, disruption of medical services and water and electricity supplies, as well as food and fuel shortages;
- Civilians, often the poorest in the country, were caught in the middle of inter- and intra-gang violence, and gang clashes with the police and the UN peacekeepers; trapped communities were systematically denied access to education, health care, justice, and humanitarian assistance;
- NGOs report a high incidence of kidnappings and rape, and children face recruitment into armed groups, abduction, sexual violence, and maiming;
- 7,200 UN troops have struggled to break the cycle of violence - there is no peace agreement to enforce and the violence does not follow the typical contours or dynamics of an internal conflict.

Source: Office for the Coordination of Humanitarian Affairs (OCHA), 2004.

The humanitarian response

- The 2003 UN Appeal requested US$83 million but received only 45 percent ;
- The 2004 UN Flash Appeal achieved only 46 percent coverage, or US$16 of the US$36 million requested. The largest donors were: UK (US$2.5 million), EC (US$2.1 million), Canada (US$1.7 million), USA (US$1.5 million), and France (US$1.5 million);
- In 2006, Haiti received a total of US$25 million in humanitarian aid. The largest donors were the EC (US$10 million), USA (US$6.4 million), UK (US$3.9 million), Canada (US$2.5 million), and France (US$2.5 million);
- Donors pledged US$750 million for development programmes and government support following a request for US$600 million at a donor conference in 2006;
- The 2007 UN Transitional Appeal requested US$98 million.

Source: OCHA, Financial Tracking Service.

Haiti

Violence, Gangs, and a Fragile State on the Brink of Crisis

RICARDO SOLÉ, Independent Consultant, Development and Humanitarian Aid

Introduction*

The 2006 crisis in Haiti was not a typical internal conflict, characterised by high intensity, and clearly delineated groups or opposing parties with established territorial control and political agendas, or following obvious cleavages within society. Instead, "the situation in Haiti is not a post-conflict situation but rather a protracted and violent 20-year long transition following the end of the predatory dictatorship of the Duvaliers."[1]

In essence, the humanitarian crisis stems from the political violence and instability that accompanied struggles over state power, coupled with structural vulnerabilities, including widespread poverty, the failure of the state to provide basic public goods, and exposure to natural hazards. This combination pushed segments of the population into circumstances of humanitarian crisis. Following years of neglect by the international community, the deployment in 2004 of the United Nations Mission for the Stabilization of Haiti force (MINUS-TAH) marked a turning point for Haiti. Nevertheless, the humanitarian response in 2006 was still underfunded, poorly directed, and not sufficiently linked to addressing the country's long-term problems, leaving a large segment of the population vulnerable to humanitarian disaster.

* The opinions expressed here are those of the author and do not necessarily reflect those of DARA.

Causes and dynamics of the crisis:
An incomplete and turbulent transition

The long-term roots of the humanitarian, political, social and economic crisis that Haitians face today lie in the country's transition to independence and the corrupt and repressive dictatorships of Francois Duvalier (1957–1971) and his son Jean-Claude Duvalier (1971–1986). The dictatorships of both father and son concentrated power in the hands of the elite, maintained by private armed militias and gross human rights abuses. State institutions and even foreign aid became means to increase and preserve the wealth and power of the dictatorships' elite, while the majority of the population lived in chronic poverty.

The ousting of Jean-Claude Duvalier, followed by the country's first democratic elections in 1991, failed to bring either political stability or security for the population. In fact, the system of corruption, personalisation of power, and the use of political violence perpetrated by the police and private armed groups continued unabated. The international community, with little geo-strategic or commercial interest in the small Caribbean country, has undertaken at least six short-lived—largely ineffective—military interventions. In short, "the crisis is as much the result of a prevailing culture of violence, widespread corruption and the criminalisation of armed groups as it is of neglect by the international community."[2]

In 2004, escalating violence came to a head, with armed gangs and former police and soldiers taking the town of Gonaïves. As a result, then President Jean-Bertrand Aristide left the country, a UN-sanctioned Multinational Interim Force was deployed (succeeded on 1 June 2004 by MINUSTAH), and a transitional government was installed. However, the complex and non-traditional nature of the conflict in Haiti, including the absence of a peace agreement, meant that, at least at first, progress was slow.

Throughout 2004 and 2005, armed groups, former soldiers and police, political militias and, increasingly, criminal gangs, continued to act with impunity. Criminal gangs became not only a means of income for their members, but, paradoxically, a source of protection for local communities. This climate of lawlessness and impunity, coupled with the widespread availability of small arms and increasing influence of the drug trade, saw an increase in human rights abuses in 2005, including mob violence, arbitrary arrests, extrajudicial killings, kidnappings, and torture.

However, in 2006, the increased and more robust deployment of MINUSTAH resulted in a partial improvement in the security situation and long-awaited elections. Nevertheless, urban gang violence flourished, "rooted in a mix of politics and economics… thanks to the continued absence of state authority and the lack of socio-economic development."[3] Areas of Port-au-Prince became no-go zones for the security forces and MINUSTAH. Civilians living in these areas, often the poorest in the country, were caught in the middle of inter- and intra-gang violence, as well as gang clashes with the police and MINUSTAH. These trapped communities were systematically denied access to education, healthcare, justice, and humanitarian assistance. A high incidence of kidnappings and rapes are reported by NGOs, and children, according to a UN report, face "grave violations including systematic recruitment into armed groups, death, and maiming either through direct involvement in violence or in the crossfire, abduction and kidnapping, and sexual violence."[4]

Humanitarian impact of the crisis:
Insecurity, poverty, and environmental vulnerability

Significantly, when defining the priority concerns for those affected, the UN cited insecurity and lack of humanitarian access as the major determinants of the humanitarian consequences of the conflict,[5] and estimated that approximately 37 percent of the population (or 3 million people) were affected by the crisis. According to the 2004 UN Flash Appeal, the displacement of the population was not properly evaluated but was believed to be significant, both into and out of urban areas, depending on the security situation. Similarly, the level of disruption of basic services was not uniform, but contingent on the security situation in different areas at different times. Deteriorating security conditions resulted in looting, disruption of medical services, water and electricity supplies, and food and fuel shortages. This exposed an already vulnerable population to a range of humanitarian threats.

The 2004 security crisis exacerbated existing structural problems, in particular poverty and vulnerability to natural hazards. Haiti's political turmoil and violence, and the deterioration of state institutions have had devastating consequences for the civilian population. The Haitian Institute of Statistics and Information Technology estimated that in 2001, 56 percent of the population was living on less than a dollar a day and 76 percent on less than US$2. The World Bank estimated that GNI per capita in 2005 was US$450. By 2005, Haiti was ranked 153rd out of 177 countries by the UNDP Human Development Index, the lowest ranking country in the Western hemisphere. Public services, such as health, sanitation and education, are extremely weak. UNICEF estimated the 2005 under-five infant mortality rate at 120 per 1,000, as compared to 43 in Guatemala, the next Western hemisphere country in the Human Development Index. Furthermore, the combination of poverty and violence has resulted in waves of refugees fleeing the country and large numbers of internal displacements. For example, following the 1991 coup in which 1,500 died, 40,000 fled the country and 20,000 to 30,000 fled the capital.

Nevertheless, there were some improvements in macroeconomic indicators in 2006, with the annual economic growth rate increasing from 1.8 percent in 2004–2005 to a predicted rate of 2.7 percent in 2005–2006, compared to a low of -3.4 percent in 2004. However, it is difficult to gauge how these gains actually improved the lives of ordinary Haitians, as Haiti in 2006 was considered the most corrupt country in the world.[6]

It must be said, however, that, in many instances, the relief strategies applied did not mitigate these structural issues. Poverty is a structural problem, exacerbated, no doubt, by the political crisis. But the eradication of poverty is beyond the scope of any humanitarian response. In addition, in order to avert the humanitarian consequences of the lack of public services, donors and agencies were often prompted into substituting state capacity and obligations. This undermined accountability and the establishment of long-term institutional capacity.

As mentioned earlier, Haiti is also vulnerable to natural hazards, including hurricanes, floods, earthquakes, and landslides, the frequency and force of which are believed to be increasing due to climate change. In 2004, for example, major floods left 4,000 dead and 330,000 homes destroyed or damaged. In November 2006 floods affected areas of the country and prompted a reaction by humanitarian agencies, with ECHO mobilising US$1.9 million.[7] The population's vulnerability is exacerbated by poverty, high population density, poor infrastructure, unplanned urbanisation, deforestation and the over use of agricultural land. Given its overall condition, it is not surprising that the state itself lacks defences or capacity to prevent, mitigate, and respond to disasters.

The international donor response: Weak instruments for assisting a fragile state

According to the OCHA Financial Tracking Service (FTS), since the crisis in 2004, 17 of the 23 DAC donors[8] have provided humanitarian aid, progressively turning it towards development and institutional support.[9] The FTS for 2006 records a total of US$25 million in humanitarian aid, but since many donors follow their own strategy, it is difficult to ascertain the global picture. The largest donors were: Canada (US$15,473,299 or 59.8 percent), France (US$1,778,108 or 6.9 percent), Switzerland (US$1,618,588 or 6.3 percent), private individuals and organisations (US$1,550,021 or 6 percent) and Sweden (US$1,317,868 or 5.1 percent). In addition, the UN Central Emergency Response Fund (CERF) provided US$1 million (3.9 percent). However, humanitarian needs, as illustrated by the levels of funding received by the UN Appeals, are under-funded, while local government institutions are not ready to implement a long-term development strategy.

Already in 2003, the UN launched an Appeal, the Integrated Emergency Response Program (IERP), to address urgent humanitarian needs, and warned of the likelihood of deterioration. The IERP requested US$83 million which was only 45 percent funded. The situation deteriorated into a full blown crisis in 2004. A UN Flash Appeal was launched, but achieved only 46 percent coverage, US$16 million out of the US$35 million requested. The largest contributing donors to the Flash Appeal were: the UK (US$2.5 million or 13.6 percent), EC/ECHO (US$2.1 million or 13.1 percent), Canada (US$1.7 million or 10.3 percent), U.S. (US$1.5 million or 9.4 percent) and France (US$1.5 million or 9 percent).[10] This limited success was attributed to the poor quality and lack of consistency of the Appeal, and the UN's limited local operational capacity.[11] However, donors actually disbursed up to US$36 million in humanitarian aid, using alternative mechanisms.[12] Donors therefore directed some of the funds either bilaterally to the government or to their NGO partners on the ground. For instance, including both bilateral and Flash Appeal contributions, the US and EC/ECHO were, in fact, the largest donors in 2004.

Additionally, a donor conference—covering humanitarian but principally development and reconstruction aid—took place in 2004, garnering US$1,100 million in pledges, surpassing the initial objective of US$960 million. Needs were identified through the Interim Cooperation Framework (ICF), in which the

UN, donors, private sector, and civil society participated. However, some implementing agencies were critical of the weak civil society participation in the ICF, the too overt political agenda in support of the transitional government, and the high proportion of pledged loans, which added to the already critical debt situation of the country.[13] Moreover, many donors are believed to have contributed to independent humanitarian response activities, deducting these disbursements from their pledged funds. It is likely that the conference received greater donor support than the UN Appeal because of the broader range of activities covered, the deficiencies of the UN Appeal already mentioned, and donor interest in supporting the Haitian government and NGO partners according to their own agendas, especially following the establishment of MINUSTAH.

Another donor conference in 2006 again raised funds over the expected target; donors pledged US$750 million following a request for US$600 million, again principally for development programmes and government support. However, at a post-conference meeting in Madrid, the Prime Minister of Haiti complained publicly of the limited disbursement achieved.[14] Donor policies of disbursing funds through specific partners, often bypassing government structures, seem to have contributed to this perception.

Lastly, the UN launched in December 2006 a Transitional Appeal aimed at covering the period, from early 2007 until mid-2008, until the new government's recovery and development strategy could be put in place. The Appeal, for US$98 million, aims to support the newly elected government during the initial period of its mandate until its poverty reduction and development strategies gain momentum. So far, no data for the Appeal's rate of funding is available.

In addition to the humanitarian imperative, there have been other motivations for engagement in Haiti. As recipients of significant migration and out of concern for the added economic risk of instability in Haiti, the United States and Canada have particular sensitivity to Haiti. The U.S. justifies its involvement by its alarm at the prospect of a failed state in what has traditionally been regarded as its backyard, the possibility of political association with other hostile states, and the window of opportunity Haiti may provide for criminal organisations and drug trafficking.

Meanwhile, the EU profile seems to coincide with the general EU model: major humanitarian contributions, democratisation, and institutional support for good governance. Other donors, such as the Netherlands,

Denmark, Sweden, and Norway follow their usual profile of commitment to relief needs, the promotion of human rights, and an emphasis on linking humanitarian assistance to development and sustainability. The pragmatic approach of Norway in explicitly allowing its funds to be used by MINUSTAH in order to provide humanitarian assistance in insecure areas should be noted.

Despite poor funding for UN Appeals, the establishment in June 2004 of the long-term, robust, and well-resourced MINUSTAH mission marked a sea change in the international community's attitude towards the crisis in Haiti. Six previous UN-sanctioned interventions had been fleeting and ineffective. The original aim of MINUSTAH was to avert a full-blown crisis and to support a credible election process. However, this particular UN mission neglected (at least initially) to encourage a genuine internal process of consolidation and reform. Therefore, despite its 7,200 troops, MINUSTAH struggled to break the system of violence. Because the mission was originally conceived of in terms of traditional peacekeeping, but lacked a peace agreement to enforce, it was unable to cope with or reduce much of Haitian violence—which is not characteristic of the typical form or dynamics of an internal conflict. Traditional mechanisms, such as the Disarmament, Demobilisation and Reintegration (DDR) process have had limited success.[15]

Although it receives broad support from the international community, especially regional neighbours, MINUSTAH itself has become part of the problem.[16] Sporadic cases of mismanagement and the perception of political bias towards the government undermines its credibility and effectiveness. The increasing sense of mistrust among the population towards the UN, fuelled by a sense of occupation and lack of visible progress, is a source of genuine concern. However, MINUSTAH is involved in humanitarian activities. Recently, a guidance note was issued to clarify the roles and responsibilities of the military in support of relief activities, generally reflecting the provisions of the GHD *Principles*.

Implementation of the humanitarian response: Replacing the state?

As explained above, insecurity triggered the humanitarian crisis by interrupting the provision of basic services and supplies, and impairing humanitarian access to the most vulnerable population. The international community concluded, therefore, that the most appropriate way to address humanitarian needs was to improve security, first by means of a UN force, and second, by reinforcing the functions of the state. However, despite this long-term strategy for stabilisation, the progress towards improving the state's capacity to impose law and order has been slow and the legitimacy of the government is still weak. In the meantime, humanitarian needs have been acute since 2004, their identification weak, and the funding to address them insufficient.

The activities of relief organisations in Haiti cover the broad range of humanitarian intervention, including protection, human rights, relief, assistance in food supply, food security, health and education services, water and sanitation, and disaster preparedness. However, implementation by relief agencies has been disrupted by security concerns in some areas, preventing access. In addition, during 2006, donors responded to flood damage in some areas, exacerbating the humanitarian situation and requiring donors to increase the scope of their interventions.

The absence of a fully functioning government has constrained the response and reconstruction efforts. Most implementing agencies are committed to development strategies, although in many cases this role and activities related to it are substitutes for the responsibilities of the state. This particularly affects capacity-building initiatives, such as public health policy and disaster preparedness mechanisms. However, the election of a new government and the success of the donor conferences seem to have enhanced the possibilities for long-term strategies. Indeed, the UN 2007 Transitional Appeal explicitly focuses on strengthening local capacity and intends to bridge the period until the elected government can implement adequate measures. The general feeling is that the current situation offers a real opportunity to articulate development and reconstruction strategies that would help to mitigate the humanitarian consequences of any socio-political crisis or natural disaster.[17]

After the 2004 crisis, the Interim Cooperation Framework was intended to be a consolidated emergency plan to improve the economic situation and address the population's basic needs during the transition period, to deliver assistance as quickly as possible and to create favourable conditions for an election. The expectation was that a legitimate new government would emerge, which would serve as a recipient through which to channel aid.

However, it would appear that most needs assessments were carried out by individual agencies, with little sharing of findings or follow up. Donors generally required such ex-ante evaluations but did not contribute to the assessment effort by integrating all capacities in order to better address needs and coordinate the response.

Moreover, the UN through the IERP and Flash Appeals established its own evaluation of needs and response strategy, although for many the adequacy and quality was debatable.[18] The fact is, as mentioned earlier, donors were more ready to contribute outside the Appeal processes.

The role of the UN in Haiti is complex, and includes the provision of security, technical assistance, and coordination. Formally, the head of the UNDP acts as the UN Resident Representative and assumes the mandate of coordinating the humanitarian response. Among the UN agencies, the role of UNDP seems consolidated and accepted and coordination with MINUSTAH is reasonable.

Nevertheless, the coordination of the overall humanitarian response is considered quite poor. Even OCHA has a very weak presence and has not been properly funded. Thus, its traditional role has been lost in the complexities of the UN stabilisation force and the remaining UN agencies. However, there have been attempts to remedy this and, as a result, requests for funding for humanitarian coordination were included in the 2007 UN Transitional Appeal.

The cluster approach was not implemented in Haiti, and no real sectoral coordination was put in place, except the one chaired by government departments with technical support from the relevant UN agency. This has resulted in a very weak framework for coordination, other than for bilateral aid. In humanitarian terms, and for most donors and NGOs, this type of coordination has little impact.

Conclusion

Despite only partial funding of UN Appeals, the international response has been able to avert a more serious humanitarian disaster in Haiti. By the end of 2006, a relatively safe environment to strengthen state institutions and democratic governance had been created.

The stabilisation and legitimisation of the new government by all stakeholders and internal factions would increase the effective use of international aid in development and poverty alleviation programmes which would ultimately render humanitarian aid redundant. However, as yet, the situation is far from stable. Poverty reduction will require time, determination, and generous investments, and the issue of disaster preparedness is still poorly addressed in a highly vulnerable country.

Haiti offers us an excellent case study of the complexity of donor practices and processes, from pledges that surpass expectations to frustration at the limited commitments achieved and the lack of clear disbursement strategies, from weak financial tracking to the lack of transparent information, fragmented coordination, and the predominance of individual donors' strategies for implementation.

References

BBC. 2006. "Haiti donors in efficiency pledge." 30 November. Available at: http://news.bbc.co.uk/2/hi/americas/6197244.stm

Faubert, Carrol. 2006. "Evaluation of UNDP Assistance to Conflict-Affected Countries." New York: UNDP Evaluation Office. Available at: http://www.undp.org/eo/documents/thematic/conflict/ConflictEvaluation2006.pdf

Gauthier, Amélie. 2006. "Security in Haiti and the Madrid Donor Conference." Madrid: FRIDE.

Mobekk, Eirin. 2006. MINUSTAH: DDR and Police, Judicial and Correctional Reform in Haiti: Recommendations for Change. London: ActionAid International.

Office for the Coordination of Humanitarian Affairs. 2004. Consolidated Appeals Process (CAP): Flash Appeal 2004 for Haiti. Available at: http://www.reliefweb.int/rw/rwb.nsf/AllDocsByUNID/dede6ff35eb7cba0c1256e520053b393

———. Financial Tracking Service. Available at: http://www.reliefweb.int/FTS/

Oxfam. 2004. "World Bank, IMF and US Must Lead the Way in Haiti." Press release. 16 July. Available at: http://www.oxfamamerica.org/newsandpublications/press_releases/archive2004/press_release.2004-09-15.8077197440

Transparency International. 2006. Corruption Perception Index. Berlin.

United Nations Special Representative of the Secretary-General for Children and Armed Conflict. 2006. Report to the Security Council. 17 August 2006. New York. Available at: http://domino.un.org/UNISPAL.NSF/f45643a78fcba719852560f6005987ad/8f69b86004faedb9852571e90050497b!OpenDocument

United Nations Development Programme. 2006. Human Development Report 2006. Beyond scarcity: Power, poverty and the global water crisis. New York.

World Bank. Haiti Data Profile. Available at: http://devdata.worldbank.org/external/CPProfile.asp?PTYPE=CP&CCODE=HTI

Notes

1 Faubert, 2006.

2 Faubert, 2006, p. 69.

3 Mobekk, 2006, p. 6.

4 Report of the United Nations Special Representative of the Secretary-General for Children and Armed Conflict, 2006.

5 Office for the Coordination of Humanitarian Affairs, 2004.

6 Transparency International, 2006.

7 Floods triggered another international response in March 2007.

8 The 17 members were: the EC, the United States, the UK, Canada, France, Germany, Ireland, Switzerland, Norway, Sweden, Italy, Japan, Belgium, Netherlands, Spain, Finland, and New Zealand.

9 The DARA team learned that, although it was not registered by the FTS, humanitarian funding had also been provided by Luxembourg.

10 OCHA, Financial Tracking Service, as of 18 September 2007.

11 DARA field interviews, May–June 2007.

12 OCHA, Financial Tracking Service.

13 Oxfam, 2004.

14 BBC, 2006.

15 In 2006, only 110 participants either completed or were completing the DDR process and very few weapons, most of which were old, had been collected; estimates indicate that gangs are in possession of 6,000–13,000 weapons and that 210,000 are estimated to be in circulation in the country; see Gauthier, 2006.

16 DARA field interviews, May–June 2007.

17 DARA field interviews, May–June 2007.

18 DARA field interviews, May–June 2007.

Lebanon

AT A GLANCE

Country data *(2005 figures, unless otherwise noted)*

- 2006 Human Development Index: 0.774, ranked 78 of 177 countries
- Population (2006): 4.1 million
- GNI per capita Atlas method (2006, current US$): 5,490
- Under-five infant mortality rate: 30 per 1,000
- Population undernourished (2001–03): 3 percent
- Population with sustainable access to improved water source (2004): 100 percent
- Official development assistance (ODA): 243 million
- 2006 Corruption Perception Index: 3.6, ranked 63 of 163 countries

Sources: World Bank; United Nations Development Programme, 2006; Transparency International, 2006.

The crisis

Lebanon

- Approximately 1,200 Lebanese militants and civilians killed and 4,400 injured;
- One million people displaced; 40,000 to Cyprus, 150,000 to Syria;
- 100,000 trapped in south with declining food, water, medicine, fuel reserves;
- 107,000 homes damaged or destroyed; infrastructure damage estimated at US$3.5 billion; economic losses of US$12 billion; unemployment rose from 8-10 to 25 percent;
- 85 percent of farmers lost crops valued at approx. US$150 million; unexploded ordinance from cluster bombs killed 27 civilians since end of hostilities.

Israel

- 19 soldiers and 43 civilians killed; 894 civilians injured; 400,000 in the north displaced;
- War cost US$5.3 billion; incurred US$1.6 billion loss to economy; businesses lost US$1.4 billion;
- 12,000 buildings (incl. schools and hospitals), 6,000 homes were damaged.

Sources: International Crisis Group, 2006; Internal Displacement Monitoring Centre, 2006; UNHCR, 2006; OCHA, 2006; Lebanon Higher Relief Council; National Demining Office; Government of Lebanon; Oxfam, 2006; World Bank.

The humanitarian response

- Total humanitarian aid exceeded US$514 million (incl. projects listed/not listed in Flash Appeal); principal donors: U.S. (US$109 million / 21.1 percent); Saudi Arabia (US$63 million / 12.3 percent); EC/ECHO (US$58 million / 11.3 percent); Italy (US$33 / 6.4 percent); United Arab Emirates (US$25 million / 4.9 percent); OECD-DAC members (US$357 million / 69.4 percent of total funds);
- Gulf countries also contributed significantly with over $125 million (25 percent);
- The initial UN Flash Appeal request for $155 million was revised to $96.5 million; the total response was $119 million (total funding only to projects listed in Flash Appeal), a coverage of 123.3 percent);
- The principal donors for Flash Appeal were EC/ECHO (US$25 million or 21.1 percent), the U.S. (US$18 million or 15.0 percent), Norway (US$7 million or 5.8 percent), Canada (US$5 million or 4.5 percent), France (US$5 or 4.3 percent), and Sweden (US$5 million or 4.3 percent); members of the OECD-DAC contributed over US$98 million or 82.8 percent of total funds;
- The UN Central Emergency Response Fund (CERF) supplied $5 million for initial humanitarian operations.

Source: OCHA, Financial Tracking Service.

Lebanon
Crisis of Civilian Protection

Introduction

Both Lebanon and Israel suffered humanitarian repercussions from the 2006 July War in Lebanon between the Israel Defense Forces (IDF) and the Lebanese Party of God (Hezbollah). The ensuing humanitarian crisis was considered primarily one of "protection," with a brief emergency phase, and significant internal displacement of civilians and infrastructure destruction.

This "Second Lebanon War," lasted 34 days. A cease-fire between Hezbollah and IDF went into effect on 14 August. In early September, a strengthened UN Interim Force in Lebanon (UNIFIL II) was deployed to ensure the cessation of hostilities.

Due to the disparate levels of destruction caused by the massive military response from Israel, international institutions, national NGOs, and foreign states attempted to relieve the devastation of Lebanon. Initially characterised by its rapidity and the emphasis placed on protection issues, international humanitarian aid also emerged as increasingly politicised, irrevocably affecting the neutrality and independence of implementing agents.

Dynamics of the conflict:
Hezbollah vs. Israel and regional power politics

The 2006 Lebanon War has its roots in the broader Arab-Israeli conflict. Originating out of the first Israeli invasion of Lebanon in 1978—to combat the Palestine Liberation Organization's (PLO) use of Lebanon as a base to attack Israel—and the Islamic Revolution in Iran in 1979, Hezbollah declared its founding principles in a 1985 "Open Letter," giving as its primary *raison d'être* armed resistance against Israeli occupation. When the Lebanese Civil War (1975–1991) officially ended with the US-endorsed and Saudi-sponsored 1989 Taef Accords, Hezbollah did not disband its militia as demanded. Nor did it disarm, as stipulated in UN Security Council Resolutions 1559 and 1701. The eruption of hostilities was the result of competing international interests, regional alliances, and continued confrontations with Israel over the Shebaa Farms territory and the issue of political prisoner swaps. In the aftermath of the 2006 Lebanon War, Hezbollah has sought political leverage within the country's sectarian mix. Humanitarian aid has been used by forces both in favour and against Hezbollah to advance political ends.[1]

Since the Taef Accords, the Lebanese political system has been increasingly characterised by sectarian confessionalism, entailing a delicate balance among various religious communities in government, parliament, and the civil administration: the Prime Minister is Sunni, the Speaker of Parliament is Shia, and the President is Christian. Lebanon lacks a strong central authority, a fact which has helped to feed the power of militias, such as Hezbollah, and the development of complex sociopolitical identities and loyalties. In addition, the involvement of Syria, Israel, and the PLO, particularly during the 1970s and 1980s, are examples of complex regional and international politics. Representative of a large section of the Shia population, Hezbollah is classified as a terrorist organisation by numerous governments, including the United States and the United Kingdom—but not the EU—and maintains close connections to both Syria and Iran. Hezbollah is both a political and paramilitary organisation and has been a major force in Lebanon, having gained democratic representation in the Parliament since 1992.

The immediate political backdrop of the 2006 Lebanon War was the assassination of former Lebanese Prime Minister Rafik Hariri in February 2005, the installation of a new, Western-backed, anti-Syrian government led by Fouad Siniora following the popular protests of the Cedar Revolution, and the withdrawal of Syrian troops in the spring of 2005. This led to increasing tension between the US/Israel vision of the Greater Middle East and the Iran/Syria/Hezbollah "Shia axis." However, the trigger for the conflict was the 12 July killing on Israeli territory of three Israeli soldiers and the abduction of two others by Hezbollah.

Considered a *casus belli* by Israel, the IDF launched intensive aerial bombing of Lebanon, targeting civilian infrastructure such as the airport, roads, bridges, and energy plants. An Israeli naval blockade was established along the Lebanese coast, and repeated IDF ground invasions were attempted. In response, Hezbollah fired more than 4,000 rockets at northern Israeli towns. Both sides systematically failed to distinguish between civilian and military targets.

The hostilities came to an end on 14 August with the implementation of a UN-sponsored ceasefire called for by Security Council Resolution 1701, which does not address the causes of the conflict, including political divisions within Lebanon, the reform of state institutions, or perhaps most importantly the relevance of resolving the broader regional conflict. Though incurring substantial economic damage to Israel, the war devastated the Lebanese economy, weakened its government, and further polarised politics.

Impact of the crisis:
Civilian displacement and economic destruction

The consequences of the 34-day conflict for Lebanon were devastating. This was not a typical humanitarian crisis, but principally one of protection. Due to their proximity to military targets, Lebanese civilians were injured or died. Collateral damage also included displacement and the loss of their livelihoods.

During the conflict, some 8,600 were reported injured in Lebanon and Israel combined. In Lebanon, some 1,200 people, mostly civilians were killed, and an estimated 4,400 were injured; in Israel, 158 people, including 43 civilians, were killed, with 1,500 injured. Lebanon suffered massive infrastructure damage. At its peak, the conflict displaced up to 1.5 million people, many finding shelter in schools or with host families.[2] More than 40,000 Lebanese fled to Cyprus, 150,000 to Syria, and some 60,000 foreigners were evacuated.

Israeli bombing of key infrastructure had an immediate and long-term impact on the Lebanese population and economy. The World Bank estimates that 107,000 homes were either damaged or destroyed and infrastructure damage was estimated at US$3.5 billion. Total economic losses for Lebanon—a country already heavily indebted and ranked 78th in the UNDP Human Development Index in 2006—were estimated at US$12 billion. Losses to the Israeli economy are estimated to be close to US$7 billion. South Lebanon suffered most, and since the hostilities coincided with the harvest, around 85 percent of farmers lost crops, valued at approximately US$150 million.[3] Moreover, due to the level of destruction of infrastructure, including roads and bridges, international and Lebanese humanitarian agencies could not access the affected civilian population, many of whom lacked food, water, medicine, or fuel for transportation.

The Israeli use of cluster bombs has also had a lasting impact on South Lebanon. The UN estimated that these cluster bombs, used intensively along the Litani River, have contaminated wide areas, making the return of the displaced to villages and fields a deadly risk. According to the National Demining Office, by June 2007, 27 civilians had been killed following cessation of hostilities.

International donor response:
Strong humanitarian response, weak pressure for peace

International donors rapidly mobilised support for UN agencies and NGOs to alleviate suffering. However, the international community lacked decisiveness and unity in calling for the protection of civilians and safe humanitarian access. Therefore, for many humanitarian actors, the Lebanon crisis underlines the need to define the parameters of a protection crisis more precisely, as well as the responsibilities and actions to be taken by all relevant actors, including donors, the UN, NGOs, and civil society.

The Lebanon situation created malaise and frustration among humanitarian actors. The perception of agencies in the field was that the international community was late and weak in its public condemnation of the violations of human rights and international humanitarian law and in calling for an immediate ceasefire and the protection of humanitarian space.[4] International media coverage was very critical of the damage to infrastructure, the exodus of civilians, and the divisions in the international community. Media coverage appears to have been somewhat unbalanced, with claims made of human rights violations which were, in fact, not committed, journalists doctoring photographs, and often exaggerating and misinterpreting civilian damage and involvement.

When the war started, it was the expectation of many that the UN would intervene quickly. When it was unable to stop the hostilities, seriously tarnishing its image, neutrality, and legitimacy in the Middle East, donors stepped in, with remarkable speed and generosity. The international community contributed over US$514

million in relief assistance. This was, in part, in response to 24 July UN Flash Appeal, which requested US$155 million—revised downward to US$96.5 million following the cessation of hostilities—and the change in the humanitarian situation. The Appeal received US$119 million, representing 123.3 percent of funds requested. The UN Central Emergency Response Fund (CERF) supplied an additional US$5 million for food, medicine, logistics, and security for initial humanitarian operations. The extremely high level of funding was due to a combination of factors, including the political subtext of the response, the high degree of media coverage of the crisis, and the contributions of Arab State donors. The situation was made more complex by the fact that the Lebanese authorities did not usually have a say as to where funds were directed, which left decisions about the destination of funds in the hands of political actors. Officially, Hezbollah claims to have used the money (some US$380 million given by Iran) for reconstruction and financial compensation to the families of victims of Israeli attacks.[5]

The United States was the principal donor of humanitarian aid, with over US$109 million (21.1 percent). The next largest donors were Saudi Arabia (over US$63 million or 12.3 percent), the EC/ECHO (over US$58 million or 11.3 percent), Italy (US$33 or 6.4 percent), and United Arab Emirates (US$25 million or 4.9 percent). Members of the OECD-DAC contributed over US$357 million or 69.4 percent of the total funds. Gulf countries, referred to as "new" or "emerging" donors, contributed significantly to the crisis with over US$125 million (25 percent).

Implementing agencies in the field praised the timeliness and flexibility of donors (Principles 5 and 12 of the GHD—in particular EC/ECHO, DFID, and USAID/OFDA—for proposal design, reallocation and provision of funds.[6] As soon as needs assessments had been made, EC/ECHO announced two financial contributions, in two tranches of €10 million, on 24 and 26 July, respectively. Contracts were typically issued quickly and NGOs attributed the few delays to the significant turnover of EC/ECHO's technical assistants during the first month of the crisis. For its part, DFID announced its first financial contribution of £2 million on 20 July and a second of £2.2 million on 22 July.

However, many implementing agencies felt that donor policy was driven by political interests and not only humanitarian needs. Donor behaviour must also be seen in the light of efforts to counter the national influence of Hezbollah, and regional influence of Iran, and to support the incumbent US-backed government, within the broader context of the Middle East, in particular Israeli-Palestinian relations, the conflict in Iraq, and the global "war on terror."

Implementation of the humanitarian response: Humanitarian access and the Hezbollah dilemma

During the first emergency phase, the humanitarian priority was the evacuation of civilians and the provision of protection, food, shelter, medical attention, water and sanitation, and psycho-social support to those trapped by the fighting. Humanitarian access and space immediately became an issue. UN agencies had to negotiate prior notification with the IDF, so that convoys could move without being targeted. OCHA reported that 20 percent of planned convoys were cancelled due to problems of coordination with the IDF. In addition, humanitarian aid convoys were disrupted by heavy shelling, the destruction of roads and bridges, and the inability of drivers to get to work. The poor security situation also made it difficult to deploy needs assessment missions.[7]

During the crucial first phase of the crisis, the response came predominantly from within Lebanon. Local community networks and coping mechanisms, developed during earlier conflicts, allowed Lebanese civil society to respond immediately and effectively with basic necessities, such as food, medicine, and fuel. Two other national organisations also played an important role in the crisis, namely the Lebanese Red Cross (LRC) and Hezbollah, which mounted a well publicised campaign, using its local social networks, to address the most urgent needs of those affected, offering money to each homeless family. It is important to note that these institutions had been in place since the late 1980s, with Hezbollah offering services which the government of Lebanon was not providing to the poorer suburbs of Beirut, the Shia "belt of misery." With the 2006 war, these mechanisms went into full effect, without funding from the state. Such offers may have reinforced Hezbollah's popularity, particularly among the Shia population in Lebanon, as well as throughout the Middle East.

Nevertheless, the international community also reacted quickly, launching a large-scale response employing international humanitarian actors already present in Lebanon.

Following the ceasefire, the response had to adapt to the massive and rapid return of internally displaced persons (IDPs) and refugees, most of whom returned to their homes in South Lebanon, despite the fragility of the situation, devastation of infrastructure and homes, and the threat presented by unexploded ordnance. Return programmes included protection from submunitions, and the provision of water and sanitation, primary health care, basic materials for shelter, and psychosocial support. Later, some income-generating activities were developed. However, some implementing agencies considered the responses to be too supply-driven and materialistic. Aid was not always targeted towards needs, nor adapted to the local context. According to the Humanitarian Practice Network, "agencies need to be more sensitive to the local context, particularly given the increasing number of humanitarian responses in middle-income countries like Lebanon. It is not enough simply to roll out distributions according to the traditional model."[8]

Lebanon became a field for intense recovery and rehabilitation programmes, with multiple donors pursuing varied political and aid agendas. The presence and influence of Hezbollah remains problematic for the United States and Israel, and their Arab allies, whereas the EU does not label the Shia group "terrorist", and has adopted different means of engagement, namely through the Civil Military Cooperation concept of UNIFIL II. Some donors pressed UN agencies and NGOs not to use Hezbollah's social networks, nor to have coordination contact with them. In practical terms, this was considered unrealistic and unconstructive by field actors, as it created operational obstacles and impeded assistance to returnees in many villages.[9] Ironically, after the attack against the Spanish contingent of UNIFIL on 24 June 2007, UNIFIL has come to rely and depend on Hezbollah for "protection," after having been deployed to protect Israel against Hezbollah.

Some European countries adopted a more pragmatic approach, guided by the assessment of humanitarian needs and the understanding that collaboration with Hezbollah was inevitable and essential for effective humanitarian access. In practice, many implementing partners had contact with Hezbollah members, with donors turning a blind eye. NGOs implementing programmes with US funds faced particular problems, due to very strict guidelines. In fact, the policies emerging from the "war on terror" have created a new reality under which humanitarian organisations have to work. As a result, many implementing partners would have preferred an open dialogue with donors on this issue, to protect them against possible legal implications and avoid the politicisation of aid.

Similarly, donations by Arab States were often influenced by political considerations. Sunni Arab regimes, such as Saudi Arabia and the United Arab Emirates in particular, but also Egypt and Jordan, aimed to support the weakened Lebanese government against the Hezbollah-led opposition, which was heavily financed by Iran and Syria. Many Gulf countries are economically tied to Lebanon, particular via investment in construction and tourism, and for them quick recovery carried a financial interest.

As in many crises, coordination, one of the key GHD *Principles*, has become a major challenge. In addition to general coordination meetings, the UN introduced five clusters with weekly meetings: water and sanitation, logistics, shelter and non-food items, protection, and health. However, due to the brevity and the disruption caused by the conflict, it was difficult to hold the meetings regularly and to ensure the presence of the relevant personnel. The UN also established logistic hubs in Beirut, Damascus, Cyprus, and Tyre. While the logistics cluster, led by the World Food Programme, generally received praise, the protection cluster, led by UNHCR, has been criticised: "… the main objective of the protection cluster meetings was to produce papers for Geneva and New York. Topics discussed were often theoretical rather than practical and turnover of staff was high with five different chairs in two months. There was no agreed definition of what protection was in the context of Lebanon and so the objective for the cluster was unclear from the start."[10] Nevertheless, the UN and NGOs were generally satisfied with the cluster system, although they felt that the assessment phase should have been completed more rapidly. Finally, competition for funding was felt to have been an impediment to joint assessments and led to duplication. This was not exclusive to Lebanon, although it was exacerbated, in part, by the brevity of the crisis.

OCHA's deployment was regarded as late, with slow recruitment and strict internal security procedures having a negative impact on programme delivery.[11] Other criticisms were directed at the lack of information sharing, inappropriately targeted assistance because of inaccurate data—particularly the location and numbers of primary and secondary displacements—and poor tracking of assistance. It has also been suggested that OCHA failed to sufficiently engage local NGOs and civil society, as well as many Arab donors, due, in part, to cultural insensitivity or the lack of transparency.[12]

The general consensus was that information management could have been improved and that there were gaps and duplication where aid could have been better targeted, particularly for vulnerable groups. On 31 October 2006, OCHA declared the emergency period over and withdrew.

Conclusion

The international community was, regrettably, unable to intervene earlier than it did in the 2006 Lebanon War. In the face of the many difficulties of coordination, cooperation, and communication—caused largely by the highly political nature of foreign aid in Lebanon—the international humanitarian response did include reconstruction efforts, but these were further complicated by the weak government of Lebanon. Thus, the rapid response by Lebanese civil society was pivotal in the first days of the conflict. In its support for this protection crisis, international donors must be assessed in context of the politics of the region and in light of their aim to reduce the influence of Hezbollah, and, by extension, that of Iran. In part reflecting this motivation, the response was over-funding (123 percent of the UN Appeal).

Some donors gave strict instructions to implementing partners to avoid contact with Hezbollah, an approach considered impractical due to the organisation's deep-rooted presence in Lebanese society. This underscores the urgent need for the humanitarian response to address the legal, moral, and operational implications to comply with Principle 2 of the GHD, namely, to deliver aid according to the fundamental principles of neutrality, independence, and impartiality. Although the crisis was correctly identified as one of protection, the difficulties of humanitarian access were not sufficiently addressed. The concept, implications, and response to a protection crisis must be better defined, moreover in as non-sectarian a manner as possible. The response was also considered too supply-driven and should have given greater consideration to the local context of a middle-income country like Lebanon, and to the availability and capacity of local experts and development agencies already present. However, humanitarian agencies did recognise donor efforts to respect Principles 5, 12, and 13 of the GHD in providing timely and flexible funding.

References

Freeman, Colin. 2006. "Oxfam rejects official relief cash for Lebanon." The Telegraph.. 20 August.

Internal Displacement Monitoring Centre. 2006. "Lebanon and Israel: IDPs return following ceasefire." Available at: http://www.internal-displacement.org/idmc/website/news.nsf/(httpIDPNewsAlerts)/C17228C5DDA7F091C12571DB00524D74?OpenDocument#anchor0

International Crisis Group. 2006. "Israel/Hizbollah/Lebanon: Avoiding renewed conflict." *Middle East Report* 59. Beirut and Brussels. 1 November. Available at: http://www.crisisgroup.org/home/index.cfm?id=4480&l=1

———. 2007. "Hizbollah and the Lebanese Crisis." *Middle East Report* 69. Beirut and Brussels. 10 October. Available at: http://www.crisisgroup.org/library/documents/69_hizbollah_and_the_lebanese_crisis.pdf

Mahdi, Sarah. 2007. "Lebanon and the Near East: New Challenges, Old Dilemmas." *Humanitarian Exchange* 37. March. Available at: http://www.odihpn.org/report.asp?id=2870

Office for the Coordination of Humanitarian Affairs (OCHA). 2006a. The UN Response to the Lebanon Crisis. An OCHA Lesson Learning Paper. December 2006. Available at: ochaonline.un.org/OchaLinkClick.aspx?link=ocha&docid=34369

———. 2006b. Lebanon Crisis 2006 Interim Report: Humanitarian Response in Lebanon, 12 Jul to 30 Aug 2006. Available at ReliefWeb: http://www.reliefweb.int/rw/RWB.NSF/db900SID/YAOI-6TS8G9?OpenDocument

Oxfam. 2006. "Lebanese farmers in crisis after month of war." Press Release, 31 August 2006. Available at: www.oxfam.org/en/news/pressreleases2006/pr060728_middleeast

Reuters Alertnet. 2007. FACTBOX: "Costs of war and recovery in Lebanon and Israel." 9 July. Available at: http://www.alertnet.org/thenews/newsdesk/L08225712.htm

Transparency International. 2006. *Corruption Perception Index*. Berlin.

United Nations Development Programme. 2006. *Human Development Report 2006. Beyond scarcity: Power, poverty and the global water crisis*. New York.

United Nations High Commissioner for Refugees. 2006. *Global report 2006*. Available at: http://www.unhcr.org/gr06/index.html

World Bank, Lebanon Data Profile. Available at: http://devdata.worldbank.org/external/CPProfile.asp?PTYPE=CP&CCODE=LBN

Notes

1   See International Crisis Group, 2007.

2   International Crisis Group, 2006; UNHCR, 2006; Internal Displacement Monitoring Centre, 2006; Israel Ministry of Foreign Affairs, 2007.

3   OCHA, 2006; International Crisis Group, 2006; Oxfam, 20006.

4   DARA field interviews, July 2007; Freeman (2006) reports that, in protest against UK policy, Oxfam GB declined DFID funds, saying that, "as a humanitarian agency we have to be impartial. Our partner organisation in Lebanon told us that they would find difficulty in accepting money from the British government."

5   International Crisis Group interview with Abdel-Halim Fadlallah, 23 September 2007, from ICG, 2007, p. 20, footnote 170.

6   DARA field interviews, Lebanon, July 2007.

7   OCHA, 2006b.

8   Mahdi, 2007, p. 2.

9   DARA interviews, Lebanon, July 2007.

10   OCHA, 2006a.

11   Ibid.

12   DARA field interviews, July 2007.

Niger

AT A GLANCE

Country data *(2005 figures, unless otherwise noted)*

- 2006 Human Development Index: 0.311, ranked 177 of 177 countries
- Population (2006): 14.4 million
- GNI per capita Atlas method (2006, current US$): 260
- Life expectancy: 44.9
- Under five infant mortality rate: 256.0 per 1,000
- Population undernourished (2001–03): 32 percent
- Population with sustainable access to improved water source: 46 percent
- Primary education completion rate: 28.1 percent
- Gender-related development index (2006): 0.271, ranked 140 of 177 countries
- Official development assistance (ODA): US$515.4 million
- 2006 Corruption Perception Index: 2.3, ranked 138 of 163 countries

Sources: World Bank; United Nations Development Programme (UNDP), 2006; Transparency International, 2006.

The crisis

- Niger is one of the planet's hottest countries, with three-quarters of the country covered by desert;
- Niger suffers a food deficit every year, with malnutrition in some areas bordering emergency levels;
- 2005 food production was extremely low, due to two years of drought and a locust infestation, creating a cereal deficit of 223,448 tonnes and livestock feed deficit of 4,642,219 tonnes;
- Over 2.5 million people faced a food shortage, and a nutritional and health crisis;
- The World Food Programme (WFP) estimated that in rural areas 1.22 million people (13 percent of the population) were severely food-insecure; 1.99 million (22 percent) were moderately food-insecure; 1.91 million (20 percent) were at livelihood risk; and 4.13 million (45 percent) were in a situation of food and economic security;
- 3.3 million were affected, with the poorest, children, women, and pastoral herders most vulnerable.

Source: World Food Programme, 2005.

The humanitarian response

- The 2005 UN Appeal for West Africa (including Niger) received US$198,758,232, representing 98 percent coverage, of which 82 percent came from OECD DAC donors;
- The 2006 regional Appeal was 94 percent funded;
- The largest donors to the 2005 Niger Drought/Locust Invasion Food Security Crisis Appeal were: Saudi Arabia (US$19,570,081 or 17.3 percent), the USA (US$19,317,795 or 17.1 percent), private individuals and organisations (US$9,761,757 or 8.6 percent), Canada (US$8,185,072 or 7.2 percent), France (US$8,007,710 or 7.1 percent) and EC/ECHO (US$7,895,699 or 7 percent);
- Total humanitarian assistance in 2006 was US$243,363,823, of which DAC donors represented 69 percent, the largest the USA (21.8 percent), EC/ECHO (together 6 percent), Sweden (3.6 percent), Canada (3.1 percent) and Luxembourg (1.9 percent);
- Despite high levels of funding, the delay of almost two years between the identification of the crisis in 2004 and the distribution of aid in 2006 was disastrous for the population.

Source: OCHA, Financial Tracking Service (FTS).

Niger
A Crisis of Acute, Protracted Poverty and Vulnerability

MARTA MARAÑÓN, Deputy Director, DARA

Introduction*

The 2005–2006 crisis merged short-term natural disasters and a long-term situation of chronic vulnerability, resulting in a critical food shortage. The degree of vulnerability and poverty experienced by the majority of the population cannot be underestimated. It is therefore a structural, forgotten, chronic, and permanent crisis. The international response has been criticised for being too late, too slow, badly coordinated, and poorly directed. Significant levels of funding only began to arrive in the summer of 2005. Although the first signs of the crisis were identified as early as 2004, the majority of distribution took place in 2006. However, it is important to recognise that this crisis has generated a great deal of debate and controversy, in particular surrounding its

extent and impact, the effectiveness of the early warning systems, the diagnosis of the crisis, and the timeliness and appropriateness of the international humanitarian response. Many lessons for the implementation of the Principles of Good Humanitarian Donorship can therefore be drawn from the Niger experience, especially regarding the effectiveness of needs assessment and coordination, and linking relief and development.

Causes and humanitarian impact:
A forgotten and protracted crisis

Despite the severity of Niger's emergency, it illustrates the complexity and protracted nature of the regional

* The opinions expressed here are those of the author and do not necessarily reflect those of DARA.

crisis which affects several countries in the Saharan belt, and the challenges faced by the humanitarian actors.

Niger experiences a severe food shortage every year, with malnutrition rates in some areas bordering on the international 10 percent global acute malnutrition (GAM) level indicating an emergency. In 2005, food production was low, due to two consecutive years of drought and a locust infestation. By 2005, officials estimated cereal deficits at 223,448 tonnes and livestock feed deficits at 4,642,219 tonnes. Over 2.5 million Nigeriens[1] faced a food shortage, followed by a nutritional and health crisis.[2] A World Food Programme (WFP) survey of rural areas in October 2005 estimated that 1.22 million people (13 percent of the population) were severely food insecure; 1.99 million (22 percent) were moderately food-insecure; 1.91 million (20 percent) were at livelihood risk; and 4.13 million (45 percent) were in a situation of food and economic security.[3] Yet, crop production in 2004 was only 10 percent lower than average annual production and food was available in many markets.

However, the extent of the crisis, which groups and areas were most affected, and how the crisis should be defined—was it or was it not a famine?—were hotly debated.[4] This varied understanding of the crisis had an impact on both the response and its evaluation. For example, WFP argued that, "… this is a complex emergency, not a sudden cataclysm, like a tsunami… In technical terms Niger's President Matador Tandja may be right to say that this is not a famine… It may not be a famine, but it is an ongoing development crisis, with the need for sustained attention, even when the cameras move on somewhere else."[5] On the other hand the Humanitarian Policy Group (HPG) has argued that, "avoiding the famine label has often been convenient for those seeking to justify slow or failed responses."[6]

The 2005 crisis was, therefore, a combination of long and short-term factors, with its roots in the country's climate and terrain, its traditional rural economy and social structure, and, most significantly, widespread poverty, lack of public services, and demographic pressures. Moreover, the crisis was not an extreme or unique moment, but rather a cyclical and quasi-permanent state of affairs.[7] Nor should it be understood only as resulting from a scarcity of food across the country, but as a crisis caused by the lack of access to food, particularly by certain segments of the population. WFP has therefore suggested that, "the Niger crisis… removes the line traditionally drawn between structural and short-term crises. A permanent emergency such as Niger's under-

lines the lack of effective solutions to its underlying structural elements."[8]

Niger ranked last out of 177 countries in the UNDP's Human Development Index in both 2005 and 2006, and last in the Gender-Related Development Index and Human Poverty Index. The International Monetary Fund (IMF) estimates that 63 percent of the population lives below the poverty line, while UNICEF estimated the 2005 under-five infant mortality rate at 256 for every 1,000 children[9] illustrating the structural vulnerability of the economy and population. In addition, Niger is one of the hottest countries on the planet, with three-quarters of its surface covered by desert. Recurring droughts, overgrazing, soil erosion, deforestation, and desertification all threaten the environment and people's livelihoods.[10] This is exacerbated by a 3.2 percent population growth rate and the division of land through inheritance. Following this trend, arable land per capita will diminish from 1.2 hectares in 2005 to 0.87 in 2015.[11] This chronic environmental unsustainability is a long-term threat.

The combination of short- and long-term factors pushed many families over the brink, affecting approximately 3.3 million people, especially vulnerable groups, such as women and children. The vulnerability of women and children was in part exacerbated by the male-dominated socio-economic structures, as is often the case in situations of poverty and food crises.

In fact, the crisis did not affect all geographic regions or population groups equally. Locust swarms destroyed much of the grass used to feed livestock, causing nomadic herders to lose many of their cattle, their only source of income. As a result, they could not afford the rising cost of food. Many were forced to sell what livestock they had, incur unsustainable debts, and drastically reduce food consumption, thus creating acute food insecurity and malnutrition. Nevertheless, high chronic malnutrition rates were also recorded in the wealthier southern areas, where food was more widely available in markets. Gary Eilerts of USAID states that there were at least two simultaneous crises occurring in Niger.[12] He argues that the nutritional crisis in the south demonstrated characteristics common to situations of widespread poverty and was linked to increasing wage labour, indebtedness, and declining disposable income.

The crisis also interacted with political tensions and cleavages within the country, which rendered the Touareg group particularly vulnerable. Traditionally, these people, concentrated in the north, have been politically and economically marginalised, a situation which led to a violent rebellion in 1990. The Touareg's traditional nomadic herding existence, coupled with their continued marginalisation, meant that they were both more exposed to the crisis and received less help. UN sources also suggest that increased tensions are affecting humanitarian access.[13]

The international donor response: Too late and only after media exposure

International aid to Niger for the 2005–2006 nutritional crisis has been criticised for arriving six to eight months too late, far too long a delay for a country so dependent on subsistence agriculture.[14] An implementing agency stated that, "the need was already in October 2004 and they [donors] didn't arrive until the second half of 2006 when the needs had changed."[15] To make matters worse, and despite the continuing food crisis, 2006 saw widespread flooding, itself requiring humanitarian action.

The 2005 UN Consolidated Appeal Process (CAP) for West Africa, which included Niger, received US$198,758,232,[16] representing 98 percent coverage of the funds requested, 82 percent of the total from the OECD Development Assistance Committee (DAC) donors.[17] However, OCHA's Financial Tracking Service does not discriminate by country the funds dispersed in the region, which includes Burkina Faso, Chad, Mali, Mauritania, Niger, Nigeria, and Senegal. In 2006, the regional CAP was 94 percent funded, although this focussed almost exclusively on nutrition and food security.[18]

Total humanitarian assistance to the region in 2006 amounted to US$243,363,823, including the CAP and additional contributions. Of this total, DAC donors represented 69 percent, un-earmarked UN funds 10 percent, the UN Central Emergency Response Fund (CERF) 4.8 percent, and non-DAC donors and private funds the remainder. In 2006, Niger received funds from 17 of the 23 DAC members, the largest sum coming from United States (21.8 percent), EC/ECHO[19] (together 6 percent), Sweden (3.6 percent), Canada (3.1 percent), and Luxembourg (1.9 percent). In 2005, under the Niger Drought/Locust Invasion Food Security Crisis identified by the UN, the main donors were Saudi Arabia (US$19,570,081 or 17.3 percent), the United States (US$19,317,795 or 17.1 percent), private individuals and organisations (US$9,761,757 or 8.6 percent), Canada (US$8,185,072 or 7.2 percent), France

(US$8,007,710 or 7.1 percent) and EC/ECHO (US$7,895,699 or 7 percent).

Despite the eventual high levels of funding, it is crucial to recognise that the delay of almost two years between the first identification of high levels of malnutrition in 2004 and the distribution of aid on the ground in 2006 was disastrous for the population.

It is widely recognised that the media played a major role in precipitating a reaction from the international community. As Jan Egeland declared on July 22, 2005, "over the last few days, the world has finally woken up, but it took graphic images of dying children for this to happen. More money has been received over the last 10 days than over the last 10 months."[20] Despite some misrepresentation of the situation, the positive influence and impact of the media was undeniable. However, the U.S. has criticised the message sent by the media and some NGOs as too alarmist, and therefore as having contributed to rising local food prices.

It is also significant that the rapid response to the food security crisis came only when the government of Niger itself recognised its severity. But this recognition came too late for many starving families. The HPG argues that, "part of the reason for this failure [to prevent the crisis] is a long-term lack of concern by the government in the capital Niamey, in the far south of the country, for the conditions of the nomads in the north, the people who will suffer most in the long term."[21] The government was, in part, distracted by the 2004 elections, and later did not want to appear not to be in control of the situation. This attitude shifted through international pressure, the accumulating amount of evidence produced by actors on the ground—often with the participation of state institutions—and pressure from the local population. In June 2005, thousands demonstrated in the capital carrying slogans which read "We Are Hungry!" and "Free Food Distributions!" However, it must be recognised that the crisis was the first to occur following the restoration of democracy in 1999, when government crisis management mechanisms were not yet in place. In addition, some implementing agencies in the field recognised the government's improved commitment and coordination of the response.[22]

Implementation of the humanitarian response: Failures of analysis, inappropriate aid and poor government coordination

It is important to raise questions about the quality of early warning systems and needs assessment analysis of the crisis, as well as the capacity of the humanitarian actors to respond. "There has been a tendency to present this as a crisis that was predicted, but not responded to."[23] Nevertheless, while it may have been possible to foresee the crisis, it was at the time misdiagnosed.

There were a number of early warning systems. The Global Information and Early Warning System (GIEWS) of the Food and Agriculture Organization (FAO) monitors the situation throughout the growing season. The existence of the parallel Famine Early Warning System Network (FEWSNET), implemented by US organisations[24] and regional partners, reflects the lack of confidence in the FAO system. Finally, the EC has invested in improving early warning systems, including AGRHYMET, a regional weather monitoring programme. In September 2004, the Inter-Agency Standing Committee (IASC) Working Group on Early Warning–Early Action recommended strengthening national and local early warning systems in Niger. The overlaps and gaps among these various systems should be addressed in order to increase coherence, so that local communities and the local context can be better accounted for. The Humanitarian Practice Network (HPN) argues that, "analyses failed to identify which population groups were at relatively greater risk, and why… information should be analysed from a long-term perspective."[25]

There were also failures within the different analysis systems. Both the emergency plan prepared by the Dispositif National de Prévention et de Gestion de Crises Alimentaires (DNPGCA)[26] and the EMOP (Emergency and Operations Plan), prepared by WFP, failed to consider the situation affecting herders, underestimated the problem of food access, inadequately estimated the ability to obtain supplies at a regional level, and did not focus sufficient attention on the nutritional situation for a growing population.[27]

Typically, needs assessments were done with an implementing agency's own funds, often at a donor's request, except in the case of ECHO and France, which provided funds to the WFP for needs assessments. Furthermore, despite the fact that donor funding is generally based on needs assessments, it is often not proportionate to the needs identified. In fact, NGOs received far less for Niger than what they asked for, limiting the efforts of implementing agencies.[28]

The principal activity carried out by agencies was the provision of food, followed by water and sanitation, the recovery of livelihoods, health service and medical treatments, and longer-term development. However, while food aid was crucial as part of the response, it was not sufficient and more should have been done to support livelihoods, in particular for pastoralists, and to link relief to development.[29] Clearly, this would have required more funds. Furthermore, the amount of food was considered insufficient and the strategy focussed on food volumes rather than problems regarding access to food.[30] WFP only provided food aid, and the U.S., the largest donor, was largely restricted to offering food that had to be shipped from the United States and took at least four to five months to arrive.[31] In addition, as agreed by the UN and the government, food and fodder were initially only partially subsidised rather than provided for free, so as not to disrupt local markets or create dependency—a strategy which did not last long.

At the onset of the crisis, very few international NGOs had a presence in Niger. By the end of 2005, there were more than 80 implementing agencies. Today (2007), no more than 40 remain in the field. However, many agencies including WFP, CARE, and Save the Children, worked with local NGOs, such as ABC Écologie, as partners and recruited and trained local staff, whose knowledge was invaluable. ECHO has also been praised for having a permanent presence in the field and for increasing its commitment to long-term funding.

Lastly, many organisations believe there is a grave lack of attention to and funding for disaster preparedness and risk reduction. Only a few donors, such as the EC which contributes to DNPGCA, appear to be strengthening the government's capacity to prevent, prepare for, mitigate, and respond to humanitarian crises.

Coordination was also a major problem in Niger, since there was no initial government structure through which it could be carried out. The government established the Committee for Food Crisis (CCA, Comité de Crises Alimentaires) but only when agencies had already begun implementing their programmes. This resulted in confusion over the relationship between international organisations and the government, with the latter objecting to NGOs sharing information without official approval.

In addition to the CCA, there are lead coordinating agencies for different sectors, including the World

Health Organisation for health, the UN Food and Agriculture Organisation and World Food Programme for food security, and UNICEF for nutrition. There is also a Niamey-based IASC task force with representatives from donors, NGOs, and UN agencies.

Since 2006, OCHA has made the following efforts to improve coordination:

- established a Humanitarian Information Centre (CIH) and transferred it to the National Mechanism for the Prevention and Management of Food Crises;
- developed a contact list of humanitarian partners;
- created a matrix of responses to the floods and cholera epidemic;
- produced a "who does what" database;
- developed inter-agency multi-risk and avian flu contingency plans.

Nevertheless, communication between the government and humanitarian partners continued to deteriorate, and is still extremely poor. The government has complained that humanitarian agencies transmitted information to the public without first involving them. On the other hand, some NGOs believe donors did not pressure the government enough to address the reality of the crisis. Some agencies argue that the government does not want to recognise the gravity of the situation because it fears a coup if it appears weak. In effect, the government sends completely different messages to civil society, on the one hand, and to the international community, on the other.

Despite these difficulties, according to UNICEF acute malnutrition decreased from 15 to 10 percent between 2005 and 2006, illustrating that the response at least partially addressed the needs of the population, although far more was needed in both the short and long term.[32]

Conclusion

In the wake of the 2005 crises and the 2005–2006 response there are several challenges and lessons to be learned. First, although there is considerable debate and controversy surrounding the crisis in Niger, there is undeniable chronic vulnerability facing the majority of the population. This highlights the central importance of strengthening both government and local community disaster preparedness and risk reduction capacity, as laid

out in GHD Principles 8 and 9. Without funding on a long-term basis to enhance the link between relief, rehabilitation, and development, future generations will remain vulnerable to malnutrition and starvation.

Second, enhanced coordination at all levels is required, in particular between government and humanitarian partners, but also among donors and implementing agencies, both national and international.

Third, there is an urgent need to respond in a more timely, relevant and effective manner, based on more comprehensive analysis and early warning systems, with greater participation by local communities and greater appreciation for the local context. This will require better planning and greater funding. Indeed, one of the fundamental aims of the GHD is for donors to fund all emergencies on the basis of need, irrespective of political interests or media attention.

In fact, the Humanitarian Policy Group states that discussion of the need to reform the humanitarian system has engaged donors, primarily through the Good Humanitarian Donorship (GHD), as well as operational agencies, adding that "Niger shows just how far the system is from providing a timely, effective and proportionate response. The crisis is being cited as an example of why new mechanisms are needed to improve performance."[33] Fortunately, some important changes in donor behaviour seem to be taking place. The will to strengthen government capacity appears to be greater, and the main donors are moving towards longer-term funding.

References

Borrel, Annalies, Lauren Rumble, and Gillian Mathurin. 2006. "Chronic vulnerability in Niger: Implications and lessons learned." Humanitarian Practice Network. London: Overseas Development Institute. June.

Clay, E. 2005. "The Niger food crisis: How has this happened? What should be done to prevent a recurrence?" Overseas Development Institute. September.

Deen, Thalif. 2005. "UN Official Sees Language Bias Skewing Aid to Africa." Inter Press Service. 26 May.

Eilerts, Gary. 2006. "Niger 2005: Not a famine: Something much worse." ODI Humanitarian Exchange Magazine 33. March. Available at: http://www.reliefweb.int/rw/lib.nsf/db900SID/AMMF-6R9CMZ/$FILE/odihpn-gen-mar06.pdf?OpenElement

Humanitarian Policy Group. 2005. Humanitarian Issues in Niger. Humanitarian Policy Group at the Overseas Development Institute. August.

International Monetary Fund. 2005. Niger: Poverty Reduction Strategy Paper Progress Report. Washington. IMF and International Development Association. 27 January.

Loyn, David. 2005. "How many dying babies make a famine?" BBC News. 8 September.

Office for the Coordination of Humanitarian Affairs (OCHA). Financial Tracking Service. Available at: http://ocha.unog.ch/fts2/

———. West Africa 2005: List of all commitments/contributions and pledges as of 9 September 2007. Available at: http://ocha.unog.ch/fts/reports/daily/ocha_R10_E14760___07090907.pdf

Overseas Development Institute. 2005. "Beyond the blame game." Report on a meeting on Niger held in London on 4 October 2005. London.

UNICEF. 2005. "Niger food crisis increases child deaths." Press release. 12 July. Available at: http://www.unicef.org/media/media_27620.html

———. 2006. "Enquête. Nutrition et Survie de l'Enfant. Níger 2006." UNICEF and the National Statistics Institute. "Enquête sur la vulnerabilité a l'insecurité alimentaire des ménages." WFP, FAO, UNICEF, and the Système d'alerte précoce et de gestion de catatastrophes. November.

United Nations Development Programme (UNDP). 2006. Human Development Report 2006. Beyond scarcity: Power, poverty and the global water crisis. New York.

World Bank. Niger Data Profile. Available at: http://devdata.worldbank.org/external/CPProfile.asp?PTYPE=CP&CCODE=NER

World Food Programme. 2005. Emergency food security assessment in Niger: Synopsis of main findings

———. 2006. "Summary report of the evaluation of WFP's response to the crisis in Niger in 2005". WFP. July 2006. Evaluation Reports. Executive Board Documents.

Notes

1   Citizens of Niger, as distinct from "Nigerians," citizens of Nigeria.

2   In 2006, the World Health Organization declared a cholera epidemic.

3   World Food Programme, 2005.

4   See Eilerts, 2006; and Overseas Development Institute, 2005.

5   Loyn, 2005.

6   Humanitarian Policy Group, 2005.

7   According to the interviews conducted in the field, acute food crises occur every 10 years in Niger.

8   World Food Programme, 2006.

9   IMF, 2006; the poverty line is defined as living on less than US$1 per day.

10 According to the Niger National Institute of Agronomical Research (INRAN), available farm land is shrinking by as much as 200,000 hectares per year because of desertification and soil degradation; the southern movement of the Sahara is forcing many northern herders to create permanent settlements in order to retain some land.

11 Niger National Institute of Agronomical Research (INRAN).

12 Eilerts, 2006.

13 DARA field interview, May 2007

14 However, there is some disagreement within the humanitarian community as to whether the response was indeed late, depending on one's understanding of whether it was, in fact, a crisis or simply the norm; see Overseas Development Institute, 2005.

15 DARA field interview, May 2007.

16 As per OCHA West Africa 2005: List of all commitments/contributions and pledges.

17 OCHA, Financial Tracking Service.

18 Food received 120 percent of requested funding, Agriculture 73 percent, Coordination and Support Services 45 percent, Economic Recovery and Infrastructure 0 percent, Education 12 percent, Health 33 percent, Protection of Human Rights and Law 0 percent, and Water and Sanitation 11 percent.

19 European Commission Humanitarian (AID) Office.

20 Quoted in Overseas Development Institute, 2005.

21 Humanitarian Policy Group, 2005.

22 DARA field interview, May 2007.

23 See Humanitarian Policy Group, 2005.

24 Chemonics International, NASA, NOAA (National Oceanic and Atmospheric Administration), the US Department of Agriculture, and US Geological Survey.

25 Borrel et al., 2006.

26 Trans. "National Mechanism for the Prevention and Management of Food Crises."

27 World Food Programme, 2006.

28 DARA field interview, May 2007.

29 See Clay, 2005.

30 Humanitarian Policy Group, 2005.

31 Clay, 2005.

32 UNICEF, 2006.

33 Humanitarian Policy Group, 2005.

Pakistan (South Asia Earthquake)

AT A GLANCE

Country data *(2005 figures, unless otherwise noted)*

- 2006 Human Development Index: 0.539: ranked 134 of 177 countries
- Population (2006): 159 million
- GNI per capita Atlas method (2006, in current US$): US$770
- Life expectancy: 64.9
- Under five infant mortality rate: 99 per 1,000
- Population undernourished (2001–03): 23 percent
- Population with sustainable access to improved water source: 91 percent
- Primary education completion rate: 63.2 percent
- Gender-related development index (2006): 0.508, ranked 107 of 177 countries
- Official development assistance (ODA): US$1.7 billon
- 2006 Corruption Perception Index: 2.2 score, ranked 142 out of 163 countries

Sources: World Bank; UNDP, 2006a; Transparency International, 2006.

The crisis

- Earthquake 7.6 on Richter scale, centered 95 km NE of Islamabad, 8 October 2005;
- Largest natural disaster, causing 84 percent of 99,425 deaths in 2005 from natural catastrophes;
- 73,000 died (incl. 1,300 in India, 4 in Afghanistan); 128,000+ injured;
- More than 3,500,000 homeless;
- 203,579 homes destroyed;196,575 damaged or 84 percent housing stock;
- 50 percent health facilities demolished; another 25 percent damaged;
- Economic losses of US$5.2 billion, equal to IDA in preceding three years;
- Approximately 2.3 million people reliant on food aid;
- 30,000 people remained in camps until March 2007.

Sources: International Federation of the Red Cross and Red Crescent Societies (IFRC), 2006; Asian Development Bank (ADB), 2005; World Bank, 2005; World Food Programme (WFP), 2006.

The humanitarian response

- Estimated 3.2 to 3.5 million people needed immediate relief assistance;
- 11 Oct. UN Flash Appeal for US$270 million (rev. to US$550 million) for first six months of operation; after one month Appeal only 12 percent funded;in six months, over two-thirds funded;
- US$4,195,941 from CERF to International Organization for Migration (IOM) and OCHA; Pakistan third largest annual CERF recipient, or 11.5 percent of 2005 total;
- In addition to UN Appeal, donor reconstruction conference requested US$5.2 billion; international community pledged more than US$5.8 billion; France, Germany, UK, and EC pledged US$100 million+ each; U.S. and Saudi Arabia over US$500 million each;
- By June 2007, humanitarian assistance reached US$1,165,589,575, above US$1.9 billion pledged in grants and aid in-kind; top five donors: private (22.8 percent), U.S. (17.5 percent); UK (9.5 percent); Turkey (5.7 percent); EC/ECHO (5.2 percent);
- The Pakistan government deployed 50,000 troops to assist the relief work.

Sources: OCHA, 2006b; OCHA, Financial Tracking Service.

Pakistan (South Asia Earthquake)
Testing Reform of the Humanitarian System

RICCARDO POLASTRO, Evaluation Officer, DARA

Introduction*

The October 2005 South Asia earthquake was the largest natural disaster of the year,[1] accounting for 84 percent of the year's 99,425 deaths from natural catastrophes, the vast majority occurring in Pakistan.[2] The international response—one of the major humanitarian operations of 2005–2006, involving both civilian and military actors—also served as a test site for many new UN reform mechanisms for improved coordination and delivery. The crisis is therefore an excellent case study to review the application of the Principles of Good Humanitarian Donorship (GHD).

Despite the massive destruction caused by the earthquake, the humanitarian objectives outlined in the GHD *Principles*—saving lives, alleviating suffering and maintaining human dignity during, and, in the aftermath of the earthquake—were largely fulfilled. Indeed, aided by a mild winter, the relief response has been praised for having prevented the much-feared second wave of death and the massive displacement of communities into the cities.[3] In this respect, international support for the strong leadership shown by the Pakistan government and the use of military logistical capacity, reflecting GHD Principles 8 and 9, were vital. However, funding delays, shortfalls, and problems implementing the new UN coordination mechanisms raised doubts about the effectiveness and pace of the response and the transition from relief to rehabilitation and development, another key point in the GHD.[4]

Causes and humanitarian impact: The earthquake and encroaching winter

An earthquake measuring 7.6 on the Richter scale, with its epicentre near Muzaffarabad, 95 kilometers northeast of Pakistan's capital Islamabad, struck at 8:50 local time on 8 October 2005, affecting 30,000 square miles of

treacherous Himalayan terrain. Tremors were felt from Kabul to New Delhi.

The impact of the earthquake was severe in terms of loss of human life, infrastructure damage, and economic disruption. According to Pakistan's Federal Relief Commission, 73,338 people died and 128,309 were injured, making it the country's deadliest disaster and the world's seventh deadliest earthquake.[5]

Thousands of mud and concrete buildings collapsed or were damaged, while access roads were blocked and critical infrastructure destroyed. In the worst affected areas, 3.5 million people were left homeless, 600,000 rural homes were damaged or destroyed, 50 percent of health facilities flattened and another 25 percent

* The opinions expressed here are those of the author and do not necessarily reflect those of DARA.

damaged, mills and irrigation channels ruined, water sources diverted or contaminated, and electricity and water supply systems destroyed. According to the World Bank and Asian Development Bank, 203,579 homes were destroyed and a further 196,575 damaged, constituting 84 percent and 36 percent, respectively, of the housing stock in Pakistan-administered Kashmir and the North West Frontier Province.[6]

Economic losses were estimated at US$5.2 billion, according to the Asian Development Bank and the World Bank.[7] "Estimated damage was roughly equivalent to the total ODA for the preceding three years and equivalent to the amount the World Bank had lent to the country over the preceding 10 years."[8]

In addition, the quake caused considerable loss of agricultural land and production. Much of the 2005 harvest was buried under the debris, compounding the effects of widespread poverty and two years of drought. Furthermore, since households were still recovering from the disaster and almost none had planted winter wheat, approximately 2.3 million people became reliant on food aid.[9] The earthquake also caused significant long-term disruption to the traditional economy, stripping people of their livelihoods and assets, including grain, seeds, land, and livestock.

Initial estimates indicated that between 3.2 and 3.5 million people needed immediate relief assistance, including shelter, medical care, food and water, and sanitation facilities. As the crisis took place just before the Himalayan winter, the cold, lack of proper shelter, fuel and food, as well as the threat of snows blocking roads, increased the urgency of relief efforts.

International donor response: System shortfalls and bilateral support

With the number of victims rising daily, the Pakistan government issued an urgent request for international assistance. Traditional international humanitarian actors responded, totalling over 100 organisations, including UN agencies, the International Red Cross and Red Crescent Movement (IRCM), NATO and other foreign militaries.

On 11 October, the UN launched a Flash Appeal for US$270 million (later revised upward to $561 million), to cover the first six months of the operation. The UN Flash Appeal was produced in only three, as opposed to the usual eleven days. This may have limited the comprehensiveness of the data used and discussion

of the best response[10] and may, in part, explain why the Flash Appeal initially struggled to raise the necessary funds. After one month, the Appeal was only 12 percent funded. Nevertheless, it is important to recognise that it took several weeks to realise the scale of the disaster. In defence of what appeared to be the slow reaction from donors, the EC Commissioner for Development and Humanitarian Aid, Louis Michel, said on 26 October, "I am well aware that the international community is being accused of lacking generosity... But I refuse to go along with the critics. We will not strengthen the international system by blaming the donors... [T]he truth... is far more nuanced."[11] The fact that, initially, donors did not have the complete picture of the scale of the disaster influenced the extent and speed of early funding, and, in turn, the operational capacity of implementing agencies on the ground.

Within six months the Appeal was more than two-thirds funded, sufficient for the bulk of UN relief efforts. Nevertheless, according to then UN Secretary-General, "the lacklustre response by donors to the United Nations Appeal raises issues about the use of the Flash Appeal as well as donor perception of United Nations capacity to respond to disasters."[12] In essence this reflects the divide between donors' policy commitment to support the UN system, as set out in the GHD *Principles*, and funding support in practice. However, the Appeal remained the main resource mobilisation tool for UN efforts and gained support as the relief response progressed. As of June 2007, it had received US$367 million, 65 percent of the total requested.

Humanitarian organisations placed the emphasis in their critique of the operation on initial cash-flow issues and funding shortages, despite the levels of "soft" or initial commitments made.[13] For humanitarian actors engaged in life-saving operations, the sluggish start made it difficult to sustain their efforts and plan for early recovery. Slow funding of the Flash Appeal as illustrated above also temporarily hampered UN efforts, with agencies delaying or scaling down activities until funds became available.

However, from the UN Central Emergency Response Fund (CERF) US$4,195,941 was rapidly allocated in response to International Organization for Migration (IOM) and Office for the Coordination of Humanitarian Affairs (OCHA) requests. Pakistan was the third largest annual recipient of CERF, constituting 11.5 percent of the 2005 total.[14] This was useful for the coordination of the relief operation, given the initial underfunding of the UN Appeal.

In addition to the UN Appeal process, a donor reconstruction conference was held in November, requesting US$5.2 billion, with the international community pledging more than US$5.8 billion.[15] France, Germany, the UK, and the EC pledged more than US$100 million each, while the USA and Saudi Arabia each gave over US$500 million.

As many as 85 bilateral, multilateral, and private donors provided grants and in-kind humanitarian assistance in response to the disaster. As of June 2007, total humanitarian assistance to the South Asia Earthquake amounted to US$1,165,589,575, in addition to US$1.9 billion pledged in grants and aid in kind.[16] The largest donors were: private (22.8 percent), the United States (17.5 percent), the United Kingdom (9.5 percent), Turkey (5.7 percent), EC/ECHO (5.2 percent), and Norway (5 percent). The lead taken by private donors illustrates a growing trend in the humanitarian sector. Although this funding is often more flexible, less frequently earmarked, and made available more rapidly than donor funding by states, it is not governed by the GHD *Principles*.

Many donors channelled aid directly to the government, rather than through the UN. The government of Pakistan set up the Earthquake Reconstruction and Rehabilitation Authority (ERRA) to coordinate and implement the reconstruction process. It was funded up to 82 percent, a level which can be considered sufficient in comparison to the coverage provided in other major emergencies, such as the December 2003 earthquake in Bam, Iran. ERRA was staffed by a mix of civilian, military, and ex-military personnel, and had a range of specialist departments such as rural shelter, transitional relief, water and sanitation, health, and livelihoods. The effectiveness of donor support and of the government's leadership role was crucial to the delivery of the humanitarian response and the saving of lives. This was a good example of Principle 8 of the GHD in practice.[17] However, the humanitarian effort must be linked to building national capacity in disaster risk-reduction and preparedness.

The eventual high level of funds provided by donors in part reflected their response to the enormity of the disaster, the largest natural catastrophe of the year, and to media coverage of the disaster. However, it could also relate to Pakistan's global strategic importance, including its role as a key ally in the US-led war on terror, as well as the influence of the Pakistani diaspora, with the United States and the UK being the two largest donor governments.

At the national level, the humanitarian response resulted in unprecedented attention and support to the poor and remote North West Frontier Province, an area not traditionally considered an economic priority, despite the political sensitivity of Pakistan-administered Kashmir. However, even if the return of internally displaced persons marked an important step in the transition from relief to recovery, by late 2006, it was clear that more people-centred solutions were required to assist long-term recovery. This included better awareness of government initiatives to help the population, and policies directed at the needs of the more vulnerable groups, including women.[18] Furthermore, as reported by the International Committee of the Red Cross, "property issues continued to affect many who returned home. Larger infrastructure projects including new towns in Muzaffarabad and Balakot districts made slow progress."[19] Linking the humanitarian effort effectively with reconstruction is outlined in GHD (Principle 9), necessary not only for rebuilding the lives and livelihoods of the affected population, but also for increasing their capacity to respond to disasters in the future and to reducing their vulnerability.

Implementing the humanitarian response: Clusters, coordination, and leadership

Initially, 900 camps were established by the government of Pakistan, the UN, and NGOs to accommodate the 3,500,000 left homeless. However, while some moved south to Islamabad, Rawalpindi, or Lahore in the weeks following the earthquake, many others stayed and rebuilt their homes, constructing shelters from the rubble. With the arrival of winter, they were in dire need of protection from the elements. Until March 2007, approximately 30,000 people remained in 44 camps. These were closed by the government on 31 May as part of a returnees assistance programme.

Initial needs assessments and identification of priorities were carried out by the Pakistani authorities. In addition, the United Nations Disaster Assessment and Coordination Team (UNDAC) carried out a rapid assessment, followed by multi-cluster rapid air assessments, while the Pakistani military conducted assessments on the ground. Information was subsequently relayed to the Central Command for medical evacuation and delivery of humanitarian assistance.

In the immediate aftermath of the disaster, the Pakistani army and state administration conducted the search and rescue operation, with the government deploying 50,000 troops to assist the relief work. The military was responsible for coordinating the emergency response and was vital in delivering relief and logistical support, using 60 helicopters to reach isolated communities. The predominant role of the military stemmed from the militarised nature of the Pakistani a since the 1999 coup, the sensitivity of the Kashmir border, and their logistical capacity to respond to and reach isolated communities.

Strong, central government institutions were also critical to the effectiveness of the response. The Federal Relief Commission was created on 10 October to coordinate and monitor the government's relief effort. The government also established the Steering Committee for Recovery and Reconstruction, consisting of the Ministries of Finance, Economic Affairs, Planning and Foreign Affairs, as well as the UN, the World Bank, the Asian Development Bank, and a number of bilateral donors. Overall, the government and army played key roles in the delivery of aid, although even they were hampered by the mountainous geography of the area, the cold weather, and damaged or collapsed infrastructure. As the Inter-Agency Standing Committee stated, "the overall success of the relief effort to the earthquake turned on the competence and adept performance of the government of Pakistan and its military."[20] In addition, given the large-scale involvement of foreign troops, the UN deployed civil-military coordination officers and established humanitarian hubs to link with the government.

However, some NGOs considered that the centralised and militarised nature of the earthquake relief process created levels of bureaucracy which have hindered access to information on reconstruction. Traditionally, humanitarians have been wary of working with the military out of fear of compromising the principles of neutrality and impartiality. Yet, in the words of Hilary Benn, then UK Minister for International Development, "for the time being, the international community should recognise that the military has tools that the humanitarian community doesn't have, and sometimes that we need to use these to save lives."[21]

In addition to the Pakistani military, the UN played a key coordination and leadership role. Within 24 hours of the earthquake, an UNDAC team was deployed inside the country and established on-site coordination centres in Islamabad and severely affected areas. To establish geographical coordination, the UN Country Team opened five field offices, creating humanitarian

hubs to provide common services for the humanitarian community. These promptly became focal points for coordination between UN agencies and the Pakistan Federal Relief Commission, the military, institutional donors, and national and international NGOs. Field Assessment and Coordination Teams from the International Federation of the Red Cross (IFRC) coordinated closely with the UNDAC teams.

A UN Joint Logistics Centre was set up in the UN Coordination Centre in Islamabad, together with the UN Humanitarian Air Service antenna, and a Humanitarian Information Centre (HIC) was established to produce and update a who-does-what-where database. However, according to the end-users interviewed, the database was time consuming to use and sometimes lacked the relevant information. In addition, 14 international NGOs established the Pakistan Humanitarian Forum to share information and coordinate activities. Lastly, Sphere and Humanitarian Accountability Project support personnel were deployed to the field to support quality and accountability efforts among their implementing agency partners, partly funded by the UK government's Department for International Development.[22] These are good examples of the learning and accountability initiatives supported by the GHD and of the efforts made to increase the accountability of relief assistance to beneficiaries.

The Pakistan government announced on 17 October a 12-Point Plan for Relief, Recovery and Reconstruction and presented a National Plan of Action on 1 November. This ensured a coherent response, identifying responsibilities, policies and end-states for stakeholders and key players, and was supported by the international community.[23] Again, the establishment of strong government institutions to respond to the crisis was critically important, as was the support they received from donors, in line with the GHD *Principles*. The UN system undertook further needs assessments in support of government interventions, and these were, in turn, supplemented by a damage and loss assessment by the Asian Development Bank and World Bank to identify long-term reconstruction needs.

The cluster approach:
A new way of working

The international response to the earthquake became a test ground for the UN reform process, introducing the cluster approach to improve coordination, service delivery and accountability. Although this approach was to be introduced in 2006, the response to the earthquake offered an early and important trial opportunity for clusters, because of the urgency and complexity of relief efforts.

Initially ten clusters were formed: coordination, shelter, nutrition, health, water and sanitation, logistics, camp management, protection, and economic recovery and infrastructure, with education added later. Lead agencies were appointed for each cluster. However, despite increased attempts at coordination, generally assessments were carried out individually and the information was not always shared.[24]

The Inter-Agency Standing Committee has claimed that, "although the early performance of the cluster approach in Pakistan was uneven and sometimes problematic, the comments of the Country Team were generally positive and recognised its potential for an improved response. The cluster approach successfully provided a single and recognisable framework for coordination, collaboration, decision-making, and practical solutions in a chaotic operational environment."[25] However, the communication between the cluster hub and the capital was not considered fluid.[26] Moreover, the impetus behind the cluster approach waned during the transition to recovery, in part due to ERRA's lack of capacity to lead the coordination of the clusters. Lastly, clusters with designated government counterparts, such as health, performed well, while others, such as shelter and camp management, struggled to deliver until counterparts were identified. The national authorities' buy-in and adoption of the cluster system were therefore crucial to its success.

Conclusion

The international response to the Pakistan earthquake was considered a success, particularly in preventing further deaths. Moreover, many lessons which relate to the GHD *Principles* can be drawn from the experience, in particular regarding coordination with Pakistan's government and military, and the challenges of the cluster system.

In the event of a sudden onset disaster such as an earthquake, the use of CERF proved crucial in providing adequate levels of un-earmarked seed funding for the organisations coordinating each cluster, facilitating a swift response, especially given that the Flash Appeal was initially underfunded. Once the scale of the disaster was

realised, donor funding levels were good, although private sources provided the bulk of the funds given. Strong and effective coordination with national government institutions and the military was paramount in the response. The existence of an effective government disaster management body was therefore critical, as was the international support given to it. Similarly, given the logistical and coordination difficulties faced, the role of the military should not be underestimated.

Important lessons on the cluster approach and coordination were also learned. For example, joint and coordinated needs assessments are indispensable for making better use of resources and avoiding duplication and contradictions in the relief effort. In this regard, inter-cluster coordination was still a work in progress and communication could have been more fluid. However, despite these weaknesses, the potential of the cluster approach became clear. Lastly, effective coordination and needs assessments must continue into the transition to recovery stage and risk-reduction initiatives. In addition to making better use of local skills and materials and involve more local communities, donors must plan for support for the reconstruction from the early stages of the response to cover the continuum gaps.

References

Asian Development Bank and World Bank. 2005. India—Post-Tsunami Preliminary Damage and Needs Assessment. 14 March. Available at: http://www.adb.org/tsunami/india-post-tsunami-recovery.asp

Benn, Hilary. 2006. "We need an emergency service." Developments Magazine. UK Department for International Development. Available at: http://www.developments.org.uk/articles/hilary-benn-we-need-an-emergency-service/

Humanitarian Accountability Partnership. 2006. Promoting quality and accountable humanitarian services to earthquake survivors in Pakistan. Available at: http://www.hapinternational.org/pdf_word/396-HAP-Pakistan%20Report%20-%20Dec%2005%20%20Mar%2006.pdf

Independent Evaluation Group. 2006. "Hazards of Nature, Risks to Development. An IEG Evaluation of the World Bank Assistance to Natural Disasters." Available at: http://www.worldbank.org/ieg/naturaldisasters/report.html

Inter-Agency Standing Committee. 2006. Real-Time Evaluation Cluster Approach - Pakistan Earthquake. Cluster Working Group. Islamabad. 10–20 February. Available at: http://www.unhic.org/documents/IASC EvaluationofClusterApproach-Pakistan%5BFINAL%5D.pdf

International Committee of the Red Cross. 2006. Annual Report. Geneva. Available at: http://www.icrc.org/Web/Eng/siteeng0.nsf/htmlall/section_annual_report_2006?OpenDocument

International Federation of the Red Cross and Red Crescent Societies. 2006. World Disaster Report 2006. Bloomfield, CT: Kumarian Press.

———. 2007. Pakistan Earthquake Facts and Figures Sheet. 13 March. Available at: http://www.ifrc.org/Docs/pubs/disasters/pakistan-earthquake/factsfigures0307.pdf

Michel, Louis. 2005. "The European Commission's response to the earthquake in South Asia." Geneva. 26 October.

Office for the Coordination of Humanitarian Affairs (OCHA). 2006a. Annual Report: Activities and Use of Extra-Budgetary Funds. New York: United Nations. Available at: http://ochaonline.un.org/ocha2006ar/html/part1_introduction.html

———. 2006b. Final Report: Joint OCHA-DGO-UNDP Mission to Pakistan. 16–19 August. Available at: http://www.undp.org/cpr/iasc/content/docs/Sep_Links/doc_8.pdf

———. Financial Tracking Service. Available at: http://reliefweb.int/FTS/

Oxfam. 2006a. "Keeping recovery on course: Challenges facing the Pakistan earthquake response one year on." October. Available at: http://www.oxfam.org/en/files/bn0610_pakistan_earthquake_oneyear/download

———. 2006b. "Pakistan Earthquake Response Key Facts–19/02/06 to 28/02/06." (DATE)

———. 2007. "Women's Review of the Pakistan Earthquake Response." Available at: http://www.pakhumanitarianforum.com.pk/modules/cjaycontent/07-02-17%20final%20Women's%20Review%20report.pdf

Pakistan Federal Relief Commission

Transparency International. 2006. Corruption Perception Index 2006. Berlin

United Nations Development Programme. 2006a. Human Development Report 2006. Beyond scarcity: Power, poverty and the global water crisis. New York.

———. 2006b. "Moving from relief to Reconstruction and Recovery." New York: United Nations. May.

United Nations Economic and Social Council. 2006. Strengthening Emergency Relief, Rehabilitation, Reconstruction and Prevention in the Aftermath of the South Asian Earthquake Disaster. Report E/2006/67, A/61/79. New York: United Nations. 8 May.

United Nations High Commissioner for Refugees. 2005. Global Appeal, Strategies and Programmes. Available at: http://www.unhcr.org/publ/PUBL/41ab28cb0.pdf

United Nations System. 2005. Pakistan 2005 Earthquake Early Recovery Framework. November. Available at: http://www.reliefweb.int/library/documents/2005/un-pak-16nov.pdf

World Bank. 2005. "Pakistan Needs US$5.2 Billion for Earthquake Relief, Reconstruction, and Rehabilitation." Islamabad. 12 November.

———. Pakistan Data Profile. Available at: http://devdata.worldbank.org/external/CPProfile.asp?PTYPE=CP&CCODE=PAK

World Food Programme. 2006. "Food needed for 2.3 million quake survivors until April." Press release. Available at: http://www.wfp.org/english/?ModuleID=137&Key=1928)

Notes

1   According to the International Federation of the Red Cross and Red Crescent Societies World Disaster Report 2006.

2   It should be noted that until the end of 2006 Pakistan hosted the largest single refugee community (over 2.5 million Afghans) in the world, despite not being a signatory to International Refugee Law. However, because of their geographical location this population was on the whole unaffected by the 2005 earthquake.

3   See United Nations Economic and Social Council, 2006; Inter-Agency Standing Committee, 2006; Oxfam, 2006a.

4   Oxfam, 2006a.

5   Another 1,360 people died in Indian-administered Kashmir and four in Afghanistan.

6   Asian Development Bank, 2005.

7   World Bank, 2005.

8   Independent Evaluation Group, 2006.

9   World Food Programme. 2006.

10   OCHA. 2006a.

11   Michel, 2005.

12   Economic and Social Council, 2006.

13   DARA, field interview in Pakistan, May 2007.

14   OCHA, 2006a.

15   US$1.9 billion consisted of grants and aid in kind, and $3.9 billion in concessionary loans.

16   This includes funds to the UN Appeal and those channelled through other mechanisms.

17   Principle 8 reads: "Strengthen the capacity of affected countries and local communities to prevent, prepare for, mitigate and respond to humanitarian crises, with the goal of ensuring that governments and local communities are better able to meet their responsibilities and co-ordinate effectively with humanitarian partners."

18   Oxfam, 2006a.

19   International Committee of the Red Cross, 2006.

20   Inter-Agency Standing Committee, 2006.

21   Benn, 2006.

22   Humanitarian Accountability Project (2006).

23   This included integrating the UN cluster approach with the overall strategy.

24   DARA field interview, Pakistan, May 2007.

25   Inter-Agency Standing Committee, 2006.

26   DARA field interview, Pakistan, May 2007.

Sudan

AT A GLANCE

Country data *(2005 figures, unless otherwise noted)*

- 2006 Human Development Index: 0.516, ranked 141 of 177 countries
- Population (2006): 37 million
- GNI per capita Atlas method (2006, current US$): 810
- Life expectancy: 56.7
- Under five infant mortality rate: 90 per 1,000
- Population undernourished (2001-03): 27 percent
- Population with sustainable access to improved water source: 70 percent
- Primary education completion rate: 49.7 percent
- Gender-related development index (2006): 0.495, ranked 110 of 177 countries
- Official development assistance (ODA): US$1.8 billion
- 2006 Corruption Perception Index: 2.0, ranked 156 out of 163 countries

Sources: World Bank, 2006; United Nations Development Programme (UNDP), 2006; Transparency International, 2006.

The crisis

- Over 2 million people died in the conflict in the South, and 4 million fled their homes;
- Human rights violations in Darfur included use of child soldiers, systematic rape, and torture;
- Between May and end-2006, over 250,000 people were displaced; by August 2006, there were 5 million IDPs across the country, and 200,000 refugees in Chad; by October, there were 343,600 Sudanese refugees;
- Camp conditions were often inadequate and insecure; in 2006 the number of severely malnourished children rose by 20 percent;
- By the end of 2006, 3 million were reliant on humanitarian assistance; by March 2007, 4 million;
- By December 2006, 73,800 refugees returned spontaneously, an additional 18,600 with UN support;
- During August 2006, approximately 45,000 people in Blue Nile State were forced to leave their homes due to flooding; March saw outbreaks of cholera and watery diarrhoea in the South.

Sources: Internal Displacement Monitoring Centre, 2006; Watchlist on Children and Armed Conflict, 2007; and *BBC*, 2006.

The humanitarian response

- Sudan received 19.6 percent of all 2006 humanitarian aid; cf. next largest, Lebanon, with 7 percent;
- UN Sudan Work Plan world's largest humanitarian operation, reaching 4 million+; Plan requested US$1.5 billion, received 66 percent of requested funds;
- By early 2006, only 38 percent of required funding pledged or committed; by April, the World Food Programme (WFP) halved food rations; UNICEF received US$15 million of promised US$89;
- Sudan received total of US$1,225 million in 2006 donor aid; the largest DAC donors: U.S. (US$685.5 million / 47.9 percent); EC/ECHO (US$153.5 million /10.7 percent); UK (US$97.1 million / 6.8 percent); Netherlands (US$57.3 million / 4 percent); Canada (US$36.6 million / 2.6 percent); US$71.35m (5 percent) carried over from previous year and US$31m (2.2 percent) from CERF;
- Attacks on humanitarian actors rise; 12 killed between July and September 2006;
- By April 2006, one-third of IDPs in Darfur without assistance due to increasing insecurity; in July, 470,000 people without food.

Sources: OCHA, Financial Tracking Service; BBC, 2006; Amnesty International, 2006.

Sudan
From One Crisis to Another

Introduction

The humanitarian operation in Sudan in 2006, the largest in the world, addressed three distinct, but interrelated conflicts, characterised by brutality, gross human rights violations, and massive civilian displacement. The violence exacerbated conditions of widespread poverty, environmental degradation, and competition for scarce resources, as well as vulnerability to disease and natural hazards. With each of the conflicts at differing stages, the year witnessed continued instability, with Darfur experiencing renewed violence and a deterioration of the humanitarian situation.

In addition to the largest volume of humanitarian aid, Sudan also received much international attention, from the media, NGOs, civil society, and the international community. Political, strategic and commercial interests in Sudan divided the international community's attitude and response to the crises, which illustrates the complex and critical relationship between international political and humanitarian efforts. There was a marked contrast between the failure to halt the violence in Darfur and the start of recovery efforts in the South. Failure to protect humanitarian space in Darfur had tragic consequences for the population, as implementing agencies became targets of violence and many withdrew.

Causes and Dynamics of the Crises:
Three conflicts with common roots

In 2006, Sudan was wracked by three armed conflicts: one in the South, another in the West (Darfur), and a third in the East. Their shared causes included Sudan's colonial past, ethnic and religious tensions, the centralisation of power and resources in the capital (Khartoum), marginalisation of the South, West, and East, and competition over resources (land, water, and oil). Conflict over scarce resources between nomadic and sedentary tribes, desertification, the erosion of agricultural and grazing lands, and pervasive poverty added to the explosive mix. These factors were compounded by the virtual absence of social services from the state (especially in marginalised areas), weak state institutions and authority, and the widespread presence of small arms. Spillover from conflicts in neighbouring states and the support of rebels by regional rivals fuelled the violence.

The civil war between North and South began in 1983, after President Jaafar Nimeiri attempted to include southern states in a federal government and impose sharia law. In the largely Christian south, this provoked the emergence of the rebel Sudan People's Liberation Movement/Army (SPLM/A) rebel group, which receives support from Uganda. The conflict was fuelled by ethnic divisions between the African South and Arab North and competition over power and resources, including oil. After 21 years of conflict, the Comprehensive Peace Agreement (CPA) was signed in January 2005, due in part to the work of the Kenyan-led regional Intergovernmental Authority on Development and pressure by Western governments, particularly the United States. The CPA granted southern Sudan dependent autonomy for six years, after which a referendum on full independence, or secession, was to be held, and permission given for the deployment of a UN peacekeeping force (UNMIS). However, as the CPA is fragile and many of its terms have not been implemented (including the lifting of sharia law and the more equitable sharing of oil revenues), sporadic fighting continued into 2006.

The situation in the South is further complicated by the presence of the Ugandan rebel group the Lord's Resistance Army (LRA), supported by Khartoum, which has waged brutal guerrilla warfare for over 20 years. Despite peace talks, the LRA continued to threaten civilians in the South throughout 2006. Localised disputes, in part due to the cyclical movement of cattle herders in the dry season, have further aggravated the situation.

The conflict in Darfur broke out in 2003 with the emergence of the rebel forces, the Sudan Liberation Army/Movement (SLA) and the Justice and Equality Movement (JEM). The violence which erupted followed ethnic and tribal cleavages and was driven by localised competition for resources between pastoralists (largely Arab) and agriculturalists (largely African). In response, the government of Sudan (GoS) armed traditional militias from Arab tribes, the Janjaweed. The violence was characterised by attacks on villages who were thought to be supporting the rebels, first by aerial bombardment by government troops, followed by attacks by the Janjaweed. All sides in the conflict committed grave human rights violations.

The government has opposed international involvement, particularly under the UN, and the 7,000 strong African Union Mission in Sudan (AMIS), deployed in 2004, is under-strength and ineffective. Following a split in the SLA, in May 2005 the GoS signed the Darfur Peace Agreement (DPA) with one of the rebel groups. This was rejected by the other armed groups, resulting in violence between signatory and non-signatory rebels. Further rebel splits and deteriorating command structures added to the violence and lawlessness. 2006 also saw breaches of the UN arms embargo and continued government support to the Janjaweed. The situation was further complicated by the interaction of the crisis with conflicts in neighbouring Chad and the Central African Republic. In 2006, violence increased in intensity and frequency.

Although less intense, the Eastern conflict is also fuelled by the perceived marginalisation of the region, with its repeated, acute livelihood crises. In June 2006, the Eastern Sudan Peace Agreement (ESPA) was signed between the Eastern Front rebel groups and the GoS. This included a power-sharing agreement and a more equitable distribution of resources. Despite the lifting of the state of emergency, sporadic pockets of violence continued and the agreement has been only partially implemented.

Humanitarian Impact of the Crises:
Regional needs and increasing crisis in Darfur

The Sudanese conflicts have been characterised by attacks by all actors on civilians, human rights violations, and massive forced population displacements.

As of August 2006, there were an estimated 5 million internally displaced people (IDP) across the country.[1] The UNHCR estimated that as of October 2006, there were 343,600 Sudanese refugees outside the country.[2] Although some have begun to return to the South, most IDPs and refugees live in precarious conditions. For example, OCHA estimates that 48 percent of IDP children in Khartoum do not go to school,[3] and in August 2006, the government forcibly evicted 12,000 IDPs from the Dar al-Salam settlement.

Displacement, along with the destruction of homes, livelihoods, and infrastructure has made millions in the Sudan dependent on humanitarian aid, further increasing the vulnerability of the population. In fact, Sudan ranked 141 of 177 countries in the 2006 UNDP Human Development Index.[4] Large areas of the country are exposed to natural hazards such as floods, droughts, and locust infestations, which exacerbate food insecurity, displacement, and public health problems. During August 2006, approximately 45,000 people in Blue Nile State were forced to leave their homes due to flooding. February and March 2006 saw outbreaks of cholera and watery diarrhoea in the South, with poor sanitation and overcrowding blamed for an estimated 209 deaths.

Over 2 million people died directly or indirectly as a result of the conflict in the South, and some 4 million were forced from their homes. However, the UN estimated that by August 2006, from 1 to 1.2 million IDPs had spontaneously returned to their villages, some fleeing violence in other areas. By December, 73,800 refugees had also returned spontaneously, and a further 18,600 with UN support. Yet, the pace of return was not matched by the level of assistance needed. For many, the presence of landmines and armed groups made coming back to their homes a hazardous undertaking, complicated by the lack of food and water. The destruction in the South has been almost total, creating immense vulnerability, with few or no services or livelihood opportunities and scarce food and water. One doctor served every 100,000 people and less than 40 percent of the population has access to clean water. The main killers in these conditions are diseases such as malaria, diarrhoea, and respiratory infections.[5] Successive waves of returnees only increase the pressure on meagre resources.

Darfur has witnessed appalling brutality and human rights violations, including the use of child soldiers,[6] systematic rape and sexual abuse,[7] and torture, resulting in well over 180,000 deaths. In fact, Amnesty International argues that "human rights are at the heart of the humanitarian crisis in Darfur. Without an improvement in the protection and human rights of the people in Darfur, humanitarian aid alone will not be effective."[8]

As the violence in Darfur escalated in 2006, humanitarian access declined. Between the signing of the DPA in May and the end of 2006 over 250,000 people were displaced and hundreds of civilians killed.[9] The Internal Displacement Monitoring Centre estimated that by August 2006, there were 1.8 million IDPs, and 200,000 refugees in Chad. Camp conditions were often inadequate, and in April, UNICEF reported a rise of 20 percent in severely malnourished children.[10]

The camps themselves became targets. In October, 80,000 people fled the Gereida camp, following fighting between opposing rebel groups. Women leaving the camps in search of firewood were routinely raped by armed groups or civilians, and security within the camps deteriorated, as many had been infiltrated by armed groups. By the end of 2006, three million people—half of Darfur's 6 million people—were dependent on humanitarian assistance. By March 2007, this number had risen to 4 million.

The international donor response: Massive funding but political impasse

Sudan received approximately 19.6 percent of global humanitarian donor aid in 2006, followed by Lebanon (7 percent) and the Palestinian Territories (6.2 percent).[11] The 2006 UN Sudan Work Plan was the largest humanitarian operation in the world in terms of funding and beneficiaries, reaching over 4 million people. The Work Plan requested US$1.5 billion for humanitarian needs and US$206 million for recovery programmes. By late 2007, it had received approximately 66 percent of the funding requested.

However, according to OCHA the speed of the funding was crucial in order to launch programmes in time to avoid the logistical difficulties of the rainy season.[12] By the start of the year, only 38 percent of funding required had been pledged or committed, resulting in a shortfall of 60 percent for January. In February 2006, OCHA warned that "the short term consequences of a funding squeeze are being felt, even before the critical hunger gap period which begins in May."[13] By April, lack of funding and the deteriorating situation in Darfur meant that WFP was forced to halve food rations. UNICEF warned of severe funding shortages, having received only US$15 million of the promised US$89 million.[14]

Sudan received a total of US$1,225 million in humanitarian donor aid in 2006, with all 23 OECD-DAC members contributing. The largest DAC donors were: the U.S. (US$685.5 million or 47.9 percent), EC/ECHO (US$153.5 million or 10.7 percent), UK (US$97.1 million or 6.8 percent), the Netherlands (US$57.3 million or 4 percent), and Canada (US$36.6 million or 2.6 percent). A further US$71.35 million (5 percent) was carried over from the previous year's funding and US$31 million (2.2 percent) came from the UN Central Emergency Response Fund (CERF), funded principally by DAC donors, excluding the EC and the U.S.

Most humanitarian assistance was requested for Darfur (53 percent), followed by the South (25 percent), with other regions receiving significantly less. Regarding actual coverage, Darfur received 77.5 percent, the disputed area of Abyei 25 percent, and Khartoum and other northern areas 12 percent. This distribution was driven substantially by media exposure in the case of Darfur, and by political considerations in the South, where it was important for donors to reinforce the CPA, which they supported and helped negotiate. Arguably, too little attention was paid to humanitarian needs and too much pressure was exerted by the GoS and the government of Southern Sudan (GoSS) on IDPs to return to ensure their presence in the pending elections. Almost two-thirds of the funds received (much of it in-kind food donations from the U.S.) was assigned to food aid, with other sectors, such as basic infrastructure and resettlement receiving amounts on the order of 7 and 5 percent of the total. It is questionable if all needs were sufficiently covered.

As reflected in the high funding levels, Sudan has received significant international attention in recent years. The UN Security Council has passed 19 resolutions on Sudan since 2004, imposed a sanctions regime, and has put in place a 10,000 member peacekeeping force in the South. Darfur in particular has become the focus of the international media, championed by well-known film celebrities and writers.

Many countries have maintained tense relations with the Sudanese government, because of the country's geo-strategic and commercial importance—including its size and location, potential for regional instability, past connections to radical Islamic terrorism, and rich oil reserves. However, the international community's response to the conflicts has been divided. On one hand, China has often supported the GoS, guided by its oil interests and a foreign policy characterised by the rejection of interference in domestic matters, particularly those concerning human rights.

On the other hand, the United States and European Union have often tried to pressure the GoS, and their relations with Sudan are characterised by a complex set of political and economic issues. For example, in 1998, the presence of terrorist organisations and the bombing of its embassies in Kenya and Tanzania precipitated a missile attack by the United States. In 2005, the U.S. went so far as to call the violence in Darfur "genocide," in contrast to the more restrained language of the Security Council. However, the next year, Sudan was described by the US State Department as reflecting a "cooperative commitment" to fighting terrorism, and by 2007, was being described as a "strong partner" in the "war on terror."[15]

The United States, UK, Norway, and Italy were involved in the negotiations of the CPA. However, international diplomatic efforts resulting in the DPA have been described by some as "precipitated," "one-dimensional," and "uncoordinated."[16] Nevertheless, in August 2006, the US Congress passed the Darfur Peace and Accountability Act, which calls on the United States to pursue a solution to the conflict. Darfur has also been key in the discourse on the Responsibility to Protect, championed by, among others, Canada. The international community, and in particular the United States, has invested considerable political capital in addressing instability in Sudan.

The humanitarian response: Closing humanitarian space

Prior to 2006, there were signs of progress across the country on both the humanitarian and political fronts. The signing of the CPA and DPA offered a glimmer of hope. In Darfur, malnutrition had been halved and nearly 2 million people were provided with safe water. Early in 2006, some organisations assumed that an important part of humanitarian assistance would shift towards recovery and development. Indeed, a significant number of people returned to the South. However, the security and humanitarian situation in Darfur deteriorated alarmingly, violence continued in areas of both the South and East, and many returnees continued to require humanitarian assistance, both during and after their return.

Humanitarian activities in 2006 covered the full range of assistance, including protection, food aid, water and sanitation, disaster preparedness and response, and rehabilitation and reconstruction. In addition, the country faced other severe challenges, including outbreaks of cholera and yellow fever, and extensive flooding.

Parallel to bilateral donor funding, the Work Plan employed a number of funding mechanisms to direct resources towards those sectors which had not been well covered. A Common Humanitarian Fund (CHF) was established in early 2006, managed by OCHA, with the aim of meeting immediate or neglected needs across the country, crucial in an operation of the scale, complexity and fluidity as that of Sudan. Furthermore, it provided early funding to launch programmes more quickly than either the Appeal process or bilateral donor funding.

Nonetheless, while some NGO critics claimed that the CHF was slower and more cumbersome than bilateral funding, others felt it a positive move, allowing them to access funding which they might not otherwise receive. US$165 million was delivered through the CHF in 2006. Two other Multi-Donor Trust Funds, administered by the World Bank and supported by DAC donors were also operational in 2006, totalling US$611 million in pledged funds.

In addition to mammoth logistical difficulties and funding shortfalls, the most significant obstacle to humanitarian action in Sudan, particularly in Darfur, was increasing violence, by all parties, against not only the civilian population but also humanitarian actors. In other words, increasing need was exacerbated by deteriorating humanitarian space and access. This constituted a gross violation of both international humanitarian law and of the most fundamental humanitarian principles, as embodied in the Good Humanitarian Donorship Principles. Camps were attacked, vehicles hijacked, supplies looted, and aid workers beaten, sexually assaulted, and murdered. Direct attacks on humanitarian actors rose considerably in 2006 and between July and September 12 humanitarian workers were killed.[17] According to UNICEF, by April 2006, a third of IDPs in Darfur were without assistance due to increasing insecurity.[18] According to the WFP, in July 2006, some 470,000 people went without food aid.[19] In the East, due to the forced withdrawal of implementing agencies, two-thirds of the population in some areas went without access to health care. In the South, the November fighting between the SPLA and government forces resulted in the temporary withdrawal of humanitarian aid staff.

Declining humanitarian space and access were further exacerbated by the actions of the GoS. The UN Deputy Humanitarian Coordinator for North Sudan stated that, "from November 2005 onwards we have begun to see a roll back in the facilitation activities of Sudanese authorities… We are seeing inane bureaucratic measures being prioritised above life-saving activities."[20] Furthermore, the use by the GoS for military purposes of white aircraft—similar to those used by the UN, the African Union (AU) and humanitarian actors—blurred the line between humanitarian and military operations and jeopardised the neutrality, and therefore the security, of the humanitarian mission. NGOs and journalists who criticised the government on human rights issues were targeted for harassment. NGOs such as Amnesty International and Human Rights Watch were denied entry into the country. Similarly, UN Special Representative Jan Pronk was expelled from Sudan in October 2006. After its fifth suspension by the GoS, the Norwegian Refugee Council closed down its operations in November.

The actions of armed groups, an increase in banditry, and the proliferation of factions further threatened the security of both the civilian population and humanitarian actors.

Conclusion

Despite high levels of international political and media attention, and the largest humanitarian operation in the world, civilians continued to suffer tragically across Sudan. Although media attention and political and economic interests and engagement help to attract donor funding—calling into question the degree of respect paid to the GHD Principle of independence—it is evident that without a lasting political solution to the crisis, humanitarian aid represents, at best, temporary relief rather than a cure. A united, robust, and effective effort is required by the international community to pressure all sides to end the conflict.

Some humanitarian reforms, reflecting objectives within the GHD Principles, are proving successful, such as the use of CERF and the Pooled Fund to release funds quickly, often to low-profile programmes. These should be encouraged, as they are proving to be crucial for the alleviation of suffering.

But even a political resolution will not end the need for humanitarian aid, much less address the long-term causes of the conflict through sustainable development. Donors must continue to invest considerable political and financial resources over the long term. This funding must also be focussed on all regions and communities in the country, according to need, not political objectives. In this respect, the application of the GHD *Principles* to the Sudan crises will be critical for the country's future.

At present, observance of GHD Principles 4 and 17—respect for international humanitarian law and human rights and the facilitation of safe humanitarian access, respectively—is fundamental to saving lives, particularly in Darfur. The violence and human rights abuses perpetrated by all sides cannot be underestimated. Attacks on humanitarian space, by all sides to the conflict, are not only disastrous for the civilian population, but have served to unravel the gains made in 2005.

References

Amnesty International. 2006. "Darfur: threats to humanitarian aid." Available at: http://web.amnesty.org/library/Index/ENGAFR540312006?open&of=ENG-SDN

BBC. 2006. "Malnutrition in Darfur is on the rise again." 28 April. Available at: http://news.bbc.co.uk/2/hi/africa/4947788.stm

ENOUGH. 2007. "Darfur Monthly Report." May–June. Available at: http://www.enoughproject.org/reports/darfur_2007-05.php

Internal Displacement Monitoring Centre. 2006. "More than 5 million estimated IDPs in Sudan." Available at: http://www.internal-displacement.org/idmc/website/countries.nsf/(httpEnvelopes)/CA38A0F0F269546F802570B8005AAFAD?OpenDocument

OCHA 2006a. *Sudan Humanitarian Overview*. Vol 2(1). Available at: http://www.unsudanig.org/docs/Sudan percent20Humanitarian percent20Overview percent20Vol2 percent20Iss1Jan06.pdf

OCHA 2006b. *Sudan Humanitarian Overview*. Vol 2(2). Available at: http://www.unsudanig.org/docs/Sudan percent20Humanitarian percent20Overview percent20Vol2 percent20Iss2 percent20Feb06.pdf

Transparency International. 2006. *Corruption Perception Index*. Berlin.

United Nations Development Programme (UNDP). 2006. *Human Development Report 2006. Beyond Scarcity: Power, poverty and the global water crisis*. New York.

United Nations Development Programme. 2006. Human Development Report 2006. *Beyond Scarcity: Power, Poverty and the Global Water Crisis*. New York:

US Department of State. 2006. Country Reports on Terrorism (Sudan). Washington. 28 April. Available at: http://www.state.gov/s/ct/rls/crt/2005/64337.htm

———. 2007. Country Reports on Terrorism (Sudan). Washington. 30 April. Available at: http://www.state.gov/s/ct/rls/crt/2006/82736.htm

Watchlist on Children and Armed Conflict. 2007. "Sudan's Children at a Crossroads: An Urgent Need for Protection." Available at: http://www.watchlist.org/reports/pdf/sudan_07_final.pdf

World Bank. 2006. "Sudan Data Profile." Available at: http://devdata.worldbank.org/external/CPProfile.asp?PTYPE=CP&CCODE=SDN

Notes

1   Internal Displacement Monitoring Centre, 2006.

2   Watchlist on Children and Armed Conflict, 2007.

3   OCHA, 2006b.

4   UNDP, 2006.

5   Watchlist on Children and Armed Conflict, 2007.

6   By December 2006, 1,040 children had been removed from armed groups in the South, representing only a small proportion of those across the country.

7   Exact figures for sexual violence are impossible to ascertain but the International Rescue Committee reported that over 200 women and girls were sexually assaulted near the Kalma camp in only five weeks in 2006, more than double the rate previously reported.

8   Amnesty International, 2006.

9   By July 2007, a further 140,000 people had been displaced in Darfur (many for the second or third time) and 170,000 in Chad.

10   *BBC*, 2006

11   OCHA, Financial Tracking Service

12   OCHA. 2006b.

13   Ibid.

14   *BBC*, 2006.

15   US Department of State, 2006 and 2007.

16   By ENOUGH (the Project to Abolish Genocide and Mass Atrocities), 2007.

17   Amnesty International, 2006.

18   *BBC*, 2006.

19   Amnesty International, 2006.

20   OCHA, 2006a.

Timor-Leste

AT A GLANCE

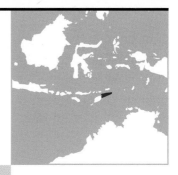

Country data *(2005 figures, unless otherwise noted)*

- 2006 Human Development Index: 0.512, ranked 142 of 177 countries
- Population (2006): 1 million
- GNI per capita Atlas method (2006, current US$): 840
- Life expectancy: 56.7
- Under-five infant mortality rate: 61.3 per 1,000
- Population undernourished (2001–2003): 8 percent
- Population with sustainable access to improved water source: 58 percent
- Primary education completion rate: NA
- Gender-related development index (2006): NA
- Official development assistance (ODA): 184.7 million
- 2006 Corruption Perception Index: 2.6, ranked 111 out of 163 countries

Sources: World Bank; United Nations Development Programme, 2006; Transparency International, 2006.

The crisis

- A strike by soldiers deteriorated into riots, looting, and clashes between political opponents, divided along east and west lines;
- The April to June violence left 37 civilians dead;
- 1,650 homes were destroyed and 2,350 damaged, in addition to destruction of infrastructure and businesses;
- 150,000 people were displaced, or 15 percent of the population;
- According to UNICEF, 15 percent of children in IDP camps suffered from malnutrition;
- The World Food Programme estimated that 57 percent of IDPs had to cease their primary income or livelihood activity.

Sources: United Nations, 2006a; UNICEF, 2006; World Food Programme, 2006.

The humanitarian response

- The largest donors of humanitarian aid were Australia (US$5,111,006 or 16.4 percent of the total), Japan (US$5,004,512 or 16.1 percent), the EC/ECHO (US$4,029,495 or 13 percent) and the UN Central Emergency Response Fund (CERF, US$3,274,047 or 10.5 percent);
- OECD-DAC members contributed US$29,337,648;
- The 2006 UN Flash Appeal requested US$24 million and eventually received US$25, 103.5 percent coverage;
- The crisis was both well funded and underfunded, with some sectors and agencies well funded and others not; the World Food Programme received 103 percent of the amount requested, while UNHCR was under-funded and had to withdraw

Source: OCHA, Financial Tracking Service.

Timor-Leste
Relapse and Open Wounds

SILVIA HIDALGO, Director, DARA

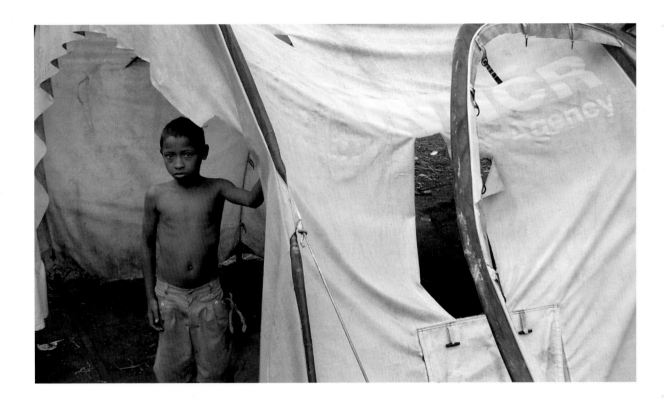

Introduction

The crisis that affected Timor-Leste in 2006 illustrates the fragility of this small, new nation and the broad range of difficulties the country and its population face. In May and June 2006, nearly seven years after the successful struggle for independence, the country was once again ravaged by unrest in the capital, Dili. This conflict polarised the nation along the lines of a supposed east-west divide and support for either former Prime Minister Mari Alkatiri or for the current and former Presidents Ramos Horta and Xanana Gusmao. These divisions were also reflected in the security forces. Street protests in Dili turned violent and were exploited by criminal gangs who looted and destroyed property. The

violence resulted in massive civilian displacement which continues today. Before this recent conflict, international intervention in the country had been praised—including by then UN Secretary-General Kofi Annan—for its exemplary nation-building and successful post-conflict development, a perspective now seen as overly optimistic.

At the government's request, international forces and the UN mission (UNMIT) filled the security vacuum and stabilised the situation. However, the humanitarian response to the 2006 crisis was both over- and underfunded, with some needs, such as food, covered much better than protection. In fact, the response was based on an unrealistic and too short-term analysis of

* The opinions expressed here are those of the author and do not necessarily reflect those of DARA.

the situation. A more long-term approach, with greater local participation and ownership is required.

Causes of the crisis:
A fragile situation and the east-west divide

The immediate origins of the 2006 crisis lay in the dismissal of the 594 of the army's 1,400 soldiers, who went on strike in February over alleged discrimination against western soldiers and officers and poor service conditions. The issue escalated and split the government, security forces, bureaucracy, and sections of the population, and eventually erupted in April and May in a series of riots, violent assaults, and political struggles.

In April, protests in Dili by the dismissed soldiers and civilian supporters turned violent, resulting in attacks on the Government Palace, and on market stalls and property belonging to easterners. However, much of the violence was instigated by street gangs and later the east-west divide was manipulated for political reasons. The police, unable or unwilling to control the situation, withdrew. In apparent violation of the Constitution, Prime Minister Alkatiri deployed the remaining soldiers to suppress the violence. Chaos ensued, in the midst of heavy automatic gunfire, and church officials alleged that 60 persons were massacred by the army—a charge subsequently proven false. The rapid deterioration of the situation, marked by the east-west divide, factionalism, and the virtual breakdown of law and order, caught Timorese and the international community by surprise.

While the east-west divide is a new phenomenon, it is rooted in inequalities of ownership by easterners and westerners and their respective access to land and property in Dili. East-west identities were popularised in the 1940s when both groups competed for limited market spaces and property. Following the 1999 independence referendum, pro-Indonesian forces forced hundreds of thousands from Dili into West Timor as refugees. Up to 30 percent of the housing in Dili was damaged—80 percent throughout the country as a whole[1]—and many formal records were destroyed. The first to return to Dili and occupy properties were predominantly from the east. The large number of returnees, housing shortages across the country, and the lack of economic activity outside Dili caused a population boom in the capital, exacerbating competition and east-west tensions.

The crisis has even deeper roots in the legacy of the brutal Indonesian occupation (1975–1999) and Timorese political rivalries. The most salient political fracture is between Prime Minister Mari Alkatiri and President Xanana Gusmao, stemming from ideological and political disputes during the occupation between the pro-independence FRETILIN (Frente Revolucionária do Timor-Leste Independente) party and its military wing FALINTIL (Forças Armadas de Libertação Nacional de Timor-Leste). This political cleavage was reflected in the formation of the new armed forces and the police force.

The crisis was also characterised by underlying structural problems, including a weak economy, poor service delivery, fragile state institutions, and a vulnerable population. Timor is one of the world's poorest nations, ranked 142 of 177 countries in the UN Human Development Index. The population is, therefore, disillusioned by the fact that independence has not improved their standard of living and that human rights abuses and corruption by state agents continue. In fact, high unemployment—up to 70 percent in Dili—is regarded as an important destabilising factor, with gangs of young men heavily involved in the violence.

A final factor in the crisis was the vulnerability of an already traumatised population, easily swayed by rumours.[2] During the crisis, Timorese were convinced that many massacres occurred and were covered up. Furthermore, the level of displacement was enormous and arguably disproportionate to the actual level of violence which occurred.

Impact of the crisis:
Displacement in a climate of fear

The most immediate impact of the 2006 crisis was the death of 37 civilians, the destruction of an estimated 1,650 homes (and a further 2,350 damaged), and the displacement of 150,000 people, mainly in Dili, representing 15 percent of the total population.[3] At one stage, the population of the Internally Displaced Persons (IDP) camps grew by 300 percent in only 24 hours. IDP camps numbered up to 52, while many displaced people took shelter in public areas, such as the central hospital, or in rural households. Those in makeshift camps required protection, food, and water and sanitation services, etc. According to UNICEF,[4] 15 percent of children in the IDP camps needed immediate treatment for malnutrition. The World Food Programme (WFP)[5] estimated that 57 percent of those displaced lost their primary income or livelihood. A year after the crisis (2007), most of the tents in which IDPs live are severely damaged and the government estimates that 5,000 new ones, at a cost of US$1 million, are needed. Access to water and sanitation in the camps also remains poor and below internationally recognised SPHERE[6] standards. In addition, food shortages occurred in camps and in households hosting displaced persons. The displacement therefore affected the situation of those in rural areas, the nation's poorest and most vulnerable even before the crisis. The climate of fear and insecurity also impeded access to some social services, such as health. Many westerners felt unsafe in the national medical hospital.[7]

The economic and human development impact of the crisis was considerable because of the already precarious situation. Timor-Leste stands at the bottom of all ASEAN[8] countries on the UN Human Development Index. For example, malnutrition rates are comparable to those of some African countries, with 60 percent of households food insecure for four months of the year. Illiteracy affects practically half of the population. Out of every 1,000 live births, around 90 children die before their first birthday and 136 before their fifth year.[9] Many of these deaths are related to malnutrition or immunisable diseases; some 58 percent of children under two years have never been immunised and 95 percent of children are not fully protected.[10]

The crisis and life in the camps exacerbated these trends. Infrastructure was damaged and property looted, including 4,000 houses, many businesses, shops, public buildings, and essential utilities. Economic activity was brought to a halt and livelihoods destroyed, with a serious effect on the government's revenue base and long-term development. Furthermore, cropping cycles were interrupted and food imports were temporarily cut off when cross-border trade with Indonesia and maritime transport were halted. As Timor-Leste is a food deficit country and relies on imports, this led to rice shortages, the population's basic staple, increasing food insecurity across the country.

As is common in humanitarian crises, women and children were disproportionately affected. According to the Human Development Report, approximately half of Timorese women in intimate relationships suffer from some form of gender violence. Because of the increasing levels of sexual and gender violence in the camps, the government is considering making protection for women and children a priority, through the introduction of Timorese camp managers and an awareness-raising campaign.[11]

Indeed, the climate of fear which fuelled the displacement still remains, and the majority of the population has suffered increased trauma due to the crisis. A year on, those displaced in camps still cite fear and insecurity as their main concern, although it is possible that the aid they receive is a perverse incentive for them to remain in the camps. The crisis and perceived insecurity also had an impact on people's freedom of movement and the free flow of goods. The existence of east-west "transit camps," located immediately to the west of Dili, illustrate this perceived insecurity. The camps were established because bus drivers from the west will not drive further east. As of June 2007, this sense of fear, compounded by the outstanding land law issue, was considered by implementing agencies and IDPs to be one of the key obstacles to recovery.[12]

International response to the crisis: The role of regional donors

Following the government's prompt request for assistance, the international response to the crisis was considered timely in stabilising the situation and responding to immediate humanitarian needs. This included the establishment of the large integrated UN mission, UNMIT, mandated to facilitate "the provision of relief and recovery assistance and access to the Timorese people in need, with a particular focus on the segment of society in the most vulnerable situation, including internally displaced and women and children."[13]

Most donors already present in Timor with development programmes at the time of the crisis also provided humanitarian funding. The majority of humanitarian aid funding (including that of the UN Appeal as well as other mechanisms) was provided by Australia (US$5,111,006 or 16.4 percent of the total), Japan (US$5,004,512 or 16.1 percent), the EC/ECHO (US$4,029,495 or 13 percent) and the UN Central Emergency Response Fund (CERF, US$3,274,047 or 10.5 percent). Humanitarian aid to Timor-Leste in 2006 from OECD-DAC members—therefore signatories to the GHD *Principles*—amounted to US$29,337,648.[14] The 2006 UN Flash Appeal requested US$24 million and eventually received US$25 million, representing 103.5 percent coverage.

Several donors, less visible in other crises, were actively engaged in Timor, including, Australia, Japan, New Zealand, and, to a lesser extent, Portugal. Some more traditional donors, such as DFID, were less in evidence, due to Australia's significant engagement.[15] Australia and New Zealand claim that geographic proximity justifies their greater involvement. They also both share an interest in promoting regional stability and have similar concerns regarding immigration issues. It should also be noted that Australia has rights to exploit the oil resources in the Timor Sea. The involvement of Portugal is explained by their historical ties and other interests, including economic and commercial linkages. Despite the fact that non-DAC Asian donors are engaged in development activities, OCHA's Financial Tracking Service indicates that only South Korea and Singapore have provided humanitarian funding, while, in contrast to development aid contributions, there is no record of Chinese funding. Other donors, such as the EC, Ireland, and Norway, are also present in Timor, despite the lack of regional interests.

The traditional donor-recipient relationship in the case of Timor is complicated by the paradox that, despite poor human development indictors, the country is regarded as wealthy. High global oil and gas prices have raised current and potential revenue inflows. Petroleum production from Bayu Undan in the Timor Sea can now fully finance an annual budget at a sustainable level of income, and as of 30 June 2007, the capital of the fund was almost US$1.4 billion. However, the government's capacity to respond to development and humanitarian needs is constrained by weak state institutions, poor delivery of social services, and severe fiscal restrictions.

Overall, as was mentioned earlier, the crisis was both well funded and underfunded, with some sectors and agencies receiving sufficient funding, and others finding it particularly difficult to access resources. This occurred partly because of donor fatigue, resulting from a lack of progress and poor assessment and planning at the onset.

Reflecting this, CERF provided US$3,274,047 (10.5 percent) of humanitarian assistance in 2006, to cover needs not addressed immediately by donors. At the beginning of the crisis, the Humanitarian Coordinator explained that, "while we have had a good response to the Flash Appeal there are critical shortfalls in the area of food supplies and health. The displaced population is incredibly vulnerable and the camps have the potential to become flashpoints if we cannot continue to provide basic humanitarian needs."[16] However, at the onset of the crisis, WFP immediately sought funding from the Australian government and in the end received 103 percent of the amount requested from seven donors.

Thus, while in the end, as in other crises, the basic areas of the Appeal, such as food aid, were well funded,

other key areas were not. For example, the UN High Commissioner for Refugees (UNHCR) is currently underfunded and has had to withdraw from the country. This presents a serious problem, for not only is it the lead agency for protection, but the official registration process of IDPs has not yet taken place. On the other hand, the International Organization for Migration (IOM) has received considerable support and has increased its protection operations. NGOs such as Oxfam are also attempting to cover the protection gap. In fact, funding was directed towards agencies viewed as most capable of absorbing the resources. Several UN agencies which experienced shortfalls were less well staffed and did not foresee the need to upgrade their capacity at the onset of the crisis. Moreover, the heads of those agencies which received the most funds, including WFP and IOM, were highly experienced.[17] Donors felt that although certain underfunded sectors were key to the response, aid was better channelled through NGOs outside the Appeal, and that limited resources were best directed at those sectors in which both priorities and capacity existed.

Implementation of the humanitarian response: Realistic and long-term local-ownership approach needed

As mentioned earlier, although the overall level and timeliness of the international response was sufficient to address immediate needs, there were some shortcomings in implementation. Among these were the following: first, assistance lacked an overall strategy and long-term perspective, as programmes and appeals failed to acknowledge that there are no short-term solutions to the internal displacement situation; second, due to the overly optimistic diagnosis of the situation, many UN agencies had not planned for the required level of presence and resources.

Reflecting this, the Timor-Leste Institute for Reconstruction Monitoring and Analysis (La'o Hamutuk) cautioned that the UN mission was "being designed in an emergency atmosphere. Although immediate humanitarian and security concerns must be dealt with, there are deeper-seated causes of the current problems, and crises will recur if they are not addressed."[18] Similarly, far from presenting a genuine strategic planning process, with analysis, strategy, and objectives being discussed and agreed in the appropriate order, the UN Consolidated Appeals Process (CAP) was an arduous process undertaken by OCHA to identify the projects of different agencies in the best possible way. In practice, the process was undermined by the absence of clear prioritisation which, however difficult, would have focussed the response and ensured greater governmental and donor engagement.

CAP projects and donor responses emphasised resource procurement, rather than substantive policy issues at the level of strategic decision making. So, for example, the issue of land titles and the housing shortage was not addressed. By way of illustration of this lack of a long-term perspective, UNHCR was overfunded in 2006 and underfunded in 2007. OCHA's departure was also partly prompted by overly optimistic assumptions regarding the relocation of IDPs. Responses to the IDP problem were inconsistent and wavered between encouragement and ultimatums. In fact, there is still no official registration of IDPs. At the same time, the humanitarian response and the registration process now foreseen have focused on the IDP issue without following a needs assessment or considering levels of vulnerability within the entire Timorese population. In contrast, a recent joint food and crop supply assessment carried out by the Food and Agriculture Organisation (FAO) and WFP highlighted the need to improve food security policies, strategies, and implementation mechanisms across the board.

While the challenge of providing aid that supports and empowers the most vulnerable is common to all crises, in Timor one finds extremely low levels of local participation, both by government agencies and the population more generally. However, judging the extent to which donors supported local government capacity is extremely difficult, given the unique context, that is, the infancy of the Timorese state.[19] Indeed, concern exists about the impact of international aid in perpetuating a sense of dependency and in providing a form of exoneration for the government, as its responsibilities are carried out by external actors. In addition, cultural and language differences made communication and cooperation between Timorese and foreign staff difficult.[20] Limited local participation, compounded by limited expatriate understanding of the specific needs of the Timorese made the task of providing the right people with the right aid all the more complex. For example, awareness of the fact that the population suffers from post-traumatic stress disorder may caution against the usual procurement-based response. Thus, efforts should not only focus on nation-building but on creating greater participation and a

sense of ownership by Timorese in order to better address their concerns.

The context of political struggles, tension, mistrust and insecurity, coupled with widespread poverty, also presented a challenge. By August, the government announced that there were 168,000 internally displaced persons, half of whom were in Dili. Charges were soon expressed that the number of IDPs was inflated, either because IDPs were double-registering, or because people who had not been displaced managed to sign up for assistance. Donors and implementation agencies were also concerned that food aid could be used for political reasons and, more recently, that aid was politicised prior to elections.[21] This happened, in part, because food can be used as currency. The fact that the number of food aid recipients has remained practically unchanged since the onset of the crisis also raises questions concerning clientelism. However, reducing rations and limiting food aid would be a difficult task given the delicate political and humanitarian situation.

An inter-agency Humanitarian Coordination Group (HCG)[22] was established in May 2006 and its work was facilitated by the existing closely knit humanitarian community. However, the UN cluster approach mechanism was never introduced. According to observers, this was largely due to lack of knowledge of the cluster system on the part of the UN country team and the heads of agencies.[23] Nevertheless, attempts were made for coordination efforts to largely follow the cluster sectors.

International aid personnel suggested that UN agencies were too caught up in coordinating themselves and in feeding information into the different echelons of the UN system.[24] Furthermore, UN personnel themselves complained that the system is still unpredictable. Finally, many feel that the UN lacks the means to develop a holistic view in order to properly coordinate efforts and assist the government and international community to develop a transition strategy.

Conclusion

A year after the crisis, the situation remains bleak for the majority of those who are still displaced and who face severely deteriorated conditions. The current humanitarian situation requires a greater effort to assess and respond to the needs of the most vulnerable.[25] There is a need to focus on the IDP issue and develop a strategy for addressing needs in a coherent manner, and for a realistic exit. If UN Appeals had better reflected humanitarian needs from the start, donors would have been better able to uphold GHD *Principles*. This is at the heart of the GHD definition of humanitarian action (Principle 1) and refers to need-based funding through Consolidated Appeals (Principle 14), the need to "allocate humanitarian funding in proportion to needs" (Principle 6), and the need to "contribute responsibly, and on the basis of burden sharing" (Principle 14).

In relation to the humanitarian response and the Principles of Good Humanitarian Donorship, the case of Timor raises several issues and related challenges. First, there is a need for greater accuracy and realism in assessments, specifically with respect to timing and duration, to ensure an appropriate response. In Timor, the challenge of building effective local capacity in a new and fragile nation was underestimated.

Second, the need to take into account the complexity of providing needs-based humanitarian aid in a context of high levels of poverty.

Third, the importance of having an overall articulated humanitarian aid strategy that prioritises actions. Donors, as all actors in Timor, would welcome far more guidance on the planning and prioritisation of programmes. In this regard, the crisis highlighted the need for greater comprehensiveness and complementarity within and between the humanitarian response and development agendas. With its newly acquired income from oil reserves, foreign donors are eager to see the government assume a greater role and responsibility in responding to needs. Therefore, while the problem of displacement remains, there has been insufficient planning and synchronisation of activities both to build effective local capacity and to provide more durable or realistic solutions to specific pressing problems. At another level, the longer-term planning must prioritise activities and sectors—namely, housing and land ownership—so as to offer durable solutions to the crisis.

Finally, beneficiary involvement is all the more critical in a situation where the population has been greatly disempowered and traumatised. The Timorese must start to develop some sense of ownership of the current processes and international donors must make this an urgent priority.

References

Harrington, Andrew. 2007. "Significant secondary occupation of land and housing following the 1999 conflict." Internal Displacement Monitoring Centre. Available at: http://www.internal-displacement.org/idmc/website/countries.nsf/(httpEnvelopes)/77421D8707B05FCEC12573280034FF8C?OpenDocument

Office for the Coordination of Humanitarian Affairs. Financial Tracking Service. Available at: http://www.reliefweb.int/FTS/

Scheiner, Charles. 2006. "Suggestions for the Next United Nations Mission in Timor-Leste." San Francisco: Nautilus Institute. 13 July.

Transparency International. 2006. *Corruption Perception Index*. Berlin.

UNICEF. 2006. "Timor-Leste: UNICEF reports malnutrition among children displaced by violence." 3 July. Available at: http://www.un.org/apps/news/story.asp?NewsID=19077&Cr=Timor&Cr1=

———. 2007. "UNICEF Humanitarian Action: Timor-Leste Donor Update." 21 March. Available at: http://www.reliefweb.int/rw/RWB.NSF/db900SID/LSGZ-6ZHKRW?OpenDocument

United Nations. 2006a. "Report of the Independent Special Commission of Inquiry for Timor-Leste." Geneva: OHCHR. 2 October. Available at: http://www.ohchr.org/english/countries/tp/docs/ColReport-English.pdf

United Nations. 2006b. Security Council Resolution 1704. New York: United Nations. 25 August. Available at: se2.isn.ch/serviceengine/FileContent?serviceID=23&fileid=5821F5DB-9DAD-0F28-44DC-40892F5A311E&lng=en

United Nations Development Programme (UNDP). 2006. "Food shortage looms in Timor-Leste." Press release. 30 June. Available at: http://www.tl.undp.org/humanitarian/press_releases.html

World Food Programme. 2006. "Emergency Food Security Assessment." 9–14 June. Available at: http://www.mtrc.gov.tl/info/files/513/Timor%20Leste%20Emergency%20Food%20Security%20Assessment.pdf

World Bank. Available at: http://devdata.worldbank.org/external/CPProfile.asp?PTYPE=CP&CCODE=TMP

Notes

1   Harrington, 2007.

2   A sign of this trauma and perception of risk is the exodus that took place in January 2005, when the population, encouraged by security personnel, fled into the mountains, fearing a tsunami; some stayed up to 10 days in the belief that Dili had been destroyed.

3   United Nations, 2006a.

4   UNICEF (2006).

5   World Food Programme, 2006.

6   The SPHERE Project, launched in 1997 by a group of humanitarian NGOs and the Red Cross and Red Crescent movement, has developed the Humanitarian Charter and Minimum Standards in Disaster Response.

7   DARA field interview, June 2007.

8   ASEAN: Association of Southeast Asian Nations.

9   UNICEF, 2007.

10 Ibid.

11 DARA field interview, June 2007.

12 DARA field interview, June 2007.

13 United Nations, 2006b.

14 97 percent of global CERF funding is provided by OECD-DAC members.

15 DARA field interview, June 2007.

16 UNDP, 2006.

17 DARA field interview, June 2007.

18 Scheiner, 2006.

19 Timor-Leste became a sovereign state on 20 May 2002.

20 DARA field interview, June 2007.

21 DARA field interview, June 2007.

22 The HCG includes members of UNDP, UNICEF, the United Nations Population Fund (UNFPA), WFP, WHO, IOM, UNHCR, the International Committee of the Red Cross (ICRC), the International Federation of Red Cross and Red Crescent Societies (IFRC) and international and local NGOs such as CARE, Caritas, Christian Children's Fund, Catholic Relief Services (CRS), Cruz Vermelha do Timor-Leste, OXFAM, Plan International, and World Vision.

23 DARA field interview, June 2007.

24 DARA field interview, June 2007.

25 The WFP/FAO mission estimated that some 210,000 to 220,000 vulnerable rural people—not exclusively IDPs—will require emergency food assistance from October 2007 to March 2008.

Summary
2006—A Year of Emergencies

JANUARY

Palestinian Territories
As a result of the Hamas victory in parliamentary elections, international aid to the Palestinians was drastically reduced. There are over 4.4 million Palestinian refugees living in Gaza, West Bank, Jordan, Lebanon, and Syria. (ECHO, *2006 Annual Review*; UNRWA)

Côte d'Ivoire
Supporters of President Gbago engaged in violent protests in Côte d'Ivoire over what they consider to be UN intervention. As a result, 500 humanitarian and peacekeeping workers were forced to leave the country. As of 2006, there were an estimated 750,000 IDPs as a result of the conflict. (WHO, *Annual Report*; BBC; OCHA)

Malawi
Flooding displaced more than 40,000 people in Malawi and impeded the distribution of much needed food aid following the drought. (BBC; CAFOD)

FEBRUARY

Algeria
In Tindouf, heavy rains and floods in south-western Algeria left approximately 60,000 Sahrawi refugees without food or shelter. (MINURSO)

Bolivia
Heavy rains caused floods and mudslides, resulting in serious damage in the provinces of Santa Cruz, Beni, and La Paz. At least 19 people were killed and according to official data, over 38,800 families were affected, 4,200 of whom were living in temporary shelters. Houses, farming activities, and road infrastructure incurred severe damage. The government estimates damages of over US$260 million. President Morales secured several million dollars of aid from international agencies and foreign governments. (*BBC*; ReliefWeb)

Zimbabwe
After five years of drought the hope for a better harvest was destroyed by torrential rains at the beginning of the February. Life expectancy in the country is just over 30 years and 20 percent of adults are infected with HIV/AIDS. (*IRIN News*; ECHO, *2006 Annual Review*)

MARCH

Liberia
Charles Taylor, Former President of Liberia was arrested on 29 March 2006 in Nigeria and faces charges of war crimes and crimes against humanity. Taylor led the opposition group, the National Patriotic Front of Liberia in the civil war from 1989–1997 which left 150,000 people dead and approximately 850,000 refugees (*BBC*; UNMIL)

Horn of Africa, Kenya, Malawi, Zambia, and Mozambique
An estimated 11 million people in the Horn of Africa (Kenya, Malawi, Zambia, and Mozambique) faced food shortages as a result of severe drought. (ECHO, *2006 Annual Review*)

APRIL

Timor-Leste
A strike by dismissed soldiers degenerated into a series of riots, looting, and clashes between political opponents over the following months, which left 37 civilians dead, 1,650 homes destroyed and 2,350 damaged, and 150,000 people displaced (15 percent of the population. (DARA Crisis Report)

Ecuador
Over two months of intensive rain flooded the coastal provinces affecting over 140,000 people, 55,000 of whom were displaced and required humanitarian assistance. (ReliefWeb)

Guinea-Bissau
Following the fighting between the Senegalese separatist group in Csamance and Guinea-Bissau soldiers, 20,000 people sought humanitarian assistance. (ECHO, 2006 Annual Review; *BBC*)

MAY

Colombia
President Uribe won a second term in office on the promise to end 40 years of internal conflict. Colombia continues to suffer from decades of internal conflict, resulting in the displacement of more than 215,000 people in 2006 alone. It is estimated that, after Sudan, Colombia has the highest number of internally displaced persons (IDPs) in the world. (DARA Crisis Report; *Consultoría para los Derechos Humanos y el Desplazamiento* [Organisation for Human Rights and Displacement]; *BBC*)

Indonesia
An earthquake of 6.2 magnitude on the Richter scale caused at least 6,500 deaths and injured 50,000 more. Over 60,000 houses were destroyed and an estimated 300,000 damaged, leaving over 200,000 homeless. (WHO, *Annual Report*; IFRC, *2006 Annual Report*)

Pakistan
The government of Pakistan closed camps housing victims of the October 2005 earthquake. It was reported that at least 73,000 people died (including 1,300 in India and 4 in Afghanistan), over 128,000 were injured and more than 3,500,000 were left homeless as a result of the earthquake. (USAID, *2006 Annual Report*)

Sudan
Despite a peace accord signed in May by the Khartoum government and the main rebel faction in Darfur, the fighting continued. The security situation deteriorated, halting the delivery of humanitarian aid. The number of humanitarian workers killed since May rose to 13, with an estimated 4.5 million IDPs across the country. (*BBC*; Internal Displacement Monitoring Centre)

JUNE

Iraq
According to the United Nations, some 100 civilians per day were killed in violence in Iraq. Since the beginning of the war in 2003, some 655,000 civilians died and an estimated 60,000 were forced to leave their homes each month. (UNHCR; BBC)

China
An estimated 5 million hectares of winter crops were lost or damaged due to increased temperatures and drought in the provinces of Yunnan, Gansu, Ningxia, Inner Mongolia, and Hebei, among the poorest regions in China. The drought affected 18,000 people. (ReliefWeb; FAO)

Chechnya
After Chechen separatist Abdul-Khalim Saydullayev was killed by Russian government forces, Dokka Umarov took over the leadership. Despite improved security in 2006, there continued to be over 160,000 IDPs in Chechnya. (ReliefWeb; BBC)

2006

JULY

Democratic Republic of the Congo
The first free presidential and parliamentary elections in 40 years were held. Described as "forgotten" and "the deadliest conflict since World War II," 4 million people died between 1996 and 2003. In 2006, an estimated 1,200 people continued to die each day and 1.4 to 1.6 million persons were still displaced and unable to return to their homes due to the continuing violence. (DARA Crisis Report)

Lebanon
The conflict between Israel and Hezbollah from 12 July to 13 August ended with the deaths of some 1,200 Lebanese militants and civilians and the deaths of 19 Israeli soldiers and 43 Israeli civilians. Over 4,000 Lebanese and 894 Israelis were injured, and more than an estimated million in both countries were displaced. (ECHO, *2006 Annual Review*; *Guardian Unlimited*; *BBC*)

North Korea
Major floods washed away thousands of hectares of cultivated land, increasing the country's severe food shortage. North Korea stopped emergency assistance in 2005 and ECHO was allowed to resume its activities in April 2006. (ECHO, *2006 Annual Review*; UNICEF)

AUGUST

Uganda
A Cessation of Hostilities Agreement between the Ugandan government and the Lord's Resistance Army was signed on 26 August 2006, ending 20 years of violence by the LRA. Two million Ugandans were internally displaced and were living in camps in Northern Uganda to escape the threat of violence. (UN *News Centre*; ECHO, *2006 Annual Review*)

Afghanistan
Some 2.5 million Afghans were affected by drought, while over 6 million suffered food insecurity. (OCHA, CAP: WHO, *Annual Report*)

India and Bangladesh
Torrential rains and floods killed an estimated 1,000 people and affected at least 20 million in India and Bangladesh. (ECHO, *2006 Annual Review*)

Central African Republic
Tried in absentia, exiled Former President Ange-Félix Patassé of Central African Republic (CAR) was found guilty of embezzlement and fraud and sentenced to 20 years of hard labour. Almost 1 million people were affected by violence in CAR, and approximately 220,000 have been forced to leave their homes. (ReliefWeb; *BBC*)

Ethiopia
More than 630 people died, 196,000 were affected, and over 34,000 were displaced in Ethiopia following heavy rains and flooding. The regions of South Omo and Amhara were reported to be the worst affected. (OCHA; ECHO, *2006 Annual Review*)

SEPTEMBER

Niger
Over 46,000 people were affected by a cholera epidemic caused by floods. Niger was ranked last of 177 countries for a second year in the UNDP Human Development Report. In 2005–2006 over 2.5 million Nigeriens faced a food shortage, followed by a nutritional and health crisis. The International Monetary Fund (IMF) estimated that 63 percent of the population were living below the poverty line, while UNICEF estimated the 2005 under-five infant mortality rate at 256 for every 1,000 children. (DARA Crisis Report; ECHO, *2006 Annual Review*)

Burundi
The last active rebel group, the Forces for National Liberation (FNL), signed a ceasefire agreement with the government in Tanzania after 13 years of civil war. The conflict caused the internal displacement of some 117,000 Burundians as well as an estimated 30,000 refugees from the Democratic Republic of Congo. (BBC; ECHO, *2006 Annual Review*)

OCTOBER

Burma
The Burmese army launched an offensive in Northern Karen State, forcing thousands of civilians to seek refuge in the eastern border refugee camps in Thailand. Some 150,000 Burmese live in Thailand as refugees. (UN News Service; ECHO, *2006 Annual Review*)

Sri Lanka
Peace talks in Geneva between the Tamil Tigers and the government failed. Since December 2005, more than 3,000 people have been killed and 200,000 are internally displaced. (ECHO, *2006 Annual Review*; *BBC*)

NOVEMBER

Nepal
A ten-year internal conflict that had killed over 12,000 and displaced 100,000 people was ended after the Nepalese Prime Minister and the Maoists had reached an agreement and signed a peace accord. (*BBC*; ECHO, *2006 Annual Review*)

Haiti
Heavy rainstorms caused major flooding affecting 18,000 people. (ECHO, *2006 Annual Review*; IFRC, *2006 Annual Report*)

DECEMBER

Chad
The UN evacuated its humanitarian staff from eastern Chad after increased attacks. As a result, aid was reduced significantly for an estimated 250,000 refugees and affected people, including 75,000 IDPs. (ECHO, *2006 Annual Review*)

Philippines
Typhoon Durian struck the Philippines, causing more than 1,000 deaths. Some 300,000 people were affected during the typhoon season. (ECHO, *2006 Annual Review*)

---

1 In 2006, the World Health Organization declared a cholera epidemic.

4

PART FOUR

Donor Profiles

Introduction

This section provides donor profiles showing the salient features of each donor's humanitarian assistance.

For each donor, there is a short summary describing the key actors involved in the delivery of its humanitarian aid programme, the policies guiding those actors, how the donor has incorporated the GHD Principles, and the donor's interaction with other humanitarian partners.

The spiderweb chart "HRI scores by pillar" shows the donor's scores on each of the five pillars of the Humanitarian Response Index (HRI) 2007, relative to the DAC average. In a Table "HRI results," the best five and worst five indicators are listed, under their corresponding pillars, giving a glimpse of a donor's strengths and weaknesses across the HRI.

Next, key figures of a donor's humanitarian aid for 2005 and 2006 are presented in the Table "Overview of humanitarian aid," which includes estimates for total humanitarian aid, made up of reported bilateral humanitarian aid and estimates of multilateral aid. Bilateral humanitarian aid for 2005 and 2006 was taken from the OECD-DAC database and is defined as "bilateral transactions … undertaken by a donor country directly with a developing country." It includes all flows, regardless of the channel, for which "the donor effectively controls the disposal of the funds by specifying or "earmarking" the recipient or other aspects of the disbursement."[1]

The data for bilateral humanitarian aid suffer from a number of drawbacks. First, it appears that the 2005 figures have largely been adjusted to conform to the recent decision by the OECD Working Party on Statistics to exclude the funding category "Refugees in donor countries" as of 2006. This category was henceforth no longer to be included as humanitarian aid (DAC 700), but, rather, counted against Official Development Assistance (ODA)-eligible expenses in donor countries (DAC 93010). However, this does not appear to be the case for the 2006 figures, as these are still preliminary and, therefore, not adjusted.

It is also not clear whether these data on bilateral humanitarian aid are consistent in their treatment of the delivery of humanitarian aid by the military and of land mine clearance—counted separately as code DAC 15250—and (in the case of EU countries) of contributions to ECHO. Because there was no OECD figure for multilateral humanitarian aid within its multilateral ODA category, it was estimated based on data supplied by UNHCR, UNICEF, WFP, UNRWA, UN/OCHA, ICRC and IFRC, and captured receipts from a given donor of unearmarked or core funding.

The "Overview" Table also lists ODA, as well as funding to the Central Emergency Response Fund (CERF), and other funds committed under flexible terms. It offers calculations of humanitarian aid per capita, as a proportion of ODA and of gross national income (GNI). Donor data are shown as a share or average of the corresponding total DAC figures.

The Table "Response times by crisis type" shows the timeliness of a donor's funding. It estimates the average number of days a donor has taken to commit or disburse funds to natural disasters and to new and ongoing complex emergencies, all of which occurred in 2005 or 2006 and were subject to a Consolidated Appeals Process (CAP). The data are taken from OCHA/FTS, a real-time database (updated daily), and are based on an early May 2007 download.

For natural disasters, the dates of disbursement or commitment were compared to crisis onset, as defined by the International Disaster Database EM-DAT, compiled by the Centre for Research on the Epidemiology of Disasters (CRED) at the Université Catholique de Louvain. For complex emergencies, the dates of disbursement or commitment were compared to the UN Appeal launch dates. Consequently, funding for natural disasters also included funding flows outside the UN Appeal process as reported in the FTS, whereas for complex emergencies, only data on funding within the Appeal were used. The three categories included 82 natural disasters, 20 new complex emergencies, and 13 ongoing complex emergencies. When funding was committed or disbursed before the launch of an Appeal or natural disaster, this was taken to be same-day funding, as was typically the case where a donor's unused funding to another crisis was being reallocated.

The pie chart in the Figure titled "Main channels of humanitarian aid" shows how a donor's 2006 humanitarian aid was apportioned to the UN, the Red Cross and NGOs, or other. The UN category encompasses humanitarian receipts by UNHCR, UNICEF, WFP, UNRWA, and UN/OCHA, and includes CERF funding collected from these agencies, funds, and programmes. The Red Cross category encompasses humanitarian receipts by IFRC and ICRC based on their data. "Other" is a residual category and includes humanitarian flows to NGOs, governments, Red Cross national societies, intergovernmental organisations, NGOs, private organisations, and foundations. Shares are taken relative to the estimates of total humanitarian aid reported in the Table entitled "Overview of humanitarian aid."

For the UN category, the absolute number on which this share is based is likely to represent a fairly accurate reflection of the donor's funding to the UN agencies, funds, and programmes. However, the calculated share may be skewed, due to the inaccuracy of the estimate for total humanitarian aid, as described above. Moreover, the Red Cross category, based on data provided by the IFRC and the ICRC, is certain to be an underestimate of the funding the donor provides to the International Red Cross and Red Crescent Movement, as it does not cover the amounts of official funding to respective Red Cross national societies based in donor countries, which, in turn, fund both the IFRC and other Red Cross national societies on a bilateral basis. To date, there is no accurate estimate available to capture these flows.

The next Table, titled "Funding per emergency," lists the top ten emergencies that received donor funding in 2006, based on OCHA/FTS data. It shows the amounts in US dollars and the percentage of funding to each emergency as a proportion of a donor's total 2006 funding reported in the FTS. For each emergency, it also provides a split of the funding channelled through an Appeal and outside an Appeal. The second pie-chart, called "Regional distribution of funding," shows the same data split across regions. The final bar chart, called "Sectoral distribution of funding," shows the same data apportioned across CAP sectors.

---

1   See OECD (2006), DCD/DAC/STAT(2006)11/FINAL, available at:
    http://www.odamoz.org.mz/extra/DAC-CRSManual.pdf

Australia

AusAID, the Australian Agency for International Development, manages the coordination and communication of humanitarian action within its wider overseas aid programme. AusAID is an administratively autonomous agency within the Foreign Affairs and Trade portfolio. Its Humanitarian Action Policy (January 2005), strongly based on the GHD Principles, guides Australia's response to emerging humanitarian needs. AusAID is increasingly integrating its humanitarian and development activities to ensure appropriate coordination, with a strong Asia-Pacific regional orientation. Australia has established regional emergency response stand-by mechanisms together with key donors in the Pacific, empowering prevention and preparedness, and capacity building for reducing vulnerability to natural disasters. If government systems are failing, Australia's assistance is channelled directly to community organisations, NGOs or other civil society organisations. Australia contributes to United Nations Consolidated Inter-Agency Appeals, the WFP, and the ICRC as well as to the work on developing guidelines on consultation and participation of crisis-affected communities such as with ALNAP.

Source: http://www.ausaid.gov.au, Development Assistance Committee (DAC) Peer Review for Australia (OECD, 2006).

HRI scores by pillar

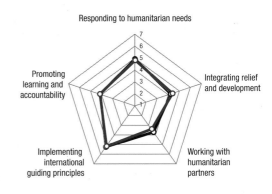

-O- Australia   -O- DAC average

HRI results

ADVANTAGES	SCORE	RANK
Integrating relief and development		
Encouraging better coordination with humanitarian partners	4.87	3
Strengthening local capacity to deal with crises	4.84	1
Strengthening resilience to cope with crises	5.30	1
Working with humanitarian partners		
Facilitating safe humanitarian access	4.73	1
Implementing international guiding principles		
Enhancing security	5.41	2

DISADVANTAGES	SCORE	RANK
Responding to humanitarian needs		
Distribution of funding relative to sector, forgotten emergency and media coverage	2.71	21
Independence	4.35	21
Neutrality	5.10	21
Implementing international guiding principles		
Affirming primary role of civilian organisations	4.56	21
Protecting human rights	5.28	21

Overview of humanitarian aid	Australia		Share of total DAC (%)	
	2005	2006[3]	2005	2006[3]
Total humanitarian aid, of which:	235.6	263.8	2.4	2.5
Bilateral humanitarian aid[1]	194.0	216.3	2.3	2.4
Multilateral humanitarian aid[2]*	41.6	39.9	2.7	3.1
Official development assistance	1,680	2,128	1.4	1.9
Funding to Central Emergency Response Fund**	n/a	7.6	n/a	2.6
Other funds committed under flexible terms[4]***	0.0	0.0	0.0	0.0
			DAC average	
Total humanitarian aid per capita (US$)	12	13	19	24
Total humanitarian aid / official development assistance (%)	14.0	12.4	8.9	9.4
Total humanitarian aid / GNI (%)	0.035	0.037	0.043	0.049

Notes: All data are given in current US$ m unless otherwise indicated.

1 Bilateral humanitarian aid is provided directly by a donor country to a recipient country and includes non-core earmarked contributions to humanitarian organisations but excludes category 'refugees in donor countries' (where 2006 data not available, estimated as average over last four years).

2 Core unearmarked humanitarian flows to UNHCR, UNICEF, WFP, UNRWA, UN/OCHA, ICRC and IFRC.

3 Preliminary; may include official support to asylum seekers in donor country.

4 Consists of IFRC's Disaster Relief Emergency Fund, Common Humanitarian Funds piloted in Sudan and Democratic Republic of Congo in 2006, Emergency Response Funds in 2006 for the DRC, Indonesia, Somalia, the Republic of Congo and Ethiopia and country Humanitarian Response Funds in 2005 for DPRK, DRC, Côte d'Ivoire and Somalia.

Sources: All data from OECD-DAC except: (*) UNHCR, UNICEF, WFP, UNRWA, UN/OCHA, ICRC and IFRC; (**) OCHA; (***) OCHA, IFRC; Common Humanitarian Fund for Sudan, Common Humanitarian Action Plan DRC 2007, US Federal Reserve.

Response times by crisis type, 2005–2006 (days)

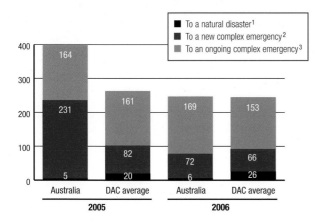

Legend:
- ■ To a natural disaster[1]
- ■ To a new complex emergency[2]
- ■ To an ongoing complex emergency[3]

2005 — Australia: 164, 231, 5
2005 — DAC average: 161, 82, 20
2006 — Australia: 169, 72, 6
2006 — DAC average: 153, 66, 26

Notes: [1]Average number of days between launch date of a UN Appeal and commitment or disbursement of funds to given ongoing emergencies. [2]Average number of days between launch date of a UN Appeal and commitment or disbursement of funds to given new emergencies. [3]Average number of days between onset of natural disaster (following CRED dates) and commitment or disbursement of funds to given natural disaster.
Source: OCHA/FTS (status early May 2007), Centre for Research on Epidemiology of Disasters (http://www.cred.be/).

Main channels of humanitarian aid, 2006

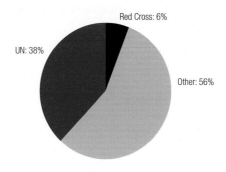

Red Cross: 6%
UN: 38%
Other: 56%

Notes: The UN category encompasses humanitarian receipts by UNHCR, UNICEF, WFP, UNRWA and UN/OCHA including CERF funding; the Red Cross category encompasses humanitarian receipts by IFRC and ICRC. 'Other' is a residual category and includes humanitarian flows to governments, Red Cross national societies, intergovernmental organisations, NGOs, private organisations and foundations. Shares are taken relative to total humanitarian aid reported in 'Overview of humanitarian aid' table.
Sources: UN/OCHA, UNICEF, WFP, UNRWA, UNHCR, ICRC, IFRC, OECD.

Funding per emergency, 2006

Crisis	US$ m	% of total	Inside an Appeal (%)	Outside an Appeal (%)
Lebanon Crisis, July	18.6	21.9	22.5	77.5
Pakistan	10.7	12.5	0.0	100.0
Sudan	10.3	12.1	90.6	9.4
Indonesia: Java Earthquake, May	5.6	6.6	13.6	86.4
Timor-Leste: Population Displacement, May	5.1	6.0	73.1	26.9
Palestinian Territories	3.6	4.2	100.0	0.0
Iraq (incl. Iraqi refugees in neighbouring countries)	3.4	4.0	0.0	100.0
Kenya	2.4	2.8	0.0	100.0
Sri Lanka	2.3	2.7	16.5	83.5
Somalia	2.1	2.4	45.8	54.2
Other	21.0	24.7	70.8	29.2
Total	85.1	100.0	44.4	55.6

Notes: Category 'Other' includes both provision of unearmarked funds (inside an Appeal to CERF and outside an Appeal) and other miscellaneous flows (only outside an Appeal) if applicable.
Source: OCHA/FTS.

Regional distribution of funding, 2006

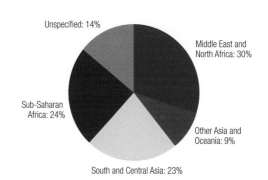

Unspecified: 14%
Middle East and North Africa: 30%
Other Asia and Oceania: 9%
South and Central Asia: 23%
Sub-Saharan Africa: 24%

Note: The number of Appeals financed per region: Europe (0), Latin America and Caribbean (0), Middle East and North Africa (2), Other Asia and Oceania (2), South and Central Asia (3), Sub-Saharan Africa (7), Unspecified (2).
Source: OCHA/FTS.

Sectoral distribution of funding, inside and outside an Appeal, 2006 (US$ m)

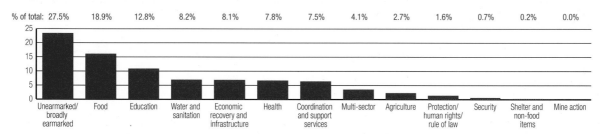

% of total: 27.5% 18.9% 12.8% 8.2% 8.1% 7.8% 7.5% 4.1% 2.7% 1.6% 0.7% 0.2% 0.0%

Categories: Unearmarked/broadly earmarked, Food, Education, Water and sanitation, Economic recovery and infrastructure, Health, Coordination and support services, Multi-sector, Agriculture, Protection/human rights/rule of law, Security, Shelter and non-food items, Mine action

Notes: 'Unearmarked/broadly earmarked' category consists of funding not yet applied by recipient agency to particular project or sector.
Source: OCHA/FTS.

Austria

The Austrian Development Cooperation and Cooperation with Eastern Europe (ADC) at the Federal Ministry for European and International Affairs sets Austria's humanitarian policy strategy and programmes. The Austrian Ministry of the Interior is in charge of coordinating international crisis response. The Austrian Development Agency (ADA) is the operational arm of the ADC, responsible for the implementation of all bilateral programmes and projects in partner countries and administering the corresponding budget. Its document, 'Internationale humanitäre Hilfe Leitlinie der Österreichischen Entwicklungs- und Ostzusammenarbeit' (June 2007) outlines Austrian humanitarian policy and is based on relevant guidelines of the EU, the OECD/DAC, international humanitarian conventions and the basic principles of GHD.

Source: http://www.ada.gv.at/, DAC Peer Review for Austria (OECD, 2004).

HRI scores by pillar

HRI results

ADVANTAGES	SCORE	RANK
Responding to humanitarian needs		
Distribution of funding relative to ECHO's GNA	6.36	4
Timely funding to onset disasters	6.15	3
Working with humanitarian partners		
Unearmarked or broadly earmarked funds	5.73	3
Implementing international guiding principles		
Implementing human rights law	5.80	3
Implementing international humanitarian law	6.40	5

DISADVANTAGES	SCORE	RANK
Responding to humanitarian needs		
Timely funding to complex emergencies	1.00	23
Integrating relief and development		
Consultation with beneficiaries on monitoring and evaluation	4.25	22
Funding to strengthen local capacity	1.02	22
Supporting long-term development aims	4.35	22
Working with humanitarian partners		
Funding UN Consolidated Inter-Agency Appeals	1.07	22

Overview of humanitarian aid	Austria 2005	Austria 2006[3]	Share of total DAC (%) 2005	Share of total DAC (%) 2006[3]
Total humanitarian aid, of which:	29.2	19.6	0.3	0.2
Bilateral humanitarian aid[1]	26.1	16.9	0.3	0.2
Multilateral humanitarian aid[2]*	3.0	2.6	0.2	0.2
Official development assistance	1,573	1,498	1.4	1.3
Funding to Central Emergency Response Fund**	n/a	0.0	n/a	0.0
Other funds committed under flexible terms[4]***	0.0	0.0	0.0	0.0
			DAC average	
Total humanitarian aid per capita (US$)	4	2	19	24
Total humanitarian aid / official development assistance (%)	1.9	1.3	8.9	9.4
Total humanitarian aid / GNI (%)	0.010	0.006	0.043	0.049

Notes: All data are given in current US$ m unless otherwise indicated.
1 Bilateral humanitarian aid is provided directly by a donor country to a recipient country and includes non-core earmarked contributions to humanitarian organisations but excludes category 'refugees in donor countries' (where 2006 data not available, estimated as average over last four years).
2 Core unearmarked humanitarian flows to UNHCR, UNICEF, WFP, UNRWA, UN/OCHA, ICRC and IFRC.
3 Preliminary; may include official support to asylum seekers in donor country.
4 Consists of IFRC's Disaster Relief Emergency Fund, Common Humanitarian Funds piloted in Sudan and Democratic Republic of Congo in 2006, Emergency Response Funds in 2006 for the DRC, Indonesia, Somalia, the Republic of Congo and Ethiopia and country Humanitarian Response Funds in 2005 for DPRK, DRC, Côte d'Ivoire and Somalia.
Sources: All data from OECD-DAC except: (*) UNHCR, UNICEF, WFP, UNRWA, UN/OCHA, ICRC and IFRC; (**) OCHA; (***) OCHA, IFRC; Common Humanitarian Fund for Sudan, Common Humanitarian Action Plan DRC 2007, US Federal Reserve.

Response times by crisis type, 2005–2006 (days)

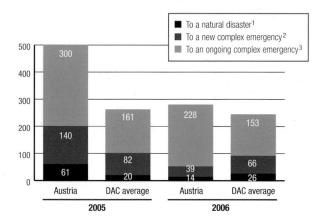

Legend:
- ■ To a natural disaster[1]
- ■ To a new complex emergency[2]
- ■ To an ongoing complex emergency[3]

2005:
- Austria: 300 / 140 / 61
- DAC average: 161 / 82 / 20

2006:
- Austria: 228 / 39 / 14
- DAC average: 153 / 66 / 26

Notes: [1]Average number of days between launch date of a UN Appeal and commitment or disbursement of funds to given ongoing emergencies. [2]Average number of days between launch date of a UN Appeal and commitment or disbursement of funds to given new emergencies. [3]Average number of days between onset of natural disaster (following CRED dates) and commitment or disbursement of funds to given natural disaster.
Source: OCHA/FTS (status early May 2007), Centre for Research on Epidemiology of Disasters (http://www.cred.be/).

Main channels of humanitarian aid, 2006

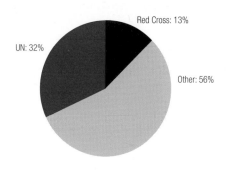

- Red Cross: 13%
- UN: 32%
- Other: 56%

Notes: The UN category encompasses humanitarian receipts by UNHCR, UNICEF, WFP, UNRWA and UN/OCHA including CERF funding; the Red Cross category encompasses humanitarian receipts by IFRC and ICRC. 'Other' is a residual category and includes humanitarian flows to governments, Red Cross national societies, intergovernmental organisations, NGOs, private organisations and foundations. Shares are taken relative to total humanitarian aid reported in 'Overview of humanitarian aid' table.
Sources: UN/OCHA, UNICEF, WFP, UNRWA, UNHCR, ICRC, IFRC, OECD.

Funding per emergency, 2006

Crisis	US$ m	% of total	Inside an Appeal (%)	Outside an Appeal (%)
Palestinian Territories	1.5	26.4	100.0	0.0
Ethiopia	0.6	11.6	0.0	100.0
Lebanon Crisis, July	0.6	11.4	0.0	100.0
Bosnia and Herzegovina	0.6	10.4	0.0	100.0
Sudan	0.4	6.9	100.0	0.0
Uganda	0.4	6.5	0.0	100.0
Kenya: Influx of Somali refugees, September	0.3	6.0	100.0	0.0
Ethiopia: Floods, August	0.3	5.8	0.0	100.0
Mozambique	0.3	5.3	0.0	100.0
Iraq (incl. Iraqi refugees in neighbouring countries)	0.1	2.5	0.0	100.0
Other	0.4	7.2	9.8	90.2
Total	5.5	100.0	40.0	60.0

Notes: Category 'Other' includes both provision of unearmarked funds (inside an Appeal to CERF and outside an Appeal) and other miscellaneous flows (only outside an Appeal) if applicable.
Source: OCHA/FTS.

Regional distribution of funding, 2006

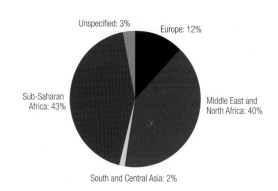

- Unspecified: 3%
- Europe: 12%
- Middle East and North Africa: 40%
- South and Central Asia: 2%
- Sub-Saharan Africa: 43%

Note: The number of Appeals financed per region: Europe (0), Latin America and Caribbean (0), Middle East and North Africa(1), Other Asia and Oceania (0), South and Central Asia (0), Sub-Saharan Africa (3), Unspecified (0).
Source: OCHA/FTS.

Sectoral distribution of funding, inside and outside an Appeal, 2006 (US$ m)

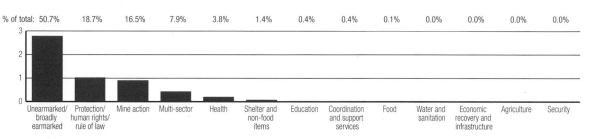

% of total: 50.7% / 18.7% / 16.5% / 7.9% / 3.8% / 1.4% / 0.4% / 0.4% / 0.1% / 0.0% / 0.0% / 0.0% / 0.0%

Categories: Unearmarked/broadly earmarked / Protection/human rights/rule of law / Mine action / Multi-sector / Health / Shelter and non-food items / Education / Coordination and support services / Food / Water and sanitation / Economic recovery and infrastructure / Agriculture / Security

Notes: 'Unearmarked/broadly earmarked' category consists of funding not yet applied by recipient agency to particular project or sector.
Source: OCHA/FTS.

Belgium

Both the Ministry for Foreign Affairs and the Ministry for Development Cooperation are responsible for Belgian humanitarian aid, which is administered by the Department for Special Programmes, focussing on emergency aid, rehabilitation and food aid and prevention, and the Department for Multilateral and European Programmes, both within the Directorate-General for Development Cooperation (DGDC). There are some other special programmes related to humanitarian assistance, in particular the Belgian Survival Fund, which exclusively finances programmes in Africa aimed at ensuring the survival of people threatened by hunger, under nourishment, poverty, and exclusion in countries faced with food shortage.

Source: http://www.dgcd.be/, DAC Peer Review for Belgium (OECD, 2005).

HRI scores by pillar

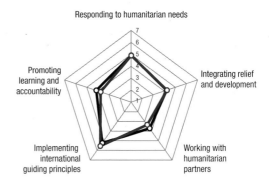

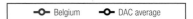

HRI results

ADVANTAGES	SCORE	RANK
Integrating relief and development		
Consultation with beneficiaries on design and implementation	5.26	2
Strengthening preparedness	5.38	1
Working with humanitarian partners		
Funding Red Cross Movement	7.00	1
Learning and accountability		
Encouraging regular evaluations	5.80	2
Supporting learning and accountability initiatives	5.59	2

DISADVANTAGES	SCORE	RANK
Responding to humanitarian needs		
Distribution of funding relative to historical ties and geographical proximity	1.00	22
Integrating relief and development		
Encouraging better coordination with humanitarian partners	3.91	20
Working with humanitarian partners		
Donor preparedness in implementation of humanitarian action	4.17	21
Promoting role of NGOs	5.12	20
Learning and accountability		
Number of evaluations	1.00	20

Overview of humanitarian aid	Belgium		Share of total DAC (%)	
	2005	2006[3]	2005	2006[3]
Total humanitarian aid, of which:	74.6	99.9	0.8	1.0
Bilateral humanitarian aid[1]	65.7	86.4	0.8	1.0
Multilateral humanitarian aid[2]*	8.9	10.8	0.6	0.9
Official development assistance	1,963	1,978	1.7	1.7
Funding to Central Emergency Response Fund**	n/a	2.7	n/a	0.9
Other funds committed under flexible terms[4]***	0.0	1.9	0.0	0.7
			DAC average	
Total humanitarian aid per capita (US$)	7	9	19	24
Total humanitarian aid / official development assistance (%)	3.8	5.1	8.9	9.4
Total humanitarian aid / GNI (%)	0.020	0.025	0.043	0.049

Notes: All data are given in current US$ m unless otherwise indicated.
1 Bilateral humanitarian aid is provided directly by a donor country to a recipient country and includes non-core earmarked contributions to humanitarian organisations but excludes category 'refugees in donor countries' (where 2006 data not available, estimated as average over last four years).
2 Core unearmarked humanitarian flows to UNHCR, UNICEF, WFP, UNRWA, UN/OCHA, ICRC and IFRC.
3 Preliminary; may include official support to asylum seekers in donor country.
4 Consists of IFRC's Disaster Relief Emergency Fund, Common Humanitarian Funds piloted in Sudan and Democratic Republic of Congo in 2006, Emergency Response Funds in 2006 for the DRC, Indonesia, Somalia, the Republic of Congo and Ethiopia and country Humanitarian Response Funds in 2005 for DPRK, DRC, Côte d'Ivoire and Somalia.
Sources: All data from OECD-DAC except: (*) UNHCR, UNICEF, WFP, UNRWA, UN/OCHA, ICRC and IFRC; (**) OCHA; (***) OCHA, IFRC; Common Humanitarian Fund for Sudan, Common Humanitarian Action Plan DRC 2007, US Federal Reserve.

Response times by crisis type, 2005–2006 (days)

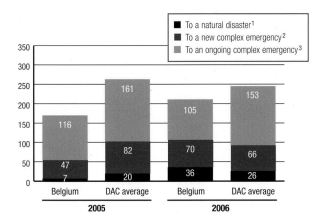

Legend:
- ■ To a natural disaster[1]
- ■ To a new complex emergency[2]
- ■ To an ongoing complex emergency[3]

2005: Belgium — 116, 47, 7; DAC average — 161, 82, 20
2006: Belgium — 105, 70, 36; DAC average — 153, 66, 26

Notes: [1]Average number of days between launch date of a UN Appeal and commitment or disbursement of funds to given ongoing emergencies. [2]Average number of days between launch date of a UN Appeal and commitment or disbursement of funds to given new emergencies. [3]Average number of days between onset of natural disaster (following CRED dates) and commitment or disbursement of funds to given natural disaster.
Source: OCHA/FTS (status early May 2007), Centre for Research on Epidemiology of Disasters (http://www.cred.be/).

Main channels of humanitarian aid, 2006

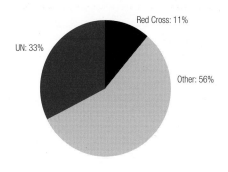

Red Cross: 11%
UN: 33%
Other: 56%

Notes: The UN category encompasses humanitarian receipts by UNHCR, UNICEF, WFP, UNRWA and UN/OCHA including CERF funding; the Red Cross category encompasses humanitarian receipts by IFRC and ICRC. 'Other' is a residual category and includes humanitarian flows to governments, Red Cross national societies, intergovernmental organisations, NGOs, private organisations and foundations. Shares are taken relative to total humanitarian aid reported in 'Overview of humanitarian aid' table.
Sources: UN/OCHA, UNICEF, WFP, UNRWA, UNHCR, ICRC, IFRC, OECD.

Funding per emergency, 2006

Crisis	US$ m	% of total	Inside an Appeal (%)	Outside an Appeal (%)
Democratic Republic of Congo	20.2	30.9	64.1	35.9
Palestinian Territories	8.9	13.6	14.8	85.2
Burundi	6.3	9.7	58.4	41.6
Great Lakes Region	5.8	8.9	100.0	0.0
Lebanon Crisis, July	1.9	2.9	33.6	66.4
Rwanda	1.8	2.8	0.0	100.0
Sudan	1.6	2.5	37.6	62.4
Uganda	1.5	2.3	65.0	35.0
Somalia	1.4	2.1	45.7	54.3
West Africa	1.4	2.1	100.0	0.0
Other	14.6	22.3	35.7	64.3
Total	65.5	100.0	50.8	49.2

Notes: Category 'Other' includes both provision of unearmarked funds (inside an Appeal to CERF and outside an Appeal) and other miscellaneous flows (only outside an Appeal) if applicable.
Source: OCHA/FTS.

Regional distribution of funding, 2006

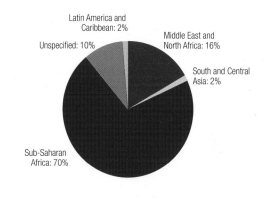

Latin America and Caribbean: 2%
Unspecified: 10%
Middle East and North Africa: 16%
South and Central Asia: 2%
Sub-Saharan Africa: 70%

Note: The number of Appeals financed per region: Europe (0), Latin America and Caribbean (0), Middle East and North Africa (2), Other Asia and Oceania (0), South and Central Asia (1), Sub-Saharan Africa (10), Unspecified (1).
Source: OCHA/FTS.

Sectoral distribution of funding, inside and outside an Appeal, 2006 (US$ m)

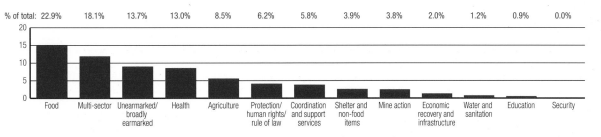

% of total: 22.9% 18.1% 13.7% 13.0% 8.5% 6.2% 5.8% 3.9% 3.8% 2.0% 1.2% 0.9% 0.0%

Food; Multi-sector; Unearmarked/broadly earmarked; Health; Agriculture; Protection/human rights/rule of law; Coordination and support services; Shelter and non-food items; Mine action; Economic recovery and infrastructure; Water and sanitation; Education; Security

Notes: 'Unearmarked/broadly earmarked' category consists of funding not yet applied by recipient agency to particular project or sector.
Source: OCHA/FTS.

Canada

The Ministry of Foreign Affairs is responsible for humanitarian policy and also plays a coordinating role in natural disasters. Canada's humanitarian aid programme is managed by the International Humanitarian Assistance and Food Aid Division of the Canadian International Development Agency (CIDA) as part of the Ministry of International Cooperation. CIDA has a small field presence which is development-focussed. The Department of National Defence has a crisis cell with its Rapid Disaster Assessment and Response Team. Finally, the Department of Immigration coordinates support to refugees. Canada's humanitarian aid policy is broadly aligned with the GHD Principles and the government has also formulated a GHD Domestic Implementation Plan.

Source: CIDA, http://www.acdi-cida.gc.ca, DAC Peer Review for Canada (OECD, 2002), GHD Domestic Implementation Plan for Canada.

HRI scores by pillar

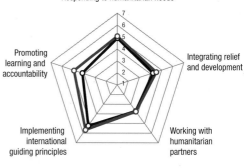

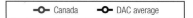

HRI results

ADVANTAGES	SCORE	RANK
Integrating relief and development		
Funding to international disaster risk reduction mechanisms	4.08	3
Strengthening preparedness	5.38	2
Working with humanitarian partners		
Funding Red Cross Movement	7.00	1
Implementing international guiding principles		
Implementing human rights law	5.80	3
Learning and accountability		
Number of evaluations	5.48	3

DISADVANTAGES	SCORE	RANK
Responding to humanitarian needs		
Distribution of funding relative to sector, forgotten emergency and media coverage	3.07	18
Integrating relief and development		
Funding to strengthen local capacity	2.06	18
Strengthening resilience to cope with crises	4.50	17
Working with humanitarian partners		
Flexible funding	4.75	17
Reducing earmarking	4.51	16

Overview of humanitarian aid	Canada 2005	Canada 2006[3]	Share of total DAC (%) 2005	Share of total DAC (%) 2006[3]
Total humanitarian aid, of which:	270.7	323.9	2.7	3.1
Bilateral humanitarian aid[1]	165.8	238.0	2.0	2.7
Multilateral humanitarian aid[2]*	104.8	63.9	6.8	5.0
Official development assistance	3,756	3,713	3.2	3.3
Funding to Central Emergency Response Fund**	n/a	21.9	n/a	7.6
Other funds committed under flexible terms[4]***	0.0	3.1	0.1	1.1
			DAC average	
Total humanitarian aid per capita (US$)	8	10	19	24
Total humanitarian aid / official development assistance (%)	7.2	8.7	8.9	9.4
Total humanitarian aid / GNI (%)	0.024	0.026	0.043	0.049

Notes: All data are given in current US$ m unless otherwise indicated.
1 Bilateral humanitarian aid is provided directly by a donor country to a recipient country and includes non-core earmarked contributions to humanitarian organisations but excludes category 'refugees in donor countries' (where 2006 data not available, estimated as average over last four years).
2 Core unearmarked humanitarian flows to UNHCR, UNICEF, WFP, UNRWA, UN/OCHA, ICRC and IFRC.
3 Preliminary; may include official support to asylum seekers in donor country.
4 Consists of IFRC's Disaster Relief Emergency Fund, Common Humanitarian Funds piloted in Sudan and Democratic Republic of Congo in 2006, Emergency Response Funds in 2006 for the DRC, Indonesia, Somalia, the Republic of Congo and Ethiopia and country Humanitarian Response Funds in 2005 for DPRK, DRC, Côte d'Ivoire and Somalia.
Sources: All data from OECD-DAC except: (*) UNHCR, UNICEF, WFP, UNRWA, UN/OCHA, ICRC and IFRC; (**) OCHA; (***) OCHA, IFRC; Common Humanitarian Fund for Sudan, Common Humanitarian Action Plan DRC 2007, US Federal Reserve.

Response times by crisis type, 2005–2006 (days)

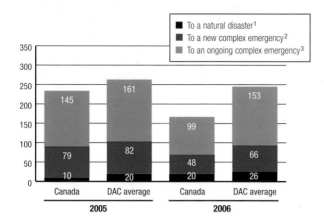

Legend:
- ■ To a natural disaster[1]
- ■ To a new complex emergency[2]
- ■ To an ongoing complex emergency[3]

2005
- Canada: 10 / 79 / 145
- DAC average: 20 / 82 / 161

2006
- Canada: 20 / 48 / 99
- DAC average: 26 / 66 / 153

Notes: [1]Average number of days between launch date of a UN Appeal and commitment or disbursement of funds to given ongoing emergencies. [2]Average number of days between launch date of a UN Appeal and commitment or disbursement of funds to given new emergencies. [3]Average number of days between onset of natural disaster (following CRED dates) and commitment or disbursement of funds to given natural disaster.
Source: OCHA/FTS (status early May 2007), Centre for Research on Epidemiology of Disasters (http://www.cred.be/).

Main channels of humanitarian aid, 2006

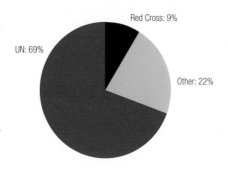

- Red Cross: 9%
- UN: 69%
- Other: 22%

Notes: The UN category encompasses humanitarian receipts by UNHCR, UNICEF, WFP, UNRWA and UN/OCHA including CERF funding; the Red Cross category encompasses humanitarian receipts by IFRC and ICRC. 'Other' is a residual category and includes humanitarian flows to governments, Red Cross national societies, intergovernmental organisations, NGOs, private organisations and foundations. Shares are taken relative to total humanitarian aid reported in 'Overview of humanitarian aid' table.
Sources: UN/OCHA, UNICEF, WFP, UNRWA, UNHCR, ICRC, IFRC, OECD.

Funding per emergency, 2006

Crisis	US$ m	% of total	Inside an Appeal (%)	Outside an Appeal (%)
Sudan	36.6	14.9	89.9	10.1
Haiti	15.5	6.3	0.0	100.0
Ethiopia	14.4	5.8	100.0	0.0
Palestinian Territories	12.4	5.0	100.0	0.0
Lebanon Crisis, July	11.1	4.5	47.9	52.1
Pakistan	10.1	4.1	0.0	100.0
Democratic Republic of Congo	9.7	4.0	95.5	4.5
West Africa	7.5	3.0	100.0	0.0
Uganda	7.4	3.0	94.1	5.9
Somalia	5.7	2.3	73.4	26.6
Other	**115.4**	**47.0**	**38.6**	**61.4**
Total	**245.6**	**100.0**	**55.9**	**44.1**

Notes: Category 'Other' includes both provision of unearmarked funds (inside an Appeal to CERF and outside an Appeal) and other miscellaneous flows (only outside an Appeal) if applicable.
Source: OCHA/FTS.

Regional distribution of funding, 2006

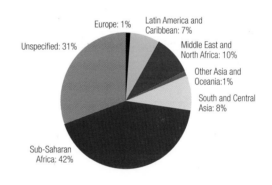

- Europe: 1%
- Latin America and Caribbean: 7%
- Middle East and North Africa: 10%
- Other Asia and Oceania: 1%
- South and Central Asia: 8%
- Sub-Saharan Africa: 42%
- Unspecified: 31%

Note: The number of Appeals financed per region: Europe (1), Latin America and Caribbean (0), Middle East and North Africa (2), Other Asia and Oceania (2), South and Central Asia (3), Sub-Saharan Africa (13), Unspecified (2).
Source: OCHA/FTS.

Sectoral distribution of funding, inside and outside an Appeal, 2006 (US$ m)

% of total: 49.2% | 33.4% | 5.4% | 3.0% | 2.8% | 1.4% | 1.1% | 1.1% | 1.1% | 0.8% | 0.7% | 0.0% | 0.0%

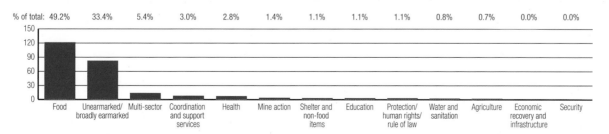

Categories: Food | Unearmarked/ broadly earmarked | Multi-sector | Coordination and support services | Health | Mine action | Shelter and non-food items | Education | Protection/ human rights/ rule of law | Water and sanitation | Agriculture | Economic recovery and infrastructure | Security

Notes: 'Unearmarked/broadly earmarked' category consists of funding not yet applied by recipient agency to particular project or sector.
Source: OCHA/FTS.

Denmark

The Ministry of Foreign Affairs, its agency DANIDA and the Ministry of Defence all play a role in humanitarian action. DANIDA does not have an operational capacity of its own and does not conduct its own needs assessment, relying instead on multilateral organisations and national NGOs to deliver its humanitarian aid. Danish humanitarian assistance is guided by its strategy document (Strategic Priorities in Danish Humanitarian Assistance, 2002) which predates the GHD Principles. It contains a strong rights perspective, is oriented toward protecting vulnerable groups and IDPs and integrating relief and development, including building local and regional capacity and prevention issues. Denmark has formulated a GHD Domestic Implementation Plan. The Humanitarian Contact Group, which brings together Danish public and private organisations, is the central body for planning and coordinating Danish humanitarian assistance. Denmark's International Humanitarian Service is part of international emergency preparedness efforts, and has a roster of 200 Danish people on standby and funds emergency response mechanisms established by Danish NGOs. Denmark commits approximately a quarter of its humanitarian flows through multi-year framework agreements to major humanitarian agencies.

Source: http://www.um.dk/, DAC Peer Review for Denmark (OECD, 2007), GHD Domestic Implementation Plan for Denmark.

HRI scores by pillar

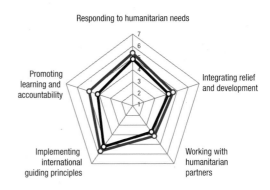

HRI results

ADVANTAGES	SCORE	RANK
Responding to humanitarian needs		
Timely funding	6.05	1
Integrating relief and development		
Strengthening local capacity to deal with crises	4.84	2
Strengthening resilience to cope with crises	5.05	2
Working with humanitarian partners		
Longer-term funding arrangements	4.60	1
Promoting role of NGOs	6.14	1

DISADVANTAGES	SCORE	RANK
Responding to humanitarian needs		
Commitment to ongoing crises	4.55	15
Funding in proportion to need	4.82	15
Funding to priority sectors	3.62	20
Independence	5.32	13
Working with humanitarian partners		
Predictability of funding (hard data)	2.74	13

Overview of humanitarian aid

	Denmark 2005	Denmark 2006[3]	Share of total DAC (%) 2005	Share of total DAC (%) 2006[3]
Total humanitarian aid, of which:	210.1	218.4	2.1	2.1
Bilateral humanitarian aid[1]	155.4	151.0	1.9	1.7
Multilateral humanitarian aid[2]*	54.7	59.0	3.5	4.6
Official development assistance	2,109	2,236	1.8	2.0
Funding to Central Emergency Response Fund**	n/a	8.4	n/a	2.9
Other funds committed under flexible terms[4]***	0.2	0.2	1.1	0.1
			DAC average	
Total humanitarian aid per capita (US$)	39	40	19	24
Total humanitarian aid / official development assistance (%)	10.0	9.8	8.9	9.4
Total humanitarian aid / GNI (%)	0.081	0.078	0.043	0.049

Notes: All data are given in current US$ m unless otherwise indicated.
1 Bilateral humanitarian aid is provided directly by a donor country to a recipient country and includes non-core earmarked contributions to humanitarian organisations but excludes category 'refugees in donor countries' (where 2006 data not available, estimated as average over last four years).
2 Core unearmarked humanitarian flows to UNHCR, UNICEF, WFP, UNRWA, UN/OCHA, ICRC and IFRC.
3 Preliminary; may include official support to asylum seekers in donor country.
4 Consists of IFRC's Disaster Relief Emergency Fund, Common Humanitarian Funds piloted in Sudan and Democratic Republic of Congo in 2006, Emergency Response Funds in 2006 for the DRC, Indonesia, Somalia, the Republic of Congo and Ethiopia and country Humanitarian Response Funds in 2005 for DPRK, DRC, Côte d'Ivoire and Somalia.
Sources: All data from OECD-DAC except: (*) UNHCR, UNICEF, WFP, UNRWA, UN/OCHA, ICRC and IFRC; (**) OCHA; (***) OCHA, IFRC; Common Humanitarian Fund for Sudan, Common Humanitarian Action Plan DRC 2007, US Federal Reserve.

Response times by crisis type, 2005–2006 (days)

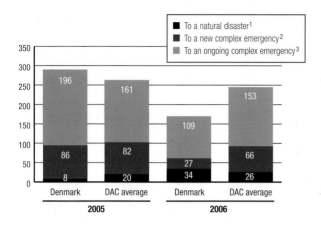

Legend:
- ■ To a natural disaster[1]
- ■ To a new complex emergency[2]
- ■ To an ongoing complex emergency[3]

2005: Denmark — 196, 86, 8; DAC average — 161, 82, 20
2006: Denmark — 109, 27, 34; DAC average — 153, 66, 26

Notes: [1]Average number of days between launch date of a UN Appeal and commitment or disbursement of funds to given ongoing emergencies. [2]Average number of days between launch date of a UN Appeal and commitment or disbursement of funds to given new emergencies. [3]Average number of days between onset of natural disaster (following CRED dates) and commitment or disbursement of funds to given natural disaster.
Source: OCHA/FTS (status early May 2007), Centre for Research on Epidemiology of Disasters (http://www.cred.be/).

Main channels of humanitarian aid, 2006

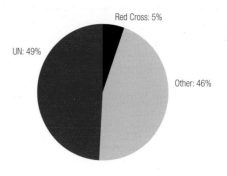

UN: 49%, Red Cross: 5%, Other: 46%

Notes: The UN category encompasses humanitarian receipts by UNHCR, UNICEF, WFP, UNRWA and UN/OCHA including CERF funding; the Red Cross category encompasses humanitarian receipts by IFRC and ICRC. 'Other' is a residual category and includes humanitarian flows to governments, Red Cross national societies, intergovernmental organisations, NGOs, private organisations and foundations. Shares are taken relative to total humanitarian aid reported in 'Overview of humanitarian aid' table.
Sources: UN/OCHA, UNICEF, WFP, UNRWA, UNHCR, ICRC, IFRC, OECD.

Funding per emergency, 2006

Crisis	US$ m	% of total	Inside an Appeal (%)	Outside an Appeal (%)
Sudan	29.4	15.4	53.7	46.3
Palestinian Territories	18.3	9.6	17.7	82.3
Afghanistan	7.1	3.7	0.0	100.0
Somalia	5.9	3.1	59.5	40.5
Iraq (incl. Iraqi refugees in neighbouring countries)	5.5	2.9	0.0	100.0
Angola	5.5	2.9	0.0	100.0
Sri Lanka	5.1	2.7	0.0	100.0
Kenya	4.6	2.4	0.0	100.0
Liberia	4.3	2.3	0.0	100.0
Lebanon Crisis, July	4.0	2.1	63.6	36.4
Other	101.0	52.9	22.1	77.9
Total	190.9	100.0	24.8	75.2

Notes: Category 'Other' includes both provision of unearmarked funds (inside an Appeal to CERF and outside an Appeal) and other miscellaneous flows (only outside an Appeal) if applicable.
Source: OCHA/FTS.

Regional distribution of funding, 2006

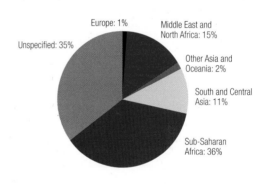

Europe: 1%, Unspecified: 35%, Middle East and North Africa: 15%, Other Asia and Oceania: 2%, South and Central Asia: 11%, Sub-Saharan Africa: 36%

Note: The number of Appeals financed per region are: Europe (1), Latin America and Caribbean (0), Middle East and North Africa (2), Other Asia and Oceania (0), South and Central Asia (2), Sub-Saharan Africa (9), Unspecified (2).
Source: OCHA/FTS.

Sectoral distribution of funding, inside and outside an Appeal, 2006 (US$ m)

% of total: 39.5% 27.2% 6.6% 6.1% 4.0% 4.0% 3.7% 3.4% 2.8% 1.5% 0.9% 0.3% 0.0%

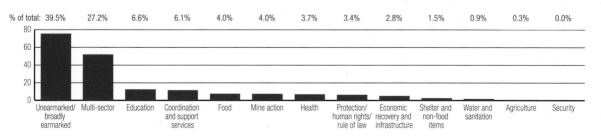

Unearmarked/broadly earmarked, Multi-sector, Education, Coordination and support services, Food, Mine action, Health, Protection/human rights/rule of law, Economic recovery and infrastructure, Shelter and non-food items, Water and sanitation, Agriculture, Security

Notes: 'Unearmarked/broadly earmarked' category consists of funding not yet applied by recipient agency to particular project or sector.
Source: OCHA/FTS.

European Commission

The European Commission's relief assistance is provided primarily through its Humanitarian Aid Department (ECHO). This aid is complementary to individual European Union (EU) countries' humanitarian assistance and makes up roughly half of the EU's total humanitarian funding. ECHO's mandate is defined in Council Regulation (EC No. 1257/96), which embraces the basic principles of humanitarian aid. Its current strategy is contained in its Operational Strategy document (SEC(2006) 1626) and reflects a growing commitment to GHD, in line with the current process underway that is expected to lead to a declaration 'Towards a European Consensus on Humanitarian Aid' by late 2007, which would provide the opportunity for the new Member States of the EU to commit themselves to the GHD. ECHO has a large field presence including 43 field offices and conducts its own needs assessments on which its financing decisions are based and on the basis of which it earmarks its aid. Its fast-track primary emergency decision allows it to provide up to €3m almost immediately to respond to sudden crises. In recent years, ECHO has redirected more of its aid budget to the multilateral organisations but NGOs continue to play an important role in delivering its aid.

Sources: ECHO, DAC Peer Review for the EC (OECD, 2007).

HRI scores by pillar

-O- European Commission   -O- DAC average

HRI results

ADVANTAGES	SCORE	RANK
Working with humanitarian partners		
Funding to NGOs	7.00	1
Predictability of funding	7.00	1
Learning and accountability		
Encouraging regular evaluations	5.86	1
Number of evaluations	7.00	1
Support to main accountability initiatives	7.00	1

DISADVANTAGES	SCORE	RANK
Responding to humanitarian needs		
Neutrality	5.70	17
Reallocation of funds from other crises	3.05	22
Timely funding to onset disasters	1.83	22
Working with humanitarian partners		
Flexible funding	4.47	19
Unearmarked or broadly earmarked funds	1.00	23

Overview of humanitarian aid	European Commission		Share of total DAC (%)	
	2005	2006[3]	2005	2006[3]
Total humanitarian aid, of which:	1,319.8	1,287.2	13.4	12.2
Bilateral humanitarian aid[1]	1,166.4	1,155.8	14.0	12.9
Multilateral humanitarian aid[2]*	153.4	131.4	9.9	10.3
Official development assistance	9,390	10,245	8.1	9.0
Funding to Central Emergency Response Fund**	n/a	0.0	n/a	0.0
Other funds committed under flexible terms[4]***	0.0	0.0	0.0	0.0
			DAC average	
Total humanitarian aid per capita (US$)	3	3	19	24
Total humanitarian aid / official development assistance (%)	14.1	12.6	8.9	9.4
Total humanitarian aid / GNI (%)	0.010	0.010	0.043	0.049

Notes: All data are given in current US$ m unless otherwise indicated.

1   Bilateral humanitarian aid is provided directly by a donor country to a recipient country and includes non-core earmarked contributions to humanitarian organisations but excludes category 'refugees in donor countries' (where 2006 data not available, estimated as average over last four years).

2   Core unearmarked humanitarian flows to UNHCR, UNICEF, WFP, UNRWA, UN/OCHA, ICRC and IFRC.

3   Preliminary; may include official support to asylum seekers in donor country.

4   Consists of IFRC's Disaster Relief Emergency Fund, Common Humanitarian Funds piloted in Sudan and Democratic Republic of Congo in 2006, Emergency Response Funds in 2006 for the DRC, Indonesia, Somalia, the Republic of Congo and Ethiopia and country Humanitarian Response Funds in 2005 for DPRK, DRC, Côte d'Ivoire and Somalia.

Sources: All data from OECD-DAC except: (*) UNHCR, UNICEF, WFP, UNRWA, UN/OCHA, ICRC and IFRC; (**) OCHA; (***) OCHA, IFRC; Common Humanitarian Fund for Sudan, Common Humanitarian Action Plan DRC 2007, US Federal Reserve.

Response times by crisis type, 2005–2006 (days)

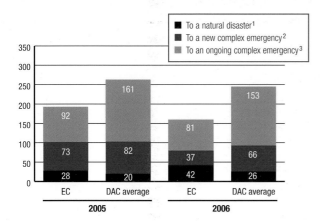

Legend:
- To a natural disaster[1]
- To a new complex emergency[2]
- To an ongoing complex emergency[3]

2005: EC — 28, 73, 92; DAC average — 20, 82, 161
2006: EC — 42, 37, 81; DAC average — 26, 66, 153

Notes: [1]Average number of days between launch date of a UN Appeal and commitment or disbursement of funds to given ongoing emergencies. [2]Average number of days between launch date of a UN Appeal and commitment or disbursement of funds to given new emergencies. [3]Average number of days between onset of natural disaster (following CRED dates) and commitment or disbursement of funds to given natural disaster.
Source: OCHA/FTS (status early May 2007), Centre for Research on Epidemiology of Disasters (http://www.cred.be/).

Main channels of humanitarian aid, 2006

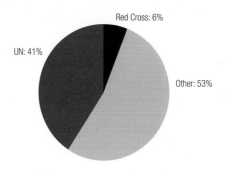

Red Cross: 6%
UN: 41%
Other: 53%

Notes: The UN category encompasses humanitarian receipts by UNHCR, UNICEF, WFP, UNRWA and UN/OCHA including CERF funding; the Red Cross category encompasses humanitarian receipts by IFRC and ICRC. 'Other' is a residual category and includes humanitarian flows to governments, Red Cross national societies, intergovernmental organisations, NGOs, private organisations and foundations. Shares are taken relative to total humanitarian aid reported in 'Overview of humanitarian aid' table.
Sources: UN/OCHA, UNICEF, WFP, UNRWA, UNHCR, ICRC, IFRC, OECD.

Funding per emergency, 2006

Crisis	US$ m	% of total	Inside an Appeal (%)	Outside an Appeal (%)
Sudan	154.1	17.1	76.2	23.8
Palestinian Territories	105.7	11.7	67.6	32.4
Democratic Republic of Congo	64.8	7.2	87.3	12.7
Lebanon Crisis, July	57.6	6.4	43.7	56.3
Zimbabwe	48.9	5.4	84.4	15.6
North Caucasus	37.6	4.2	63.0	37.0
Somalia	30.5	3.4	24.4	75.6
Uganda	28.0	3.1	43.7	56.3
Liberia	24.2	2.7	41.2	58.8
Nepal	22.6	2.5	67.9	32.1
Other	**327.8**	**36.4**	**24.2**	**75.8**
Total	**901.9**	**100.0**	**51.0**	**49.0**

Notes: Category 'Other' includes both provision of unearmarked funds (inside an Appeal to CERF and outside an Appeal) and other miscellaneous flows (only outside an Appeal) if applicable.
Source: OCHA/FTS.

Regional distribution of funding, 2006

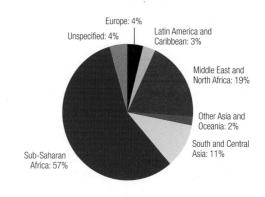

Europe: 4%
Unspecified: 4%
Latin America and Caribbean: 3%
Middle East and North Africa: 19%
Other Asia and Oceania: 2%
South and Central Asia: 11%
Sub-Saharan Africa: 57%

Note: The number of Appeals financed per region: Europe (2), Latin America and Caribbean (0), Middle East and North Africa (4), Other Asia and Oceania (2), South and Central Asia (3), Sub-Saharan Africa (21), Unspecified (0).
]Source: OCHA/FTS.

Sectoral distribution of funding, inside and outside an Appeal, 2006 (US$ m)

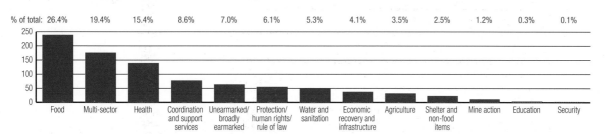

% of total: 26.4% | 19.4% | 15.4% | 8.6% | 7.0% | 6.1% | 5.3% | 4.1% | 3.5% | 2.5% | 1.2% | 0.3% | 0.1%

Food | Multi-sector | Health | Coordination and support services | Unearmarked/broadly earmarked | Protection/human rights/rule of law | Water and sanitation | Economic recovery and infrastructure | Agriculture | Shelter and non-food items | Mine action | Education | Security

Notes: 'Unearmarked/broadly earmarked' category consists of funding not yet applied by recipient agency to particular project or sector.
Source: OCHA/FTS.

Finland

The Unit for Humanitarian Assistance within the Ministry for Foreign Affairs is in charge of Finnish humanitarian assistance. The Civil Protection Mechanism under the Ministry of the Interior also has a mandate for specific international humanitarian interventions. The Ministry of Foreign Affairs is not an implementing agency and works mainly through multilateral channels and through exclusively Finnish NGOs and on the basis of their needs assessments. Until very recently, Finland's humanitarian assistance strategy was embedded within its overall development policy (Development Policy Government Resolution, 2004) but made no explicit mention of GHD Principles. In April 2007, the MFA adopted a new policy framework (Humanitarian Assistance Guidelines, 2007) that is firmly based on the GHD Principles.

Source: Ministry of Foreign Affairs, http://formin.finland.fi/, DAC Peer Review of Finland (OECD, 2003).

HRI scores by pillar

HRI results

ADVANTAGES	SCORE	RANK
Working with humanitarian partners		
Flexible funding	5.35	3
Funding IFRC Appeals	4.66	4
Funding Red Cross Movement	7.00	1
Supporting effective coordination efforts	5.19	5
Learning and accountability		
Funding of other accountability initiatives	7.00	1

DISADVANTAGES	SCORE	RANK
Responding to humanitarian needs		
Commitment to ongoing crises	3.80	23
Funding in proportion to need	4.33	21
Integrating relief and development		
Encouraging better coordination with humanitarian partners	3.71	22
Strengthening preparedness	4.00	22
Working with humanitarian partners		
Facilitating safe humanitarian access	3.18	21

Overview of humanitarian aid	Finland			Share of total DAC (%)	
	2005	2006[3]		2005	2006[3]
Total humanitarian aid, of which:	97.5	101.0		1.0	1.0
Bilateral humanitarian aid[1]	74.4	74.6		0.9	0.8
Multilateral humanitarian aid[2]*	23.1	21.3		1.5	1.7
Official development assistance	902	826		0.8	0.7
Funding to Central Emergency Response Fund**	n/a	5.2		n/a	1.8
Other funds committed under flexible terms[4]***	0.0	0.0		0.0	0.0
				DAC average	
Total humanitarian aid per capita (US$)	19	19		19	24
Total humanitarian aid / official development assistance (%)	10.8	12.2		8.9	9.4
Total humanitarian aid / GNI (%)	0.050	0.048		0.043	0.049

Notes: All data are given in current US$ m unless otherwise indicated.
1 Bilateral humanitarian aid is provided directly by a donor country to a recipient country and includes non-core earmarked contributions to humanitarian organisations but excludes category 'refugees in donor countries' (where 2006 data not available, estimated as average over last four years).
2 Core unearmarked humanitarian flows to UNHCR, UNICEF, WFP, UNRWA, UN/OCHA, ICRC and IFRC.
3 Preliminary; may include official support to asylum seekers in donor country.
4 Consists of IFRC's Disaster Relief Emergency Fund, Common Humanitarian Funds piloted in Sudan and Democratic Republic of Congo in 2006, Emergency Response Funds in 2006 for the DRC, Indonesia, Somalia, the Republic of Congo and Ethiopia and country Humanitarian Response Funds in 2005 for DPRK, DRC, Côte d'Ivoire and Somalia.
Sources: All data from OECD-DAC except: (*) UNHCR, UNICEF, WFP, UNRWA, UN/OCHA, ICRC and IFRC; (**) OCHA; (***) OCHA, IFRC; Common Humanitarian Fund for Sudan, Common Humanitarian Action Plan DRC 2007, US Federal Reserve.

Response times by crisis type, 2005–2006 (days)

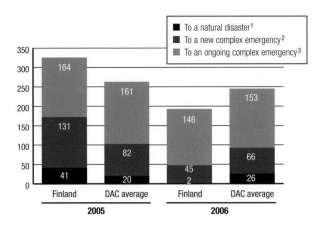

Legend:
- ■ To a natural disaster[1]
- ■ To a new complex emergency[2]
- ■ To an ongoing complex emergency[3]

2005 — Finland: 41, 131, 164; DAC average: 20, 82, 161
2006 — Finland: 2, 45, 146; DAC average: 26, 66, 153

Notes: [1]Average number of days between launch date of a UN Appeal and commitment or disbursement of funds to given ongoing emergencies. [2]Average number of days between launch date of a UN Appeal and commitment or disbursement of funds to given new emergencies. [3]Average number of days between onset of natural disaster (following CRED dates) and commitment or disbursement of funds to given natural disaster.
Source: OCHA/FTS (status early May 2007), Centre for Research on Epidemiology of Disasters (http://www.cred.be/).

Main channels of humanitarian aid, 2006

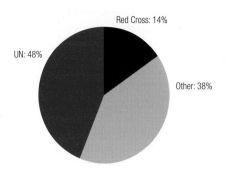

Red Cross: 14%
UN: 48%
Other: 38%

Notes: The UN category encompasses humanitarian receipts by UNHCR, UNICEF, WFP, UNRWA and UN/OCHA including CERF funding; the Red Cross category encompasses humanitarian receipts by IFRC and ICRC. 'Other' is a residual category and includes humanitarian flows to governments, Red Cross national societies, intergovernmental organisations, NGOs, private organisations and foundations. Shares are taken relative to total humanitarian aid reported in 'Overview of humanitarian aid' table.
Sources: UN/OCHA, UNICEF, WFP, UNRWA, UNHCR, ICRC, IFRC, OECD.

Funding per emergency, 2006

Crisis	US$ m	% of total	Inside an Appeal (%)	Outside an Appeal (%)
Palestinian Territories	8.9	12.2	44.2	55.8
Sudan	5.7	7.9	40.5	59.5
Democratic Republic of Congo	5.2	7.1	53.3	46.7
Southern Africa	3.8	5.2	0.0	100.0
Lebanon Crisis, July	3.7	5.0	82.9	17.1
Uganda	3.7	5.0	86.1	13.9
Somalia	2.4	3.3	89.3	10.7
Afghanistan	1.7	2.3	0.0	100.0
Kenya	1.6	2.2	0.0	100.0
Burundi	1.3	1.8	100.0	0.0
Other	**35.0**	**48.1**	**28.8**	**71.2**
Total	**72.8**	**100.0**	**39.4**	**60.6**

Notes: Category 'Other' includes both provision of unearmarked funds (inside an Appeal to CERF and outside an Appeal) and other miscellaneous flows (only outside an Appeal) if applicable.
Source: OCHA/FTS.

Regional distribution of funding, 2006

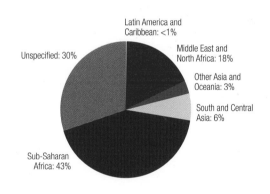

Latin America and Caribbean: <1%
Unspecified: 30%
Middle East and North Africa: 18%
Other Asia and Oceania: 3%
South and Central Asia: 6%
Sub-Saharan Africa: 43%

Note: The number of Appeals financed per region: Europe (0), Latin America and Caribbean (0), Middle East and North Africa (2), Other Asia and Oceania (0), South and Central Asia (1), Sub-Saharan Africa (9), Unspecified (2).
Source: OCHA/FTS.

Sectoral distribution of funding, inside and outside an Appeal, 2006 (US$ m)

% of total: 27.9% 27.1% 13.4% 9.1% 8.4% 6.9% 2.1% 1.8% 1.6% 1.4% 0.4% 0.0% 0.0%

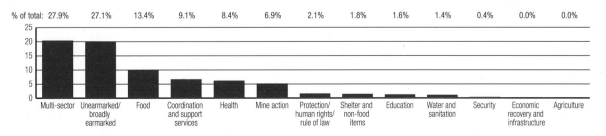

Multi-sector, Unearmarked/broadly earmarked, Food, Coordination and support services, Health, Mine action, Protection/human rights/rule of law, Shelter and non-food items, Education, Water and sanitation, Security, Economic recovery and infrastructure, Agriculture

Notes: 'Unearmarked/broadly earmarked' category consists of funding not yet applied by recipient agency to particular project or sector.
Source: OCHA/FTS.

France

The Ministry of Foreign Affairs is in charge of humanitarian action through two departments, the Délégation à l'Action Humanitaire (DAH), coordinating humanitarian action and the United Nations and International Organisation Division, which is in charge of multilateral aid. The Ministry of Development Co-operation also has a role to play in rehabilitation, governance and mine clearance. France performs bilateral humanitarian needs assessments with teams of six to eight experts, in coordination with their local embassies. In addition to needs, the decision to fund a crisis is also influenced by historical and linguistic ties and the political context. Based on a progressive alert system, an inter-ministerial operational group meets on a regular basis to assess individual crises. NGOs are only funded where other donors are involved. Although it is possible to fund international NGOs, in practice, French humanitarian funds primarily support French NGOs. The business community is also engaged in funding humanitarian emergencies and has benefited from tax breaks instituted in 2003 for this purpose.

Source: Ministry of Foreign Affairs, http://www.diplomatie.gouv.fr/

HRI scores by pillar

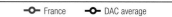

HRI results

ADVANTAGES	SCORE	RANK
Responding to humanitarian needs		
Commitment to ongoing crises	5.18	1
Timely funding to onset disasters	5.81	5
Implementing international guiding principles		
Implementing human rights law	5.80	3
Implementing international humanitarian law	6.70	2
Learning and accountability		
Funding of other accountability initiatives	3.54	4

DISADVANTAGES	SCORE	RANK
Responding to humanitarian needs		
Impartiality	4.77	22
Independence	4.17	22
Integrating relief and development		
Funding to strengthen local capacity	1.00	23
Strengthening resilience to cope with crises	3.38	22
Working with humanitarian partners		
Funding IFRC Appeals	1.00	22

Overview of humanitarian aid	France 2005	France 2006[3]	Share of total DAC (%) 2005	Share of total DAC (%) 2006[3]
Total humanitarian aid, of which:	58.2	749.7	0.6	7.1
Bilateral humanitarian aid[1]	27.9	715.9	0.3	8.0
Multilateral humanitarian aid[2]*	30.3	32.5	2.0	2.6
Official development assistance	10,026	10,448	8.6	9.1
Funding to Central Emergency Response Fund**	n/a	1.3	n/a	0.4
Other funds committed under flexible terms[4]***	0.0	0.0	0.0	0.0
			DAC average	
Total humanitarian aid per capita (US$)	1	12	19	24
Total humanitarian aid / official development assistance (%)	0.6	7.2	8.9	9.4
Total humanitarian aid / GNI (%)	0.003	0.033	0.043	0.049

Notes: All data are given in current US$ m unless otherwise indicated.

1 Bilateral humanitarian aid is provided directly by a donor country to a recipient country and includes non-core earmarked contributions to humanitarian organisations but excludes category 'refugees in donor countries' (where 2006 data not available, estimated as average over last four years).

2 Core unearmarked humanitarian flows to UNHCR, UNICEF, WFP, UNRWA, UN/OCHA, ICRC and IFRC.

3 Preliminary; may include official support to asylum seekers in donor country.

4 Consists of IFRC's Disaster Relief Emergency Fund, Common Humanitarian Funds piloted in Sudan and Democratic Republic of Congo in 2006, Emergency Response Funds in 2006 for the DRC, Indonesia, Somalia, the Republic of Congo and Ethiopia and country Humanitarian Response Funds in 2005 for DPRK, DRC, Côte d'Ivoire and Somalia.

Sources: All data from OECD-DAC except: (*) UNHCR, UNICEF, WFP, UNRWA, UN/OCHA, ICRC and IFRC; (**) OCHA; (***) OCHA, IFRC; Common Humanitarian Fund for Sudan, Common Humanitarian Action Plan DRC 2007, US Federal Reserve.

Response times by crisis type, 2005–2006 (days)

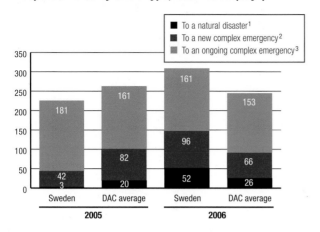

Legend:
- ■ To a natural disaster[1]
- ■ To a new complex emergency[2]
- ■ To an ongoing complex emergency[3]

2005
- Sweden: 181, 3, 42
- DAC average: 161, 20, 82

2006
- Sweden: 161, 52, 96
- DAC average: 153, 26, 66

Notes: [1]Average number of days between launch date of a UN Appeal and commitment or disbursement of funds to given ongoing emergencies. [2]Average number of days between launch date of a UN Appeal and commitment or disbursement of funds to given new emergencies. [3]Average number of days between onset of natural disaster (following CRED dates) and commitment or disbursement of funds to given natural disaster.
Source: OCHA/FTS (status early May 2007), Centre for Research on Epidemiology of Disasters (http://www.cred.be/).

Main channels of humanitarian aid, 2006

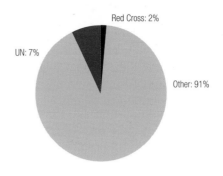

Red Cross: 2%
UN: 7%
Other: 91%

Notes: The UN category encompasses humanitarian receipts by UNHCR, UNICEF, WFP, UNRWA and UN/OCHA including CERF funding; the Red Cross category encompasses humanitarian receipts by IFRC and ICRC. 'Other' is a residual category and includes humanitarian flows to governments, Red Cross national societies, intergovernmental organisations, NGOs, private organisations and foundations. Shares are taken relative to total humanitarian aid reported in 'Overview of humanitarian aid' table.
Sources: UN/OCHA, UNICEF, WFP, UNRWA, UNHCR, ICRC, IFRC, OECD.

Funding per emergency, 2006

Crisis	US$ m	% of total	Inside an Appeal (%)	Outside an Appeal (%)
Lebanon Crisis, July	22.3	22.8	22.8	77.2
Palestinian Territories	11.1	11.4	18.3	81.7
Chad	6.0	6.2	74.4	25.6
Sudan	4.9	5.0	58.3	41.7
Niger	4.1	4.2	0.0	100.0
West Africa	3.7	3.8	100.0	0.0
Central African Republic	2.9	2.9	93.6	6.4
Democratic Republic of Congo	2.9	2.9	57.4	42.6
Uganda	2.5	2.5	64.7	35.3
Yemen	2.0	2.0	0.0	100.0
Other	**35.3**	**36.1**	**13.2**	**86.8**
Total	**97.8**	**100.0**	**29.5**	**70.5**

Notes: Category 'Other' includes both provision of unearmarked funds (inside an Appeal to CERF and outside an Appeal) and other miscellaneous flows (only outside an Appeal) if applicable.
Source: OCHA/FTS.

Regional distribution of funding, 2006

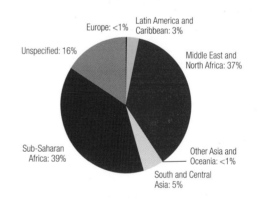

Europe: <1%
Latin America and Caribbean: 3%
Unspecified: 16%
Middle East and North Africa: 37%
Sub-Saharan Africa: 39%
Other Asia and Oceania: <1%
South and Central Asia: 5%

Note: The number of Appeals financed per region: Europe (0), Latin America and Caribbean (0), Middle East and North Africa (2), Other Asia and Oceania (0), South and Central Asia (2), Sub-Saharan Africa (12), Unspecified (1).
Source: OCHA/FTS.

Sectoral distribution of funding, inside and outside an Appeal, 2006 (US$ m)

% of total: 31.6% 14.8% 14.7% 12.7% 12.0% 5.6% 3.4% 3.0% 1.7% 0.5% 0.1% 0.0% 0.0%

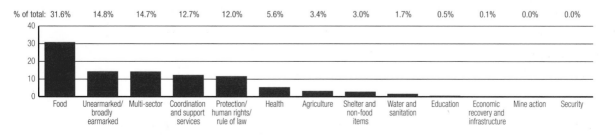

Food | Unearmarked/ broadly earmarked | Multi-sector | Coordination and support services | Protection/ human rights/ rule of law | Health | Agriculture | Shelter and non-food items | Water and sanitation | Education | Economic recovery and infrastructure | Mine action | Security

Notes: 'Unearmarked/broadly earmarked' category consists of funding not yet applied by recipient agency to particular project or sector.
Source: OCHA/FTS.

Germany

The Humanitarian Task Force within the Federal Foreign Office (FFO) is responsible for emergency response, humanitarian mine action, and also for providing some funds for disaster risk reduction. The Ministry for Economic Cooperation and Development (BMZ) oversees the integration of relief and development activities. The FFO prepares a special humanitarian report to parliament on a four-year cycle ('Bericht der Bundesregierung über die deutsche humanitäre Hilfe im Ausland 2002 bis 2005'), outlining its main policies. This document expressly mentions the GHD Principles as the basis for its humanitarian action. National and international NGOs receive a large share of German aid and many are present at bi-monthly coordination meetings with the FFO but do not benefit from framework agreements. The FFO relies primarily on needs assessments by NGOs, and on additional information from their embassies, ECHO, the Red Cross Movement or the UN. Humanitarian aid funding is earmarked by law to concrete programmes although some UN agencies can receive unearmarked funds. The BMZ can offer three-year funding programmes that are renewed annually.

Source: Federal Foreign Office, http://www.auswaertiges-amt.de, DAC Peer Review for Germany (OECD, 2006).

HRI scores by pillar

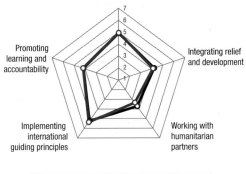

Germany — DAC average

HRI results

ADVANTAGES	SCORE	RANK
Working with humanitarian partners		
Funding to NGOs	7.00	1
Promoting role of NGOs	5.86	5
Implementing international guiding principles		
Affirming primary role of civilian organisations	5.82	4
Implementing international humanitarian law	6.40	5
Learning and accountability		
Supporting accountability in humanitarian action	5.92	3

DISADVANTAGES	SCORE	RANK
Responding to humanitarian needs		
Commitment to ongoing crises	4.31	19
Timely funding to complex emergencies	2.65	20
Working with humanitarian partners		
Funding CERF	1.00	19
Funding UN Consolidated Inter-Agency Appeals	1.17	19
Unearmarked or broadly earmarked funds	1.60	21

Overview of humanitarian aid	Germany		Share of total DAC (%)	
	2005	2006[3]	2005	2006[3]
Total humanitarian aid, of which:	332.8	291.1	3.4	2.8
Bilateral humanitarian aid[1]	316.6	273.8	3.8	3.1
Multilateral humanitarian aid[2]*	16.2	17.3	1.1	1.4
Official development assistance	10,082	10,351	8.7	9.1
Funding to Central Emergency Response Fund**	n/a	0.0	n/a	0.0
Other funds committed under flexible terms[4]***	0.0	0.0	0.0	0.0
			DAC average	
Total humanitarian aid per capita (US$)	4	4	19	24
Total humanitarian aid / official development assistance (%)	3.3	2.8	8.9	9.4
Total humanitarian aid / GNI (%)	0.012	0.010	0.043	0.049

Notes: All data are given in current US$ m unless otherwise indicated.
1 Bilateral humanitarian aid is provided directly by a donor country to a recipient country and includes non-core earmarked contributions to humanitarian organisations but excludes category 'refugees in donor countries' (where 2006 data not available, estimated as average over last four years).
2 Core unearmarked humanitarian flows to UNHCR, UNICEF, WFP, UNRWA, UN/OCHA, ICRC and IFRC.
3 Preliminary; may include official support to asylum seekers in donor country.
4 Consists of IFRC's Disaster Relief Emergency Fund, Common Humanitarian Funds piloted in Sudan and Democratic Republic of Congo in 2006, Emergency Response Funds in 2006 for the DRC, Indonesia, Somalia, the Republic of Congo and Ethiopia and country Humanitarian Response Funds in 2005 for DPRK, DRC, Côte d'Ivoire and Somalia.
Sources: All data from OECD-DAC except: (*) UNHCR, UNICEF, WFP, UNRWA, UN/OCHA, ICRC and IFRC; (**) OCHA; (***) OCHA, IFRC; Common Humanitarian Fund for Sudan, Common Humanitarian Action Plan DRC 2007, US Federal Reserve.

Response times by crisis type, 2005–2006 (days)

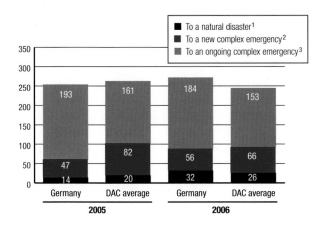

Notes: [1]Average number of days between launch date of a UN Appeal and commitment or disbursement of funds to given ongoing emergencies. [2]Average number of days between launch date of a UN Appeal and commitment or disbursement of funds to given new emergencies. [3]Average number of days between onset of natural disaster (following CRED dates) and commitment or disbursement of funds to given natural disaster.
Source: OCHA/FTS (status early May 2007), Centre for Research on Epidemiology of Disasters (http://www.cred.be/).

Main channels of humanitarian aid, 2006

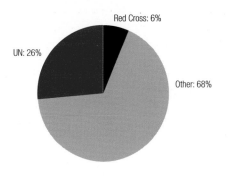

Notes: The UN category encompasses humanitarian receipts by UNHCR, UNICEF, WFP, UNRWA and UN/OCHA including CERF funding; the Red Cross category encompasses humanitarian receipts by IFRC and ICRC. 'Other' is a residual category and includes humanitarian flows to governments, Red Cross national societies, intergovernmental organisations, NGOs, private organisations and foundations. Shares are taken relative to total humanitarian aid reported in 'Overview of humanitarian aid' table.
Sources: UN/OCHA, UNICEF, WFP, UNRWA, UNHCR, ICRC, IFRC, OECD.

Funding per emergency, 2006

Crisis	US$ m	% of total	Inside an Appeal (%)	Outside an Appeal (%)
Sudan	16.9	9.1	33.9	66.1
Afghanistan	16.4	8.8	0.0	100.0
Democratic Republic of Congo	13.6	7.3	41.9	58.1
Chad	8.8	4.7	46.2	53.8
Uganda	8.3	4.5	15.1	84.9
Palestinian Territories	8.0	4.3	39.0	61.0
Great Lakes Region	7.2	3.9	35.5	64.5
Lebanon Crisis, July	6.1	3.3	62.1	37.9
Somalia	5.8	3.1	48.1	51.9
Bosnia and Herzegovina	4.9	2.7	0.0	100.0
Other	89.6	48.3	9.4	90.6
Total	185.6	100.0	20.1	79.9

Notes: Category 'Other' includes both provision of unearmarked funds (inside an Appeal to CERF and outside an Appeal) and other miscellaneous flows (only outside an Appeal) if applicable.
Source: OCHA/FTS.

Regional distribution of funding, 2006

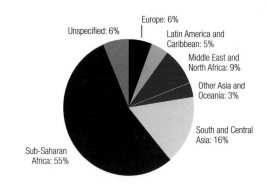

Note: The number of Appeals financed per region: Europe (1), Latin America and Caribbean (0), Middle East and North Africa (2), Other Asia and Oceania (1), South and Central Asia (3). Sub-Saharan Africa (14), Unspecified (0).
Source: OCHA/FTS.

Sectoral distribution of funding, inside and outside an Appeal, 2006 (US$ m)

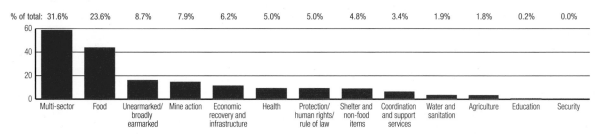

Notes: 'Unearmarked/broadly earmarked' category consists of funding not yet applied by recipient agency to particular project or sector.
Source: OCHA/FTS.

Greece

The Foreign Ministry's International Development Cooperation Department (Hellenic Aid) is responsible for monitoring, coordinating, supervising and promoting humanitarian assistance. Humanitarian aid is structured under two pillars: emergency humanitarian and food programmes (which can be more protracted and address multi-year crises) and emergency distress relief activities, such as the provision of gifts in-kind, mobilisation of Greek civil society and provision of support, personnel, and other resources from other ministries, particularly Defence and the Ministries of Health and Civil Protection. Policies and principles underpinning Greek humanitarian assistance are set out within the five-year programme approved by the Inter-Ministerial Committee (EOSDOS). Annual planning is based on this framework, with Hellenic Aid requesting proposals for its humanitarian programme, identifying countries and sectoral priorities which should guide implementing organisations. Greek does not carry out formal needs assessment, relying on large NGOs for this purpose and, if relevant on the Greek diaspora of a particular country. By law, Hellenic Aid can only finance Greek or international NGOs and requires NGOs to have a local partner in affected countries. Its contributions to multilateral organisations are typically earmarked.

Source: Hellenic Aid, DAC Peer Review for Greece (OECD, 2006).

HRI scores by pillar

HRI results

ADVANTAGES	SCORE	RANK
Responding to humanitarian needs		
Funding to priority sectors	4.85	11
Working with humanitarian partners		
Funding quick disbursement mechanisms	1.00	10
Implementing international guiding principles		
Implementing human rights law	4.60	12

DISADVANTAGES	SCORE	RANK
Responding to humanitarian needs		
Funding in proportion to need	3.80	23
Impartiality	4.76	23
Integrating relief and development		
Strengthening preparedness	3.29	23
Working with humanitarian partners		
Predictability of funding (Survey)	3.44	23
Learning and accountability		
Supporting accountability in humanitarian action	4.82	23

Overview of humanitarian aid	Greece 2005	Greece 2006[3]	Share of total DAC (%) 2005	2006[3]
Total humanitarian aid, of which:	19.3	21.7	0.2	0.2
Bilateral humanitarian aid[1]	17.1	19.2	0.2	0.2
Multilateral humanitarian aid[2]*	2.2	2.3	0.1	0.2
Official development assistance	384	424	0.3	0.4
Funding to Central Emergency Response Fund**	n/a	0.1	n/a	0.0
Other funds committed under flexible terms[4]***	0.0	0.0	0.0	0.0
			DAC average	
Total humanitarian aid per capita (US$)	2	2	19	24
Total humanitarian aid / official development assistance (%)	5.0	5.1	8.9	9.4
Total humanitarian aid / GNI (%)	0.009	0.009	0.043	0.049

Notes: All data are given in current US$ m unless otherwise indicated.
1 Bilateral humanitarian aid is provided directly by a donor country to a recipient country and includes non-core earmarked contributions to humanitarian organisations but excludes category 'refugees in donor countries' (where 2006 data not available, estimated as average over last four years).
2 Core unearmarked humanitarian flows to UNHCR, UNICEF, WFP, UNRWA, UN/OCHA, ICRC and IFRC.
3 Preliminary; may include official support to asylum seekers in donor country.
4 Consists of IFRC's Disaster Relief Emergency Fund, Common Humanitarian Funds piloted in Sudan and Democratic Republic of Congo in 2006, Emergency Response Funds in 2006 for the DRC, Indonesia, Somalia, the Republic of Congo and Ethiopia and country Humanitarian Response Funds in 2005 for DPRK, DRC, Côte d'Ivoire and Somalia.
Sources: All data from OECD-DAC except: (*) UNHCR, UNICEF, WFP, UNRWA, UN/OCHA, ICRC and IFRC; (**) OCHA; (***) OCHA, IFRC; Common Humanitarian Fund for Sudan, Common Humanitarian Action Plan DRC 2007, US Federal Reserve.

Response times by crisis type, 2005–2006 (days)

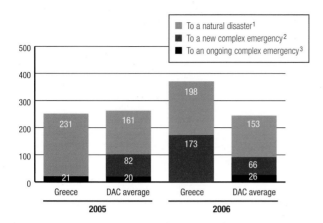

- ■ To a natural disaster[1]
- ■ To a new complex emergency[2]
- ■ To an ongoing complex emergency[3]

Notes: [1]Average number of days between launch date of a UN Appeal and commitment or disbursement of funds to given ongoing emergencies. [2]Average number of days between launch date of a UN Appeal and commitment or disbursement of funds to given new emergencies. In 2005, Greece did not commit or disburse funds to new emergencies. [3]Average number of days between onset of natural disaster (following CRED dates) and commitment or disbursement of funds to given natural disaster. In 2006, Greece committed or disbursed funds to natural disasters at onset.
Source: OCHA/FTS (status early May 2007), Centre for Research on Epidemiology of Disasters (http://www.cred.be/).

Main channels of humanitarian aid, 2006

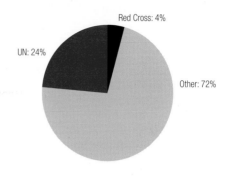

Notes: The UN category encompasses humanitarian receipts by UNHCR, UNICEF, WFP, UNRWA and UN/OCHA including CERF funding; the Red Cross category encompasses humanitarian receipts by IFRC and ICRC. 'Other' is a residual category and includes humanitarian flows to governments, Red Cross national societies, intergovernmental organisations, NGOs, private organisations and foundations. Shares are taken relative to total humanitarian aid reported in 'Overview of humanitarian aid' table.
Sources: UN/OCHA, UNICEF, WFP, UNRWA, UNHCR, ICRC, IFRC, OECD.

Funding per emergency, 2006

Crisis	US$ m	% of total	Inside an Appeal (%)	Outside an Appeal (%)
Lebanon Crisis, July	2.52	53.80	13.14	86.86
Democratic Republic of Congo	0.66	14.05	100.00	0.00
West Africa	0.62	13.28	100.00	0.00
Sudan	0.25	5.36	100.00	0.00
Indonesia: Java Earthquake, May	0.25	5.30	0.00	100.00
Palestinian Territories	0.18	3.75	100.00	0.00
Central African Republic	0.07	1.56	100.00	0.00
Zimbabwe	0.06	1.34	100.00	0.00
Burundi	0.05	1.01	100.00	0.00
Other	**0.03**	**0.56**	**0.00**	**100.00**
Total	**4.69**	**100.00**	**47.41**	**52.59**

Notes: Category 'Other' includes both provision of unearmarked funds (inside an Appeal to CERF and outside an Appeal) and other miscellaneous flows (only outside an Appeal) if applicable.
Source: OCHA/FTS.

Regional distribution of funding, 2006

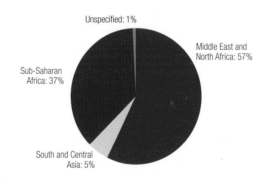

Note: The number of Appeals financed per region: Europe (0), Latin America and Caribbean (0), Middle East and North Africa (2), Other Asia and Oceania (0), South and Central Asia (0), Sub-Saharan Africa (6), Unspecified (0).
Source: OCHA/FTS.

Sectoral distribution of funding, inside and outside an Appeal, 2006 (US$ m)

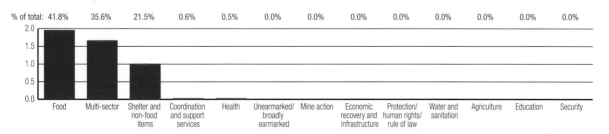

| % of total: | 41.8% | 35.6% | 21.5% | 0.6% | 0.5% | 0.0% | 0.0% | 0.0% | 0.0% | 0.0% | 0.0% | 0.0% | 0.0% |

Food / Multi-sector / Shelter and non-food items / Coordination and support services / Health / Unearmarked/broadly earmarked / Mine action / Economic recovery and infrastructure / Protection/human rights/rule of law / Water and sanitation / Agriculture / Education / Security

Notes: 'Unearmarked/broadly earmarked' category consists of funding not yet applied by recipient agency to particular project or sector.
Source: OCHA/FTS.

Ireland

Irish Aid, the official development co-operation programme managed by the Department of Foreign Affairs has primary responsibility for the government's overall international humanitarian response. In addition, the Irish Defence Forces and the Department of Agriculture have minor roles. Irish humanitarian assistance is guided by the Government White Paper on Irish Aid (2007), which fully embraces the GHD Principles. Ireland also has a GHD Domestic Implementation Plan. Irish Aid's priorities are to target needs and forgotten emergencies. It works with all partners, including governments and local organisations, Irish and international NGOs, as well as the Red Cross Movement and multilateral organisations. Irish aid places a strong emphasis on disaster risk reduction and preparedness.

Source: Irish Aid, http://www.irishaid.gov.ie, GHD Domestic Implementation Plan for Ireland.

HRI scores by pillar

HRI results

ADVANTAGES	SCORE	RANK
Responding to humanitarian needs		
Independence	6.13	1
Timely funding to complex emergencies	6.40	2
Integrating relief and development		
Funding to strengthen local capacity	7.00	1
Working with humanitarian partners		
Funding to NGOs	7.00	1
Learning and accountability		
Support to main accountability initiatives	6.33	2

DISADVANTAGES	SCORE	RANK
Responding to humanitarian needs		
Timely funding to onset disasters	2.39	21
Integrating relief and development		
Encouraging better coordination with humanitarian partners	3.96	19
Strengthening local capacity to deal with crises	3.95	19
Working with humanitarian partners		
Supporting UNDAC	1.00	19
Learning and accountability		
Supporting accountability in humanitarian action	5.43	19

Overview of humanitarian aid	Ireland 2005	Ireland 2006[3]	Share of total DAC (%) 2005	Share of total DAC (%) 2006[3]
Total humanitarian aid, of which:	88.4	189.9	0.9	1.8
Bilateral humanitarian aid[1]	63.9	136.1	0.8	1.5
Multilateral humanitarian aid[2]*	24.5	41.2	1.6	3.2
Official development assistance	719	997	0.6	0.9
Funding to Central Emergency Response Fund**	n/a	12.6	n/a	4.4
Other funds committed under flexible terms[4]***	0.5	3.8	3.1	1.3
			DAC average	
Total humanitarian aid per capita (US$)	22	45	19	24
Total humanitarian aid / official development assistance (%)	12.3	19.0	8.9	9.4
Total humanitarian aid / GNI (%)	0.052	0.102	0.043	0.049

Notes: All data are given in current US$ m unless otherwise indicated.
1 Bilateral humanitarian aid is provided directly by a donor country to a recipient country and includes non-core earmarked contributions to humanitarian organisations but excludes category 'refugees in donor countries' (where 2006 data not available, estimated as average over last four years).
2 Core unearmarked humanitarian flows to UNHCR, UNICEF, WFP, UNRWA, UN/OCHA, ICRC and IFRC.
3 Preliminary; may include official support to asylum seekers in donor country.
4 Consists of IFRC's Disaster Relief Emergency Fund, Common Humanitarian Funds piloted in Sudan and Democratic Republic of Congo in 2006, Emergency Response Funds in 2006 for the DRC, Indonesia, Somalia, the Republic of Congo and Ethiopia and country Humanitarian Response Funds in 2005 for DPRK, DRC, Côte d'Ivoire and Somalia.
Sources: All data from OECD-DAC except: (*) UNHCR, UNICEF, WFP, UNRWA, UN/OCHA, ICRC and IFRC; (**) OCHA; (***) OCHA, IFRC; Common Humanitarian Fund for Sudan, Common Humanitarian Action Plan DRC 2007, US Federal Reserve.

Response times by crisis type, 2005–2006 (days)

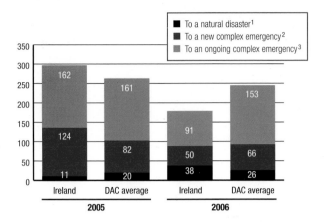

Legend:
- To a natural disaster[1]
- To a new complex emergency[2]
- To an ongoing complex emergency[3]

2005 — Ireland: 162, 124, 11
2005 — DAC average: 161, 82, 20
2006 — Ireland: 91, 50, 38
2006 — DAC average: 153, 66, 26

Notes: [1]Average number of days between launch date of a UN Appeal and commitment or disbursement of funds to given ongoing emergencies. [2]Average number of days between launch date of a UN Appeal and commitment or disbursement of funds to given new emergencies. [3]Average number of days between onset of natural disaster (following CRED dates) and commitment or disbursement of funds to given natural disaster.
Source: OCHA/FTS (status early May 2007), Centre for Research on Epidemiology of Disasters (http://www.cred.be/).

Main channels of humanitarian aid, 2006

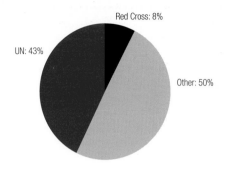

Red Cross: 8%
UN: 43%
Other: 50%

Notes: The UN category encompasses humanitarian receipts by UNHCR, UNICEF, WFP, UNRWA and UN/OCHA including CERF funding; the Red Cross category encompasses humanitarian receipts by IFRC and ICRC. 'Other' is a residual category and includes humanitarian flows to governments, Red Cross national societies, intergovernmental organisations, NGOs, private organisations and foundations. Shares are taken relative to total humanitarian aid reported in 'Overview of humanitarian aid' table.
Sources: UN/OCHA, UNICEF, WFP, UNRWA, UNHCR, ICRC, IFRC, OECD.

Funding per emergency, 2006

Crisis	US$ m	% of total	Inside an Appeal (%)	Outside an Appeal (%)
Sudan	11.1	8.3	63.2	36.8
Democratic Republic of Congo	7.1	5.3	85.0	15.0
Kenya	6.5	4.9	0.0	100.0
Zimbabwe	6.1	4.6	78.3	21.7
Somalia	5.7	4.3	45.9	54.1
Liberia	5.6	4.2	44.4	55.6
Sierra Leone	5.4	4.1	0.0	100.0
Palestinian Territories	5.4	4.1	14.1	85.9
Uganda	5.0	3.8	79.9	20.1
Great Lakes Region	3.7	2.8	83.0	17.0
Other	71.6	53.7	38.7	61.3
Total	133.3	100.0	43.9	56.1

Notes: Category 'Other' includes both provision of unearmarked funds (inside an Appeal to CERF and outside an Appeal) and other miscellaneous flows (only outside an Appeal) if applicable.
Source: OCHA/FTS.

Regional distribution of funding, 2006

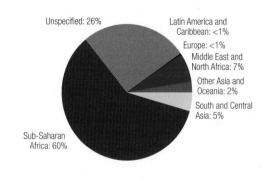

Unspecified: 26%
Latin America and Caribbean: <1%
Europe: <1%
Middle East and North Africa: 7%
Other Asia and Oceania: 2%
South and Central Asia: 5%
Sub-Saharan Africa: 60%

Note: The number of Appeals financed per region: Europe (1), Latin America and Caribbean (0), Middle East and North Africa (2), Other Asia and Oceania (1), South and Central Asia (4), Sub-Saharan Africa (17), Unspecified (2).
Source: OCHA/FTS.

Sectoral distribution of funding, inside and outside an Appeal, 2006 (US$ m)

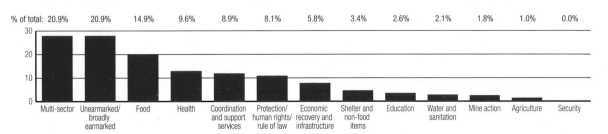

% of total: 20.9% 20.9% 14.9% 9.6% 8.9% 8.1% 5.8% 3.4% 2.6% 2.1% 1.8% 1.0% 0.0%

Multi-sector | Unearmarked/broadly earmarked | Food | Health | Coordination and support services | Protection/human rights/rule of law | Economic recovery and infrastructure | Shelter and non-food items | Education | Water and sanitation | Mine action | Agriculture | Security

Notes: 'Unearmarked/broadly earmarked' category consists of funding not yet applied by recipient agency to particular project or sector.
Source: OCHA/FTS.

Italy

Humanitarian assistance is conducted by the Ministry of Foreign Affairs (DGCS). In order to maintain full flexibility to adapt different responses to different crises, the DGCS does not have a defined strategy for humanitarian aid but is generally guided by the EC Code of Conduct and the EC Consensus on Humanitarian Aid. Italy does not have a crisis cell on permanent call or standby and does not actively participate in needs assessments, relying to a very large extent on UN sources for this purpose. However, funding to crises appears to be less guided by needs, as the DGCS endeavours to specialise on a small number of interventions where it can make a difference. Consequently, it targets those countries which it has prior experience in. Legally, the DGCS can fund all NGOs, but in practice, it prefers Italian NGOs. It does not have multi-year funding arrangements in place, but in practice can informally commit to extending programmes.

Source: Ministry of Foreign Affairs.

HRI scores by pillar

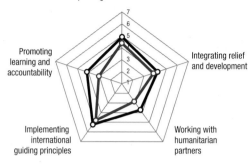

- Italy
- DAC average

HRI results

ADVANTAGES	SCORE	RANK
Responding to humanitarian needs		
Funding in proportion to need	5.13	4
Integrating relief and development		
Funding to international disaster risk reduction mechanisms	2.53	9
Working with humanitarian partners		
Flexible funding	5.27	5
Reducing earmarking	4.75	9
Implementing international guiding principles		
Implementing human rights law	5.80	3

DISADVANTAGES	SCORE	RANK
Responding to humanitarian needs		
Timely funding	4.33	22
Integrating relief and development		
Strengthening local capacity to deal with crises	3.54	22
Implementing international guiding principles		
Protecting human rights	5.25	22
Enhancing security	4.18	23
Engagement in risk mitigation	4.81	22

Overview of humanitarian aid	Italy		Share of total DAC (%)	
	2005	2006[3]	2005	2006[3]
Total humanitarian aid, of which:	87.5	89.1	0.9	0.8
Bilateral humanitarian aid[1]	66.6	74.6	0.8	0.8
Multilateral humanitarian aid[2]*	20.9	14.5	1.4	1.1
Official development assistance	5,091	3,672	4.4	3.2
Funding to Central Emergency Response Fund**	n/a	0.0	n/a	0.0
Other funds committed under flexible terms[4]***	0.0	0.0	0.0	0.0
			DAC average	
Total humanitarian aid per capita (US$)	1	2	19	24
Total humanitarian aid / official development assistance (%)	1.7	2.4	8.9	9.4
Total humanitarian aid / GNI (%)	0.005	0.005	0.043	0.049

Notes: All data are given in current US$ m unless otherwise indicated.

1 Bilateral humanitarian aid is provided directly by a donor country to a recipient country and includes non-core earmarked contributions to humanitarian organisations but excludes category 'refugees in donor countries' (where 2006 data not available, estimated as average over last four years).

2 Core unearmarked humanitarian flows to UNHCR, UNICEF, WFP, UNRWA, UN/OCHA, ICRC and IFRC.

3 Preliminary; may include official support to asylum seekers in donor country.

4 Consists of IFRC's Disaster Relief Emergency Fund, Common Humanitarian Funds piloted in Sudan and Democratic Republic of Congo in 2006, Emergency Response Funds in 2006 for the DRC, Indonesia, Somalia, the Republic of Congo and Ethiopia and country Humanitarian Response Funds in 2005 for DPRK, DRC, Côte d'Ivoire and Somalia.

Sources: All data from OECD-DAC except: (*) UNHCR, UNICEF, WFP, UNRWA, UN/OCHA, ICRC and IFRC; (**) OCHA; (***) OCHA, IFRC; Common Humanitarian Fund for Sudan, Common Humanitarian Action Plan DRC 2007, US Federal Reserve.

Response times by crisis type, 2005–2006 (days)

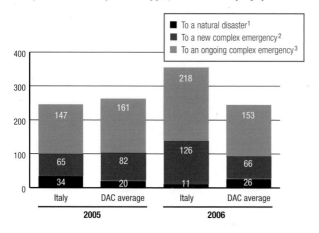

- To a natural disaster[1]
- To a new complex emergency[2]
- To an ongoing complex emergency[3]

Notes: [1]Average number of days between launch date of a UN Appeal and commitment or disbursement of funds to given ongoing emergencies. [2]Average number of days between launch date of a UN Appeal and commitment or disbursement of funds to given new emergencies. [3]Average number of days between onset of natural disaster (following CRED dates) and commitment or disbursement of funds to given natural disaster.
Source: OCHA/FTS (status early May 2007), Centre for Research on Epidemiology of Disasters (http://www.cred.be/).

Main channels of humanitarian aid, 2006

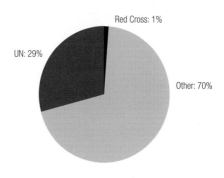

Red Cross: 1%
UN: 29%
Other: 70%

Notes: The UN category encompasses humanitarian receipts by UNHCR, UNICEF, WFP, UNRWA and UN/OCHA including CERF funding; the Red Cross category encompasses humanitarian receipts by IFRC and ICRC. 'Other' includes humanitarian flows to governments, Red Cross national societies, intergovernmental organisations, NGOs, private organisations and foundations reported in OCHA/FTS. Shares are taken relative to total of three categories.
Sources: UN/OCHA, UNICEF, WFP, UNRWA, UNHCR, ICRC, IFRC, OECD.

Funding per emergency, 2006

Crisis	US$ m	% of total	Inside an Appeal (%)	Outside an Appeal (%)
Lebanon Crisis, July	33.2	33.2	0.8	99.2
Afghanistan	9.5	9.5	0.0	100.0
Sudan	6.5	6.5	79.2	20.8
Somalia	3.8	3.8	53.1	46.9
Mauritania	3.6	3.6	0.0	100.0
Ethiopia	3.5	3.5	63.4	36.6
Palestinian Territories	2.9	2.9	1.3	98.7
Bangladesh	2.6	2.6	0.0	100.0
Iraq (incl. Iraqi refugees in neighbouring countries)	2.2	2.2	0.0	100.0
Pakistan	2.0	2.1	0.0	100.0
Other	30.0	30.0	15.3	84.7
Total	**99.8**	**100.0**	**14.3**	**85.7**

Notes: Category 'Other' includes both provision of unearmarked funds (inside an Appeal to CERF and outside an Appeal) and other miscellaneous flows (only outside an Appeal) if applicable.
Source: OCHA/FTS.

Regional distribution of funding, 2006

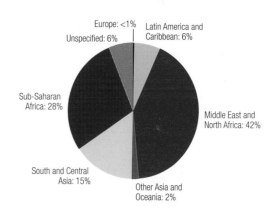

Europe: <1%
Unspecified: 6%
Latin America and Caribbean: 6%
Sub-Saharan Africa: 28%
Middle East and North Africa: 42%
South and Central Asia: 15%
Other Asia and Oceania: 2%

Note: The number of Appeals financed per region: Europe (0), Latin America and Caribbean (0), Middle East and North Africa (2), Other Asia and Oceania (1), South and Central Asia (1), Sub-Saharan Africa (10), Unspecified (0).
Source: OCHA/FTS.

Sectoral distribution of funding, inside and outside an Appeal, 2006 (US$ m)

% of total: 33.0% 28.0% 22.8% 7.4% 3.8% 2.8% 0.6% 0.6% 0.5% 0.4% 0.0% 0.0% 0.0%

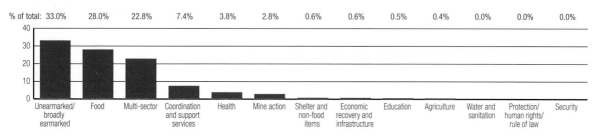

Unearmarked/broadly earmarked, Food, Multi-sector, Coordination and support services, Health, Mine action, Shelter and non-food items, Economic recovery and infrastructure, Education, Agriculture, Water and sanitation, Protection/human rights/rule of law, Security

Notes: 'Unearmarked/broadly earmarked' category consists of funding not yet applied by recipient agency to particular project or sector.
Source: OCHA/FTS.

Japan

The main actors in humanitarian conflict-related assistance are the Ministry of Foreign Affairs and the Japan International Cooperation Agency (JICA). The latter is in charge of grant aid and technical assistance and falls under the portfolio of the MFA. Japan's humanitarian assistance is underpinned by the 1987 Law Concerning the Dispatch of Japan Disaster Relief Teams (JDR Law), which provides a comprehensive basis for international disaster relief but restricts its scope to natural disasters and man-made disasters other than those arising from conflict. In the early 1990s, the Japanese government enacted another law, in connection with UN Peacekeeping Operations, which expanded its international humanitarian relief operations. Since 2000, policies have shifted to emphasise the importance of integrating relief and development, which has now become a priority area. Most humanitarian assistance is channelled through UN agencies, although Japan has recently begun to increase its support for NGOs and to diversify its areas of assistance. JDR teams that are sent out to major disaster areas around the globe specialise in SAR operations and provide medical care or undertake rehabilitation work.

Source: DAC Peer Review for Japan (OECD, 2004), Overseas Development Institute.

HRI scores by pillar

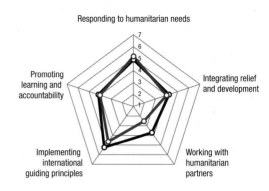

HRI results

ADVANTAGES	SCORE	RANK
Responding to humanitarian needs		
Distribution of funding relative to historical ties and geographical proximity	6.40	3
Funding to priority sectors	6.44	3
Timely funding to onset disasters	6.55	2
Integrating relief and development		
Funding to international disaster risk reduction mechanisms	3.35	5
Learning and accountability		
Funding of other accountability initiatives	4.19	3

DISADVANTAGES	SCORE	RANK
Working with humanitarian partners		
Facilitating safe humanitarian access	3.00	22
Flexible funding (Survey)	3.59	23
Funding ICRC Appeals	1.00	23
Promoting role of NGOs	4.87	21
Reducing earmarking	3.37	23

Overview of humanitarian aid

	Japan 2005	Japan 2006[3]	Share of total DAC (%) 2005	Share of total DAC (%) 2006[3]
Total humanitarian aid, of which:	640.0	58.7	6.5	0.6
Bilateral humanitarian aid[1]	515.9	8.9	6.2	0.1
Multilateral humanitarian aid[2]*	124.1	42.4	8.0	3.3
Official development assistance	13,147	11,608	11.3	10.2
Funding to Central Emergency Response Fund**	n/a	7.5	n/a	2.6
Other funds committed under flexible terms[4]***	0.0	0.0	0.0	0.0

	Japan 2005	Japan 2006[3]	DAC average 2005	DAC average 2006[3]
Total humanitarian aid per capita (US$)	5	0	19	24
Total humanitarian aid / official development assistance (%)	4.9	0.5	8.9	9.4
Total humanitarian aid / GNI (%)	0.014	0.001	0.043	0.049

Notes: All data are given in current US$ m unless otherwise indicated.

1 Bilateral humanitarian aid is provided directly by a donor country to a recipient country and includes non-core earmarked contributions to humanitarian organisations but excludes category 'refugees in donor countries' (where 2006 data not available, estimated as average over last four years).

2 Core unearmarked humanitarian flows to UNHCR, UNICEF, WFP, UNRWA, UN/OCHA, ICRC and IFRC.

3 Preliminary; may include official support to asylum seekers in donor country.

4 Consists of IFRC's Disaster Relief Emergency Fund, Common Humanitarian Funds piloted in Sudan and Democratic Republic of Congo in 2006, Emergency Response Funds in 2006 for the DRC, Indonesia, Somalia, the Republic of Congo and Ethiopia and country Humanitarian Response Funds in 2005 for DPRK, DRC, Côte d'Ivoire and Somalia.

Sources: All data from OECD-DAC except: (*) UNHCR, UNICEF, WFP, UNRWA, UN/OCHA, ICRC and IFRC; (**) OCHA; (***) OCHA, IFRC; Common Humanitarian Fund for Sudan, Common Humanitarian Action Plan DRC 2007, US Federal Reserve.

Response times by crisis type, 2005–2006 (days)

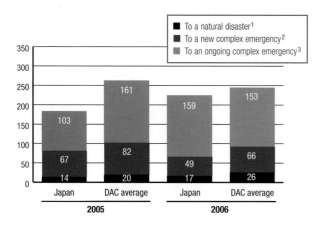

Legend:
- ■ To a natural disaster[1]
- ■ To a new complex emergency[2]
- ■ To an ongoing complex emergency[3]

2005 — Japan: 14, 67, 103; DAC average: 20, 82, 161
2006 — Japan: 17, 49, 159; DAC average: 26, 66, 153

Notes: [1]Average number of days between launch date of a UN Appeal and commitment or disbursement of funds to given ongoing emergencies. [2]Average number of days between launch date of a UN Appeal and commitment or disbursement of funds to given new emergencies. [3]Average number of days between onset of natural disaster (following CRED dates) and commitment or disbursement of funds to given natural disaster.
Source: OCHA/FTS (status early May 2007), Centre for Research on Epidemiology of Disasters (http://www.cred.be/).

Main channels of humanitarian aid, 2006

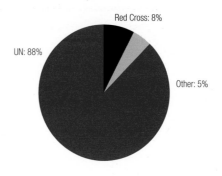

UN: 88%, Red Cross: 8%, Other: 5%

Notes: The UN category encompasses humanitarian receipts by UNHCR, UNICEF, WFP, UNRWA and UN/OCHA including CERF funding; the Red Cross category encompasses humanitarian receipts by IFRC and ICRC. 'Other' includes humanitarian flows to governments, Red Cross national societies, intergovernmental organisations, NGOs, private organisations and foundations reported in OCHA/FTS. Shares are taken relative to total of three categories.
Sources: UN/OCHA, UNICEF, WFP, UNRWA, UNHCR, ICRC, IFRC, OECD.

Funding per emergency, 2006

Crisis	US$ m	% of total	Inside an Appeal (%)	Outside an Appeal (%)
Palestinian Territories	29.5	17.5	59.6	40.4
Sudan	25.7	15.2	78.7	21.3
Democratic Republic of Congo	12.7	7.5	100.0	0.0
Liberia	11.9	7.1	100.0	0.0
Burundi	10.8	6.4	100.0	0.0
Chad	6.0	3.5	100.0	0.0
Great Lakes Region	5.5	3.3	100.0	0.0
Indonesia: Java Earthquake, May	5.4	3.2	22.3	77.7
Timor-Leste: Population Displacement - May	5.0	3.0	100.0	0.0
Kenya	4.7	2.8	0.0	100.0
Other	51.3	30.4	62.2	37.8
Total	168.4	100.0	72.9	27.1

Notes: Category 'Other' includes both provision of unearmarked funds (inside an Appeal to CERF and outside an Appeal) and other miscellaneous flows (only outside an Appeal) if applicable.
Source: OCHA/FTS.

Regional distribution of funding, 2006

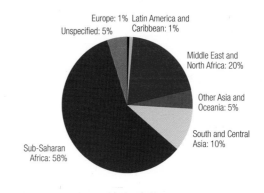

Europe: 1%; Unspecified: 5%; Latin America and Caribbean: 1%; Middle East and North Africa: 20%; Other Asia and Oceania: 5%; South and Central Asia: 10%; Sub-Saharan Africa: 58%

Note: The number of Appeals financed per region: Europe (1), Latin America and Caribbean (0), Middle East and North Africa (2), Other Asia and Oceania (1), South and Central Asia (3), Sub-Saharan Africa (14), Unspecified (1).
Source: OCHA/FTS.

Sectoral distribution of funding, inside and outside an Appeal, 2006 (US$ m)

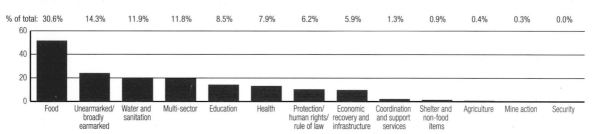

% of total: 30.6% Food, 14.3% Unearmarked/broadly earmarked, 11.9% Water and sanitation, 11.8% Multi-sector, 8.5% Education, 7.9% Health, 6.2% Protection/human rights/rule of law, 5.9% Economic recovery and infrastructure, 1.3% Coordination and support services, 0.9% Shelter and non-food items, 0.4% Agriculture, 0.3% Mine action, 0.0% Security

Notes: 'Unearmarked/broadly earmarked' category consists of funding not yet applied by recipient agency to particular project or sector.
Source: OCHA/FTS.

The Humanitarian Response Index 2007

Luxembourg

The key actor is the Development Cooperation under the Ministry of Foreign Affairs. Luxembourg's humanitarian aid policy is guided by its recent General Humanitarian Strategy. The MFA does not perform its own needs assessments due to limited capacity but relies on assessments by the UN and the Red Cross Movement. In allocating its funding, the MFA places highest emphasis on needs, as well as whether the country is a development partner, reflecting the priority is gives to integrating relief and development activities. It has a crisis cell on permanent call. Luxembourg is a strong supporter of the UN. It was among the first countries to support the establishment of the CERF and is part of the OCHA donor support group. The MFA has instituted four-year contracts with key humanitarian organisations such as the ICRC, the WFP and UNHCR, with a strong focus on forgotten emergencies. Technically, the MFA can fund foreign NGOs but in practice, this is of limited significance. MSF and Caritas receive most of the funding going through the NGO channel. This collaboration was accompanied in 2002 by a 50 percent increase in Luxembourg's budgetary contribution to these organisations.

Source: Ministry of Foreign Affairs, DAC Peer Review for Luxembourg (OECD, 2003).

HRI scores by pillar

HRI results

ADVANTAGES	SCORE	RANK
Working with humanitarian partners		
Facilitating safe humanitarian access	4.38	2
Funding CERF	7.00	1
Funding ICRC Appeals	7.00	1
Funding UN Consolidated Inter-Agency Appeals	7.00	1
Implementing international guiding principles		
Affirming primary role of civilian organisations	6.19	1

DISADVANTAGES	SCORE	RANK
Integrating relief and development		
Encouraging better coordination with humanitarian partners	3.73	21
Working with humanitarian partners		
Predictability of funding (hard data)	1.63	20
Implementing international guiding principles		
Implementing international humanitarian law	3.70	21
Learning and accountability		
Support to main accountability initiatives	1.00	20
Supporting accountability in humanitarian action	5.32	20

Overview of humanitarian aid	Luxembourg		Share of total DAC (%)	
	2005	2006[3]	2005	2006[3]
Total humanitarian aid, of which:	24.6	44.1	0.2	0.4
Bilateral humanitarian aid[1]	16.3	34.0	0.2	0.4
Multilateral humanitarian aid[2]*	8.3	6.1	0.5	0.5
Official development assistance	256	291	0.2	0.3
Funding to Central Emergency Response Fund**	n/a	4.0	n/a	1.4
Other funds committed under flexible terms[4]***	0.0	0.0	0.0	0.0
			DAC average	
Total humanitarian aid per capita (US$)	55	96	19	24
Total humanitarian aid / official development assistance (%)	9.6	15.1	8.9	9.4
Total humanitarian aid / GNI (%)	0.082	0.135	0.043	0.049

Notes: All data are given in current US$ m unless otherwise indicated.

1 Bilateral humanitarian aid is provided directly by a donor country to a recipient country and includes non-core earmarked contributions to humanitarian organisations but excludes category 'refugees in donor countries' (where 2006 data not available, estimated as average over last four years).

2 Core unearmarked humanitarian flows to UNHCR, UNICEF, WFP, UNRWA, UN/OCHA, ICRC and IFRC.

3 Preliminary; may include official support to asylum seekers in donor country.

4 Consists of IFRC's Disaster Relief Emergency Fund, Common Humanitarian Funds piloted in Sudan and Democratic Republic of Congo in 2006, Emergency Response Funds in 2006 for the DRC, Indonesia, Somalia, the Republic of Congo and Ethiopia and country Humanitarian Response Funds in 2005 for DPRK, DRC, Côte d'Ivoire and Somalia.

Sources: All data from OECD-DAC except: (*) UNHCR, UNICEF, WFP, UNRWA, UN/OCHA, ICRC and IFRC; (**) OCHA; (***) OCHA, IFRC; Common Humanitarian Fund for Sudan, Common Humanitarian Action Plan DRC 2007, US Federal Reserve.

Response times by crisis type, 2005–2006 (days)

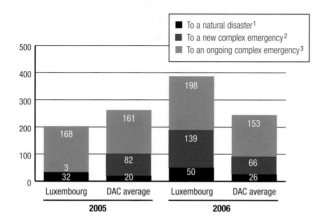

Legend:
- To a natural disaster [1]
- To a new complex emergency [2]
- To an ongoing complex emergency [3]

2005 — Luxembourg: 168, 3, 32; DAC average: 161, 82, 20

2006 — Luxembourg: 198, 139, 50; DAC average: 153, 66, 26

Notes: [1]Average number of days between launch date of a UN Appeal and commitment or disbursement of funds to given ongoing emergencies. [2]Average number of days between launch date of a UN Appeal and commitment or disbursement of funds to given new emergencies. [3]Average number of days between onset of natural disaster (following CRED dates) and commitment or disbursement of funds to given natural disaster.
Source: OCHA/FTS (status early May 2007), Centre for Research on Epidemiology of Disasters (http://www.cred.be/).

Main channels of humanitarian aid, 2006

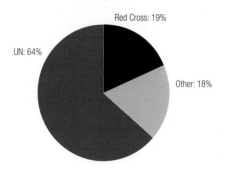

- Red Cross: 19%
- UN: 64%
- Other: 18%

Notes: The UN category encompasses humanitarian receipts by UNHCR, UNICEF, WFP, UNRWA and UN/OCHA including CERF funding; the Red Cross category encompasses humanitarian receipts by IFRC and ICRC. 'Other' is a residual category and includes humanitarian flows to governments, Red Cross national societies, intergovernmental organisations, NGOs, private organisations and foundations. Shares are taken relative to total humanitarian aid reported in 'Overview of humanitarian aid' table.
Sources: UN/OCHA, UNICEF, WFP, UNRWA, UNHCR, ICRC, IFRC, OECD.

Donor Profiles: Luxembourg

Funding per emergency in 2006

Crisis	US$ m	% of total	Inside an Appeal (%)	Outside an Appeal (%)
West Africa	4.6	24.1	100.0	0.0
Sudan	1.4	7.6	82.3	17.7
Iraq (incl. Iraqi refugees in neighbouring countries)	1.1	5.7	0.0	100.0
Lebanon Crisis July	1.1	5.6	70.8	29.2
Democratic Republic of Congo	0.9	4.7	100.0	0.0
Somalia	0.7	3.4	100.0	0.0
Indonesia: Java Earthquake May	0.6	3.0	88.9	11.1
Pakistan	0.5	2.8	0.0	100.0
Chad	0.4	2.3	70.2	29.8
Kenya	0.4	2.2	0.0	100.0
Other	**7.4**	**38.6**	**73.6**	**26.4**
Total	**19.1**	**100.0**	**75.1**	**24.9**

Notes: Category 'Other' includes both provision of unearmarked funds (inside an Appeal to CERF and outside an Appeal) and other miscellaneous flows (only outside an Appeal) if applicable.
Source: OCHA/FTS.

Regional distribution of funding, 2006

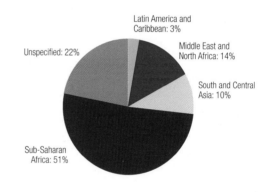

- Latin America and Caribbean: 3%
- Middle East and North Africa: 14%
- South and Central Asia: 10%
- Sub-Saharan Africa: 51%
- Unspecified: 22%

Note: The number of Appeals financed per region: Europe (0), Latin America and Caribbean (0), Middle East and North Africa (2), Other Asia and Oceania (0), South and Central Asia (2), Sub-Saharan Africa (9), Unspecified (1).
Source: OCHA/FTS.

Sectoral distribution of funding, inside and outside an Appeal, 2006 (US$ m)

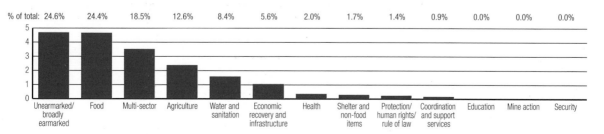

% of total: 24.6%, 24.4%, 18.5%, 12.6%, 8.4%, 5.6%, 2.0%, 1.7%, 1.4%, 0.9%, 0.0%, 0.0%, 0.0%

Categories: Unearmarked/broadly earmarked, Food, Multi-sector, Agriculture, Water and sanitation, Economic recovery and infrastructure, Health, Shelter and non-food items, Protection/human rights/rule of law, Coordination and support services, Education, Mine action, Security

Notes: 'Unearmarked/broadly earmarked' category consists of funding not yet applied by recipient agency to particular project or sector.
Source: OCHA/FTS.

Netherlands

The Humanitarian Aid Division of the Ministry of Foreign Affairs is in charge of the humanitarian portfolio and is accountable to both the Ministers of Foreign Affairs and of Development Cooperation. Other ministries can play minor roles but become involved only at the request of the MFA and under its coordination. The MFA is currently in the process of developing a formal humanitarian action, which will incorporate the GHD Principles, and is expected to be ready at the end of 2007. The Netherlands has formulated a GHD Domestic Implementation Plan. It is one of the countries instrumental to the formulation of the GHD Principles. The MFA does not perform its own needs assessments, relying in particular on the UN, and cross-checking other sources such as ECHO, the IFRC, DFID, its embassies and NGOs. The Netherlands hardly ever gives direct bilateral humanitarian aid to governments. Instead, it nearly always works through international partners, such as the UN and Red Cross; in 2006, it was the second largest contributor to CERF in absolute terms. NGOs are pre-screened for reliability, implementation capacity and willingness to cooperate with the UN. The Dutch humanitarian aid programme gives increasing emphasis to post-crisis contexts and the integration of relief and development. In 2005, a Memorandum on post conflict reconstruction was published jointly by the Ministries of Foreign Affairs, Defence and Economic Affairs. The Netherlands provides needs-based, flexible and predictable humanitarian support.

Source: Ministry of Foreign Affairs, http://www.minbuza.nl, DAC Peer Review of the Netherlands (OECD, 2006), GHD Domestic Implementation Plan for the Netherlands.

HRI scores by pillar

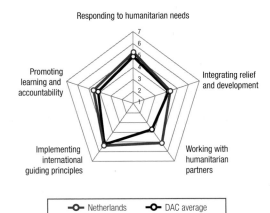

HRI results

ADVANTAGES	SCORE	RANK
Working with humanitarian partners		
Funding quick disbursement mechanisms	7.00	1
Funding Red Cross Movement	7.00	1
Predictability of funding (Survey)	5.81	2
Supporting contingency planning and capacity building efforts	4.49	1
Unearmarked or broadly earmarked funds	7.00	1

DISADVANTAGES	SCORE	RANK
Responding to humanitarian needs		
Commitment to ongoing crises	4.50	16
Independence	5.12	15
Neutrality	5.80	16
Integrating relief and development		
Encouraging better coordination with humanitarian partners	4.15	15
Working with humanitarian partners		
Donor preparedness in implementation of humanitarian action	4.58	17

Overview of humanitarian aid

	Netherlands 2005	Netherlands 2006[3]	Share of total DAC (%) 2005	Share of total DAC (%) 2006[3]
Total humanitarian aid, of which:	611.9	868.6	6.2	8.3
Bilateral humanitarian aid[1]	408.4	634.1	4.9	7.1
Multilateral humanitarian aid[2]*	203.5	182.7	13.2	14.4
Official development assistance	5,115	5,452	4.4	4.8
Funding to Central Emergency Response Fund**	n/a	51.9	n/a	18.0
Other funds committed under flexible terms[4]***	0.8	71.3	5.5	25.4
			DAC average	
Total humanitarian aid per capita (US$)	37	53	19	24
Total humanitarian aid / official development assistance (%)	12.0	15.9	8.9	9.4
Total humanitarian aid / GNI (%)	0.098	0.128	0.043	0.049

Notes: All data are given in current US$ m unless otherwise indicated.
1 Bilateral humanitarian aid is provided directly by a donor country to a recipient country and includes non-core earmarked contributions to humanitarian organisations but excludes category 'refugees in donor countries' (where 2006 data not available, estimated as average over last four years).
2 Core unearmarked humanitarian flows to UNHCR, UNICEF, WFP, UNRWA, UN/OCHA, ICRC and IFRC.
3 Preliminary; may include official support to asylum seekers in donor country.
4 Consists of IFRC's Disaster Relief Emergency Fund, Common Humanitarian Funds piloted in Sudan and Democratic Republic of Congo in 2006, Emergency Response Funds in 2006 for the DRC, Indonesia, Somalia, the Republic of Congo and Ethiopia and country Humanitarian Response Funds in 2005 for DPRK, DRC, Côte d'Ivoire and Somalia.
Sources: All data from OECD-DAC except: (*) UNHCR, UNICEF, WFP, UNRWA, UN/OCHA, ICRC and IFRC; (**) OCHA; (***) OCHA, IFRC; Common Humanitarian Fund for Sudan, Common Humanitarian Action Plan DRC 2007, US Federal Reserve.

Response times by crisis type, 2005–2006 (days)

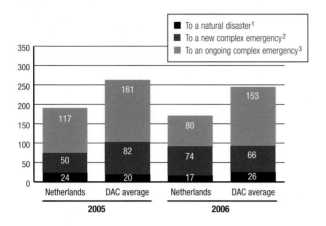

- To a natural disaster[1]
- To a new complex emergency[2]
- To an ongoing complex emergency[3]

	Netherlands	DAC average	Netherlands	DAC average
2005	117 / 50 / 24	161 / 82 / 20		
2006			80 / 74 / 17	153 / 66 / 26

Notes: [1]Average number of days between launch date of a UN Appeal and commitment or disbursement of funds to given ongoing emergencies. [2]Average number of days between launch date of a UN Appeal and commitment or disbursement of funds to given new emergencies. [3]Average number of days between onset of natural disaster (following CRED dates) and commitment or disbursement of funds to given natural disaster.
Source: OCHA/FTS (status early May 2007), Centre for Research on Epidemiology of Disasters (http://www.cred.be/).

Main channels of humanitarian aid, 2006

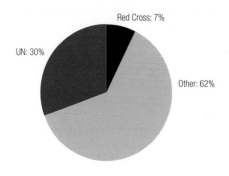

Red Cross: 7%
UN: 30%
Other: 62%

Notes: The UN category encompasses humanitarian receipts by UNHCR, UNICEF, WFP, UNRWA and UN/OCHA including CERF funding; the Red Cross category encompasses humanitarian receipts by IFRC and ICRC. 'Other' is a residual category and includes humanitarian flows to governments, Red Cross national societies, intergovernmental organisations, NGOs, private organisations and foundations. Shares are taken relative to total humanitarian aid reported in 'Overview of humanitarian aid' table.
Sources: UN/OCHA, UNICEF, WFP, UNRWA, UNHCR, ICRC, IFRC, OECD.

Funding per emergency, 2006

Crisis	US$ m	% of total	Inside an Appeal (%)	Outside an Appeal (%)
Sudan	57.3	16.8	86.2	13.8
Uganda	19.1	5.6	80.6	19.4
Democratic Republic of Congo	18.2	5.3	90.7	9.3
Somalia	17.0	5.0	87.5	12.5
Horn of Africa	13.9	4.1	63.0	37.0
Pakistan	11.3	3.3	0.0	100.0
Afghanistan	10.4	3.0	0.0	100.0
Ethiopia	8.6	2.5	91.3	8.7
Lebanon Crisis, July	8.4	2.5	56.6	43.4
Palestinian Territories	7.4	2.2	73.5	26.5
Other	**169.2**	**49.6**	**48.4**	**51.6**
Total	**340.8**	**100.0**	**60.1**	**39.9**

Notes: Category 'Other' includes both provision of unearmarked funds (inside an Appeal to CERF and outside an Appeal) and other miscellaneous flows (only outside an Appeal) if applicable.
Source: OCHA/FTS.

Regional distribution of funding, 2006

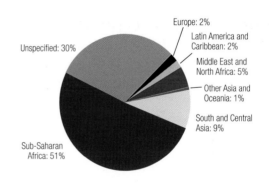

Europe: 2%
Latin America and Caribbean: 2%
Middle East and North Africa: 5%
Other Asia and Oceania: 1%
South and Central Asia: 9%
Sub-Saharan Africa: 51%
Unspecified: 30%

Note: The number of Appeals financed per region: Europe (1), Latin America and Caribbean (0), Middle East and North Africa (2), Other Asia and Oceania (0), South and Central Asia (4), Sub-Saharan Africa (14), Unspecified (2).
Source: OCHA/FTS.

Sectoral distribution of funding, inside and outside an Appeal, 2006 (US$ m)

% of total: 50.8% 13.3% 11.9% 5.1% 3.8% 3.1% 2.7% 2.5% 2.3% 2.0% 1.2% 1.1% 0.1%

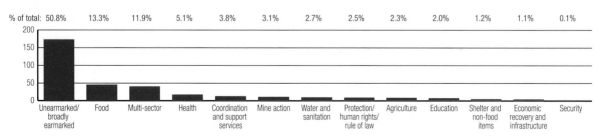

Unearmarked/broadly earmarked · Food · Multi-sector · Health · Coordination and support services · Mine action · Water and sanitation · Protection/human rights/rule of law · Agriculture · Education · Shelter and non-food items · Economic recovery and infrastructure · Security

Notes: 'Unearmarked/broadly earmarked' category consists of funding not yet applied by recipient agency to particular project or sector.
Source: OCHA/FTS.

New Zealand

The Ministry of Foreign Affairs and Trade is responsible for humanitarian assistance, administered by NZAID. Due to NZAID's semi-autonomy, its mandate extends beyond aid management and implementation, providing contestable policy advice meaning that its views may differ from those of the MFA. The independent International Development Advisory Committee (IDAC) established in early 2004 also plays a role in defining broader policy issues, including by undertaking public consultation and contracting research. The MFA meets regularly with representatives from CID, the umbrella organisation for New Zealand NGOs. Within NZAID's humanitarian pro-gramme, the NGO funding window for emergency and disaster relief has been estab-lished to channel support via New Zealand NGOs to their partners in disaster and emergency situations. A number of NGO activities, including from civil society organi-sations in partner countries, can be funded directly under NZAID bilateral and region-al programmes. NZAID has formal four-year strategic relationship agreements with four major NGOs, which include core-funding covering up to 95 per cent of organisa-tions' budgets.

Source: DAC Peer Review for New Zealand (OECD, 2005).

HRI scores by pillar

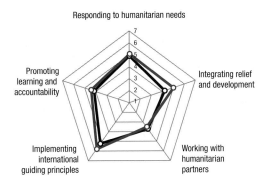

New Zealand   DAC average

HRI results

ADVANTAGES	SCORE	RANK
Responding to humanitarian needs		
Alleviation of suffering	6.17	1
Impartiality	6.39	1
Integrating relief and development		
Funding to international disaster risk reduction mechanisms	7.00	1
Working with humanitarian partners		
Flexible funding	5.76	1
Learning and accountability		
Funding of other accountability initiatives	7.00	1

DISADVANTAGES	SCORE	RANK
Responding to humanitarian needs		
Distribution of funding relative to sector, forgotten emergency and media coverage	1.50	22
Timely funding to complex emergencies	2.23	21
Integrating relief and development		
Consultation with beneficiaries on monitoring and evaluation	4.33	21
Working with humanitarian partners		
Funding CERF	1.00	19
Learning and accountability		
Number of evaluations	1.36	19

Overview of humanitarian aid	New Zealand 2005	New Zealand 2006[3]	Share of total DAC (%) 2005	Share of total DAC (%) 2006[3]
Total humanitarian aid, of which:	57.0	22.2	0.6	0.2
Bilateral humanitarian aid[1]	52.9	16.4	0.6	0.2
Multilateral humanitarian aid[2]*	4.1	5.7	0.3	0.5
Official development assistance	274	257	0.2	0.2
Funding to Central Emergency Response Fund**	n/a	0.0	n/a	0.0
Other funds committed under flexible terms[4]***	0.0	0.0	0.0	0.0
			DAC average	
Total humanitarian aid per capita (US$)	14	5	19	24
Total humanitarian aid / official development assistance (%)	20.9	8.6	8.9	9.4
Total humanitarian aid / GNI (%)	0.057	0.023	0.043	0.049

Notes: All data are given in current US$ m unless otherwise indicated.

1 Bilateral humanitarian aid is provided directly by a donor country to a recipient country and includes non-core earmarked contributions to humanitarian organisations but excludes category 'refugees in donor countries' (where 2006 data not available, estimated as average over last four years).

2 Core unearmarked humanitarian flows to UNHCR, UNICEF, WFP, UNRWA, UN/OCHA, ICRC and IFRC.

3 Preliminary; may include official support to asylum seekers in donor country.

4 Consists of IFRC's Disaster Relief Emergency Fund, Common Humanitarian Funds piloted in Sudan and Democratic Republic of Congo in 2006, Emergency Response Funds in 2006 for the DRC, Indonesia, Somalia, the Republic of Congo and Ethiopia and country Humanitarian Response Funds in 2005 for DPRK, DRC, Côte d'Ivoire and Somalia.

Sources: All data from OECD-DAC except: (*) UNHCR, UNICEF, WFP, UNRWA, UN/OCHA, ICRC and IFRC; (**) OCHA; (***) OCHA, IFRC; Common Humanitarian Fund for Sudan, Common Humanitarian Action Plan DRC 2007, US Federal Reserve.

Response times by crisis type, 2005–2006 (days)

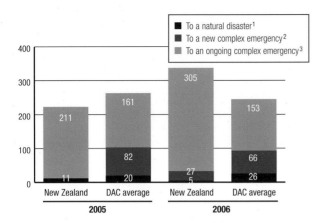

- ■ To a natural disaster[1]
- ■ To a new complex emergency[2]
- ■ To an ongoing complex emergency[3]

Notes: [1]Average number of days between launch date of a UN Appeal and commitment or disbursement of funds to given ongoing emergencies. [2]Average number of days between launch date of a UN Appeal and commitment or disbursement of funds to given new emergencies. In 2005, New Zealand did not commit or disburse funds to new emergencies. [3]Average number of days between onset of natural disaster (following CRED dates) and commitment or disbursement of funds to given natural disaster.
Source: OCHA/FTS (status early May 2007), Centre for Research on Epidemiology of Disasters (http://www.cred.be/).

Main channels of humanitarian aid, 2006

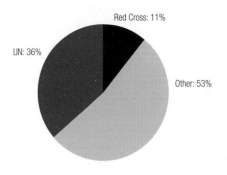

- Red Cross: 11%
- UN: 36%
- Other: 53%

Notes: The UN category encompasses humanitarian receipts by UNHCR, UNICEF, WFP, UNRWA and UN/OCHA including CERF funding; the Red Cross category encompasses humanitarian receipts by IFRC and ICRC. 'Other' is a residual category and includes humanitarian flows to governments, Red Cross national societies, intergovernmental organisations, NGOs, private organisations and foundations. Shares are taken relative to total humanitarian aid reported in 'Overview of humanitarian aid' table.
Sources: UN/OCHA, UNICEF, WFP, UNRWA, UNHCR, ICRC, IFRC, OECD.

Funding per emergency, 2006

Crisis	US$ m	% of total	Inside an Appeal (%)	Outside an Appeal (%)
Sudan	1.2	25.6	100.0	0.0
Lebanon Crisis, July	0.8	16.3	100.0	0.0
Palestinian Territories	0.5	10.2	100.0	0.0
Timor-Leste: Population Displacement, May	0.4	7.4	0.0	100.0
Indonesia: Java Earthquake, May	0.3	6.5	100.0	0.0
DPR of Korea	0.2	3.9	0.0	100.0
Philippines: Landslides, February	0.1	2.8	0.0	100.0
Nepal	0.1	2.7	100.0	0.0
Tanzania (United Republic of)	0.1	2.1	0.0	100.0
Timor-Leste	0.1	2.0	0.0	100.0
Other	1.0	20.4	0.0	100.0
Total	4.9	100.0	61.3	38.7

Notes: Category 'Other' includes both provision of unearmarked funds (inside an Appeal to CERF and outside an Appeal) and other miscellaneous flows (only outside an Appeal) if applicable.
Source: OCHA/FTS.

Regional distribution of funding, 2006

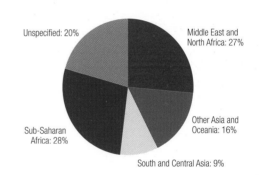

- Unspecified: 20%
- Middle East and North Africa: 27%
- Other Asia and Oceania: 16%
- South and Central Asia: 9%
- Sub-Saharan Africa: 28%

Note: The number of Appeals financed per region: Europe (0), Latin America and Caribbean (0), Middle East and North Africa (2), Other Asia and Oceania (0), South and Central Asia (2), Sub-Saharan Africa (1), Unspecified (0).
Source: OCHA/FTS.

Sectoral distribution of funding, inside and outside an Appeal, 2006 (US$ m)

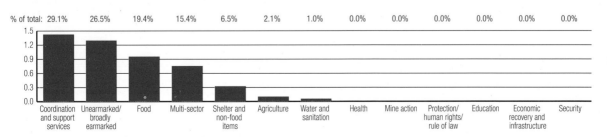

% of total: 29.1% 26.5% 19.4% 15.4% 6.5% 2.1% 1.0% 0.0% 0.0% 0.0% 0.0% 0.0% 0.0%

Coordination and support services | Unearmarked/broadly earmarked | Food | Multi-sector | Shelter and non-food items | Agriculture | Water and sanitation | Health | Mine action | Protection/human rights/rule of law | Education | Economic recovery and infrastructure | Security

Notes: 'Unearmarked/broadly earmarked' category consists of funding not yet applied by recipient agency to particular project or sector.
Source: OCHA/FTS.

Norway

The Ministry of Foreign Affairs is responsible for the management, policy formulation and administration of humanitarian action, understood to include conflict resolution. The portfolio is split among the MFA's Department for Global Affairs, with a mandate to respond to armed conflicts and natural disasters; the Regional Department in charge of transitional assistance; and the International Development Policy Department overseeing peace-building activities. Norway has a long tradition of involvement in humanitarian action and conflict resolution. Its actions are not guided by a formal policy document other than its annual budget submission to Parliament (Storting). Norway relies on UN needs assessments, backed by the MFA's internal and NGOs' assessments. It is a major contributor to the multilateral agencies and their Appeals and is a member of the OCHA Donor Support Group. It regards the CERF and clusters as important tools for increased coordination. It provides unearmarked funding to the protection programmes of the ICRC and UNHCR. Norway's national and international NGO partners are actively encouraged to involve beneficiaries in the projects. Through the Norwegian Emergency Preparedness System, Norway has a strong emergency response capacity, offering personnel, services and relief products.

Source: Ministry of Foreign Affairs, DAC Peer Review for Norway (OECD, 2005).

HRI scores by pillar

HRI results

ADVANTAGES	SCORE	RANK
Responding to humanitarian needs		
Funding in proportion to need	5.23	2
Integrating relief and development		
Funding to international disaster risk reduction mechanisms	4.30	2
Working with humanitarian partners		
Funding CERF	7.00	1
Funding quick disbursement mechanisms	7.00	1
Implementing international guiding principles		
Implementing international humanitarian law	6.70	2

DISADVANTAGES	SCORE	RANK
Responding to humanitarian needs		
Funding to priority sectors	4.29	17
Working with humanitarian partners		
Supporting contingency planning and capacity building efforts	3.61	16
Learning and accountability		
Encouraging regular evaluations	5.39	15
Funding of other accountability initiatives	1.00	17
Supporting learning and accountability initiatives	5.13	16

Overview of humanitarian aid

	Norway 2005	Norway 2006[3]	Share of total DAC (%) 2005	Share of total DAC (%) 2006[3]
Total humanitarian aid, of which:	476.0	466.7	4.8	4.4
Bilateral humanitarian aid[1]	343.7	362.8	4.1	4.1
Multilateral humanitarian aid[2]*	132.3	74.0	8.6	5.8
Official development assistance	2,786	2,946	2.4	2.6
Funding to Central Emergency Response Fund**	n/a	30.0	n/a	10.4
Other funds committed under flexible terms[4]***	0.3	17.1	2.2	6.1

			DAC average	
Total humanitarian aid per capita (US$)	103	100	19	24
Total humanitarian aid / official development assistance (%)	17.1	15.8	8.9	9.4
Total humanitarian aid / GNI (%)	0.160	0.140	0.043	0.049

Notes: All data are given in current US$ m unless otherwise indicated.

1 Bilateral humanitarian aid is provided directly by a donor country to a recipient country and includes non-core earmarked contributions to humanitarian organisations but excludes category 'refugees in donor countries' (where 2006 data not available, estimated as average over last four years).

2 Core unearmarked humanitarian flows to UNHCR, UNICEF, WFP, UNRWA, UN/OCHA, ICRC and IFRC.

3 Preliminary; may include official support to asylum seekers in donor country.

4 Consists of IFRC's Disaster Relief Emergency Fund, Common Humanitarian Funds piloted in Sudan and Democratic Republic of Congo in 2006, Emergency Response Funds in 2006 for the DRC, Indonesia, Somalia, the Republic of Congo and Ethiopia and country Humanitarian Response Funds in 2005 for DPRK, DRC, Côte d'Ivoire and Somalia.

Sources: All data from OECD-DAC except: (*) UNHCR, UNICEF, WFP, UNRWA, UN/OCHA, ICRC and IFRC; (**) OCHA; (***) OCHA, IFRC; Common Humanitarian Fund for Sudan, Common Humanitarian Action Plan DRC 2007, US Federal Reserve.

Response times by crisis type, 2005–2006 (days)

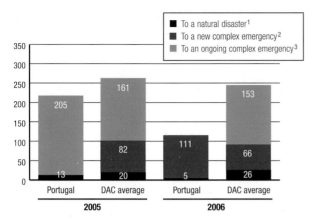

Notes: [1]Average number of days between launch date of a UN Appeal and commitment or disbursement of funds to given ongoing emergencies. In 2006, Portugal did not commit or disbursed funds to ongoing emergencies. [2]Average number of days between launch date of a UN Appeal and commitment or disbursement of funds to given new emergencies. In 2005, Portugal committed or disbursed funds to new emergencies on the Appeal launch date. [3]Average number of days between onset of natural disaster (following CRED dates) and commitment or disbursement of funds to given natural disaster.
Source: OCHA/FTS (status early May 2007), Centre for Research on Epidemiology of Disasters (http://www.cred.be/).

Main channels of humanitarian aid, 2006

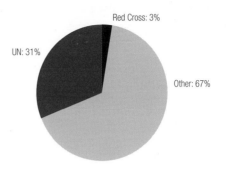

Notes: The UN category encompasses humanitarian receipts by UNHCR, UNICEF, WFP, UNRWA and UN/OCHA including CERF funding; the Red Cross category encompasses humanitarian receipts by IFRC and ICRC. 'Other' is a residual category and includes humanitarian flows to governments, Red Cross national societies, intergovernmental organisations, NGOs, private organisations and foundations. Shares are taken relative to total humanitarian aid reported in 'Overview of humanitarian aid' table.
Sources: UN/OCHA, UNICEF, WFP, UNRWA, UNHCR, ICRC, IFRC, OECD.

Funding per emergency, 2006

Crisis	US$ m	% of total	Inside an Appeal (%)	Outside an Appeal (%)
Indonesia	2.0	35.2	0.0	100.0
Sri Lanka	1.3	22.5	0.0	100.0
Malaysia	0.4	7.8	0.0	100.0
Maldives	0.4	7.0	0.0	100.0
Mozambique	0.4	6.4	0.0	100.0
Lebanon Crisis, July	0.3	4.6	100.0	0.0
Seychelles	0.2	3.4	0.0	100.0
Thailand	0.2	3.3	0.0	100.0
Algeria: Floods, February	0.1	1.6	0.0	100.0
Sao Tome and Principe	0.1	1.3	0.0	100.0
Other	**0.4**	**7.1**	**78.6**	**21.4**
Total	**5.6**	**100.0**	**10.1**	**89.9**

Notes: Category 'Other' includes both provision of unearmarked funds (inside an Appeal to CERF and outside an Appeal) and other miscellaneous flows (only outside an Appeal) if applicable.
Source: OCHA/FTS.

Regional distribution of funding, 2006

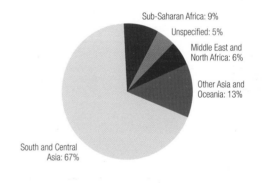

Note: The number of Appeals financed per region: Europe (0), Latin America and Caribbean (0), Middle East and North Africa (1), Other Asia and Oceania (0), South and Central Asia (0), Sub-Saharan Africa (1), Unspecified (1).
Source: OCHA/FTS.

Sectoral distribution of funding, inside and outside an Appeal, 2006 (US$ m)

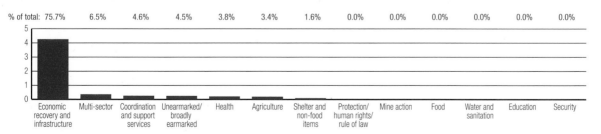

Notes: 'Unearmarked/broadly earmarked' category consists of funding not yet applied by recipient agency to particular project or sector.
Source: OCHA/FTS.

Spain

The Spanish Agency for International Cooperation (AECI) of the Ministry of Foreign Affairs and Cooperation is responsible for the coordination of humanitarian assistance. Ministries of Health and Defence play a smaller role in humanitarian and emergency response on behalf of the Spanish government. Spanish humanitarian assistance prioritises prevention, preparedness, and rehabilitation projects. Aid is channelled through multilateral organisations and Spanish NGOs.

Source: Ministry of Foreign Affairs and Cooperation, http://www.aeci.es

HRI scores by pillar

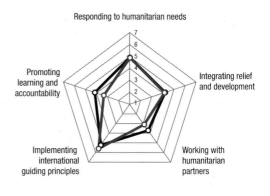

-O- Spain   -O- DAC average

HRI results

ADVANTAGES	SCORE	RANK
Responding to humanitarian needs		
Distribution of funding relative to sector, forgotten emergency and media coverage	6.05	3
Funding in proportion to need	5.23	1
Neutrality	6.31	2
Working with humanitarian partners		
Promoting role of NGOs	5.92	3
Implementing international guiding principles		
Implementing human rights law	7.00	1

DISADVANTAGES	SCORE	RANK
Responding to humanitarian needs		
Funding to priority sectors	2.15	22
Integrating relief and development		
Funding to strengthen local capacity	1.30	21
Working with humanitarian partners		
Funding IFRC Appeals	1.04	21
Implementing international guiding principles		
Engagement in risk mitigation	5.08	20
Learning and accountability		
Support to main accountability initiatives	1.00	20

Overview of humanitarian aid

	Spain 2005	Spain 2006[3]	Share of total DAC (%) 2005	Share of total DAC (%) 2006[3]
Total humanitarian aid, of which:	126.4	195.6	1.3	1.9
Bilateral humanitarian aid[1]	114.4	143.5	1.4	1.6
Multilateral humanitarian aid[2]*	12.0	42.2	0.8	3.3
Official development assistance	3,018	3,814	2.6	3.3
Funding to Central Emergency Response Fund**	n/a	10.0	n/a	3.5
Other funds committed under flexible terms[4]***	0.0	0.0	0.0	0.0
			DAC average	
Total humanitarian aid per capita (US$)	3	4	19	24
Total humanitarian aid / official development assistance (%)	4.2	5.1	8.9	9.4
Total humanitarian aid / GNI (%)	0.011	0.016	0.043	0.049

Notes: All data are given in current US$ m unless otherwise indicated.

1　Bilateral humanitarian aid is provided directly by a donor country to a recipient country and includes non-core earmarked contributions to humanitarian organisations but excludes category 'refugees in donor countries' (where 2006 data not available, estimated as average over last four years).

2　Core unearmarked humanitarian flows to UNHCR, UNICEF, WFP, UNRWA, UN/OCHA, ICRC and IFRC.

3　Preliminary; may include official support to asylum seekers in donor country.

4　Consists of IFRC's Disaster Relief Emergency Fund, Common Humanitarian Funds piloted in Sudan and Democratic Republic of Congo in 2006, Emergency Response Funds in 2006 for the DRC, Indonesia, Somalia, the Republic of Congo and Ethiopia and country Humanitarian Response Funds in 2005 for DPRK, DRC, Côte d'Ivoire and Somalia.

Sources: All data from OECD-DAC except: (*) UNHCR, UNICEF, WFP, UNRWA, UN/OCHA, ICRC and IFRC; (**) OCHA; (***) OCHA, IFRC; Common Humanitarian Fund for Sudan, Common Humanitarian Action Plan DRC 2007, US Federal Reserve.

Response times by crisis type, 2005–2006 (days)

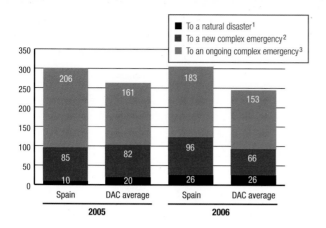

Legend:
- ■ To a natural disaster[1]
- ■ To a new complex emergency[2]
- ■ To an ongoing complex emergency[3]

2005
- Spain: 206 / 85 / 10
- DAC average: 161 / 82 / 20

2006
- Spain: 183 / 96 / 26
- DAC average: 153 / 66 / 26

Notes: [1]Average number of days between launch date of a UN Appeal and commitment or disbursement of funds to given ongoing emergencies. [2]Average number of days between launch date of a UN Appeal and commitment or disbursement of funds to given new emergencies. [3]Average number of days between onset of natural disaster (following CRED dates) and commitment or disbursement of funds to given natural disaster.
Source: OCHA/FTS (status early May 2007), Centre for Research on Epidemiology of Disasters (http://www.cred.be/).

Main channels of humanitarian aid, 2006

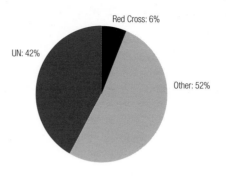

- Red Cross: 6%
- UN: 42%
- Other: 52%

Notes: The UN category encompasses humanitarian receipts by UNHCR, UNICEF, WFP, UNRWA and UN/OCHA including CERF funding; the Red Cross category encompasses humanitarian receipts by IFRC and ICRC. 'Other' is a residual category and includes humanitarian flows to governments, Red Cross national societies, intergovernmental organisations, NGOs, private organisations and foundations. Shares are taken relative to total humanitarian aid reported in 'Overview of humanitarian aid' table.
Sources: UN/OCHA, UNICEF, WFP, UNRWA, UNHCR, ICRC, IFRC, OECD.

Funding per emergency, 2006

Crisis	US$ m	% of total	Inside an Appeal (%)	Outside an Appeal (%)
Palestinian Territories	6.9	10.3	63.1	36.9
Lebanon Crisis, July	5.5	8.2	48.7	51.3
Sudan	5.5	8.2	55.3	44.7
Democratic Republic of Congo	4.0	6.0	93.7	6.3
Algeria	3.3	5.0	0.0	100.0
Guatemala	3.3	4.9	0.0	100.0
Chad	2.6	3.8	35.0	65.0
West Africa	1.7	2.5	100.0	0.0
Somalia: Floods, November	1.5	2.3	0.0	100.0
Zimbabwe	1.4	2.1	96.4	3.6
Other	**31.3**	**46.8**	**43.5**	**56.5**
Total	**66.8**	**100.0**	**46.8**	**53.2**

Notes: Category 'Other' includes both provision of unearmarked funds (inside an Appeal to CERF and outside an Appeal) and other miscellaneous flows (only outside an Appeal) if applicable.
Source: OCHA/FTS.

Regional distribution of funding, 2006

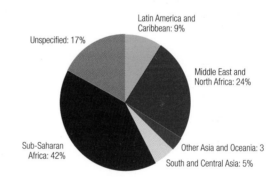

- Latin America and Caribbean: 9%
- Unspecified: 17%
- Middle East and North Africa: 24%
- Sub-Saharan Africa: 42%
- Other Asia and Oceania: 3
- South and Central Asia: 5%

Note: The number of Appeals financed per region: Europe (0), Latin America and Caribbean (0), Middle East and North Africa (2), Other Asia and Oceania (0), South and Central Asia (1), Sub-Saharan Africa (13), Unspecified (1).
Source: OCHA/FTS.

Sectoral distribution of funding, inside and outside an Appeal, 2006 (US$ m)

% of total: 26.6% | 18.8% | 18.1% | 10.1% | 7.3% | 5.1% | 4.2% | 4.0% | 3.1% | 1.4% | 1.4% | 0.0% | 0.0%

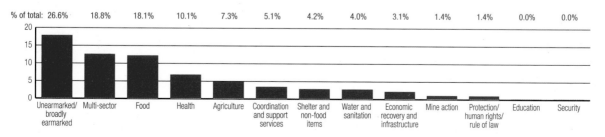

Categories: Unearmarked/broadly earmarked | Multi-sector | Food | Health | Agriculture | Coordination and support services | Shelter and non-food items | Water and sanitation | Economic recovery and infrastructure | Mine action | Protection/human rights/rule of law | Education | Security

Notes: 'Unearmarked/broadly earmarked' category consists of funding not yet applied by recipient agency to particular project or sector.
Source: OCHA/FTS.

Sweden

Swedish humanitarian aid management is shared between the Ministry of Foreign Affairs, responsible for policy development and coordination of humanitarian aid, and the Swedish International Development Cooperation Agency (SIDA), overseeing implementation and follow-up. In addition, the Swedish Rescue Services Agency under the Ministry of Defence may be called upon to implement humanitarian action. Sweden's humanitarian assistance policy (Humanitarian Aid Policy, 2004) fully embraces the GHD Principles and incorporates a strong rights perspective. The policy provides guidance on preventive measures for natural disasters, conflict prevention and the relationship to development cooperation. Sweden has been a key promoter of the GHD initiative and has formulated a GHD Domestic Implementation Plan. Sweden provides substantial support to multilateral organisations and was the third-largest donor to the CERF in 2006. SIDA offers multi-year funding arrangements running up to three years. SIDA primarily directs its support to Swedish NGOs but can also fund foreign NGOs. A select number of Swedish NGOs also have access to rapid-response funds for contingencies.

Source: Ministry of Foreign Affairs, SIDA, DAC Peer Review for Sweden (OECD, 2005), GHD Domestic Implementation Plan for Sweden.

HRI scores by pillar

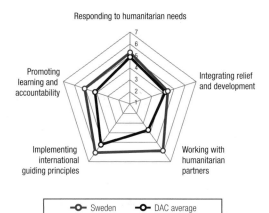

HRI results

ADVANTAGES	SCORE	RANK
Responding to humanitarian needs		
Distribution of funding relative to sector, forgotten emergency and media coverage	7.00	1
Working with humanitarian partners		
Funding CERF	7.00	1
Funding UN Consolidated Inter-Agency Appeals	7.00	1
Reducing earmarking	5.63	1
Learning and accountability		
Supporting learning and accountability initiatives	5.62	1

DISADVANTAGES	SCORE	RANK
Responding to humanitarian needs		
Funding to priority sectors	1.00	23
Integrating relief and development		
Consultation with beneficiaries on design and implementation	4.74	14
Consultation with beneficiaries on monitoring and evaluation	4.98	14
Supporting long-term development aims	4.90	15
Learning and accountability		
Encouraging regular evaluations	5.43	13

Overview of humanitarian aid	Sweden		Share of total DAC (%)	
	2005	2006[3]	2005	2006[3]
Total humanitarian aid, of which:	409.7	634.1	4.1	6.0
Bilateral humanitarian aid[1]	261.5	459.4	3.1	5.1
Multilateral humanitarian aid[2]*	148.3	133.6	9.6	10.5
Official development assistance	3,362	3,967	2.9	3.5
Funding to Central Emergency Response Fund**	n/a	41.1	n/a	14.3
Other funds committed under flexible terms[4]***	4.9	28.0	33.1	10.0
			DAC average	
Total humanitarian aid per capita (US$)	45	70	19	24
Total humanitarian aid / official development assistance (%)	12.2	16.0	8.9	9
Total humanitarian aid / GNI (%)	0.115	0.164	0.043	0.0490

Notes: All data are given in current US$ m unless otherwise indicated.

1 Bilateral humanitarian aid is provided directly by a donor country to a recipient country and includes non-core earmarked contributions to humanitarian organisations but excludes category 'refugees in donor countries' (where 2006 data not available, estimated as average over last four years).

2 Core unearmarked humanitarian flows to UNHCR, UNICEF, WFP, UNRWA, UN/OCHA, ICRC and IFRC.

3 Preliminary; may include official support to asylum seekers in donor country.

4 Consists of IFRC's Disaster Relief Emergency Fund, Common Humanitarian Funds piloted in Sudan and Democratic Republic of Congo in 2006, Emergency Response Funds in 2006 for the DRC, Indonesia, Somalia, the Republic of Congo and Ethiopia and country Humanitarian Response Funds in 2005 for DPRK, DRC, Côte d'Ivoire and Somalia.

Sources: All data from OECD-DAC except: (*) UNHCR, UNICEF, WFP, UNRWA, UN/OCHA, ICRC and IFRC; (**) OCHA; (***) OCHA, IFRC; Common Humanitarian Fund for Sudan, Common Humanitarian Action Plan DRC 2007, US Federal Reserve.

Response times by crisis type, 2005–2006 (days)

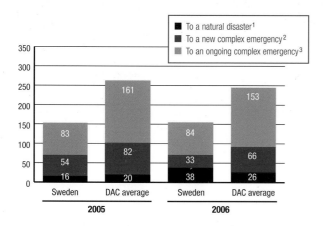

- ■ To a natural disaster[1]
- ■ To a new complex emergency[2]
- ■ To an ongoing complex emergency[3]

2005
- Sweden: 16, 54, 83
- DAC average: 20, 82, 161

2006
- Sweden: 38, 33, 84
- DAC average: 26, 66, 153

Notes: [1]Average number of days between launch date of a UN Appeal and commitment or disbursement of funds to given ongoing emergencies. [2]Average number of days between launch date of a UN Appeal and commitment or disbursement of funds to given new emergencies. [3]Average number of days between onset of natural disaster (following CRED dates) and commitment or disbursement of funds to given natural disaster.
Source: OCHA/FTS (status early May 2007), Centre for Research on Epidemiology of Disasters (http://www.cred.be/).

Main channels of humanitarian aid, 2006

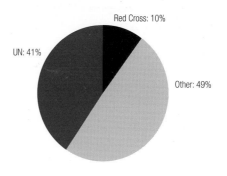

- Red Cross: 10%
- UN: 41%
- Other: 49%

Notes: The UN category encompasses humanitarian receipts by UNHCR, UNICEF, WFP, UNRWA and UN/OCHA including CERF funding; the Red Cross category encompasses humanitarian receipts by IFRC and ICRC. 'Other' is a residual category and includes humanitarian flows to governments, Red Cross national societies, intergovernmental organisations, NGOs, private organisations and foundations. Shares are taken relative to total humanitarian aid reported in 'Overview of humanitarian aid' table.
Sources: UN/OCHA, UNICEF, WFP, UNRWA, UNHCR, ICRC, IFRC, OECD.

Funding per emergency, 2006

Crisis	US$ m	% of total	Inside an Appeal (%)	Outside an Appeal (%)
Palestinian Territories	58.6	16.3	25.4	74.6
Sudan	31.9	8.9	56.5	43.5
Democratic Republic of Congo	19.5	5.4	78.2	21.8
Lebanon July	13.2	3.7	38.3	61.7
Somalia	9.8	2.7	76.7	23.3
Uganda	9.6	2.7	88.7	11.3
West Africa	8.8	2.4	55.3	44.7
Liberia	8.6	2.4	80.4	19.6
Côte d'Ivoire	6.9	1.9	36.7	63.3
Zimbabwe	6.5	1.8	87.0	13.0
Other	**186.9**	**51.9**	**40.7**	**59.3**
Total	**360.3**	**100.0**	**45.9**	**54.1**

Notes: Category 'Other' includes both provision of unearmarked funds (inside an Appeal to CERF and outside an Appeal) and other miscellaneous flows (only outside an Appeal) if applicable.
Source: OCHA/FTS.

Regional distribution of funding, 2006

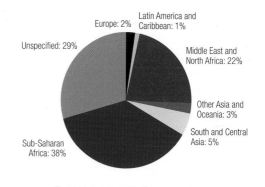

- Europe: 2%
- Latin America and Caribbean: 1%
- Unspecified: 29%
- Middle East and North Africa: 22%
- Other Asia and Oceania: 3%
- South and Central Asia: 5%
- Sub-Saharan Africa: 38%

Note: The number of Appeals financed per region: Europe (1), Latin America and Caribbean (0), Middle East and North Africa (2), Other Asia and Oceania (2), South and Central Asia (4), Sub-Saharan Africa (18), Unspecified (2).
Source: OCHA/FTS.

Sectoral distribution of funding, inside and outside an Appeal, 2006 (US$ m)

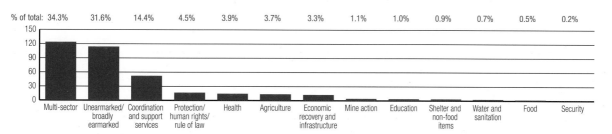

% of total: 34.3% | 31.6% | 14.4% | 4.5% | 3.9% | 3.7% | 3.3% | 1.1% | 1.0% | 0.9% | 0.7% | 0.5% | 0.2%

Multi-sector | Unearmarked/ broadly earmarked | Coordination and support services | Protection/ human rights/ rule of law | Health | Agriculture | Economic recovery and infrastructure | Mine action | Education | Shelter and non-food items | Water and sanitation | Food | Security

Notes: 'Unearmarked/broadly earmarked' category consists of funding not yet applied by recipient agency to particular project or sector.
Source: OCHA/FTS.

Switzerland

The overall responsibility for Swiss humanitarian action rests with the Humanitarian Aid Department, a Branch of the Swiss Agency for Development and cooperation (SDC), itself a Directorate General of the Ministry of Foreign Affairs. Under its leadership, other actors, including the Swiss Army, assume subsidiary roles. Switzerland's Humanitarian Action Strategy ('Humanitäre Hilfe des Bundes, Strategie 2010) is based on a 1976 Law on Humanitarian Aid, focussing on emergency relief (rapid response), prevention and preparedness, recovery and reconstruction and advocacy. These serve to anchor humanitarian aid firmly within IHL and humanitarian principles. The Strategy refers in passing to the GHD. SDC is both a donor and an implementing agency, managing the delivery of approximately one-sixth of the annual humanitarian aid budget. Switzerland has a long humanitarian tradition and hosts many of the large multilateral humanitarian organisations that also receive strong financial backing from SDC. The humanitarian budget is channelled in roughly equal measure to bilateral programmes or Swiss NGOs (although foreign NGOs can be funded in principle), to the Red Cross Movement and to the UN. SDC offers multi-year contracts for prevention and preparedness, recovery and reconstruction issues that last between 3-5 years.

Source: Swiss Agency for Development and Cooperation, DAC Peer Review for Switzerland (OECD, 2005)

HRI scores by pillar

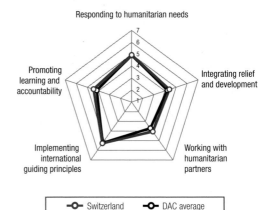

HRI results

ADVANTAGES	SCORE	RANK
Responding to humanitarian needs		
Impartiality	6.06	2
Integrating relief and development		
Funding to strengthen local capacity	4.07	2
Working with humanitarian partners		
Funding Red Cross Movement	7.00	1
Promoting role of NGOs	6.13	2
Learning and accountability		
Support to main accountability initiatives	6.33	2

DISADVANTAGES	SCORE	RANK
Responding to humanitarian needs		
Distribution of funding relative to ECHO's GNA	2.46	22
Funding to priority sectors	3.05	21
Timely funding to onset disasters	3.30	19
Implementing international guiding principles		
Implementing human rights law	3.40	19
Learning and accountability		
Supporting accountability in humanitarian action	5.10	22

Overview of humanitarian aid	Switzerland		Share of total DAC (%)	
	2005	2006[3]	2005	2006[3]
Total humanitarian aid, of which:	267.4	255.2	2.7	2.4
Bilateral humanitarian aid[1]	191.7	173.4	2.3	1.9
Multilateral humanitarian aid[2]*	75.7	77.9	4.9	6.1
Official development assistance	1,767	1,647	1.5	1.4
Funding to Central Emergency Response Fund**	n/a	3.9	n/a	1.4
Other funds committed under flexible terms[4]***	0.0	0.2	0.0	0.1
			DAC average	
Total humanitarian aid per capita (US$)	36	34	19	24
Total humanitarian aid / official development assistance (%)	15.1	15.5	8.9	9
Total humanitarian aid / GNI (%)	0.067	0.061	0.043	0.049

Notes: All data are given in current US$ m unless otherwise indicated.
1   Bilateral humanitarian aid is provided directly by a donor country to a recipient country and includes non-core earmarked contributions to humanitarian organisations but excludes category 'refugees in donor countries' (where 2006 data not available, estimated as average over last four years).
2   Core unearmarked humanitarian flows to UNHCR, UNICEF, WFP, UNRWA, UN/OCHA, ICRC and IFRC.
3   Preliminary; may include official support to asylum seekers in donor country.
4   Consists of IFRC's Disaster Relief Emergency Fund, Common Humanitarian Funds piloted in Sudan and Democratic Republic of Congo in 2006, Emergency Response Funds in 2006 for the DRC, Indonesia, Somalia, the Republic of Congo and Ethiopia and country Humanitarian Response Funds in 2005 for DPRK, DRC, Côte d'Ivoire and Somalia.
Sources: All data from OECD-DAC except: (*) UNHCR, UNICEF, WFP, UNRWA, UN/OCHA, ICRC and IFRC; (**) OCHA; (***) OCHA, IFRC; Common Humanitarian Fund for Sudan, Common Humanitarian Action Plan DRC 2007, US Federal Reserve.

Response times by crisis type, 2005–2006 (days)

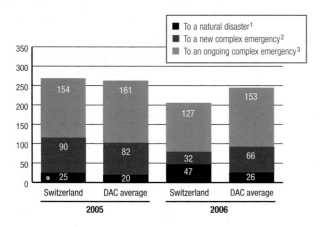

Legend:
- ■ To a natural disaster[1]
- ■ To a new complex emergency[2]
- ■ To an ongoing complex emergency[3]

	Switzerland 2005	DAC average 2005	Switzerland 2006	DAC average 2006
To an ongoing complex emergency	154	161	127	153
To a new complex emergency	90	82	32	66
To a natural disaster	25	20	47	26

Notes: [1]Average number of days between launch date of a UN Appeal and commitment or disbursement of funds to given ongoing emergencies. [2]Average number of days between launch date of a UN Appeal and commitment or disbursement of funds to given new emergencies. [3]Average number of days between onset of natural disaster (following CRED dates) and commitment or disbursement of funds to given natural disaster.
Source: OCHA/FTS (status early May 2007), Centre for Research on Epidemiology of Disasters (http://www.cred.be/).

Main channels of humanitarian aid, 2006

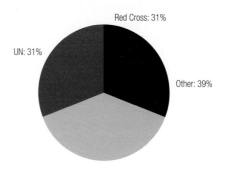

Red Cross: 31%
UN: 31%
Other: 39%

Notes: The UN category encompasses humanitarian receipts by UNHCR, UNICEF, WFP, UNRWA and UN/OCHA including CERF funding; the Red Cross category encompasses humanitarian receipts by IFRC and ICRC. 'Other' is a residual category and includes humanitarian flows to governments, Red Cross national societies, intergovernmental organisations, NGOs, private organisations and foundations. Shares are taken relative to total humanitarian aid reported in 'Overview of humanitarian aid' table.
Sources: UN/OCHA, UNICEF, WFP, UNRWA, UNHCR, ICRC, IFRC, OECD.

Funding per emergency, 2006

Crisis	US$ m	% of total	Inside an Appeal (%)	Outside an Appeal (%)
Palestinian Territories	16.2	6.1	33.4	66.6
Lebanon Crisis, July	15.4	5.8	0.0	100.0
Sudan	8.1	3.1	55.2	44.8
North Caucasus	5.7	2.2	70.6	29.4
Liberia	5.6	2.1	36.8	63.2
Sri Lanka	4.6	1.7	8.8	91.2
Pakistan	4.4	1.7	0.0	100.0
Belarus	4.2	1.6	0.0	100.0
West Africa	3.8	1.4	98.0	2.0
South Caucasus	3.8	1.4	0.0	100.0
Other	192.7	72.9	8.0	92.0
Total	**264.4**	**100.0**	**13.4**	**86.6**

Notes: Category 'Other' includes both provision of unearmarked funds (inside an Appeal to CERF and outside an Appeal) and other miscellaneous flows (only outside an Appeal) if applicable.
Source: OCHA/FTS.

Regional distribution of funding, 2006

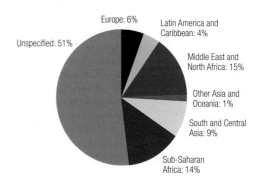

Europe: 6%
Latin America and Caribbean: 4%
Unspecified: 51%
Middle East and North Africa: 15%
Other Asia and Oceania: 1%
South and Central Asia: 9%
Sub-Saharan Africa: 14%

Note: The number of Appeals financed per region: Europe (1), Latin America and Caribbean (0), Middle East and North Africa (1), Other Asia and Oceania (0), South and Central Asia (3), Sub-Saharan Africa (10), Unspecified (1).
Source: OCHA/FTS.

Sectoral distribution of funding, inside and outside an Appeal, 2006 (US$ m)

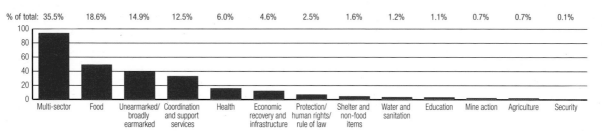

% of total: 35.5% | 18.6% | 14.9% | 12.5% | 6.0% | 4.6% | 2.5% | 1.6% | 1.2% | 1.1% | 0.7% | 0.7% | 0.1%

Categories: Multi-sector | Food | Unearmarked/broadly earmarked | Coordination and support services | Health | Economic recovery and infrastructure | Protection/human rights/rule of law | Shelter and non-food items | Water and sanitation | Education | Mine action | Agriculture | Security

Notes: 'Unearmarked/broadly earmarked' category consists of funding not yet applied by recipient agency to particular project or sector.
Source: OCHA/FTS.

United Kingdom

The Department for International Development (DFID) is in charge of humanitarian assistance. Its Conflict, Humanitarian and Security Department (CHASE), UN Conflict and Humanitarian Division, and Africa Conflict and Humanitarian Aid Unit (ACHU) share responsibilities for humanitarian action. CHASE is responsible for policy development, monitoring, and operational support; ACHU for humanitarian programmes at the regional and country level. Other entities with smaller roles include the Foreign and Commonwealth Office, the Ministry of Defence and the Cabinet Office. The UK's humanitarian assistance policy (saving lives, relieving suffering, protecting dignity: DFID's Humanitarian Policy, 2006) is strongly GHD in character. The UK has been a key supporter of the GHD and promoted the formal endorsement by the OECD/DAC of the GHD Principles, which has led to humanitarian aid being assessed within the DAC Peer Review framework. It has formulated a GHD Domestic Implementation Plan. The UK is a leading supporter of multilateral organisations and, in 2006, was the most generous donor to CERF in absolute terms and has been a key contributor to various pooled funds.

Source: Department for International Development, DAC Peer Review for UK (OECD, 2006), GHD Domestic Implementation Plan for the UK.

HRI scores by pillar

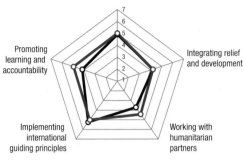

Legend: United Kingdom — DAC average

HRI results

ADVANTAGES	SCORE	RANK
Responding to humanitarian needs		
Distribution of funding relative to ECHO's GNA	7.00	1
Working with humanitarian partners		
Funding quick disbursement mechanisms	7.00	1
Predictability of funding	4.63	2
Learning and accountability		
Number of evaluations	4.97	4
Support to main accountability initiatives	6.22	4

DISADVANTAGES	SCORE	RANK
Responding to humanitarian needs		
Distribution of funding relative to historical ties and geographical proximity	1.73	21
Independence	4.92	18
Neutrality	5.42	19
Implementing international guiding principles		
Enhancing security	4.72	18
Implementing human rights law	3.40	19

Overview of humanitarian aid

	United Kingdom 2005	United Kingdom 2006[3]	Share of total DAC (%) 2005	Share of total DAC (%) 2006[3]
Total humanitarian aid, of which:	800.3	964.9	8.1	9.2
Bilateral humanitarian aid[1]	628.4	764.0	7.5	8.5
Multilateral humanitarian aid[2]*	171.9	131.0	11.1	10.3
Official development assistance	10,767	12,607	9.3	11.0
Funding to Central Emergency Response Fund**	n/a	69.9	n/a	24.3
Other funds committed under flexible terms[4]***	8.0	154.7	54.4	55.2

	United Kingdom 2005	United Kingdom 2006[3]	DAC average 2005	DAC average 2006[3]
Total humanitarian aid per capita (US$)	13	16	19	24
Total humanitarian aid / official development assistance (%)	13.1	7.7	8.9	9.4
Total humanitarian aid / GNI (%)	0.035	0.040	0.043	0.049

Notes: All data are given in current US$ m unless otherwise indicated.
1 Bilateral humanitarian aid is provided directly by a donor country to a recipient country and includes non-core earmarked contributions to humanitarian organisations but excludes category 'refugees in donor countries' (where 2006 data not available, estimated as average over last four years).
2 Core unearmarked humanitarian flows to UNHCR, UNICEF, WFP, UNRWA, UN/OCHA, ICRC and IFRC.
3 Preliminary; may include official support to asylum seekers in donor country.
4 Consists of IFRC's Disaster Relief Emergency Fund, Common Humanitarian Funds piloted in Sudan and Democratic Republic of Congo in 2006, Emergency Response Funds in 2006 for the DRC, Indonesia, Somalia, the Republic of Congo and Ethiopia and country Humanitarian Response Funds in 2005 for DPRK, DRC, Côte d'Ivoire and Somalia.
Sources: All data from OECD-DAC except: (*) UNHCR, UNICEF, WFP, UNRWA, UN/OCHA, ICRC and IFRC; (**) OCHA; (***) OCHA, IFRC; Common Humanitarian Fund for Sudan, Common Humanitarian Action Plan DRC 2007, US Federal Reserve.

Response times by crisis type, 2005–2006 (days)

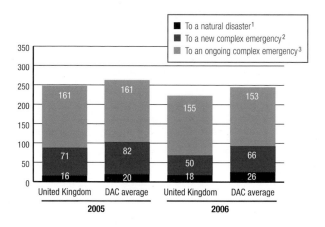

- To a natural disaster[1]
- To a new complex emergency[2]
- To an ongoing complex emergency[3]

Notes: [1]Average number of days between launch date of a UN Appeal and commitment or disbursement of funds to given ongoing emergencies. [2]Average number of days between launch date of a UN Appeal and commitment or disbursement of funds to given new emergencies. [3]Average number of days between onset of natural disaster (following CRED dates) and commitment or disbursement of funds to given natural disaster.
Source: OCHA/FTS (status early May 2007), Centre for Research on Epidemiology of Disasters (http://www.cred.be/).

Main channels of humanitarian aid, 2006

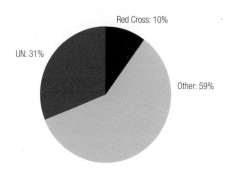

Red Cross: 10%
UN: 31%
Other: 59%

Notes: The UN category encompasses humanitarian receipts by UNHCR, UNICEF, WFP, UNRWA and UN/OCHA including CERF funding; the Red Cross category encompasses humanitarian receipts by IFRC and ICRC. 'Other' is a residual category and includes humanitarian flows to governments, Red Cross national societies, intergovernmental organisations, NGOs, private organisations and foundations. Shares are taken relative to total humanitarian aid reported in 'Overview of humanitarian aid' table.
Sources: UN/OCHA, UNICEF, WFP, UNRWA, UNHCR, ICRC, IFRC, OECD.

Funding per emergency, 2006

Crisis	US$ m	% of total	Inside an Appeal (%)	Outside an Appeal (%)
Sudan	97.1	20.4	98.9	1.1
Democratic Republic of Congo	84.3	17.7	76.2	23.8
Uganda	62.9	13.2	95.0	5.0
Zimbabwe	54.3	11.4	7.5	92.5
Somalia	25.1	5.3	77.6	22.4
Lebanon Crisis, July	19.4	4.1	25.9	74.1
Indonesia: Java Earthquake, May	9.4	2.0	69.5	30.5
Ethiopia	8.5	1.8	100.0	0.0
Great Lakes Region	6.3	1.3	100.0	0.0
Appeal for Improving Humanitarian Response Capacity: Cluster	5.6	1.2	100.0	0.0
Other	103.4	21.7	87.7	12.3
Total	**476.4**	**100.0**	**76.9**	**23.1**

Notes: Category 'Other' includes both provision of unearmarked funds (inside an Appeal to CERF and outside an Appeal) and other miscellaneous flows (only outside an Appeal) if applicable.
Source: OCHA/FTS.

Regional distribution of funding, 2006

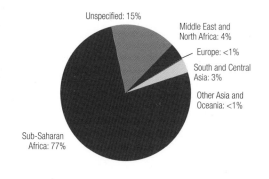

Unspecified: 15%
Middle East and North Africa: 4%
Europe: <1%
South and Central Asia: 3%
Other Asia and Oceania: <1%
Sub-Saharan Africa: 77%

Note: The number of Appeals financed per region: Europe (1), Latin America and Caribbean (0), Middle East and North Africa (1), Other Asia and Oceania (0), South and Central Asia (3), Sub-Saharan Africa (15), Unspecified (2).
Source: OCHA/FTS.

Sectoral distribution of funding, inside and outside an Appeal, 2006 (US$ m)

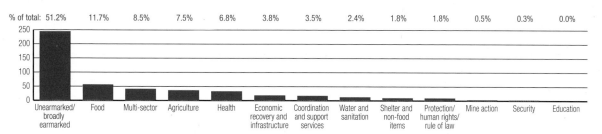

% of total: 51.2% | 11.7% | 8.5% | 7.5% | 6.8% | 3.8% | 3.5% | 2.4% | 1.8% | 1.8% | 0.5% | 0.3% | 0.0%

Unearmarked/broadly earmarked | Food | Multi-sector | Agriculture | Health | Economic recovery and infrastructure | Coordination and support services | Water and sanitation | Shelter and non-food items | Protection/human rights/rule of law | Mine action | Security | Education

Notes: 'Unearmarked/broadly earmarked' category consists of funding not yet applied by recipient agency to particular project or sector.
Source: OCHA/FTS.

United States

US humanitarian action has three central actors, the Office for Foreign Disaster Assistance (OFDA), designated as the President's Special Coordinator for International Disaster Assistance; Food for Peace (FFP), which purchases US grown commodities and distributes them to recipient countries; and the Department of State's Bureau of Population, Refugees and Migration (PRM), whose mission is to provide protection and assistance to refugees and victims of conflict and to advance US population and migration policies. The first two are part of the United States Agency for International Development (USAID), which takes the lead role in coordinating the response to humanitarian disasters. Other government departments have subsidiary roles. Due to the complex institutional structures that govern its massive humanitarian aid budget of over US$3 billion, there is no single policy strategy but the new Foreign Assistance Framework (2006) spells out a new orientation for humanitarian assistance, including a stronger emphasis on integrating relief and development. OFDA is currently working on a GHD implementation plan to be launched in October 2007. In line with its mandate, PRM's principal partners are the ICRC, UNHCR, IOM and UNRWA; OFDA works through NGOs, OCHA, UNICEF and the WFP; FFP deals mainly with the WFP and US NGOs.

Source: PRM, FFP, OFDA, DAC Peer Review for US (OECD, 2006).

HRI scores by pillar

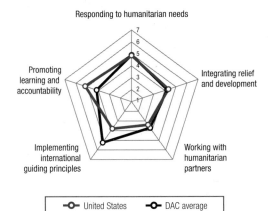

HRI results

ADVANTAGES	SCORE	RANK
Responding to humanitarian needs		
Distribution of funding relative to ECHO's GNA	6.97	2
Integrating relief and development		
Consultation with beneficiaries on monitoring and evaluation	5.51	2
Working with humanitarian partners		
Funding to NGOs	7.00	1
Learning and accountability		
Number of evaluations	6.07	2
Supporting accountability in humanitarian action	6.06	1

DISADVANTAGES	SCORE	RANK
Responding to humanitarian needs		
Funding in cash	3.98	22
Independence	3.99	23
Working with humanitarian partners		
Unearmarked or broadly earmarked funds	1.23	22
Implementing international guiding principles		
Implementing human rights law	1.00	22
Implementing international humanitarian law	1.00	22

Overview of humanitarian aid

Overview of humanitarian aid	United States			Share of total DAC (%)	
	2005	2006[3]		2005	2006[3]
Total humanitarian aid, of which:	3,627.7	3,338.3		36.7	31.8
Bilateral humanitarian aid[1]	3,450.2	3,192.9		41.4	35.7
Multilateral humanitarian aid[2]*	177.5	135.4		11.5	10.7
Official development assistance	27,622	22,739		23.8	19.9
Funding to Central Emergency Response Fund**	n/a	10.0		n/a	3.5
Other funds committed under flexible terms[4]***	0.1	0.1		0.6	0.0
				DAC average	
Total humanitarian aid per capita (US$)	12	11		19	24
Total humanitarian aid / official development assistance (%)	13.1	14.7		8.9	9.4
Total humanitarian aid / GNI (%)	0.029	0.025		0.043	0.049

Notes: All data are given in current US$ m unless otherwise indicated.

1 Bilateral humanitarian aid is provided directly by a donor country to a recipient country and includes non-core earmarked contributions to humanitarian organisations but excludes category 'refugees in donor countries' (where 2006 data not available, estimated as average over last four years).

2 Core unearmarked humanitarian flows to UNHCR, UNICEF, WFP, UNRWA, UN/OCHA, ICRC and IFRC.

3 Preliminary; may include official support to asylum seekers in donor country.

4 Consists of IFRC's Disaster Relief Emergency Fund, Common Humanitarian Funds piloted in Sudan and Democratic Republic of Congo in 2006, Emergency Response Funds in 2006 for the DRC, Indonesia, Somalia, the Republic of Congo and Ethiopia and country Humanitarian Response Funds in 2005 for DPRK, DRC, Côte d'Ivoire and Somalia.

Sources: All data from OECD-DAC except: (*) UNHCR, UNICEF, WFP, UNRWA, UN/OCHA, ICRC and IFRC; (**) OCHA; (***) OCHA, IFRC; Common Humanitarian Fund for Sudan, Common Humanitarian Action Plan DRC 2007, US Federal Reserve.

Response times by crisis type, 2005–2006 (days)

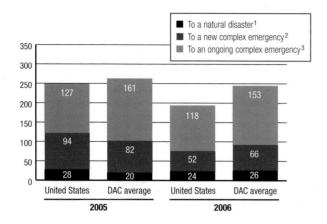

Legend:
- To a natural disaster[1]
- To a new complex emergency[2]
- To an ongoing complex emergency[3]

2005:
- United States: 28, 94, 127
- DAC average: 20, 82, 161

2006:
- United States: 24, 52, 118
- DAC average: 26, 66, 153

Notes: [1]Average number of days between launch date of a UN Appeal and commitment or disbursement of funds to given ongoing emergencies. [2]Average number of days between launch date of a UN Appeal and commitment or disbursement of funds to given new emergencies. [3]Average number of days between onset of natural disaster (following CRED dates) and commitment or disbursement of funds to given natural disaster.
Source: OCHA/FTS (status early May 2007), Centre for Research on Epidemiology of Disasters (http://www.cred.be/).

Main channels of humanitarian aid, 2006

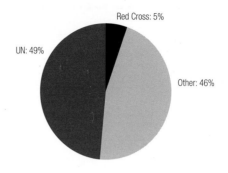

- Red Cross: 5%
- UN: 49%
- Other: 46%

Notes: The UN category encompasses humanitarian receipts by UNHCR, UNICEF, WFP, UNRWA and UN/OCHA including CERF funding; the Red Cross category encompasses humanitarian receipts by IFRC and ICRC. 'Other' is a residual category and includes humanitarian flows to governments, Red Cross national societies, intergovernmental organisations, NGOs, private organisations and foundations. Shares are taken relative to total humanitarian aid reported in 'Overview of humanitarian aid' table.
Sources: UN/OCHA, UNICEF, WFP, UNRWA, UNHCR, ICRC, IFRC, OECD.

Funding per emergency, 2006

Crisis	US$ m	% of total	Inside an Appeal (%)	Outside an Appeal (%)
Sudan	685.5	36.1	64.6	35.4
Ethiopia	238.0	12.5	57.0	43.0
Lebanon Crisis, July	106.4	5.6	16.8	83.2
Kenya	102.3	5.4	0.0	100.0
Somalia	85.0	4.5	91.6	8.4
Palestinian Territories	80.8	4.3	100.0	0.0
Democratic Republic of Congo	77.0	4.1	66.6	33.4
Chad	63.5	3.3	78.2	21.8
Uganda	54.1	2.8	82.4	17.6
West Africa	52.9	2.8	99.4	0.6
Other	**353.0**	**18.6**	**46.4**	**53.6**
Total	**1898.3**	**100.0**	**58.8**	**41.2**

Notes: Category 'Other' includes both provision of unearmarked funds (inside an Appeal to CERF and outside an Appeal) and other miscellaneous flows (only outside an Appeal) if applicable.
Source: OCHA/FTS.

Regional distribution of funding, 2006

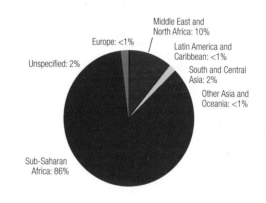

- Middle East and North Africa: 10%
- Europe: <1%
- Latin America and Caribbean: <1%
- Unspecified: 2%
- South and Central Asia: 2%
- Other Asia and Oceania: <1%
- Sub-Saharan Africa: 86%

Note: The number of Appeals financed per region: Europe (1), Latin America and Caribbean (0), Middle East and North Africa (2), Other Asia and Oceania (1), South and Central Asia (4), Sub-Saharan Africa (20), Unspecified (2).
Source: OCHA/FTS.

Sectoral distribution of funding, inside and outside an Appeal, 2006 (US$ m)

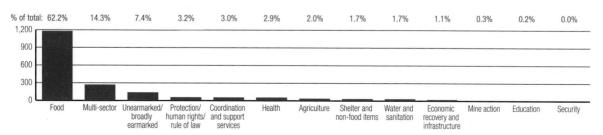

% of total: 62.2% | 14.3% | 7.4% | 3.2% | 3.0% | 2.9% | 2.0% | 1.7% | 1.7% | 1.1% | 0.3% | 0.2% | 0.0%

Categories: Food | Multi-sector | Unearmarked/broadly earmarked | Protection/human rights/rule of law | Coordination and support services | Health | Agriculture | Shelter and non-food items | Water and sanitation | Economic recovery and infrastructure | Mine action | Education | Security

Notes: 'Unearmarked/broadly earmarked' category consists of funding not yet applied by recipient agency to particular project or sector.
Source: OCHA/FTS.

Acronyms

AA ....Federal Foreign Office (Germany)

ADB................Asian Development Bank

AECI ....Spanish Agency for International Cooperation

AGHRYMET.....Agrometeorological and Hydrometeorological Programme

ALNAP............Active Learning Network for Accountability and Performance in Humanitarian Action

AMIS ....African Union Mission in Sudan

ASEAN ....Association of Southeast Asian Nations

AU ....African Union

AUC................Autodefensas Unidas de Colombia

BMZ ....Federal Ministry for Economic Cooperation and Development (Germany)

CAFOD...........Catholic Agency for Overseas Development

CAP................Consolidated Appeals Process

CARE ....Christian Action Research and Education

CCA ....Committee for Food Crisis (Comité de Crises Alimentaire)

CERF..............Central Emergency Response Fund (United Nations)

CFPJ ....Centre de Formation et de Perfectionnement des Journalistes

CHAP ....Common Humanitarian Action Plan

CHF................Common Humanitarian Fund

CIDA...............Canadian International Development Agency

CIH ....Humanitarian Information Centre

CIP ....Centre for International Policy

COHDES ....Council for Human Rights and Displacement (Colombia).

COMPAS ....Centre on Migration Policy and Society

CPA ....Comprehensive Peace Agreement (Sudan)

CRS................Catholic Relief Services

CSO ....civil society organisation

DAC................Development Assistance Committee (OECD)

DARA ....Development Assistance Research Associates

DCHA.............(Bureau for) Democracy, Conflict and Humanitarian Assistance (United States)

DCI ....Development Cooperation Ireland

DDR ....Disarmament, Demobilisation and Reintegration

DEV ....Directorate-General for Development (European Community)

DFID ....Department for International Development (UK)

DGCS.............General Direction of Development Cooperation (Italy)

DGDC.............Directorate-General for Development Cooperation (Belgium)

DI....................Development Initiatives

DMV/HH ....Humanitarian Aid Division (Netherlands)

DNPGCA ....Dispositif National de Prévention et de Gestion de Crises Alimentaires

DPA ....Darfur Peace Agreement

DRC ....Democratic Republic of Congo

EC ....European Commission

ECHO ....European Commission Humanitarian (Aid) Office

ELN ....Ejercito de Liberación Nacional (Colombia)

EMOP.............Emergency Mode Operation Plan

ENOUGH.........Campaign to Abolish Genocide and Mass Atrocities

ESPA ....Eastern Sudan Peace Agreement

EuropeAid........EuropeAid Co-operation Office (European Community)

EWS ....Early Warning System

FARC..............Fuerzas Armadas Revolucionarias de Colombia

FAO ....Food and Agriculture Organization (United Nations)

FEWSNET........Famine Early Warning System Network

FALINTIL..........Forças Armadas de Libertação Nacional de Timor Leste

FRETILIN ....Frente Revolucionária do Timor-Leste Independente

FRIDE ....Fundación para las Relaciones Internacionales y el Diálogo Exterior

FTS.................Financial Tracking System (OCHA)

GAM...............Global Acute Malnutrition

GHA ....Global Humanitarian Assistance

GHD ....Good Humanitarian Donorship

GIEWS............Global Information and Early Warning System

GoS................Government of Sudan

GoSS..............Government of Southern Sudan

HA..................Humanitarian Assistance

HAP................Humanitarian Action Plan

HAPI...............Humanitarian Accountability Partnership International

HCG...............Humanitarian Coordination Group

HDR...............Human Development Report (UNDP)

HPG...............Humanitarian Policy Group

HPN...............Humanitarian Practice Network

IASC...............Inter-Agency Standing Committee (UN)

ICF..................Interim Cooperation Framework ICG International Crisis Group

ICG.................International Crisis Group

ICRC...............International Conference of the Red Cross and Red Crescent

IDF..................Israeli Defense Force

IDMC..............Internal Displacement Monitoring Centre

IDP.................Internally Displaced Person

IERP...............Integrated Emergency Response Program

IFI...................International Financial Institutions

IFRC...............International Federation of the Red Cross and Red Crescent Societies

IHL..................International Humanitarian Law

IMF.................International Monetary Fund

INRAN............Niger National Institute of Agronomical Research

IOM................International Organization for Migration

IPAD...............Institute for Development Support (Portugal)

IRC.................International Rescue Committee

JEM................Justice and Equality Movement (Sudan)

LOD................Long-term Debt

LRA................Lord's Resistance Army (Sudan)

LRC................Lebanese Red Cross

MAS...............Muerte a Secuestradores (Colombia)

MCDA.............Military and Civil Defence Assets

MDG...............Millennium Development Goals

MFA................Ministry of Foreign Affairs

MIF.................Multinational Interim Force

MINURSO........United Nations Mission for the Referendum in Western Sahara

MINUSTAH......United Nations Stabilization Mission in Haiti (Mission des Nations Unies pour la Stabilisation en Haïti)

MOD...............Ministry of Defence

MONUC...........United Nations Mission in the Democratic Republic of Congo

MSF................Médecins Sans Frontières

NAFM.............Needs Assessment Framework Matrix

NZAid.............New Zealand Agency for International Development

OCHA.............Office for the Coordination of Humanitarian Affairs (United Nations)

ODA...............Official Development Assistance

ODI.................Overseas Development Institute

OECD-DAC.....Organisation for Economic Co-operation and Development-Development Assistance Committee

OFDA.............Office of Foreign Disaster Assistance (U.S.)

OHCHR...........Office of the High Commissioner for Human Rights (United Nations)

PLO................Palestine Liberation Organization

PRT................Provincial Reconstruction Team

RELEX............Directorate-General for External Relations (European Community)

RRM...............Rapid Reaction Mechanism

SDC...............Swiss Agency for Development and Cooperation

SEWA.............Self-Employed Women's Association (India)

SIDA...............Swedish Development Cooperation Agency

SMS...............Short Message Service

SPHERE..........Humanitarian Charter and Minimum Standards in Disaster Response

SPLM.............Sudan People's Liberation Movement (Sudan)

UNDAC...........United Nations Disaster Assessment and Coordination

UNDP.............United Nations Development Programme

UNFPA............United Nations Population Fund

UNHCR...........Office of the United Nations High Commissioner for Refugees

UNIFIL.............United Nations Interim Force in Lebanon

UNMIS............United Nations Mission in Sudan

UNMIT............United Nations Integrated Mission in Timor-Leste

UNSOSOM......United Nations Operation in Somalia

UNRWA...........United Nations Relief and Works Agency

USAID.............United States Agency for International Development

WFP...............World Food Programme

WHO..............World Health Organization

Appendix

Questionnaire on Good Practice in Humanitarian Donorship[1]

Following are the questions asked during each field visit to the relevant agencies actively working with donors, which had given them funding for that particular crisis. The target survey group included national and international NGOs, UN agencies, funds, and programmes, as well as other international organisations active in the field and involved in humanitarian action. A fuller discussion of the survey and underlying methodological issues is presented in Chapter 1 of the *Index*.

Objectives of humanitarian action

1.01 In your view, are the donor's objectives for humanitarian action consistent with saving lives, alleviating suffering, and maintaining human dignity?

Not at all	1 2 3 4 5 6 7	Completely and fully

1.02 In your view are the donor's objectives for humanitarian action consistent with strengthening preparedness for emergencies?

Not at all	1 2 3 4 5 6 7	Completely and fully

2.01 Are the donor's humanitarian actions *impartial*, meaning implemented solely on the basis of need, without discrimination between or within affected populations?

Seldom, if ever	1 2 3 4 5 6 7	Always

2.02 Are the donor's humanitarian actions *neutral*, meaning not favouring any side in an armed conflict or dispute?

No, they are biased in favour of one side	1 2 3 4 5 6 7	Totally neutral

2.03 Are the donor's humanitarian actions *independent* of political and economic objectives?

Seldom, if ever	1 2 3 4 5 6 7	Always

2.04 Are the donor's humanitarian actions *independent* of military objectives?

Seldom, if ever	1 2 3 4 5 6 7	Always

General principles

3.01 How actively is the donor engaged in humanitarian protection to reduce the risk and extent of harm to civilians and to safeguard their dignity during this crisis?

Disengaged and ineffective	1 2 3 4 5 6 7	Fully engaged and effective

3.02 How actively is the donor engaged in humanitarian protection to enhance opportunities to obtain security?

Disengaged and ineffective	1 2 3 4 5 6 7	Fully engaged and effective

4.01 In a crisis, does the donor respect and promote the protection of human rights?

Never	1 2 3 4 5 6 7	Always

5.01 To allow you to respond immediately to the most pressing humanitarian needs, the donor permits you to reallocate funds from another crisis.

Never	1 2 3 4 5 6 7	Always

5.02 To allow you to identify the most pressing humanitarian needs (in order to formulate the most appropriate response) the donor has supported your agency in its needs assessment efforts.

Never	1 2 3 4 5 6 7	Always

5.03 To allow you to respond rapidly to the most pressing humanitarian needs, the donor provides a significant portion of funding in cash.

Never	1 2 3 4 5 6 7	Always

5.04 To allow you to respond immediately to the most pressing humanitarian needs, the donor provided funding in a timely manner.

Never	1 2 3 4 5 6 7	Always

6.01 The donor's humanitarian funding is allocated in proportion to need and on the basis of needs assessments.

Never	1 2 3 4 5 6 7	Always

7.01 In the *design* and *implementation* of the humanitarian response, has the donor requested that you consult with the beneficiaries and ensure their active involvement?

Never	1 2 3 4 5 6 7	Always

7.02 In the *monitoring* and *evaluation* of the humanitarian response, has the donor requested that you consult with the beneficiaries and ensure their active involvement?

Never	1 2 3 4 5 6 7	Always

8.01 The donor has strengthened the capacity of the government to prevent, prepare for, mitigate, and respond to humanitarian crises.

Not at all	1 2 3 4 5 6 7	Very effectively

8.02 The donor has strengthened the capacity of the local communities to prevent, prepare for, mitigate, and respond to humanitarian crises.

Not at all	1 2 3 4 5 6 7	Very effectively

8.03 The donor has supported programs that increase or strengthen resilience, meaning building the capacity to cope with crises.

Not at all	1 2 3 4 5 6 7	Very effectively

8.04 The donor has ensured that governments are better able to coordinate effectively with humanitarian partners.

Strongly disagree	1 2 3 4 5 6 7	Strongly agree

8.05 More generally, the donor supports and facilitates coordination efforts.

Strongly disagree	1 2 3 4 5 6 7	Strongly agree

9.01 Has the donor provided humanitarian assistance in ways that are supportive of recovery and/or long-term development?

Not at all	1 2 3 4 5 6 7	Always

9.02 Has the donor provided humanitarian assistance to ensure the rapid recovery of sustainable livelihoods?

Not at all	1 2 3 4 5 6 7	Always

10.01 In implementing humanitarian action, the donor supports and promotes the special role of nongovernmental organisations.

Strongly disagree	1 2 3 4 5 6 7	Strongly agree

Good practices in donor financing, management, and accountability

(a) Funding

11.01 Donor support for your humanitarian action in an ongoing crisis has been affected by the needs of new crises elsewhere.

To a significant extent	1 2 3 4 5 6 7	Not at all

12.01 Funding from the donor has been provided to you:

Irregularly	1 2 3 4 5 6 7	Predictably and as per prior agreement

13.01 Has the donor reduced earmarking, or made it more flexible?

Not at all	1 2 3 4 5 6 7	Yes, clearly

13.02 Does the donor provide the necessary flexibility in the use of funds to help you adapt your program to changing needs?

| Not at all | | 1 2 3 4 5 6 7 | | Yes, clearly |

13.03 Has the donor encouraged the introduction of longer-term funding arrangements that allow you to better program assistance?

| Not at all | | 1 2 3 4 5 6 7 | | Yes, clearly |

(b) Promoting standards and enhancing implementation

15.01 The donor requests your adherence to good practice, including in your accountability, efficiency and effectiveness in implementing humanitarian action.

| Not at all | | 1 2 3 4 5 6 7 | | Frequently and insistently |

17.01 The donor is available at short notice to support you in the implementation of humanitarian action.

| Seldom or never | | 1 2 3 4 5 6 7 | | Always |

17.02 The donor has helped to facilitate safe humanitarian access.

| Rarely or never | | 1 2 3 4 5 6 7 | | Frequently |

18.01 The donor has supported mechanisms for your organisation's contingency planning.

| Never | | 1 2 3 4 5 6 7 | | Regularly |

18.02 Such support has included funds to strengthen your capacity for response.

| None | | 1 2 3 4 5 6 7 | | All that was requested |

19.01 Does the donor affirm the primary position of civilian (as opposed to military) organisations in implementing humanitarian action?

| Seldom if ever | | 1 2 3 4 5 6 7 | | Affirmed and maintained |

(c) Learning and accountability

21.01 The donor supports learning initiatives.

| Not at all | | 1 2 3 4 5 6 7 | | Extensively |

21.02 The donor supports accountability initiatives

| Not at all | | 1 2 3 4 5 6 7 | | Extensively |

22.01 The donor encourages regular evaluations.

| Never | | 1 2 3 4 5 6 7 | | Regularly |

23.01 As far as you know, the donor's reporting on official humanitarian assistance spending is:

| Inaccurate and opaque | 1 2 3 4 5 6 7 | Accurate, timely, and transparent |

23.02 As far as you know, the donor tries to follow standardised reporting for humanitarian assistance spending.

| Not at all | | 1 2 3 4 5 6 7 | | Always |

Note

1 The questionnaire reproduced in this Appendix does not include the original instructions and other supporting explanations, which need not be reproduced here.

Glossary

1. **Accountability:** Humanitarian actors are accountable to both those they seek to assist and those from whom they accept resources. All dealings with donors and beneficiaries shall reflect an attitude of openness and transparency, recognising the need to report on activities, from both a financial and an effectiveness perspective.

   See: http://www.icrc.org/web/eng/siteeng0.nsf/htmlall/57JMNB

   Accountability involves three dimensions:

   - Processes through which individuals, organisations and states make decisions that affect others;
   - Mechanisms through which individuals, organisations, and states seek to explain their decisions and actions;
   - Processes through which individuals, organisations, and states raise concerns about, and seek redress or compensation for, the consequences of the decisions and actions of others.

   See: http://www.hapinternational.org/en/page.php?IDpage=64&IDcat=10

2. **Armed conflict:** An international armed conflict means fighting between the armed forces of at least two states. It should be noted that wars of national liberation have been classified as international armed conflicts.

   According to IHL, a non-international armed conflict means fighting on the territory of a state between the regular armed forces and identifiable armed groups, or between armed groups fighting one another. To be considered a non-international armed conflict, fighting must reach a certain level of intensity and extend over a certain period of time.

   See: http://www.icrc.org/web/eng/siteeng0.nsf/htmlall/5kzf5n?open-document

3. **Beneficiaries:** Individuals and communities affected by a disaster or conflict, whose suffering and losses are intended to be relieved through humanitarian action.

4. **Capacity:** A combination of all the strengths and resources available within a community, society, or organisation that can reduce the level of risk, or the effects of a disaster. Capacity may include physical, institutional, social, or economic means as well as skilled personal or collective attributes, such as leadership and management. Capacity may also be described as *capability*.

5. **Central Emergency Response Fund (CERF):** A stand-by fund established by the United Nations to enable more timely and reliable humanitarian assistance to those affected by natural disasters and armed conflicts.

   The CERF is a tool for pre-positioning funding for humanitarian action. The CERF was established to upgrade the current Central Emergency Revolving Fund by including a grant element based on voluntary contributions by governments and private sectors such as corporations, individuals, and NGOs.

   The CERF was approved by consensus by the United Nations General Assembly on December 2005 to achieve the following objectives:

   - promote early action and response to reduce loss of life;
   - enhance response to time-critical requirements;
   - strengthen core elements of humanitarian response in underfunded crises.

   See: http://ochaonline.un.org/cerf/WhatIstheCERF/tabid/1706/Default.aspx

6. **Civil-military coordination:** The essential dialogue and interaction between civilian and military actors in humanitarian emergencies that is necessary to protect and promote humanitarian principles, avoid competition, minimise inconsistency, and, when appropriate, pursue common goals. Basic strategies range from coexistence to cooperation. Coordination is a shared responsibility facilitated by liaison and common training.

   See: www.humanitarianinfo.org/iasc/_tools/download.asp?docID=88&type=prod

7. **Civil society:** Conglomerate of individuals and groups active in society, including:

- NGOs (nongovernmental organisations) which bring people together in a common cause, such as environmental, human rights, charitable, educational and training organisations, consumer associations, etc.;
- CBOs (community-based organisations), i.e., grassroots organisations which pursue member-oriented objectives), such as youth organisations, family associations, and all organisations through which citizens participate in local and municipal life;
- the so-called labour-market players (i.e., trade unions and employer federations, also called the social partners);
- organisations representing social and economic players, which are not social partners in the strict sense of the term, such as religious communities.

See: http://ec.europa.eu/civil_society/coneccs/question.cfm?CL=en

8. **Civilians and civilian population:** Defined according to article 50 of the Protocol Additional to the Geneva Conventions of 12 August 1949, and relating to the Protection of Victims of International Armed Conflicts (Protocol I), 8 June 1977. Part IV : Civilian population #Section I—General protection against effects of hostilities #Chapter II—Civilians and civilian population, as:

> *Any person who does not belong to one of the categories of persons referred to in Article 4 A (1), (2), (3), and (6) of the Third Convention and in Article 43 of this Protocol. In case of doubt whether a person is a civilian, that person shall be considered to be a civilian.*

The civilian population comprises all persons who are civilians. The presence within the civilian population of individuals who do not come within the definition of civilians does not deprive the population of its civilian character.

See: http://www.icrc.org/ihl.nsf/WebART/470-750064?OpenDocument

9. **Cluster approach:** Introduced in December 2005, the cluster approach is one element of humanitarian reform. It identifies predictable leadership in the gap sectors/areas of response and is designed around the concept of "partnership" (i.e., "clusters") between UN agencies, NGOs, international organisations, and the International Red Cross and Red Crescent Movement (except the International Committee of the Red Cross).

Partners work together towards commonly agreed humanitarian objectives, both at the global level (preparedness, standards, tools, stockpiles, and capacity-building) and at the field level (assessment, planning, delivery, and monitoring). Eleven clusters have been created to cover the following sectors: agriculture, camp coordination/management, early recovery, education, emergency shelter, emergency telecommunications, health, logistics, nutrition, protection, and water sanitation and hygiene.

Cluster leads are responsible for ensuring that response capacity is in place and that assessment, planning, and response activities are carried out in collaboration with partners and in accordance with agreed standards and guidelines.

The approach strengthens accountability to beneficiaries through commitments to participatory and community-based approaches, improved common needs assessments and prioritisation, and better monitoring and evaluation.

See: www.humanitarianreform.org

10. **Code of Conduct for the International Red Cross and Red Crescent Movement and NGOs in Disaster Response:** The Code of Conduct, written in 1994, is a set of guiding principles for organisations involved in humanitarian activities. It seeks to safeguard high standards of behaviour and maintain independence and effectiveness in disaster relief. In the event of armed conflict, its clauses are to be interpreted and applied in conformity with international humanitarian law. It is a voluntary code, enforced by the will of organisations accepting it to maintain the standards it lays down. As of August 2007, the Code of Conduct was signed by 427 organisations worldwide.

See: http://www.icrc.org/web/eng/siteeng0.nsf/htmlall/p1067?opendocument

11. **Common Humanitarian Action Plan (CHAP):** A strategic plan for humanitarian response in a given country or region. It provides:

- A common analysis of the context in which humanitarian takes place;
- An assessment of needs;
- Best, worst, and most likely scenarios;
- Identification of roles and responsibilities, i.e., who does what and where;
- A clear statement of longer-term objectives and goals; and
- A framework for monitoring the strategy and revising it if necessary.

The CHAP is the foundation for developing a Consolidated Appeal, and is as such part of the Coordinated Appeals Process (CAP).

See: http://ochaonline.un.org/cap2005/webpage.asp?MenuID=7888&Page=1241

12. **Common Humanitarian Funds (CHFs):** A new humanitarian financing instrument being piloted in Sudan (since 2005) and the Democratic Republic of Congo (since 2006). It provides a mechanism allowing donors to put money into a central fund to support humanitarian action in a particular country. The UN Humanitarian Coordinator can then draw on this fund to underwrite strategic priorities quickly and

easily. Rather than making bilateral decisions in support of agencies within the CAP, funding decisions are deferred to the Humanitarian Coordinator and his team, using the CHAP as a central strategic tool. A total of seven donors have participated in the funds in DRC and Sudan.

See: http://www.humanitarianreform.org/humanitarianreform/Default.aspx?tabid=204

13. **Complex emergency:** A humanitarian crisis in a country, region or society where there is total or considerable breakdown of authority, resulting from internal or external conflict, which requires an international response that goes beyond the mandate or capacity of any single agency and/or the ongoing United Nations country program.

Such "complex emergencies" are typically characterised by: extensive violence and loss of life; massive displacements of people; widespread damage to societies and economies; the need for large-scale, multi-faceted humanitarian assistance; the hindrance or prevention of humanitarian assistance by political and military constraints; significant security risks for humanitarian relief workers in some areas.

See: www.humanitarianinfo.org/iasc/_tools/download.asp?docID=88&type=prod

14. **Consolidated Appeal:** A reference document on the humanitarian strategy, programme and funding requirements in response to a major or complex emergency.

See: www.reliefweb.int/cap

15. **Consolidated Appeal Process (CAP)/ UN Consolidated Inter-Agency Appeals Process:** An inclusive and coordinated programming cycle through which national, regional, and international relief systems mobilise to respond to selected major or complex emergencies that require a system-wide response to humanitarian crisis. A common humanitarian strategy is elaborated through the CAP along with an action plan to implement this strategy. Projects included in the CAP support the humanitarian strategy. CAP serves to promote a coordinated strategy and a common fundraising platform, and advocate for humanitarian principles.

Its cycle includes: strategic planning leading to a Common Humanitarian Action Plan (CHAP); resource mobilisation (leading to a Consolidated Appeal or a Flash Appeal); coordinated programme implementation; joint monitoring and evaluation; revision, if necessary; and reporting on results.

See: www.reliefweb.int/cap

16. **Coordination:** The systematic use of policy instruments to deliver humanitarian assistance in a cohesive and effective manner. Such instruments include strategic planning, gathering data and managing information, mobilising resources and ensuring accountability, orchestrating a functional division of labour, negotiating and maintaining a serviceable framework with host political authorities, and providing

leadership. See Minear, L., Chelliah., U, Crisp, J., Mackinlay, J. and Weiss, T. (1992) UN Coordination of the International Humanitarian Response to the Gulf Crisis 1990–1992 (Thomas J. Watson Institute for International Studies: Providence, Rhode Island) Occasional Paper 13).

See: http://ochaonline.un.org/Coordination/tabid/1085/Default.aspx

17. **Coping capacity:** The means by which people or organisations use available resources and abilities to face adverse consequences that could lead to a disaster. In general, this involves managing resources, both in normal times, as well as during crises or adverse conditions. The strengthening of coping capacities usually builds resilience to withstand the effects of natural and human-induced hazards.

18. **Crisis (humanitarian):** Any situation in which there is an exceptional and widespread threat to human life, health, or subsistence. Such crises tend to occur in situations of vulnerability, in which a number of pre-existing factors (poverty, inequality, lack of access to basic services) are further exacerbated by a natural disaster or armed conflict which vastly increases their destructive effects.

See: http://www.escolapau.org/img/programas/alerta/alerta/alerta07006i.pdf

19. **Disaster:** A serious disruption of the functioning of a community or a society causing widespread human, material, economic or environmental losses which exceed the ability of the affected community or society to cope using its own resources.

It is a function of the risk process, that is, a combination of hazards, conditions of vulnerability, and insufficient capacity or measures to reduce the potential negative consequences of risk.

We can distinguish natural disasters such as droughts, earthquakes, floods, hurricanes, cyclones, typhoons, volcanic eruptions, etc., from man-made disasters which refer to disastrous occurrences, either sudden or long-term. Sudden, man made disasters include structural, building, and mine collapse, when this occurs independently, that is, without outside force.

See: http://www.unisdr.org/eng/library/lib-terminology-eng%20home.htm and http://www.ifrc.org/what/disasters/Types/index.asp

20. **Disaster preparedness:** Activities and measures taken in advance to ensure effective response to the impact of hazards, including the issuance of timely and effective early warnings, and the temporary evacuation of people and property from threatened locations.

See: http://www.unisdr.org/eng/library/lib-terminology-eng%20home.htm

21. **Disaster risk management:** The systematic process of using administrative decisions, organisation, operational skills, and capacities to implement policies, strategies and the coping capability of the society and community to lessen the impact of natural hazards and related environmental and technological disasters. This comprises different activities, such as structural and non-structural measures to avoid (prevention) or limit (mitigation and preparedness) the adverse effects of hazards.

22. **Early warning:** The provision of timely and effective information, through identified institutions, that allows individuals exposed to a hazard to take action to avoid or reduce their risk and prepare for effective response. (same source as above)

23. **Disaster risk reduction (disaster reduction):** The conceptual framework of elements which minimise vulnerability and disaster risk throughout a society to avoid (prevent) or limit (mitigate and be prepared for) the adverse impacts of hazards, within the broad context of sustainable development.

    See: http://www.unisdr.org/eng/library/lib-terminology-eng%20home.htm

24. **Early warning systems:** include a chain of concerns, namely: understanding and mapping the hazard; monitoring and forecasting impending events; processing and disseminating understandable warnings to political authorities and the population, and undertaking appropriate and timely actions in response to the warnings. *(same source as above)*

25. **Emergency:** An emergency is a "crisis" which calls for immediate humanitarian response.

    See: http://www.humanitarianinfo.org/iasc/content/default.asp and http://www.unisdr.org/eng/library/lib-terminology-eng%20home.htm

26. **Evaluation of Humanitarian Action (EHA):** A systematic and impartial examination of humanitarian action intended to draw lessons to improve policy and practice and enhance accountability. EHA is:

    - Commissioned by or in cooperation with the organisation(s) whose performance is being evaluated;
    - Undertaken either by a team of non-employees (external) or by a mixed team of non-employees (external) and employees (internal) from the commissioning organisation and/or the organisation being evaluated;
    - An assessment of policy and/or practice against recognised criteria (e.g., the DAC criteria);
    - A description of findings, conclusions, and recommendations.

    See: http://www.alnap.org/themes/evaluation.htm

27. **Famine:** A catastrophic food shortage affecting large numbers of people due to climatic, environmental, and socio-economic causes. The cause of the famine may produce great migrations to less affected areas.

    See: http://www.ifrc.org/what/disasters/Types/drought/

28. **Financial Tracking Service (FTS):** A global, real-time database which records all reported international humanitarian aid, including that for NGOs and the Red Cross/Red Crescent Movement, bilateral aid, in-kind aid, and private donations. FTS focuses particularly on Consolidated and Flash Appeals, both because they cover the major humanitarian crises, and because their funding requirements are well defined. This allows FTS to indicate to what extent populations in crisis receive humanitarian aid in proportion to needs. FTS is managed by the UN Office for Coordination of Humanitarian Affairs (OCHA). All FTS data are provided by donors or recipient organisations.

    See: http://ocha.unog.ch/fts2/

29. **Flash Appeal (UN):** The Flash Appeal is a tool for structuring a coordinated humanitarian response for the first three to six months of an emergency. The UN Humanitarian Coordinator triggers it in consultation with all stakeholders. The Flash Appeal is issued within one week of an emergency. It provides a concise overview of urgent life-saving needs and may include recovery projects that can be implemented within the time frame of the Appeal.

    See: http://ochaonline.un.org/cap2005/webpage.asp?MenuID=9196&Page=1483

30. **Fragile states:** States which fail to provide basic services to poor people because they are unwilling or unable to do so. Such states are unable or unwilling to harness domestic and international resources effectively for poverty reduction.

    See: http://www.oecd.org/dataoecd/30/62/34041714.pdf and http://stats.oecd.org/glossary/detail.asp?ID=7235

31. **Good Humanitarian Donorship (GHD):** An initiative undertaken in 2003 by a group of donors for the purpose of setting standards for donor actions, aimed at achieving efficient and principled humanitarian assistance funding. During the first meeting in Stockholm on June 17 2003 the members produced the following tools:

    GHD Principles: Declaration of 23 principles endorsed by the OECD-DAC members;

    GHD Implementation Plan: Created by several DAC countries to apply the Good Humanitarian Donorship Principles domestically;

GHD DAC Peer Review: Process to evaluate each other's development programmes, and monitor their corresponding policies and interventions. Peer reviews take place every four years and are conducted by two DAC members and the DAC Secretariat.

The GHD Country Pilots in the Democratic Republic of the Congo and Burundi were conducted in the framework of this initiative to apply the Principles of Good Humanitarian Donorship in real situations. The United Kingdom spearheaded the country pilot in Burundi, and the United States and Belgium led the pilot in the Democratic Republic of Congo.

See: www.goodhumanitariandonorship.org

32. **Humanitarian access:** Where protection is not available from national authorities or controlling non-state actors, vulnerable populations have a right to receive international protection and assistance from an impartial humanitarian relief operation. Such action is subject to the consent of the state or parties concerned and does not prescribe coercive measures in the event of refusal, however unwarranted.

    See: www.ochaonline.un.org

33. **Humanitarian action:** Humanitarian action includes the protection of civilians and those no longer taking part in hostilities, and the provision of food, water and sanitation, shelter, health services, and other items of assistance, undertaken for the benefit of affected people and to facilitate the return to normal lives and livelihoods.

    Humanitarian action should be guided by the humanitarian principles of *humanity*, meaning the centrality of saving human lives and alleviating suffering wherever it is found; *impartiality*, meaning the implementation of actions solely on the basis of need, without discrimination between or within affected populations; *neutrality*, meaning that humanitarian action must not favour any side in an armed conflict or other dispute where such action is carried out; and *independence*, meaning the autonomy of humanitarian objectives from the political, economic, military, or other objectives that any actor may hold with regard to areas where humanitarian action is being implemented. GHD Principles 1, 2, 3.

    See: www.goodhumanitariandonorship.org

34. **Humanitarian reform:** Humanitarian reform aims to dramatically enhance humanitarian response capacity, predictability, accountability, and partnership. It represents an ambitious effort by the international humanitarian community to reach more beneficiaries with more comprehensive, needs-based relief and protection, in a more effective and timely manner.

    The reform has four main objectives:

    - Sufficient humanitarian response capacity and enhanced leadership, accountability, and pre-

    dictability in "gap" sectors/areas of response, ensuring trained staff, adequate commonly-accessible stockpiles, surge capacity, agreed standards and guidelines;
    - Adequate, timely, and flexible humanitarian financing, including through the Central Emergency Response Fund;
    - Improved humanitarian coordination and leadership, a more effective Humanitarian Coordinator (HC) system, more strategic leadership, and coordination at the sectoral and intersectoral level;
    - More effective partnerships between UN and non-UN humanitarian actors.

    See: http://www.humanitarianreform.org/humanitarianreform/ Default.aspx?tabid=109

35. **Humanitarian space:** The area in which humanitarian actors operate on the ground to access those in need of assistance without compromising the safety of aid workers. To maintain humanitarian access, humanitarian space must be respected.

    See: www.ochaonline.un.org

36. **Humanitarian system:** Comprises all humanitarian actors.

37. **Humanity[1]:** Born initially out of the desire to bring assistance without discrimination to the wounded on the battlefield, this principle seeks in its national and international application to prevent and alleviate human suffering wherever it may be found. Its purpose is to protect life and health and to ensure respect for the human being. It promotes mutual understanding, friendship, cooperation, and lasting peace amongst all peoples.

    See: http://www.ifrc.org/what/values/principles/humanity.asp

38. **Hyogo Declaration:** The Hyogo Declaration is the result of negotiations during the World Conference on Disaster Reduction in January 2005. In the Declaration, the delegates recognise the interrelated nature of disaster reduction, poverty eradication, and sustainable development and agree to promote a culture of disaster prevention and resilience through risk assessments, early warning systems, etc.

    See: http://www.unisdr.org/wcdr/intergover/official-doc/L-docs/Hyogo-framework-for-action-english.pdf

39. **Impartiality[1] (non-legal):** Serving people or making decisions about people based only on their needs, without consideration of nationality, race, religious beliefs, social class, or political opinions

    See: http://www.ehl.icrc.org/images/stories/resources/glossary_e.pdf

40. **Independence[1]:** Humanitarian assistance and humanitarian actors, while auxiliaries in the humanitarian services of their

governments and subject to the laws of their respective countries, must always be autonomous, so that the assistance may be given in accordance with the principles of impartiality and neutrality.

See: www.ifrc.org

41. **Internally displaced persons (IDPs):** Persons or groups of persons who have been forced or obliged to leave their homes or habitual residence as a result of, or in order to avoid, the effects of armed conflict, situations of generalised violence, violations of human rights, or natural or man-made disasters, and who have not crossed an internationally recognised state border. A series of 30 non-binding "Guiding Principles on Internal Displacement" based on refugee law, human rights law, and international humanitarian law articulate standards for protection, assistance, and solutions for such internally displaced persons.

See: www.ochaonline.un.org

42. **International humanitarian law (IHL):** A body of rules that seeks, for humanitarian reasons, to limit the effects of armed conflict. It protects persons who are not, or are no longer participating in, hostilities and restricts the means and methods of warfare by prohibiting weapons that make no distinction between combatants and civilians or weapons and methods of warfare which cause unnecessary injury, suffering and/or damage. The rules are to be observed not only by governments and their armed forces, but also by armed opposition groups and any other parties to a conflict. The four Geneva Conventions of 1949 and their two Additional Protocols of 1977 are the principal instruments of humanitarian law. IHL is also known as the law of war or the law of armed conflict, and is part of international law. However, it does not regulate the use of force, which is governed by an important, but distinct, part of international law set out in the UN Charter.

See: www.ochaonline.un.org

43. **Livelihoods:** Those capabilities, assets (both material and social resources), and activities required for a means of living. A livelihood is sustainable when it can cope with and recover from stresses and shocks, maintain or enhance its capabilities and assets, and provide net benefits to other livelihoods locally and more widely, both in the present and in the future, while not undermining the natural resource base.

See: http://www.fao.org/sd/pe4_en.htm

44. **Malnutrition:** A major health problem, especially in developing countries. A clean water supply, sanitation, and hygiene, given their direct impact on the incidence of infectious disease, especially diarrhoea, are important for preventing malnutrition. Both malnutrition and inadequate water supply and sanitation are linked to poverty. The impact of repeated or persistent diarrhoea on nutrition-related poverty and the effect of malnutrition on susceptibility to infectious diarrhoea

are reinforcing elements of the same vicious circle, especially among children in developing countries.

See: http://www.who.int/water_sanitation_health/diseases/malnutrition/en/

45. **Millennium Development Goals (MDG):** The eight Millennium Development Goals range from halving extreme poverty to halting the spread of HIV/AIDS and providing universal primary education—all by the target date of 2015—form a blueprint agreed to by all the world's countries and leading development institutions. They have galvanised unprecedented efforts to meet the needs of the world's poorest people.

The eight MDGs are:

Goal 1: Eradicate extreme poverty and hunger
Goal 2: Achieve universal primary education
Goal 3: Promote gender equality and empower women
Goal 4: Reduce child mortality
Goal 5: Improve maternal health
Goal 6: Combat HIV/AIDS, malaria, and other diseases
Goal 7: Ensure environmental sustainability
Goal 8: Develop a Global Partnership for Development

See: http://www.un.org/millenniumgoals/

46. **Needs:** In any disaster there are two sets of needs to be met: the first concerning immediate life support, and the second concerning more long-term rehabilitation. Although the degree and importance of these basic needs may vary in magnitude and priority from one disaster to another, they are often the same:

- Search and rescue;
- Sufficient shelter (including "mobile shelter," clothing);
- Adequate food;
- Safe and adequate water supply and disposal;
- Health and social care;
- Protection from violence and harassment.

Disaster relief is one aspect of the broad spectrum of humanitarian assistance.

See: http://www.reliefweb.int/ocha_ol/programs/response/mcdunet/0guidad.html

47. **Needs Assessment Framework** (NAF): Joint needs assessments, with a view to improving the overall prioritisation of response.

See: http://ochaonline.un.org/cap2005/GetBin.asp?DocID=1540

48. **Neutrality[1]:** In order to continue to enjoy the confidence of all, humanitarian actors may not take sides in hostilities or engage at any time in controversies of a political, racial, religious, or ideological nature.

See: http://www.icrc.org/web/eng/siteeng0.nsf/html/57JN2Z

49. Official Development Assistance (ODA): Official financing flows are administered with the objective of promoting the economic development and welfare of developing countries. ODA is concessional in character—that is, below market rate—with a grant element of at least 25 percent of the total (using a fixed 10 percent rate of discount). By convention, ODA flows consist of contributions by donor government agencies to developing countries (bilateral ODA), and also to multilateral institutions. ODA receipts comprise disbursements by bilateral donors and multilateral institutions. Lending by export credit agencies for the sole purpose of export promotion is excluded.

See: http://stats.oecd.org/glossary/detail.asp?ID=6043

50. Organisation for Economic Co-operation and Development-Development Assistance Committee (OECD-DAC): is the principal body through which the OECD deals with issues related to cooperation with developing countries.

See: http://www.oecd.org/department/0,2688,en_2649_33721_1_1_1_1_1,00.html

51. Recovery (early): Recovery focuses on restoring the capacity of national institutions and communities after a crisis. Early recovery is that which begins in a humanitarian relief setting immediately following a natural disaster or armed conflict. Guided by development principles, the early recovery phase aims to generate self-sustaining, nationally-owned processes to stabilise human security and address underlying risks that contributed to the crisis.

See: http://www.undp.org/cpr/we_do/_recovery.shtml

52. Unearmarked contribution: In contrast to those which are earmarked, contributions (or commitment) for which the donor does not require that funds be used for a specific project, sector, crisis, or country, leaving the recipient organisation to decide on allocation of funds to specific projects. Because there are degrees of earmarking (e.g., to a country, crisis, or sector), FTS treats as unearmarked any funding that is not earmarked at the country level. For example, funding earmarked to "Africa" or to "East Africa" is treated as unearmarked on OCHA's Financial Tracking System. A growing phenomenon is funding not even earmarked to a particular recipient agency, e.g., directed towards the UN Central Emergency Response Fund, or to a Consolidated Appeal to be distributed by the UN Resident Coordinator's office among various appeal projects and agencies.

See: http://www.unisdr.org/eng/library/lib-terminology-eng%20home.htm

Note

1 The principles of humanity, impartiality, independence, and neutrality are among the seven Fundamental Principles espoused by the National Red Cross and Red Crescent Societies, the International Committee of the Red Cross and the International Federation of the Red Cross and Red Crescent Societies.

About the Authors

LAURA ALTINGER

As Research Director of the Humanitarian Response Index, Dr. Altinger has played a key role in defining the methodology of the Index and the associated indicators. Prior to joining DARA, Laura served as Senior Economist and Associate Director at the World Economic Forum in Geneva where she contributed to a number of publications and underlying indices, including the Global Competitiveness Report 2006–7, the Global Gender Gap Study 2006–7, the Latin America Review 2006, and the Global Information Technology Report 2006. Prior to this, she worked for the United Nations (2000–2006) to produce various editions of the Economic Survey of Europe, and has held past positions at the European Commission and the Council of the European Union. Laura is currently on leave from the United Nations. She holds a Ph.D. from the London Business School, a Graduate Diploma of Law from the College of Law, London, an MSc in Economics and Econometrics from Bristol University, and an MA from the University of Cambridge.

SARAH CLIFFE

Sarah Cliffe has led the World Bank Fragile and Conflict-Affected Countries Group at the World Bank since 2002. She has worked for the last 15 years in post-conflict countries, in South Africa, Rwanda, Burundi, Ethiopia, Indonesia, East Timor, Afghanistan, Liberia, Sudan, and Haiti. Prior to joining the Bank, she worked for the United Nations Development Programme in Rwanda, the Government of South Africa, and the Congress of South African Trade Unions, as well as for a major management consultancy company in the United Kingdom on public sector reform issues. Since joining the Bank, her work has included post-conflict reconstruction, community-driven development, and civil service reform. She was Chief of Mission for the World Bank programme in Timor-Leste from 1999 to 2002.

She holds degrees in History and Economic Development from Cambridge and Columbia Universities.

JAN EGELAND

Jan Egeland served as Under-Secretary-General for Humanitarian Affairs and Emergency Relief Coordinator from 2003 until December 2006. In this capacity, he led the joint efforts of the humanitarian community to provide relief in the wake of the earthquake in Bam, Iran, the Indian Ocean earthquakes and tsunami, the South Asia earthquake, the drought in West Africa, and drought and flooding in the Horn of Africa. He also coordinated relief efforts in neglected and forgotten crises, in Uganda, Somalia, the Democratic Republic of the Congo, Darfur, Sudan, Colombia, Lebanon, and the Palestinian Territories. He was particularly involved with the reform of OCHA and its Central Emergency Response Fund, with raising awareness of gender mainstreaming, sexual exploitation and violence, and internal displacement. Prior to joining OCHA, he was Secretary-General of the Norwegian Red Cross. From 1999 to 2002, he served as the UN Secretary-General's Special Adviser on Colombia. From 1990 to 1997, he was Norwegian State Secretary in the Ministry of Foreign Affairs, and participated in a number of peace processes, including the Norwegian channel between Israel and the PLO in 1992 (leading to the 1993 Oslo Accord), the UN-led peace talks (resulting in the 1996 ceasefire agreement between the Guatemalan government and the guerrillas), and in the host delegation for the 1997 treaty to ban landmines. Mr. Egeland holds an MA in Political Science from the University of Oslo, was a Fulbright Scholar at the University of California, Berkeley, and a fellow at the International Peace Research Institute, Oslo, and the Truman Institute for the Advancement of Peace, Jerusalem.

GILLES GASSER

Gilles Gasser is a journalist and independent consultant, specialising in humanitarian aid issues and communication. He was head of mission of the NGO Equilibre in Bosnia and Herzegovina from 1993 to 1996 and later worked as an expert from 1997 to 2000 in the humanitarian offices of the European Commission in Sarajevo, Tirana, and Pristina. He has undertaken studies for the Tsunami Evaluation Coalition, "Conversations on Democracy" for the Club of Madrid, and various projects with Fundación para las Relaciones Internacionales y el Diálogo Exterior (FRIDE). As a journalist he has travelled to Belfast, New Caledonia, Israel, the Palestinian Territories, El Salvador, Guatemala, Brazil, and the Dominican Republic.

SILVIA HIDALGO

Silvia Hidalgo is Director and co-founder of DARA. She was Head of the ECHO (European Commission Humanitarian Office) office in Sarajevo (1996–1998) and regional Coordinator for the Spanish Red Cross in Central America in the aftermath of Hurricane Mitch. She served as Desk Officer for Bosnia Herzegovina at ECHO in Brussels (1993–1995). She has participated in humanitarian action evaluations across four continents and has worked as a consultant in vulnerability surveys, studies of domestic violence, rural development, participatory management, disaster prevention and mitigation, and new tools in development assistance. Ms. Hidalgo is a member of the European Evaluation Society and the Active Learning Network for Accountability and Performance in Humanitarian Action (ALNAP). A member of Fundación para las Relaciones Internacionales y el Diálogo Exterior (FRIDE), she has been its Director since 2005. Her areas of expertise are humanitarian action, problems related to migration and return, and the evaluation of development aid. She holds a BA in Economics and Political Science and an MA in International Relations from the University of Pennsylvania.

AUGUSTO LOPEZ-CLAROS

Augusto López-Claros is Project Director for the Humanitarian Response Index. He was Chief Economist and Director of the Global Competitiveness Programme at the World Economic Forum in Geneva during the period 2003–2006. In this capacity, he served as Editor of the Forum's Global Competitiveness Report. Before joining the Forum, he was Executive Director and Senior International Economist with Lehman Brothers International (London), and Resident Representative of the International Monetary Fund in the Russian Federation (Moscow) from 1992 to 1995. Prior to joining the IMF, he was professor of economics at the University of Chile in Santiago. He has written and lectured extensively in South America, the United States, Europe, and Asia on a broad range of subjects, including aspects of economic reform in transition economies, economic integration, interdependence and cooperation, governance, peace, and the role of international organisations. He is the founder of EFD–Global Consulting Network, an international consultancy specialising in economic, financial, and development issues. Dr. López-Claros received his Ph.D. in Economics from Duke University and a diploma in Mathematical Statistics from Cambridge University.

MARTA MARAÑON

Marta Marañón has been the Deputy Director of DARA since 2003. She is an evaluation expert committed to improving the quality of aid and the empowerment of its beneficiaries, with evaluation experience in the fields of international development, humanitarian action, capacity building, and organisational performance, having worked in a variety of complex situations. She has conducted evaluations in Brazil, Colombia, Mexico, Morocco, Algeria, Mauritania, Niger, Kenya, and Uzbekistan. Ms. Marañón is the founder of the Educación Activa Foundation and is a member of the Royal Geographic Society, UK. She is also a member of the European Evaluation Society and the International Development Evaluation Association (IDEA). Her areas of expertise include the fields of environmental sustainability, sustainable livelihoods, community and rural development, disaster risk reduction, and education. She holds a BA in Geography and three MA degrees, in Landscape and Land Use Management, Cultural Management, and Evaluation of Public Policies and Programmes.

MICHEL OGRIZEK

Michel Ogrizek has been an international consultant in strategic communications, counselling international institutions and global corporations for more than 20 years. Trained in medicine, he first served as chief medical officer at the French Ministry of Cooperation operating in Sahara, Chad, Congo, and Central Africa, and later as medical and public affairs director for the region of Africa and Canada at Warner-Lambert. He was a trainer for Médecins Sans Frontières (Doctors Without Borders), training young doctors to serve in conflict and remote zones. Turning his attention to issues of communication, Dr. Ogrizek served as Vice Chairman of Edelman, where he assumed responsibility for the worldwide corporate network and supervised global practices in risk issues and crisis management, finance, employee engagement, health, and First&42nd, Edelman's management consultancy. Before joining Edelman, he was successively Managing Board Director and Head of Communications at the World Economic Forum (Geneva), Managing Director and Global Head of Marketing and Communications at UBS Warburg (London), and Global Head of Corporate Relations at Unilever (London and Rotterdam). He also served as President and CEO of Edelman's European operations, President and CEO of Hill & Knowlton, France, Head of Eurosciences, and Director of Healthcare, Environment, Issues, and Crisis Management at the public relations firm Burson-Marsteller. After receiving his MD (specialising in tropical medicine) from the University of Paris in 1974, he was a postdoctoral research associate in Medical Anthropology at the University of California, Berkeley.

CHARLES PETRIE

Charles Petrie is the current United Nations Humanitarian Coordinator, having held senior policy and operational responsibilities with the UN in conflict settings for 18 years. As Chief of the UN Emergency Unit in Sudan (1989–92), he battled the international community's impotence at the authorities' denial of the Nuba Mountain massacres and the forced eviction of the displaced in Khartoum. Frustrated by the inaction, he requested transfer to the new principled intervention in Somalia, where, as senior humanitarian advisor to the United Nations humanitarian coordinator, UNOSOM from 1992 to 1994, he was at the centre of the failed US-led international intervention. In May 1994, as part of the small team supporting General Romeo Dallaire, he witnessed the full horrors of the genocide in Rwanda. In 1995, he served in New York as Chief of the UN Africa II Section, but soon returned to the field, where he assumed the responsibilities of Special

Assistant to the Commissioner General of UNRWA in the Middle East. During the war in the Congo, he was sent on a two-week assignment to gauge the intentions of the Congolese rebels. The two weeks lasted three years and, from 1998 to 2001, he served as the Senior Humanitarian Advisor in rebel held portions of the DRC, at the time a forgotten tragedy. In 2001, he initially served as advisor to a senior Afghan Minister (Dr. Ashraf Ghani), and subsequently became the Director of Policy and Planning for the UN mission in Afghanistan. In July 2003, he was UN Resident Coordinator and UNDP Resident Representative in the Union of Myanmar.

RICCARDO POLASTRO

Riccardo Polastro has served as Evaluation Officer with DARA since September 2006. He worked for 14 years in the humanitarian and development sector in over 40 countries, carrying out missions for the United Nations, the Red Cross and Red Crescent Movement, diverse NGOs, and donors. His recent work includes *Inter-Agency Real-Time Evaluation of the Response to the Floods and Cyclone in Mozambique*, multi-country partnership evaluations for ECHO with IFRC and with UNHCR, and the study entitled "Quality and Accountabilities Complementarities." He lectures in development studies at the MA level at several universities. His key areas of expertise include strategic and operational planning, programme management, assessment, monitoring and evaluation, peace-building (including human rights, democracy, and the strengthening of civil society), rehabilitation, reintegration and reconstruction following natural disasters or violent conflicts, and local capacity building and decentralised cooperation.

JOHAN SCHAAR

In February 2005, Johan Schaar was named Special Representative of the Secretary-General for the Tsunami Operation at the International Federation of Red Cross and Red Crescent Societies. In this capacity, he was responsible for all matters related to the Federation's operation for tsunami survivors, representing the IFRC and all contributing national Red Cross and Red Crescent Societies in international high level coordination mechanisms with other international actors, such as the UN, the development banks, and NGOs. Prior to his appointment as Special

Representative, Dr. Schaar served for 15 years with the Swedish Red Cross and the IFRC, both in headquarters and in the field in Asia, first with the Swedish Committee for Afghanistan in the early 1990s, and later gaining experience in Pakistan, Vietnam, and Kuala Lumpur, as Head of the Federation's South-East Asia Regional Delegation. From 2000 to 2004, he was Head of Division for Humanitarian Assistance and Conflict Management in the Swedish Development Cooperation Agency (SIDA). He holds a Ph.D. in Agricultural Sciences.

RICARDO SOLÉ

Ricardo Solé is an international consultant specialising in humanitarian aid. He was Regional Health Coordinator of the European Commission Humanitarian Office (ECHO) in Jordan (2006–2007), giving technical assistance to the Country Offices in Lebanon, Yemen, Algeria, Tajikistan, and the Palestinian Territories. He was Head of the ECHO office in Angola (2001–2002) and Colombia (2000–2001), and ECHO Health Coordinator in Albania-FRY (1999) and Bosnia and Herzegovina (1996–1997). Mr. Sole has also served as Coordinator for the Palestinian Territories at the World Health Organization office in Jerusalem and Gaza (2002–2003). He has participated in humanitarian action evaluations in Colombia, Haiti, Guatemala, Brazil, Albania, Kenya, Burundi, Afghanistan, Mali, and Niger for various international organisations. In Spain, he worked for the Andalusian Health Service for a period of ten years, designing and implementing health programmes. He holds an MD degree in Internal Medicine and an MA in Public Health and Health Management from the University of Granada, and a specialisation degree in Evaluation of Health Programmes in Complex Emergencies from the London School of Tropical Medicine and Hygiene.